pfSense: The Definitive Guide

The Definitive Guide to the pfSense Open Source Firewall and Router Distribution

Christopher M. Buechler and Jim Pingle

D1737088

pfSense: The Definitive Guide
The Definitive Guide to the pfSense Open Source Firewall and Router Distribution
By Christopher M. Buechler and Jim Pingle

Publisher: Reed Media Services
Editor: Jeremy C. Reed
October 2009

Cover design by Holger Bauer

ISBN: 978-0-9790342-8-2

Contents

List of Figures

List of Tables

Foreword

My friends and co-workers know that I build firewalls. At least once a month someone says "My company needs a firewall with X and Y, and the price quotes I've gotten are tens of thousands of dollars. Can you help us out?"

Anyone who builds firewalls knows this question could be more realistically phrased as "Could you please come over one evening and slap together some equipment for me, then let me randomly interrupt you for the next three to five years to have you install new features, debug problems, set up features I didn't know enough to request, attend meetings to resolve problems that can't possibly be firewall issues but someone thinks might be the firewall, and identify solutions for my innumerable unknown requirements? Oh, and be sure to test every possible use case before deploying anything."

Refusing these requests makes me seem churlish. Accepting these requests ruins my cheerful demeanor. For a long time, I wouldn't build firewalls except for my employer.

pfSense lets me be a nicer person without having to actually work at it.

With pfSense I can deploy a firewall in just a few hours — and most of that is running cables and explaining the difference between "inside" and "outside." pfSense's extensive documentation and user community offers me an easy answer to questions — "did you look that up?" If pfSense doesn't support a feature, chances are I couldn't support it either.

But pfSense supports everything I could ask for, and with a friendly interface to boot. The wide userbase means that features are tested in many different environments and generally "just work," even when interacting with the CEO's kids' Windows ME PC connected to the Internet by Ethernet over ATM over carrier pigeon. Best of all, pfSense is built on much of the same software I'd use myself. I trust the underlying FreeBSD operating system to be secure, stable, and efficient.

Security updates? Just click a button and reboot.

Your need new features? Just turn them on. pfSense handles clustering, traffic shaping, load balancing, integration with your existing equipment through RADIUS, IPsec, PPTP, monitoring, dynamic DNS, and more.

Big-name industry suppliers charge outrageous fees to support what pfSense freely provides. If your employer insists on paying for support contracts, or if you just feel more secure knowing you can pick up the phone and scream for help, you can get pfSense support agreements very reasonably. If you don't need a support contract, I happen to know that Chris, Jim, or anyone else with a pfSense commit bit will let grateful pfSense users buy them a beer or six.

Personally, I don't build firewalls from scratch any more. When I need a firewall, I use pfSense.

—Michael W. Lucas

Preface

Welcome to *The Definitive Guide to pfSense*. Written by pfSense co-founder Chris Buechler and pfSense consultant Jim Pingle, this book covers installation and basic configuration through advanced networking and firewalling with the popular open source firewall and router distribution.

This book is designed to be a friendly step-by-step guide to common networking and security tasks, plus a thorough reference of pfSense's capabilities. The Definitive Guide to pfSense covers the following subjects:

- An introduction to pfSense and its features.

- Hardware and system planning.

- Installing and upgrading pfSense.

- Using the web-based configuration interface.

- Backup and restoration.

- Firewalling fundamentals and defining and troubleshooting rules.

- Port forwarding and Network Address Translation.

- General networking and routing configuration.

- Bridging, Virtual LANs (VLANs), and Multi-WAN.

- Virtual Private Networks using IPsec, PPTP, and OpenVPN.

- Traffic shaping and load balancing.

- Wireless networking and captive portal setups.

- Redundant firewalls and High Availability.

- Various network related services.

- System monitoring, logging, traffic analysis, sniffing, packet capturing, and troubleshooting.

- Software package and third-party software installations and upgrades.

At the end of this book, you'll find a menu guide with the standard menu choices available in pfSense and a detailed index.

Authors

Chris Buechler

Chris is one of the founders of the pfSense project, and one of its most active developers. He has been working in the IT industry for over a decade, working extensively with firewalls and FreeBSD for most of that time. He has provided security, network, and related services for organizations in the public and private sector, ranging from small organizations to Fortune 500 companies and large public sector organizations. He currently makes a living helping organizations with pfSense related needs including network design, deployment planning, configuration assistance, conversion from existing firewalls, development and more. He is based in Louisville, Kentucky USA and provides services for customers around the world. He holds numerous industry certifications including the CISSP, SSCP, MCSE, and CCNA amongst others. His personal web page can be found at `http://chrisbuechler.com`.

Jim Pingle

Jim has been working with FreeBSD for over ten years, professionally for the past six years. Currently as a system administrator at HPC Internet Services, a local ISP in Bedford, Indiana, USA he works with FreeBSD servers, various routing equipment and circuits, and of course pfSense-based firewalls both internally and for many customers. Jim has a Bachelor's degree in Information Systems from Indiana-Purdue Fort Wayne, and graduated in 2002. He also contributes to several Open Source projects besides pfSense, most notably RoundCube Webmail and glTail.

When away from the computer, Jim also enjoys spending time with his family, reading, taking pictures, and being a television addict. His personal web page can be found at `http://pingle.org`.

Acknowledgements

This book, and pfSense itself would not be possible without a great team of developers, contributors, corporate supporters, and a wonderful community. The project has received code contributions from more than 100 people, with 29 people having contributed considerably enough to obtain commit access. Hundreds have contributed financially, with hardware, and other needed resources. Thousands more have done their part to support the project by helping others on the mailing list, forum, and IRC. Our thanks to everyone who has done their part to make the project the great success it has become.

Book Cover Design

Thanks to Holger Bauer for the design of the cover. Holger was one of the first contributors to the project, having done much of the work on theming, graphics, and is the creator of the backgrounds we have used on our presentations at six BSD conferences over the past five years.

pfSense Developers

The current active pfSense development team, listed in order of seniority.

- Co-Founder Scott Ullrich
- Co-Founder Chris Buechler
- Bill Marquette
- Holger Bauer
- Erik Kristensen
- Seth Mos
- Scott Dale
- Martin Fuchs
- Ermal Luçi
- Matthew Grooms
- Mark Crane
- Rob Zelaya
- Renato Botelho

We would also like to thank all FreeBSD developers, and specifically, those developers who have assisted considerably with pfSense.

- Max Laier
- Christian S.J. Peron
- Andrew Thompson
- Bjoern A. Zeeb

Personal Acknowledgements

From Chris

I must give my wife thanks and considerable credit for the completion of this book, and the success of the project in general. This book and the project have lead to countless long days and nights, and months without a day's break, and her support has been crucial.

I would also like to thank the many companies who have purchased our support and reseller subscriptions, allowing me to make the jump to working full time on the project in early 2009.

I must also thank Jim for jumping in on this book and providing considerable help in completing it. It's been two years in the making, and far more work than I had imagined. It may have been obsolete before it got finished if it weren't for his assistance over the past several months. Also thanks to Jeremy Reed, our editor and publisher, for his assistance with the book.

Lastly, my thanks to everyone who has contributed to the pfSense project in any fashion, especially the developers who have given huge amounts of time to the project over the past five years.

From Jim

I would like to thank my wife and son, who put up with me throughout my participation in the writing process. Without them, I would have gone crazy a long time ago.

I would also like to thank my boss, Rick Yaney of HPC Internet Services, for being supportive of pfSense, FreeBSD, and Open Source software in general.

The entire pfSense community is deserving of even more thanks as well, it is the best and most supportive group of Open Source software users and contributors I have ever encountered.

Reviewers

The following individuals provided much-needed feedback and insight to help improve the book and its accuracy. Listed in alphabetical order by last name.

- Jon Bruce

- Mark Foster

- Bryan Irvine

- Warren Midgley

- Eirik Øverby

Feedback

The publisher and authors encourage your feedback for this book and the pfSense distribution. Please send your suggestions, criticism and/or praise for The Definitive Guide to pfSense book to info@reedmedia.net. The publisher's webpage for the book is at `http://www.reedmedia.net/books/pfsense/`.

For general feedback related to the pfSense project, please post to the forum or mailing list. Links to these resources can be found at `http://pfsense.org/support`.

Typographic Conventions

Throughout the book a few conventions are used to denote certain concepts, information, or actions. The following list gives examples of how these are formatted in the book.

Menu Selections
Firewall → Rules

GUI Item Labels/Names
Destination

Buttons
Apply Changes

Prompt for input
Do you want to proceed?

Input from the user
Rule Description

File Names
/boot/loader.conf

Names of commands or programs
gzip

Commands Typed at a shell prompt

```
# ls -l
```

Items that must be replaced with values specific to your setup
192.168.1.1

Special Notes

Note
Watch out for this!

Long literal lines in output examples may be split with the ↩ (hookleftarrow). Long shell command-line examples may be split using the backslash (\) for shell line continuation.

Chapter 1

Introduction

pfSense is a free, open source customized distribution of FreeBSD tailored for use as a firewall and router, entirely managed in an easy to use web interface. This web interface is known as the web-based GUI configurator, or WebGUI for short. No FreeBSD knowledge is required to deploy and use pfSense, and in fact the majority of the user base has never used FreeBSD outside of pfSense. In addition to being a powerful, flexible firewalling and routing platform, it includes a long list of related features and a package system allowing further expandability without adding bloat and potential security vulnerabilities to the base distribution. pfSense is a popular project with more than 1 million downloads since its inception, and proven in countless installations ranging from small home networks protecting a single computer to large corporations, universities and other organizations protecting thousands of network devices.

1.1   Project Inception

This project was founded in 2004 by Chris Buechler and Scott Ullrich. Chris had been contributing to m0n0wall for some time before that, and found it to be a great solution. However, while thrilled with the project, many users longed for more capabilities than can be accommodated in a project strictly focused towards embedded devices and their limited hardware resources. Enter pfSense. Modern embedded hardware is also well supported and popular with pfSense today. In 2004, there were numerous embedded solutions with 64 MB RAM that couldn't be accommodated with the desired feature set of pfSense.

1.2   What does pfSense stand for/mean?

The project ran for a couple months with no name. In fact, the FreeBSD jail that runs our CVS server is still called `projectx`.

Scott and Chris were the only two members of the project at the time, as its founders. We ran through numerous possibilities, with the primary difficulty being finding something with domain names available. Scott came up with pfSense, pf being the packet filtering software used, as in making sense of PF.

Chris' response was less than enthusiastic. But after a couple weeks with no better options, we went with it. It was even said "well, we can always change it."

Since then, a name change was considered amongst the developers, without gaining any traction as most people were indifferent and nobody felt a compelling need for change. In mid 2007, a discussion of naming was initiated by a blog post, and the overwhelming response from the community via email and blog comments was "keep the name!"

1.3   Why FreeBSD?

Since many of the core components in pfSense come from OpenBSD, you may wonder why we chose FreeBSD rather than OpenBSD. There were numerous factors under consideration when choosing an OS for this project. This section outlines the primary reasons for choosing FreeBSD.

1.3.1   Wireless Support

We knew wireless support would be a critical feature for many users. At the time this project was founded in 2004, OpenBSD's wireless support was very limited. Its driver support was much more limited than FreeBSD's, and it had no support for important things such as WPA (Wi-Fi Protected Access) and WPA2 with no plans of ever implementing such support at the time. Some of this has changed since 2004, but FreeBSD remains ahead in wireless capabilities.

1.3.2   Network Performance

FreeBSD's network performance is significantly better than that of OpenBSD. For small to mid sized deployments, this generally isn't of any concern, as upper scalability is the primary issue in OpenBSD. One of the pfSense developers manages several hundred OpenBSD PF firewalls, and has had to switch his high load systems over to FreeBSD PF systems to handle the high packets per second rate required in portions of his network. This has become less of an issue in OpenBSD since 2004, but still holds true.

1.3.3   Familiarity and ease of fork

Since the pfSense code base started from m0n0wall, which is based on FreeBSD, it was easier to stay with FreeBSD. Changing the OS would require modifying nearly every part of the system. Scott and Chris, the founders, are also most familiar with FreeBSD and had previously worked together on a now-defunct commercial FreeBSD-based firewall solution. This in and of itself wasn't a compelling reason, but combined with the previous two factors it was just another thing to point us in this direction.

1.3.4   Alternative Operating System Support

At this time, there are no plans to support any other operating systems, simply for reasons of resource constraints. It would be a considerable undertaking to port to any of the other BSDs as we do rely on some functionality that is only available in FreeBSD, which would have to be completely refactored.

1.4 Common Deployments

pfSense is used in about every type and size of network environment imaginable, and is almost certainly suitable for your network whether it contains one computer, or thousands. This section will outline the most common deployments.

1.4.1 Perimeter Firewall

The most common deployment of pfSense is as a perimeter firewall, with an Internet connection plugged into the WAN side, and the internal network on the LAN side.

pfSense accommodates networks with more complex needs, such as multiple Internet connections, multiple LAN networks, multiple DMZ networks, etc.

Some users also add BGP (Border Gateway Protocol) capabilities to provide connection redundancy and load balancing. This is described further in Chapter 8.

1.4.2 LAN or WAN Router

The second most common deployment of pfSense is as a LAN or WAN router. This is a separate role from the perimeter firewall in midsized to large networks, and can be integrated into the perimeter firewall in smaller environments.

1.4.2.1 LAN Router

In larger networks utilizing multiple internal network segments, pfSense is a proven solution to connect these internal segments. This is most commonly deployed via the use of VLANs with 802.1Q trunking, which will be described in Chapter 10. Multiple Ethernet interfaces are also used in some environments.

Note

In environments requiring more than 3 Gbps of sustained throughput, or more than 500,000 packets per second, no router based on commodity hardware offers adequate performance. Such environments need to deploy layer 3 switches (routing done in hardware by the switch) or high end ASIC-based routers. As commodity hardware increases in performance, and general purpose operating systems like FreeBSD improve packet processing capabilities in line with what new hardware capabilities can support, scalability will continue to improve with time.

1.4.2.2 WAN Router

For WAN services providing an Ethernet port to the customer, pfSense is a great solution for private WAN routers. It offers all the functionality most networks require and at a much lower price point than big name commercial offerings.

1.4.3 Wireless Access Point

Many deploy pfSense strictly as a wireless access point. Wireless capabilities can also be added to any of the other types of deployments.

1.4.4 Special Purpose Appliances

Many deploy pfSense as a special purpose appliance. The following are four scenarios we know of, and there are sure to be many similar cases we are not aware of. Most any of the functionality of pfSense can be utilized in an appliance-type deployment. You may find something unique to your environment where this type of deployment is a great fit. As the project has matured, there has been considerable focus on using it as an appliance building framework, especially in the 2.0 release. Some special purpose appliances will be made available in the future.

1.4.4.1 VPN Appliance

Some users drop in pfSense as a VPN appliance behind an existing firewall, to add VPN capabilities without creating any disruption in the existing firewall infrastructure. Most pfSense VPN deployments also act as a perimeter firewall, but this is a better fit in some circumstances.

1.4.4.2 DNS Server Appliance

pfSense offers a DNS (Domain Name System) server package based on TinyDNS, a small, fast, secure DNS server. It isn't laden with features, so it isn't able to be used for some purposes such as Microsoft Active Directory, but it's a great fit for hosting public Internet DNS. Remember the DNS vulnerability chatter in July 2008? Daniel J. Bernstein, the author of TinyDNS, is credited with the original idea and implementation of randomized source ports in the DNS resolver, the resolution to that vulnerability. In fact, TinyDNS was the only major DNS server that did not need to be patched in July 2008. It has used randomized source ports since its inception. Several years ago, Bernstein even put $1000 USD of his own money on the line for the first person to find a privilege escalation security hole. It remains unclaimed. If you're hosting only public Internet DNS, TinyDNS should be strongly considered. The pfSense package also adds failover capabilities.

1.4.4.3 Sniffer Appliance

One user was looking for a sniffer appliance to deploy to a number of branch office locations. Commercial sniffer appliances are available with numerous bells and whistles, but at a very significant cost especially when multiplied by a number of branch locations. pfSense offers a web interface for **tcpdump** that allows the downloading of the resulting pcap file when the capture is finished. This enables this company to capture packets on a branch network, download the resulting capture file, and open it in Wireshark for analysis.

pfSense is not nearly as fancy as commercial sniffer appliances, but offers adequate functionality for many purposes at a vastly lower cost.

For more information on using the packet capture features of pfSense, see Chapter 25.

1.4.4.4 DHCP Server Appliance

One user deploys pfSense installs strictly as DHCP (Dynamic Host Configuration Protocol) servers to hand out IP addresses for its network. In most environments this probably does not make much sense. But in this case, the user's staff were already familiar and comfortable with pfSense and this enabled further deployments without additional training for the administrators, which was an important consideration in this deployment.

1.5 Versions

This section describes the different pfSense releases available currently and in the past.

1.5.1 1.2.3 Release

This is the recommended release for all installations at the time of this writing. It is widely tested and deployed, and because it is the newest 1.2.x release it is the only release that will receive bug fix releases and any necessary security fix releases on 1.2.x in the future. The 1.2.3 release provided a number of bug fixes and enhancements from 1.2.2, and updated the base OS to FreeBSD 7.2. You can find the current recommended release by browsing to www.pfsense.org/versions. References in this book to 1.2 mostly include every 1.2.x release, though some things mentioned in this book only exist in 1.2.3 and later releases.

1.5.2 1.2, 1.2.1, 1.2.2 Releases

1.2 was the first stable release in the 1.2 line of releases, and was made available on February 25, 2008. The 1.2.1 update provided a number of bug fixes and some minor security fixes, and updated the base OS to FreeBSD 7.0. The 1.2.2 release added a few bug fixes.

1.5.3 1.0 Release

This was the first release of pfSense classified as stable. It was released on October 4, 2006, with a follow up 1.0.1 bug fix release on October 20, 2006. Though we know of installs still running some early alpha versions and countless sites still running 1.0, it is no longer supported and we strongly recommend all users upgrade to 1.2.3. 1.0.1 contains several minor security vulnerabilities fixed in either 1.2 or 1.2.1.

1.5.4 Snapshot Releases

The pfSense snapshot server builds a new image from the code currently in our source code repository every two hours. These are primarily for developers and users testing bug fixes at the request of a developer. Snapshots may not always be available, depending on the point in the release cycle. Shortly after the 1.2 release, the snapshots were taken offline as the build infrastructure was updated to FreeBSD 7.0 and the 1.3 (at the time, now 2.0) release was prepared for the first publicly available releases. Similar situations may exist in the future. You can see what snapshots, if any, are available by visiting the snapshot server.

1.5.5   2.0 Release

The pfSense 2.0 release (formerly known as 1.3) is currently available for testing, and is alpha quality at the time of this writing. It contains numerous significant enhancements, many of which are still a work in progress. A stable release, or at least release candidate production quality status is expected in late 2009 or early 2010. It will be based on FreeBSD 8.0, so this schedule is somewhat dependent on FreeBSD's release schedule.

1.6   Platforms

pfSense offers three platforms suitable for three different types of deployments. This section covers each, and which you should choose.

1.6.1   Live CD

The Live CD platform allows you to run directly from the CD without installing to a hard drive or Compact Flash card. The configuration can be saved on a floppy disk or USB flash drive. The CD is not frequently accessed after boot since the system runs primarily from RAM at that point, but should not be removed from a running system. In most circumstances, this should only be used as an evaluation of the software with your particular hardware. Many people do use it long term, but we recommend using full installs instead. Live CD users cannot use packages, and the historical performance graphs are lost at restart.

1.6.2   Full Install

The live CD includes an installer option to install pfSense to the hard drive on your system. This is the preferred means of running pfSense. The entire hard drive must be overwritten; dual booting with another OS is not supported. Full installs are recommended for most deployments. From download statistics we can surmise at least 80% of all pfSense deployments are full installs. Most of the developers use full installs primarily if not entirely. Hence it's the most widely tested and best supported version. It does not have some of the limitations of the other platforms.

1.6.3   Embedded

The embedded version is specifically tailored for use with any hardware using Compact Flash (CF) rather than a hard drive. CF cards can only handle a limited number of writes, so the embedded version runs read only from CF, with read/write filesystems as RAM disks. Even with that limitation, they are widely supported in embedded hardware and via IDE-to-CF converters. Though CF cards are smaller than a traditional ATA hard drive connector, the number of pins is the same and they are compatible. This makes it easier to implement for devices which already support IDE. CF being solid state media, you also don't have the potential failure of a spinning disk to worry about.

Embedded systems are popular for many reasons, but the most compelling ones are that they typically have few if any moving parts, and they consume much less power and produce less heat than larger systems while still performing well enough for the needs of most networks. In this case, less moving parts means less points of failure, less heat, and they can run completely silent.

Historically, embedded has been a second class citizen with pfSense, as full installs have been the primary focus of the project. This has changed with the next generation of embedded, based on NanoBSD.

One drawback of embedded systems is that some of the historical graphing data in RRDtool is lost if the system is not shut down cleanly. For example, a power outage will cause some graph data loss. This does not affect functionality, but will leave blank spots in your historical graphs.

1.6.3.1　Old Embedded (pre-1.2.3 release)

Packages were not supported on the older embedded versions 1.2.2 and before. Older embedded upgrades also did not always work reliably. The only 100% guaranteed reliable means of upgrading embedded installs was to backup the configuration, re-flash the CF, and restore the configuration. These limitations have all been eliminated in the new embedded setup.

1.6.3.2　NanoBSD Embedded

NanoBSD is a standard means of building FreeBSD in an embedded friendly fashion. It supports dual firmware, and is reliably upgradeable. At the time of this writing, NanoBSD embedded is fully functional and being used in production by some of our developers. There will be a 1.2.x release using this embedded methodology, at which time the old embedded will be discontinued. 2.0 will only use the new embedded methodology.

In addition to multiple firmware support enabling switching between two different installs, this brings two additional important benefits. Packages will also be supported, for those suitable for an embedded environment. It also allows cross-building for hardware architectures other than x86, with MIPS and potentially ARM platforms being supported in the future.

1.7　Networking Concepts

While this is not an introductory to networking book, there are certain networking concepts that are important to understand. This portion of the book will not provide adequate coverage for those lacking basic fundamental networking knowledge. If you do not possess this knowledge, you will likely need to seek additional introductory networking material.

Readers with significant knowledge of public and private IP addressing, IP subnetting, CIDR notation and CIDR summarization can skip to the next chapter.

1.7.1   Understanding Public and Private IP Addresses

There are two types of IP addresses found in most networks — public and private.

1.7.1.1   Private IP Addresses

Private IP addresses are those within a reserved subnet, for internal use only. The network standard RFC 1918 defines reserved IP subnets for use in private networks (Table 1.1). In most environments, a private IP subnet from RFC 1918 is chosen and used on all internal network devices, which are then connected to the Internet through a firewall or router implementing Network Address Translation (NAT), such as pfSense. NAT will be explained further in Chapter 7.

CIDR Range	IP Address Range
10.0.0.0/8	10.0.0.0 - 10.255.255.255
172.16.0.0/12	172.16.0.0 - 172.31.255.255
192.168.0.0/16	192.168.0.0 - 192.168.255.255

Table 1.1: RFC 1918 Private IP Address Space

There are other reserved ranges such as 1.0.0.0/8 and 2.0.0.0/8 but these are not permanently reserved like the RFC 1918 addresses. Though it may be tempting to use these, the likelihood of their being allocated to real, routable locations increases as IPv4 space becomes more scarce. You should also avoid using 169.254.0.0/16, which according to RFC 3927 is reserved for "Link-Local" autoconfiguration — but *should not* be assigned by DHCP or manually. There is more than enough address space set aside by RFC 1918, as shown in Table 1.1, so there is little incentive to deviate from that list. We have encountered networks with all manner of improper addressing, and it will lead to problems — it isn't a question of "if", but "when" problems will occur. If you find yourself working on an existing network using an improper address space, it is best to correct the addressing as soon as possible. A complete list of special-use IPv4 networks may be found in RFC 3330.

1.7.1.2   Public IP Addresses

Public IP addresses are those assigned by your ISP for all but the biggest networks. Networks requiring hundreds or thousands of public IP addresses commonly have address space assigned directly from the Regional Internet Registry covering their region of the world. Regional Internet Registries are the organizations that oversee allocation and registration of public IP address in their designated region of the world.

Most residential Internet connections come with a single public IP address, while most business class connections come with an option of using multiple public IPs if necessary. A single public IP is adequate in many circumstances and can be used in conjunction with NAT to connect hundreds of privately addressed systems to the Internet. Content throughout this book will help you determine the number of public IPs your network requires.

1.7.2 IP Subnetting Concepts

When configuring the TCP/IP settings on a device, a subnet mask must be specified. This mask enables the system to determine which IP addresses are on the local network, and which must be reached by a gateway in the system's routing table. The default LAN IP of 192.168.1.1 with a mask of 255.255.255.0, or /24 in CIDR notation, has a network address of 192.168.1.0/24. CIDR is discussed in Section 1.7.4.

1.7.3 IP Address, Subnet and Gateway Configuration

The TCP/IP configuration of a host consists of three primary things — address, subnet mask and gateway. The IP address and subnet mask combined is how the host knows which IP addresses are on its local network. For any addresses outside the local network, traffic is sent (routed) to the configured default gateway which must know how to reach the desired destination. An exception to this rule is a static route, which instructs a router or system on how to contact specific non-local subnets reachable via locally connected routers. This list of gateways and static routes is kept on each host in its routing table. To see the routing table used by pfSense, see Section 8.4.1. More information about routing can be found in Chapter 8.

In a typical pfSense deployment, hosts will be assigned an IP address within the LAN range of pfSense, the same subnet mask as the LAN interface of pfSense, and use pfSense's LAN IP as their default gateway. The same applies to hosts connected to an interface other than LAN, using the appropriate configuration for the interface to which the device is connected.

Hosts within a single network communicate directly with each other with no involvement from the default gateway. This means no firewall, including pfSense, can control host to host communication within a network segment. If this functionality is required, hosts either need to be segmented via the use of multiple switches or VLANs, or equivalent switch functionality like PVLAN needs to be employed. VLANs are covered in Chapter 10.

1.7.4 Understanding CIDR Subnet Mask Notation

pfSense uses a subnet mask format you may not be familiar with. Rather than the common 255.x.x.x, it uses CIDR (Classless InterDomain Routing) notation.

You can refer to Table 1.2 to find the CIDR equivalent of your subnet mask.

1.7.4.1 So where do these CIDR numbers come from anyway?

The CIDR number comes from the number of ones in the subnet mask when converted to binary.

The common subnet mask 255.255.255.0 is 11111111.11111111.11111111.00000000 in binary. This adds up to 24 ones, or /24 (pronounced 'slash twenty four').

A subnet mask of 255.255.255.192 is 11111111.11111111.11111111.11000000 in binary, or 26 ones, hence a /26.

Subnet Mask	CIDR Prefix	Total IP Addresses	Usable IP Addresses	Number of /24 networks
255.255.255.255	/32	1	1	1/256th
255.255.255.254	/31	2	0	1/128th
255.255.255.252	/30	4	2	1/64th
255.255.255.248	/29	8	6	1/32nd
255.255.255.240	/28	16	14	1/16th
255.255.255.224	/27	32	30	1/8th
255.255.255.192	/26	64	62	1/4th
255.255.255.128	/25	128	126	1 half
255.255.255.0	/24	256	254	1
255.255.254.0	/23	512	510	2
255.255.252.0	/22	1024	1022	4
255.255.248.0	/21	2048	2046	8
255.255.240.0	/20	4096	4094	16
255.255.224.0	/19	8192	8190	32
255.255.192.0	/18	16,384	16,382	64
255.255.128.0	/17	32,768	32,766	128
255.255.0.0	/16	65,536	65,534	256
255.254.0.0	/15	131,072	131,070	512
255.252.0.0	/14	262,144	262,142	1024
255.248.0.0	/13	524,288	524,286	2048
255.240.0.0	/12	1,048,576	1,048,574	4096
255.224.0.0	/11	2,097,152	2,097,150	8192
255.192.0.0	/10	4,194,304	4,194,302	16,384
255.128.0.0	/9	8,388,608	8,388,606	32,768
255.0.0.0	/8	16,777,216	16,777,214	65,536
254.0.0.0	/7	33,554,432	33,554,430	131,072
252.0.0.0	/6	67,108,864	67,108,862	262,144
248.0.0.0	/5	134,217,728	134,217,726	1,048,576
240.0.0.0	/4	268,435,456	268,435,454	2,097,152
224.0.0.0	/3	536,870,912	536,870,910	4,194,304
192.0.0.0	/2	1,073,741,824	1,073,741,822	8,388,608
128.0.0.0	/1	2,147,483,648	2,147,483,646	16,777,216
0.0.0.0	/0	4,294,967,296	4,294,967,294	33,554,432

Table 1.2: CIDR Subnet Table

1.7.5 CIDR Summarization

In addition to specifying subnet masks, CIDR can also be employed for IP or network summarization purposes. The "Total IP Addresses" column in the CIDR subnet table indicates how many addresses a given CIDR mask will summarize. For network summarization purposes, the "Number of /24 networks" column is useful. CIDR summarization can be used in several parts of the pfSense web interface, including firewall rules, NAT, virtual IPs, IPsec, static routes, and more.

IPs or networks that can be contained within a single CIDR mask are known as CIDR summarizable.

When designing a network you should ensure all private IP subnets in use at a particular location are CIDR summarizable. For example, if you need three /24 subnets at one location, use a /22 network subnetted into four /24 networks. The following table shows the four /24 subnets you can use with the subnet 10.70.64.0/22.

10.70.64.0/22 split into /24 networks
10.70.64.0/24
10.70.65.0/24
10.70.66.0/24
10.70.67.0/24

Table 1.3: CIDR Route Summarization

This helps keep routing more manageable for multi-site networks (those connected to another physical location via the use of a private WAN circuit or VPN). With CIDR summarizable subnets, you have one route destination that covers all the networks at each location. Without it, you have several different destination networks per location.

Now, if you aren't a subnetting guru, you're probably wondering how the heck I came up with the previous table. Start by choosing a CIDR prefix for your network, according to the number of networks you will require. Then pick a /24 network that you want to use. For that example, I chose 10.70.64.0/24. I know from memory that x.x.64.0/24 will be first /24 network in a /22, but you don't have to pick the first network. You can easily calculate this using the tools available on the subnetmask.info website.

One of the tools will convert from dotted decimal to CIDR mask, and vice versa, this function is shown in Figure 1.1. If you didn't have Table 1.2 from earlier in this chapter in front of you, you could convert your chosen CIDR prefix to dotted decimal notation using this tool. Enter a CIDR prefix and click the Calculate button to its right, or enter a dotted decimal mask and click the Calculate button to its right.

Figure 1.1: Subnet Mask Converter

Armed with the dotted decimal mask, now go to the Network/Node Calculator section. Put in the subnet mask and one of the /24 networks you want to use. Then click Calculate. The bottom boxes will fill in, and show you the range covered by that particular /24, which you can see in Figure 1.2. In this case, the network address will be 10.70.64.0/22, and you can see that the usable /24 networks will be 64 through 67. "Broadcast address" isn't relevant terminology when you are using this tool to determine a CIDR range, that is simply the highest address within the range.

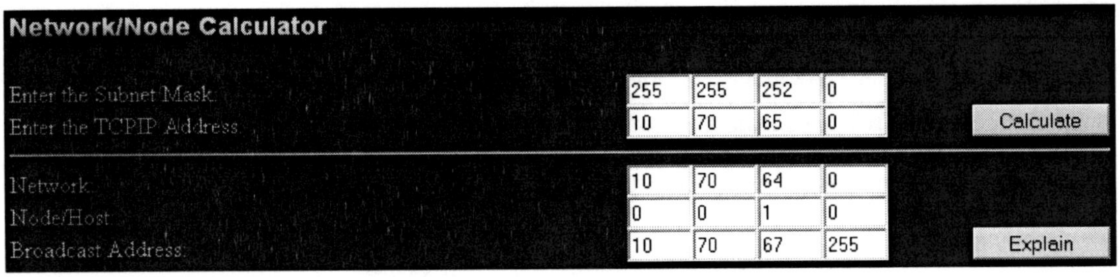

Figure 1.2: Network/Node Calculator

1.7.5.1   Finding a matching CIDR network

If you have a range of IP addresses you wish to summarize, the pfSense Tools Appliance includes **cidr_range.pl**, a Perl script that calculates the CIDR networks required to summarize a range of IP addresses. If you run it without any arguments, you will see its usage instructions.

```
# cidr_range.pl
Usage:  cidr_range.pl <first IP> <last IP>
```

If you want to summarize 192.168.1.13 through 192.168.1.20, run cidr_range.pl as follows.

```
# cidr_range.pl 192.168.1.13 192.168.1.20
192.168.1.13/32
192.168.1.14/31
192.168.1.16/30
192.168.1.20/32
```

This shows it will take four CIDR ranges to include only 192.168.1.13 through 192.168.1.20. If you look back at the CIDR table, a /29 mask covers 8 IP addresses, and this is 8 IP addresses, so why won't one /29 suffice? The answer is because you cannot pick an arbitrary starting address for a CIDR range. If you go plug 192.168.1.13 and 255.255.255.248 into the Network/Node Calculator on subnetmask.info, you will see the /29 network that contains 192.168.1.13 is 192.168.1.8/29 with a range of .8 through .15 (Figure 1.3).

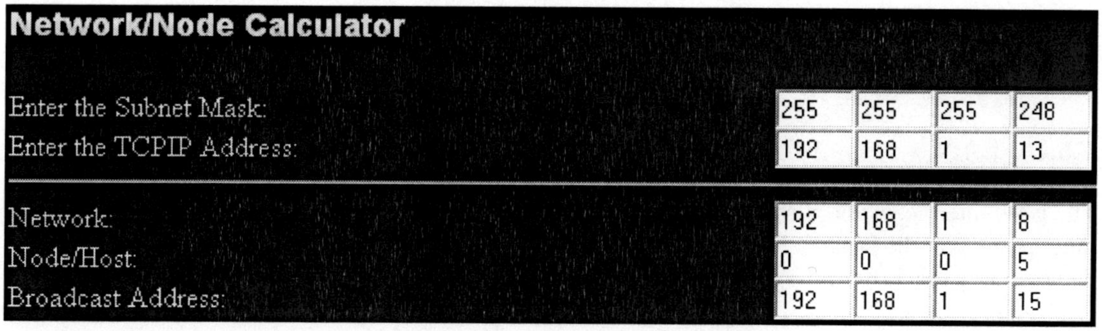

Network/Node Calculator

Enter the Subnet Mask:	255	255	255	248
Enter the TCPIP Address:	192	168	1	13
Network:	192	168	1	8
Node/Host:	0	0	0	5
Broadcast Address:	192	168	1	15

Figure 1.3: Network/Node Calculator Example

If you don't necessarily need an exact match, you can plug in numbers to the Network/Node Calculator to get close to your desired summarization.

1.7.6 Broadcast Domains

A broadcast domain is the portion of a network sharing the same layer two network segment. In a network with a single switch, the broadcast domain is that entire switch. In a network with multiple interconnected switches without the use of VLANs, the broadcast domain includes all of those switches.

A single broadcast domain *can* contain more than one IP subnet, however that is generally not considered good network design. IP subnets should be segregated into separate broadcast domains via the use of separate switches, or VLANs.

Broadcast domains can be combined by bridging two network interfaces together, but care must be taken to avoid switch loops in this scenario. There are also some proxies for certain protocols which do not combine broadcast domains but will give the same effect, such as a DHCP relay which relays DHCP requests into another interface's broadcast domain. More information on broadcast domains and how to combine them can be found in Chapter 9.

1.8 Interface Naming Terminology

This section describes the interface naming terminology used in pfSense and FreeBSD. Most people are familiar with the two basic network divisions: "WAN" and "LAN", but there can be as many segments as you can imagine. You are only limited by the number of interfaces (or VLANs) you have at your disposal.

While discussing the interface names, the topic of network segmentation also comes to mind. It is a good practice to keep different sets of systems apart from each other. For example, you don't want your publicly-accessible web server on the same network as your LAN. If the server was compromised, the attacker could easily reach any system on your LAN. If you have dedicated database servers, these can be isolated from everything else and secured from everything except the servers which need database access. As with the previous example, a compromised web server would not endanger the database servers nearly as much as if they were on the same segment without a firewall in between.

1.8.1 LAN

The LAN interface is the first internal interface on your firewall. Short for Local Area Network, it is most commonly the private side of a router which often utilizes a private IP address scheme. In small deployments, this is typically the only internal interface.

1.8.2 WAN

The WAN interface is used for your Internet connection, or primary Internet connection in a multi-WAN deployment. Short for Wide Area Network, it is the untrusted public network outside of your router. Connections from the Internet will come in through the WAN interface.

1.8.3 OPT

OPT or Optional interfaces refer to any interfaces connected to local networks other than LAN. OPT interfaces are commonly used for second LAN segments, DMZ segments, wireless networks and more.

1.8.4 OPT WAN

OPT WAN refers to Internet connections using an OPT interface, either those configured for DHCP or specifying a gateway IP address. This is discussed in detail in Chapter 11.

1.8.5 DMZ

Short for demilitarized zone. The term was borrowed from its military meaning, which refers to a sort of buffer between a protected area and a war zone. In networking, it is an area where your public servers reside that is reachable from the Internet via the WAN, but is also isolated from the LAN so that a compromise in the DMZ does not endanger systems in other segments.

Some companies misuse the term "DMZ" in their firewall products in reference to 1:1 NAT on the WAN IP which exposes a host on the LAN. There is more information on that subject in Section 7.3.3.

1.8.6 FreeBSD interface naming

FreeBSD names its interfaces by the network driver used, followed by a number starting at 0 and incrementing by one for each additional interface using that driver. For example, a common driver is fxp, used by Intel Pro/100 cards. The first Pro/100 card in a system will be fxp0, the second is fxp1, and so on. Other common ones are em (Intel Pro/1000), bge (various Broadcom chipsets), rl (Realtek 8129/8139), amongst numerous others. If your system mixes a Pro/100 card and a Realtek 8139, your interfaces will be fxp0 and rl0 respectively. Interface assignments and naming are further covered in Chapter 3.

1.9 Finding Information and Getting Help

This section offers guidance on finding information in this book, and on pfSense in general, as well as providing resources on where to get further help if needed.

1.9.1 Finding Information

The easiest way to find information on a specific topic in this book is to check the Index. All the most common features and deployments of pfSense are covered in this book, and the Index will help you find the section or sections where a specific topic is covered.

If you cannot find the information you seek in this book, there is a wealth of additional information and user experiences available on the various pfsense.org sites. The best way to search all these sites is to head to Google, type in the terms you are looking for, and append **site:pfsense.org** to your query. This will search the website, forum, cvstrac, wikis, etc. — all official sources of information. There is a wealth of information available on the forum, and this is the best way of searching it. This will also locate information in the freely available portions of this book.

1.9.2 Getting Help

The pfSense project offers several ways to get help, including a forum, documentation wiki, mailing lists and IRC (Internet Relay Chat, ##pfSense on irc.freenode.net). Commercial support is also available via subscription from the founders of the pfSense project on the pfSense Portal. You can find more information on all these support avenues on the Obtaining Support page on the pfSense site.

Chapter 2

Hardware

pfSense is compatible with any hardware that is supported by the FreeBSD version in use, on i386 hardware platforms. Alternate hardware architectures such as PowerPC, MIPS, ARM, SPARC, etc. are not supported at this time. The new embedded may bring MIPS and ARM support sometime in 2009, though it is not available at the time of this writing. There is also not currently a 64 bit release, though the 32 bit release runs fine on 64 bit hardware. A 64 bit release will come in the future for 2.0, and is currently undergoing testing by developers. To date it has not been a priority because the only benefit it offers in relation to firewalling is the ability to address more memory, and even the largest pfSense installs protecting thousands of machines do not use 4 GB RAM.

2.1 Hardware Compatibility

The best resource for determining compatible hardware is the FreeBSD Hardware Notes for the release version used by the pfSense release you are installing. pfSense 1.2.3 is based on FreeBSD 7.2, therefore a definitive reference on compatible hardware would be the hardware notes at `http://www.freebsd.org/releases/7.2R/hardware.html`. The more general FreeBSD hardware FAQ is another good resource to use for helping hardware selection. It can be found at `http://www.freebsd.org/doc/en_US.ISO8859-1/books/faq/hardware.html`. This section will provide guidance on the best supported hardware available for purposes of firewalling and routing. The primary consideration and only recommendation outside of the hardware notes is for network adapters.

2.1.1 Network Adapters

Virtually all wired Ethernet cards (NICs) are supported by pfSense. However, not all network adapters are created equal. The hardware used can vary greatly in quality from one manufacturer to another, and in some cases, while FreeBSD may support a particular NIC, the driver support may be poor with a specific implementation of the chipset.

Intel Pro/100 and Pro/1000 NICs are the most commonly recommended because they have solid driver support in FreeBSD written by Intel employees, and perform well. On the other end of the spectrum,

Realtek 8139 `rl` cards are extremely common but very poor quality hardware. A snippet of a comment in the source code for this driver tells the story — "The RealTek 8139 PCI NIC redefines the meaning of 'low end.' This is probably the worst PCI Ethernet controller ever made, with the possible exception of the FEAST chip made by SMC." Exacerbating the issue is the fact that numerous manufacturers incorporate this chipset in their NICs, with widely varying degrees of quality. You will find 8139 cards built into some embedded hardware, and those generally are reliable and function properly. Of the various PCI cards that exist, some work fine, and some have various things that are broken. VLANs may not work properly or at all, and promiscuous mode required for bridging may not work, amongst many other possibilities.

If you have NICs available and are building a system from spare parts, it is worthwhile to try what you have on hand. Many times they will work fine. If you are looking to buy hardware for your deployment, go with Intel cards. In networks where reliability and performance are of the utmost concern, don't skimp on costs by using whatever NICs you happen to have lying around (unless those happen to be Intels).

If using VLANs, ensure you select adapters that support VLAN processing in hardware. This is discussed in Chapter 10.

2.1.1.1   USB Network Adapters

Many USB network adapters are supported, but generally not recommended. They perform poorly, especially on systems that do not support USB 2.0, or with adapters that are strictly USB 1.1. USB NICs are great in a pinch, or when adding network connectivity to a desktop PC, and are fine for some home firewall deployments, but for reliable performance in the datacenter they should not be considered.

2.1.1.2   Wireless Adapters

Supported wireless adapters and recommendations are covered in Section 18.1.2.

2.2   Minimum Hardware Requirements

The following outlines the minimum hardware requirements for pfSense 1.2.3. Note the minimum requirements are not suitable for all environments; see Section 2.4 for hardware sizing guidance.

2.2.1   Base Requirements

The following requirements are common to all the pfSense platforms.

- CPU — 100 MHz or faster
- RAM — 128 MB or more

2.2.2 Platform-Specific Requirements

Requirements specific to individual platforms follow.

2.2.2.1 Live CD

- CD-ROM drive
- USB flash drive or floppy drive to store configuration file

2.2.2.2 Full installation

- CD-ROM for initial installation
- 1 GB or larger hard drive

2.2.2.3 NanoBSD Embedded

- 512 MB or larger Compact Flash card
- Serial port for console
- Null modem cable to connect to console port

2.3 Hardware Selection

Open source operating systems can induce numerous headaches with hardware compatibility. While a particular piece of hardware may be supported, a specific implementation of it may not function properly, or certain combinations of hardware may not work. This isn't limited to FreeBSD (and hence pfSense) — Linux distributions also suffer the same fate. In more than a decade of experience using BSD and various Linux distributions on a wide variety of hardware, I have seen this countless times. Some systems that work fine with Windows won't work at all with BSD or Linux, some work fine with BSD but not Linux, some with Linux but not BSD. If you happen to run into hardware related problems, Section 3.5.4 offers tips that will solve these issues in some instances.

2.3.1 Preventing hardware headaches

This section offers some tips on avoiding hardware troubles.

2.3.1.1 Use the hardware the developers use

Over the years, several hardware vendors have donated much needed test equipment to our developers. By using equipment from these vendors, you ensure the device you are purchasing is well tested, and if FreeBSD regressions affecting the hardware occur in the future, they will be fixed before you even knew they existed. We encourage our user base to support the companies that support the project. We are also in the planning stages of offering direct hardware sales, offering pre-installed hardware platforms we use, and know to be rock solid and fully compatible. Visit `http://www.pfsense.org/vendors` for the most up to date information on recommended hardware vendors.

2.3.1.2   Search for the experiences of others

If you are using a piece of hardware from a major manufacturer, if you type its make, model, and `site:pfsense.org` into Google, there is a high probability you will find someone who has tried or is using that hardware. You also may want to try searching for the make, model, and `pfSense` to find experiences people have reported on other websites or the mailing list archives. Reports of failure shouldn't necessarily be considered definitive, as a single user's problems on a particular system could be the result of defective hardware or another anomaly rather than incompatibility. Repeating these same searches with `FreeBSD` instead of pfSense may also turn up useful user experiences.

2.4   Hardware Sizing Guidance

When sizing hardware for use with pfSense, two main factors need to be considered: throughput required and features that will be used. The coming sections cover these considerations.

2.4.1   Throughput Considerations

If you require less than 10 Mbps of throughput, you can get by with the minimum requirements. For higher throughput requirements we recommend following these guidelines, based on our extensive testing and deployment experience. These guidelines offer a bit of breathing room because you never want to run your hardware to its full capacity for extended periods.

Your choice of network card has a significant impact on the maximum achievable throughput, depending on the speed of your CPU. Table 2.1 shows the maximum achievable throughput using two Realtek 8139 NICs compared to two Intel Pro/1000 GT Desktop NICs for hardware platforms with PCI slots.

2.4.1.1   Performance difference by network adapter type

Your choice of NIC will have a significant impact on performance. Cheap low end cards like Realteks will consume significantly more CPU than good quality cards such as Intel. Your first bottleneck with firewall throughput will be your CPU. You can get significantly more throughput out of a given CPU using a better quality NIC, as shown in Table 2.1 with the slower CPUs. If you have a CPU capable of significantly more throughput than you require, your choice of NICs will have little to no impact on throughput, though lesser quality NICs may prove unreliable in some circumstances.

2.4.1.2   Sizing for gigabit throughput

When sizing for gigabit deployments, you first need to determine how much throughput you really need — 1 Gbps wire speed or just more than 100 Mbps. In many networks there are no systems capable of

CPU	Onboard Max Throughput (Mbps)	Realtek Max Throughput (Mbps)	Pro/1000 Max Throughput (Mbps)
Pentium MMX 200 MHz	n/a	25 Mbps	40 Mbps
WRAP — 266 MHz Geode	24 Mbps	n/a	n/a
ALIX — 500 MHz Geode	85 Mbps	n/a	n/a
VIA 1 GHz	93 Mbps (100 Mb wire speed)	n/a	n/a
Netgate Hamakua (1 GHz Celeron)	250 Mbps	n/a	n/a
Pentium II 350 MHz	n/a	51 Mbps	64 Mbps
Pentium III 700 MHz	n/a	84 Mbps	217 Mbps
Pentium 4 1.7 GHz	n/a	93 Mbps (100 Mb wire speed)	365 Mbps

Table 2.1: Maximum Throughput by CPU

filling 1 Gbps with data from disk, as the systems' disk I/O is incapable of such performance. If you just want to be able to hit 200 Mbps, any 1 GHz system with good quality NICs will suffice. For up to 400-500 Mbps, an older 2-3 GHz server will suffice.

2.4.1.3 Sizing for multiple gigabits per second deployments

The numbers in Table 2.1 stop at a relatively low level because that's the extent of what we can reasonably test in our lab. Testing multiple Gbps capable servers requires the servers and several systems capable of pushing 1 Gbps wire speed. We don't have adequate equipment for that scale of testing. But that's not to say that pfSense isn't suitable in such an environment; in fact it's used in numerous deployments pushing in excess of 1 Gbps.

When sizing for multi-Gbps deployments, the primary factor is packets per second, not Gbps. You will hit the limit of FreeBSD and today's fastest quad core server hardware at around 500,000 packets per second (pps). How much throughput this will equate to depends on your network environment, with some references provided in Table 2.2.

Frame size	Throughput at 500Kpps
64 bytes	244 Mbps
500 bytes	1.87 Gbps
1000 bytes	3.73 Gbps
1500 bytes	5.59 Gbps

Table 2.2: 500,000 pps throughput at various frame sizes

For deployments looking to achieve 1 Gbps wire speed between two interfaces, a Pentium 4 3 GHz or faster CPU with PCI-X or PCI-e NICs must be used. PCI will allow you to achieve several hundred

Mbps, but PCI bus speed limitations will prevent you from achieving wire speed performance with two 1 Gbps NICs.

If you are sizing hardware for something capable of gigabit wire speed performance on multiple interfaces, get a new server with a quad core processor and PCI-e NICs and you will be in good shape. If you need to push more than 500,000 packets per second, you may exceed the capacity of commodity PC hardware to push packets. Refer to Section 1.4.2.1 for more information.

2.4.2   Feature Considerations

Most features do not factor into hardware sizing, though a few have significant impact on hardware utilization.

2.4.2.1   Large State Tables

The firewall state table is where active network connections through the firewall are tracked, with each connection consuming one state. States are covered further in Chapter 6. Environments requiring large numbers of simultaneous connections (and hence states) will require additional RAM. Each state takes approximately 1 KB of RAM. Table 2.3 provides a guideline for the amount of memory required for a large number of states. Keep in mind this is solely the memory used for the state tracking, the other components of pfSense will require at least 32-48 MB additional RAM on top of this and possibly more depending on the features in use.

States	RAM Required
100,000	~97 MB
500,000	~488 MB
1,000,000	~976 MB
3,000,000	~2900 MB

Table 2.3: Large State Table RAM Consumption

2.4.2.2   VPN (all types)

The question people usually ask about VPN is "how many connections can my hardware handle?" That is a secondary factor in most deployments, of lesser consideration. The primary consideration in hardware sizing for VPN is throughput required.

The encrypting and decrypting of network traffic with all types of VPNs is very CPU intensive. pfSense offers six cipher options for use with IPsec: DES, 3DES, Blowfish, CAST128, AES and AES 256. The various ciphers perform differently, and the maximum throughput of your firewall is dependent on the cipher used. 3DES is widely used because of its interoperability with nearly every IPsec device, however it is the slowest of all the ciphers supported by pfSense in absence of a hardware crypto accelerator. Hardware crypto accelerators such as supported cards from Hifn greatly increase maximum VPN throughput, and largely eliminate the performance difference between ciphers. Table 2.4 shows

Encryption Protocol	Maximum Throughput	Maximum Throughput (with Hifn)
DES	13.7 Mbps	34.6 Mbps
3DES	8.4 Mbps	34.3 Mbps
Blowfish	16.5 Mbps	not accelerated (no change)
CAST128	16.3 Mbps	not accelerated (no change)
AES	19.4 Mbps	34.2 Mbps
AES 256	13.5 Mbps	34.2 Mbps

Table 2.4: IPsec Throughput by Cipher — ALIX

the maximum throughput by cipher for PC Engines ALIX hardware (500 MHz Geode) without and with a Soekris vpn1411 Hifn crypto accelerator.

Table 2.5 shows the maximum IPsec throughput by CPU for the Blowfish cipher, to illustrate maximum throughput capacity of various CPUs.

CPU	Blowfish Throughput (Mbps)
Pentium II 350	12.4 Mbps
ALIX (500 MHz)	16.5 Mbps
Pentium III 700	32.9 Mbps
Pentium 4 1.7 GHz	53.9 Mbps

Table 2.5: IPsec Throughput by CPU

Hardware crypto accelerators should be used where high bandwidth through IPsec is required, except with dual or quad core CPUs, as those CPUs perform crypto faster than an accelerator by avoiding communicating on the PCI bus.

2.4.2.3   Packages

Some packages have a significant impact on the hardware requirements in your environment.

2.4.2.3.1   Snort

Snort, the network intrusion detection system available in the pfSense package system, can require a significant amount of RAM, depending on your configuration. 256 MB should be considered a minimum, and some configurations may need 1 GB or more.

2.4.2.3.2   Squid

Squid is a caching proxy HTTP server available as a pfSense package, and disk I/O performance is an important consideration for Squid users since it determines cache performance. In contrast, for most users of pfSense it is largely irrelevant since the only significant impact that disk speed has on pfSense is boot time and upgrade time; it has no relevance to network throughput or other normal operation.

In small environments, even for Squid, any hard drive will suffice. For 200+ user deployments using Squid, you should consider 10K RPM SATA or SCSI disks. Use 15K RPM SCSI or SAS disks for best performance in large environments.

pfSense supports most hardware RAID controllers found in server hardware. The use of RAID 10 on your RAID arrays can further improve Squid performance, and would be recommended for deployments with thousands of users.

Chapter 3

Installing and Upgrading

The hardware has been chosen, along with the pfSense version and platform to be used. Now it is time to download the appropriate pfSense release and install it on the target device. After downloading the proper version, continue to the section that describes installing the platform that has been chosen: Full Install or Embedded. If something should go wrong during the process, see Section 3.5 later in the chapter.

In this chapter, we also talk about recovery installation methods and how to upgrade pfSense. Recovery installations (Section 3.6) are ways to reinstall pfSense with an existing configuration, typically with minimal downtime. Upgrading pfSense (Section 3.7) will keep your system current, add new features, or fix bugs. Upgrading is a fairly painless process which can be accomplished in several different ways.

3.1 Downloading pfSense

Browse to www.pfsense.org and click the **Downloads** link. On the Downloads page, click the link for new installations. This will lead to the mirror selection page. Pick a mirror geographically close to your location for best performance. Once a mirror has been selected, a directory listing will appear with the current pfSense release files for new installations.

For Live CD or full installations, download the `.iso` file. The 1.2.3 release file name is `pfSense-1.2.3-LiveCD-Installer.iso`. There is also a MD5 file available by the same name, but ending in `.md5`. This file contains a hash of the ISO, which can be used to ensure the download completed properly.

For embedded installations, download the `.img.gz` file. The 1.2.3 release file name is `pfSense-1.2.3-nanobsd-size.img.gz`, where *size* is one of 512M, 1G, 2G, or 4G, to reflect the size of CF card for which that image was intended (sizes are in M for megabyte and G for gigabyte). Typically you would want to match the size of the image to the size of your CF card, but you can use a smaller size image on a larger CF card such as a 1G image on a 2G CF card. This file is a gzipped image. You need not extract the file, as the installation process described later in this chapter will handle that.

If at any point in the installation something does not go as described, check Section 3.5.

3.1.1 Verifying the integrity of the download

The accompanying MD5 file can be used to verify the download completed successfully, and that an official release is being used.

3.1.1.1 MD5 verification on Windows

Windows users may install HashTab or a similar program to view MD5 hashes for any given file. With HashTab installed, right click on the downloaded file and there will be a File Hashes tab containing the MD5 hash, among others. The generated MD5 hash can be compared with the contents of the `.md5` file downloaded from the pfSense website, which is viewable in any plain text editor such as Notepad.

3.1.1.2 MD5 verification on BSD and Linux

The **md5** command comes standard on FreeBSD, and many other UNIX and UNIX-like operating systems. An MD5 hash may be generated by running the following command from within the directory containing the downloaded file:

```
# md5 pfSense-1.2.3-LiveCD-Installer.iso
```

Compare the resulting hash with the contents of the `.md5` file downloaded from the pfSense website. (Gnu or Linux systems provide a **md5sum** command that works similarly.)

3.1.1.3 MD5 verification on OS X

OS X also includes the **md5** command just like FreeBSD, but there are also GUI applications available such as MD5 from Eternal Storms.

3.2 Full Installation

This section describes the process of installing pfSense to a hard drive. In a nutshell, this involves booting from the Live CD, performing some basic configuration, and then invoking the installer from the CD. If you encounter problems while trying to boot or install from CD, see Section 3.5 later in the chapter.

Note

If the target hardware does not have a CD-ROM drive, a different machine may be used to install on the target hard drive. See Alternate Installation Techniques (Section 3.4) for more information.

3.2.1 Preparing the CD

A CD will need to be burned from the ISO image downloaded in the previous section. Since the downloaded file is a CD image, it will need to be burned appropriately for image files — *not* as a data CD containing the single ISO file. Procedures for doing so will vary by OS and software available.

3.2.1.1 Burning in Windows

Virtually every major CD burning software package for Windows includes the ability to burn ISO images. Refer to the documentation of the CD burning program being used. A Google search with the name of the burning software and "**burn iso**" should help to locate instructions.

3.2.1.1.1 Burning with Nero

It is easy to burn ISO images with Nero. Start by right clicking on the ISO file, then click Open With, and select Nero. The first time this is done, it may be necessary to select Chose Default Program and then pick Nero from the list. This same process should work with other commercial CD burning software.

3.2.1.1.2 Burning with ISO Recorder

If using Windows XP, 2003, or Vista, the freely available ISO Recorder tool may be used. Download and install the appropriate version of ISO Recorder for the operating system being used, then browse to the folder on the drive containing the pfSense ISO, right click on it, and click Copy image to CD.

3.2.1.1.3 Other Free Burning Software

Other free options for Windows users include CDBurnerXP, InfraRecorder and burnatonce (bao), among others. Before downloading and installing any program, check its feature list to make sure it is capable of burning an ISO image.

3.2.1.2 Burning in Linux

Linux distributions such as Ubuntu typically include some form of GUI CD burning application that can handle ISO images. If one is integrated with the window manager, right click on the ISO file and choose Write disc to. Other popular choices include K3B and Brasero Disc Burner.

If there is not a GUI burning program installed, it may still be possible to burn from the command line. First, determine the burning device's SCSI ID/LUN (Logical Unit Number) with the following command:

```
# cdrecord --scanbus
Cdrecord-Clone 2.01 (i686-pc-linux-gnu) Copyright (C) 1995-2004 Jörg ↩
    Schilling
Linux sg driver version: 3.1.25
Using libscg version 'schily-0.8'.
scsibus0:
    0,0,0 100) 'LITE-ON ' 'COMBO LTC-48161H' 'KH0F' Removable CD-ROM
```

Note the SCSI ID/LUN is *0, 0, 0*. Burn the image as in the following example, replacing **<max speed>** with the speed of the burner and *lun* with the SCSI ID/LUN of your recorder:

```
# cdrecord --dev=lun --speed=<max speed> \
    pfSense-1.2.3-LiveCD-Installer.iso
```

3.2.1.3   Burning in FreeBSD

FreeBSD includes the burncd program in its base system which can be used to burn ISO images like
so.

```
# burncd -s max -e data pfSense-1.2.3-LiveCD-Installer.iso fixate
```

For more information on creating CDs in FreeBSD, please see the entry for CD burning in the *FreeBSD
Handbook* at `http://www.freebsd.org/doc/en/books/handbook/creating-cds.html`.

3.2.1.4   Verifying the CD

Now that the CD is prepared, verify it was burned properly by viewing the files contained on the CD.
More than 20 folders should be visible, including bin, boot, cf, conf, and more. If only one large ISO
file is seen, the CD was not burned properly. Repeat the steps listed earlier for burning a CD, and be
sure to burn the ISO file as a CD image and not as a data file.

3.2.2   Booting the CD

Now power on the target system and place the CD into the drive. pfSense should begin to boot, and
will show an assign interfaces prompt which is covered in a following section.

3.2.2.1   Specifying Boot Order in BIOS

If the target system did not boot from the CD, the most likely reason is that the CD-ROM drive was
not early enough in the list of boot media in the BIOS. Many newer motherboards also allow bringing
up a one time boot menu by pressing a key during POST, commonly **Esc** or **F12**.

Failing that, change the boot order in the BIOS. First, power on the system and enter the BIOS setup.
It is typically found under a Boot or Boot Priority heading, but could be anywhere. If booting from CD-
ROM is not enabled, or has a lower priority than booting from the hard drive and the drive contains
another OS, the system will not boot from the pfSense CD. Consult the motherboard manual for more
detailed information on altering the boot order.

3.2.3   Assigning Interfaces

After the pfSense Live CD has completed the boot process, the system will prompt for interface assignment as in Figure 3.1. This is where the network cards installed in the system are given their roles
as WAN, LAN, and Optional interfaces (OPT1, OPT2 ... OPTn).

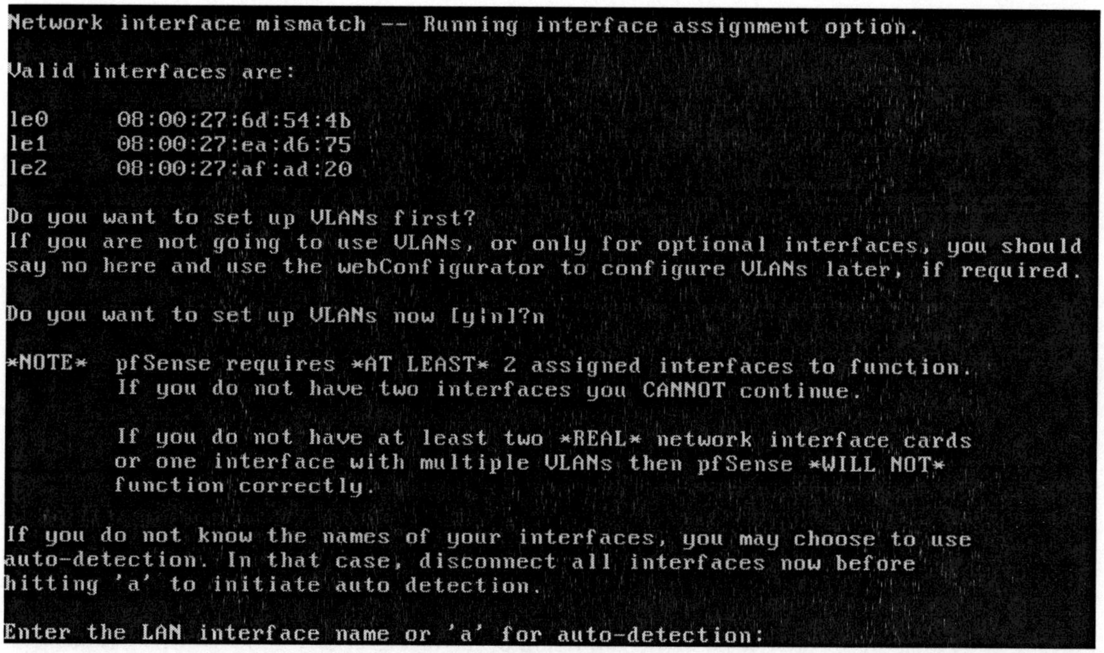

```
Network interface mismatch -- Running interface assignment option.

Valid interfaces are:

le0      08:00:27:6d:54:4b
le1      08:00:27:ea:d6:75
le2      08:00:27:af:ad:20

Do you want to set up VLANs first?
If you are not going to use VLANs, or only for optional interfaces, you should
say no here and use the webConfigurator to configure VLANs later, if required.

Do you want to set up VLANs now [y|n]?n

*NOTE*   pfSense requires *AT LEAST* 2 assigned interfaces to function.
         If you do not have two interfaces you CANNOT continue.

         If you do not have at least two *REAL* network interface cards
         or one interface with multiple VLANs then pfSense *WILL NOT*
         function correctly.

If you do not know the names of your interfaces, you may choose to use
auto-detection. In that case, disconnect all interfaces now before
hitting 'a' to initiate auto detection.

Enter the LAN interface name or 'a' for auto-detection:
```

Figure 3.1: Interface Assignment Screen

A list of network interfaces and their MAC addresses that were located on the system will appear, along with an indication of their link state if that is supported by the network card. The link state is denoted by "(up)" appearing after the MAC address if a link is detected on that interface. The MAC (Media Access Control) address of a network card is a unique identifier assigned to each card, and no two network cards should have the same MAC address. (In practice, this is not quite true, MAC address duplication does happen fairly often.) After that, a prompt will show up for VLAN configuration. If VLANs are desired, see Chapter 10 later in the book for details of their setup and usage. Otherwise, type **n** and press enter.

The LAN interface is configured first. As pfSense 1.2.3 requires at least two network cards, a dilemma may present itself: How to tell which is which? If the identity of each card is already known, simply enter the proper device names for each interface. If the difference between network cards is unknown, the easiest way to figure it out would be to use the auto-detection feature.

For automatic interface assignment, first unplug all network cables from the system, then type **a** and press enter. Now plug a network cable into the interface that should connect to the LAN, and press enter. If all went well, pfSense should know now which interface to use for the LAN. The same process may be repeated for the WAN, and any optional interfaces that will be needed. If a message is displayed such as No link-up detected, see the Section 3.5 for more information on sorting out network card identities.

After the interfaces have been configured, a prompt will appear asking Do you want to proceed?. If the network interface assignment appears correct, type **y**, then press enter. If the assignment is not right, type **n** and press enter to repeat this process.

3.2.4   Installing to the Hard Drive

Once the interface assignment is complete, a menu will appear with additional tasks that may be performed. To install pfSense to the hard drive of this system, choose option **99** which will launch the installation process.

The first screen to appear will ask to adjust console settings. Unless an alternate language keyboard is being used, choose Accept These Settings and move on to the next step.

Next, a list of tasks will be presented. If there is only one hard drive installed on the system and you do not need to set any other custom options, Quick/Easy Install may be chosen. This will install to the first hard drive it finds and accept all of the default options. A confirmation dialog will be shown. Press OK to continue or Cancel to return to the previous menu. The installation will proceed and only stop to prompt for which kernel should be installed.

If you chose to use the Quick/Easy Install option, skip ahead to Table 3.1 for kernel choices. Otherwise, pick the first option: Install pfSense to perform a custom installation and continue on through the rest of this section.

Now pick the hard drive to which pfSense will be installed. Each hard drive attached to the system should be shown, along with any supported RAID or gmirror volumes. Select the drive with the up and down arrows, then press enter. If no drives are found or the incorrect drives are shown, it is possible that the desired drive is attached to an unsupported controller or a controller set for an unsupported mode in the BIOS. See Section 3.5 for help.

The next step is to format the drive that was just chosen. Unless it is known for certain that the drive contains a usable FreeBSD partition, select Format This Disk and press enter. Otherwise, choose Skip this step. When presented with the Disk Geometry screen, it is best to choose Use this geometry. It is possible to override this if more correct values are known, but in most cases the defaults are correct. A confirmation screen will be shown, at which point the Format <drive name> option must be chosen to continue.

Note

This is a good place to stop and ensure that the correct drive has been selected, as there is no turning back once this action has been performed. *Everything on the disk will be destroyed.*

Dual booting with another operating system is possible for advanced users who know how to manually configure such things, but such configurations are not officially supported and will not be detailed here.

Partitioning follows, and you should simply accept the defaults by choosing Accept and Create, then choosing Yes, partition at the next screen.

A prompt is then shown for installing bootblocks. This is what will allow the hard drive to boot. Install Bootblocks will already be selected (an X appears in that column next to the drive being configured). Packet Mode may or may not be needed, depending on the hardware combination in use. Some newer hardware and larger drives will work better with packet mode enabled, and older hardware may prefer packet mode disabled. Leave the defaults selected unless they do not work on your system for some reason. Now select Accept and Install Bootblocks and press enter. A confirmation box will appear with the result of that command, and if it succeeded, press enter one more time to proceed.

Select the partition on which to install pfSense at the next screen that comes up. If the defaults were used as suggested, there is likely only one choice. If multiple choices appear, pick the one that was created for pfSense. Another confirmation window will appear reporting the success of the formatting process.

Subpartitions may now be created, but again the defaults on this screen will be acceptable for nearly all uses. Some people prefer to have separate subpartitions for /var, /tmp, and so on but this is not necessary, and you should not do so unless you have a considerable understanding of the space requirements specific to your installation. If you are performing a full install to flash-based media like a CF card or USB thumb drive, be sure to remove the swap partition. Make the desired changes, and then select Accept and Create.

Now sit back, wait, and have a few sips of coffee while the installation process copies pfSense to the target location. After the installation process has finished its work, there is a final prompt to select which kernel to install on the target system. There are four options available, each with its own purpose:

Kernel Type	Purpose/Description
Symmetric Multiprocessing Kernel	Used for systems which have multiple cores or processors.
Uniprocessor Kernel	Used for systems that have only one processor
Embedded Kernel	Disables VGA console and keyboard, uses serial console.
Developers Kernel	Includes debugging options useful for developers.

Table 3.1: Kernel Choices

When in doubt, either the Uniprocessor Kernel (UP) or the Symmetric Multiprocessing Kernel (SMP) should work, regardless of the number of processors available. There are rare issues where certain hardware, regardless of the number of processors, will not function reliably or at all with the uniprocessor kernel but works fine with the SMP kernel, as well as vice versa. Should you encounter problems, try switching your kernel from SMP to uniprocessor or vice versa.

When the installation is complete, select Reboot, and then once the system has restarted, remove the CD before the boot process begins.

Congratulations, pfSense is now fully installed!

3.3 Embedded Installation

The embedded version is released as a disk image, which must be written out to a Compact Flash card (CF) using **physdiskwrite** or **dd**. After the image is written, it is then placed in the target device and configured.

Note

Be **very careful** when doing this!! If this is run this on a machine containing other hard drives it is possible to select the wrong drive and overwrite a portion of that drive with pfSense. This renders the disk completely unreadable except to certain disk recovery programs, and that is hit and miss at best. **physdiskwrite** for Windows contains a safety check that will not allow overwriting a drive larger than 800 MB without a specific option at the command line. The safest way to install pfSense to a CF is through USB redirection with VMware, discussed later in this chapter in the Alternate Installation Techniques section (Section 3.4).

Again, **be very careful when doing this!** I stress this because I know of multiple people who have mistyped a disk and overwritten a hard drive. This can happen to anybody, including the other founder of pfSense, who accidentally overwrote his 1 TB data drive instead of his CF with a pfSense image.

3.3.1 Embedded Installation in Windows

The **physdiskwrite** program by Manuel Kasper, author of m0n0wall, is the preferred means of writing the pfSense image to CF in Windows. It can be downloaded from the m0n0wall website. Save it somewhere on the PC being used, such as `C:\tools` or another convenient location. If another location is chosen, substitute `C:\tools` in the example with the directory where `physdiskwrite.exe` has been placed.

Note

There is also a GUI available for **physdiskwrite** called PhysGUI, but the only available version as of this writing was in German. That said, the GUI is simple enough to use that it may not be a barrier for many people. In fact, it may prove easier to use, even in a foreign language, than the command line version is in English. For example, identifying the proper device is a much simpler task. It is also available from the m0n0wall website.

In Windows Vista or Windows 7, **physdiskwrite** must be launched from a command prompt run as administrator. Simply having administrator rights is not enough. The easiest way to do this is to click the Start button, then type **cmd** in the search box. Right click on `cmd.exe` when it pops up and choose Run as Administrator. The **physdiskwrite** program may then be run from that command prompt without any problems. Running it from a command prompt which has not been run as administrator will result in no disks being found.

To use **physdiskwrite**, first start a command prompt.

Then change to the directory containing `physdiskwrite.exe` and run it followed by the path to the `pfSense.img.gz` file downloaded earlier. After running the command, a prompt with a list of drives attached to the system will appear. The safest way to ensure the correct drive is chosen would be to run **physdiskwrite** before inserting the CF, record the output, then press Ctrl-C to exit. Insert the CF and run **physdiskwrite** again, comparing the output to the previous run. The disk shown now that was not shown previously is the CF. The number of cylinders ("cyl" in **physdiskwrite** output) may also be used to help indicate the proper drive. The 512 MB CF used in the following example has 63 cylinders, while the hard drives all have over 30,000. Also remember that **physdiskwrite** has a safety mechanism that will not overwrite a disk larger than 2 GB without specifying -u after the **physdiskwrite** command.

After selecting the disk to write, **physdiskwrite** will write out the image. This will take between two to ten minutes on a fast machine with USB 2.0 and a USB 2.0 CF writer. If the system or CF writer is only USB 1.1, expect it to take several times longer due to the very low speed of USB 1.1.

The following is a practical example of using **physdiskwrite** to write a pfSense image.

```
Microsoft Windows [Version 6.0.6001]
Copyright (c) 2006 Microsoft Corporation.  All rights reserved.

C:\Windows\system32> cd \tools

C:\tools> physdiskwrite.exe c:\temp\pfSense-1.2.3-nanobsd-512M.img.gz

physdiskwrite v0.5.1 by Manuel Kasper <mk@neon1.net>

Searching for physical drives...

Information for \\.\PhysicalDrive0:
    Windows:        cyl: 36481
                    tpc: 255
                    spt: 63

Information for \\.\PhysicalDrive1:
    Windows:        cyl: 30401
                    tpc: 255
                    spt: 63

Information for \\.\PhysicalDrive2:
    Windows:        cyl: 63
                    tpc: 255
                    spt: 63

Information for \\.\PhysicalDrive3:
DeviceIoControl() failed on \\.\PhysicalDrive3.

Information for \\.\PhysicalDrive4:
DeviceIoControl() failed on \\.\PhysicalDrive4.

Information for \\.\PhysicalDrive5:
DeviceIoControl() failed on \\.\PhysicalDrive5.

Information for \\.\PhysicalDrive6:
    Windows:        cyl: 30515
                    tpc: 255
                    spt: 63

Information for \\.\PhysicalDrive7:
    Windows:        cyl: 0
                    tpc: 0
                    spt: 0
```

```
Which disk do you want to write? (0..7) 2
About to overwrite the contents of disk 2 with new data. Proceed? (y/n)   ↵
    y
Found compressed image file
122441728/122441728 bytes written in total

C:\tools>
```

After **physdiskwrite** has completed, the CF may be removed from the writer and placed in the target hardware.

Note

The written CF contains BSD filesystem formatted partitions that are not readable in Windows. Windows will claim the drive needs to be formatted should you try to access it. Do not do so, simply move the CF to the target hardware. There is no way to view the contents of the written CF in Windows.

3.3.2   Embedded Installation in Linux

Embedded installation in Linux is accomplished by piping the **gunzip** output from the image to **dd**.

```
# gunzip -c pfSense-1.2.3-nanobsd.img.gz | dd of=/dev/hdX bs=16k
```

where X specifies the IDE device name of the CF card or IDE disk (check with **hdparm -i /dev/hdX**) — some adapters, particularly USB, may show up under SCSI emulation as /dev/sdX.

Ignore the warning about trailing garbage — it's because of the digital signature.

3.3.3   Embedded Installation in FreeBSD

gzip piped to **dd** will write the image out to CF in FreeBSD. Before starting, you will need to know the device name which corresponds to the CF card in use. If a hard drive or CF-to-IDE adapter is being used, it may be an ad device such as ad0. Check the output of **dmesg** or /var/log/messages. If a USB CF reader is being used, it may be a da device such as da0, check /var/log/messages after plugging in the card reader, it should report which device was added.

To image the card, you should be able to decompress the image and copy it to the card in one step:

```
# gzip -dc pfSense-1.2.3-nanobsd.img.gz | dd of=/dev/adX obs=64k
```

Ignore the warning about trailing garbage — it's because of the digital signature.

If the imaging stops short or errors off after only transferring a small amount of data, you may need to decompress the image first:

```
# gunzip pfSense-1.2.3-nanobsd.img.gz
# dd if=pfSense-1.2.3-nanobsd.img of=/dev/adX obs=64k
```

3.3.4 Embedded Installation in Mac OS X

This process has been tested on Mac OS X 10.3.9 and later, up to and including Snow Leopard/10.6. It is recommended that you disconnect all disks except for your startup disk before carrying out this procedure, as an error in specifying the drive to be written to could cause data loss.

- Plug in your CF reader with CF card inserted.

- If Mac OS X pops up a message saying that the card could not be read, click Ignore.

- Open Disk Utility.

- Select any Partitions of your CF Card that are mounted, and click the unmount button. The partitions should now appear greyed out.

- Select your CF Card Reader in the left-hand column, and click the Info button.

- Note the 'Disk Identifier': e.g. 'disk1'.

- Open Terminal.

- Change to the directory containing the pfSense image.

- Use this command, replacing *disk[n]* with the disk identifier found above:

```
# gzcat pfSense-1.2.3-nanobsd.img.gz | dd of=/dev/disk[n] bs=16k
```

There is also the following alternative to accomplish this entirely from the command line.

```
$ diskutil list
/dev/disk0
   #:                       TYPE NAME                  SIZE       IDENTIFIER
   0:      GUID_partition_scheme                      *298.1 Gi   disk0
   1:                        EFI                        200.0 Mi   disk0s1
   2:                  Apple_HFS Macintosh HD           297.8 Gi   disk0s2
/dev/disk1
   #:                       TYPE NAME                  SIZE       IDENTIFIER
   0:    CD_partition_scheme 30 Days To Great French  *521.4 Mi   disk1
   1:                      CD_DA                        7.8 Mi     disk1s1
   2:                      CD_DA                        7.8 Mi     disk1s2
   3:                      CD_DA                        18.2 Mi    disk1s3
   4:                      CD_DA                        13.8 Mi    disk1s4
   5:                      CD_DA                        14.0 Mi    disk1s5
   6:                      CD_DA                        12.1 Mi    disk1s6
   7:                      CD_DA                        14.2 Mi    disk1s7
   8:                      CD_DA                        21.5 Mi    disk1s8
   9:                      CD_DA                        16.6 Mi    disk1s9
  10:                      CD_DA                        14.7 Mi    disk1s10
  11:                      CD_DA                        24.3 Mi    disk1s11
  12:                      CD_DA                        16.6 Mi    disk1s12
  13:                      CD_DA                        22.4 Mi    disk1s13
  14:                      CD_DA                        14.7 Mi    disk1s14
```

```
    15:                  CD_DA                        20.5 Mi    disk1s15
    16:                  CD_DA                        19.4 Mi    disk1s16
    17:                  CD_DA                        15.3 Mi    disk1s17
    18:                  CD_DA                        17.9 Mi    disk1s18
    19:                  CD_DA                        18.2 Mi    disk1s19
    20:                  CD_DA                        16.0 Mi    disk1s20
    21:                  CD_DA                        26.8 Mi    disk1s21
    22:                  CD_DA                        18.8 Mi    disk1s22
    23:                  CD_DA                        21.7 Mi    disk1s23
    24:                  CD_DA                        14.5 Mi    disk1s24
    25:                  CD_DA                        22.2 Mi    disk1s25
    26:                  CD_DA                        16.7 Mi    disk1s26
    27:                  CD_DA                        20.9 Mi    disk1s27
    28:                  CD_DA                        16.0 Mi    disk1s28
    29:                  CD_DA                        20.8 Mi    disk1s29
    30:                  CD_DA                        17.1 Mi    disk1s30
/dev/disk2
    #:                  TYPE NAME                     SIZE       IDENTIFIER
    0:    GUID_partition_scheme                    *90.0 Mi    disk2
    1:            Apple_HFS Processing               90.0 Mi    disk2s1
/dev/disk3
    #:                  TYPE NAME                     SIZE       IDENTIFIER
    0:   FDisk_partition_scheme                    *978.5 Mi   disk3
    1:          DOS_FAT_32 UNTITLED                 978.4 Mi   disk3s1
$ diskutil umount disk3s1
$ gzcat pfsense-embedded.img.gz | dd of=/dev/disk3s1 bs=16k
7665+1 records in
7665+1 records out
125587456 bytes transferred in 188.525272 secs (666157 bytes/sec)
```

3.3.5   Completing the Embedded Installation

Now that the CF contains a pfSense image, it can be placed into the target device, but it may still need some configuration. Users of ALIX and Soekris 5501 hardware can skip this section, as they use vr(4)-based network controllers, and the default embedded installation assumes that vr0 is LAN and vr1 is WAN. These ports should be labeled on the hardware. If you want to reassign these interfaces from the console instead of the WebGUI, continue on.

3.3.5.1   Connect a Serial Cable

First, a null modem serial cable should be connected between the device and a PC. Depending on the serial port and cable being used, a serial cable gender changer may also be necessary to match the available ports. If a real null modem serial cable is unavailable, there are also null modem adapters that will convert a standard serial cable into a null modem cable.

3.3.5.2 Start a Serial Client

On the PC being used to configure the embedded device, a serial client program must be used. Some popular clients for Windows are Hyperterminal, which should be on almost any XP installation, and PuTTY, which is free and much more reliable. On Linux, `minicom` should be present in most distribution package systems. On FreeBSD, simply use the built-in program `tip`. Typing **tip com1** will connect to the first serial port. Disconnect by typing "**~.**" at the start of a line.

Whichever serial client is used, ensure that it is set for the proper Speed (9600), Data Bits (8), Parity (No), and Stop Bits (1). This is typically written as 9600/8/N/1. Some embedded units default to a faster speed. PC Engines WRAP and ALIX default to 38400/8/N/1 and Soekris hardware defaults to 19200/8/N/1. Many serial clients default to 9600/8/N/1, so adjusting these settings may not be necessary. You will need to use 9600/8/N/1 with pfSense regardless of the setting of your hardware. For hardware using speeds other than 9600, you will likely want to change the baud rate to 9600 in the BIOS setup so the BIOS and pfSense are both accessible with the same settings. Refer to the manual for your hardware for information on setting its baud rate.

3.3.5.3 Assign Network Interfaces

After the device is powered on and the boot process has started, a prompt will be shown for VLANs and assigning network interfaces. This step was covered earlier under Section 3.2.3 for automatic detection, and later in Section 3.5.3.1 for manually assigning interfaces.

Once the interfaces have been assigned, the system should be ready to configure via the WebGUI.

3.4 Alternate Installation Techniques

This section describes some alternate methods of installation that may be easier for some deployments.

3.4.1 Installation with drive in a different machine

If it is difficult or impossible to add a CD-ROM drive to the target hardware, another system may be utilized to install pfSense on the target hard drive. The drive may then be moved to the original machine.

When prompted with `Assign Interfaces` during the live CD boot, choose **n** for VLANs and type **exit** at the assign LAN interface prompt to skip interface assignment. Then proceed through the installation normally. A prompt will appear in the installer for configuring network settings, and this may be skipped as well. After installation, allow the machine to restart and power it off once it returns to the BIOS screen. Remove the hard drive from the installation machine and place it into the target system. After boot, it will prompt for interface assignment and then the rest of the configuration may be performed as usual.

3.4.1.1   Boot failure after moving drive to target machine

If the machine used to perform the install assigned the drive with a different device name than the target device, the system will halt booting at a `mountroot>` prompt. This can happen if the install was performed with the drive on the secondary IDE port and in the target hardware it resides on the primary IDE port. In the case of VMware, the USB adapter may be detected as a SCSI device while the target hardware uses IDE.

If this problem is encountered, the system will stop booting and sit at a `mountroot>` prompt, as in this example:

```
Timecounter "TSC" frequency 431646144 Hz quality 800
Timecounters tick every 10.000 msec
Fast IPsec: Initialized Security Association Processing.
ad0: 3906MB <HMS360404D5CF00 DN4OCA2A> at ata0-master UDMA33
Trying to mount root from ufs:/dev/ad2s1a

Manual root filesystem specification:
  <fstype>:<device>  Mount <device> using filesystem <fstype>
                       eg. ufs:da0s1a
  ?                  List valid disk boot devices
  <empty line>       Abort manual input

mountroot> ufs:ad0s1a
Trying to mount root from ufs:ad0s1a


    ___
   ___/ f \
  / p \___/ Sense
  \___/    \
      \___/
```

The system is trying to mount the drive by the wrong device name, such as `ad2`. A line just above the `mountroot` prompt should list the real location of the drive, such as `ad0`. To continue the boot process, type in the correct device name. In this case, **ufs:ad0s1a**. Just replace *ad0* in that line with the device name of the hard drive as shown above this prompt. Make a note of the proper device name, as it will be needed for the next step.

Now that the system has booted, one more change is needed. The filesystem table in `/etc/fstab` needs to be updated with the proper device. To change this in the WebGUI, browse to Diagnostics → Edit file, and open `/etc/fstab`. Replace each instance of the device name in that file and save your changes. Reboot to verify the change.

For those familiar with command line operations, to change this at the command line choose option **8** once the console menu loads to enter to start a shell. This example uses the **vi** editor. If **vi** is not a desirable choice, **ee** is also available and has on-screen help.

Now enter the command to edit the `fstab` file.

```
# vi /etc/fstab
```

The contents of the file will appear. It will look something like this:

```
# Device              Mountpoint      FStype   Options        Dump    Pass#
/dev/ad2s1a          /               ufs      rw             1       1
```

Make the necessary changes. In this example, the incorrect device is `ad2`, this should be changed to `ad0`:

```
# Device              Mountpoint      FStype   Options        Dump    Pass#
/dev/ad0s1a          /               ufs      rw             1       1
```

Now save the file and quit the editor. (**Esc**, then `:wq!` if **vi** was used.)

3.4.2 Full Installation in VMware with USB Redirection

You can use the USB redirection in VMware Player and Workstation to install to a hard drive. Most any USB to IDE or SFF (Small Form Factor) IDE adapter will work for this purpose. The following instructions are specific to VMware Workstation 6.0 and earlier.

- Create a VM with USB redirection.

- Unplug your CF writer from your PC.

- Plug your CF/Microdrive into your CF writer.

- Start the virtual machine, and click inside the VM to give it focus.

- Plug the CF writer into your PC. The VM will pick up the USB device, and the pfSense installer CD will recognize the CF/Microdrive as a hard drive.

- Continue through the installation the same as a normal Full Install.

In VMware Workstation 6.5, you will see an icon for each USB device on the host along the bottom of the VMware window. Click the device and click `Connect (Disconnect from host)` to use it inside your VM. Refer to the VMware documentation for more information on USB redirection.

3.4.3 Embedded Installation in VMware with USB Redirection

The embedded image may also be written in VMware using its USB redirection. This is a safer option as it makes it impossible to overwrite disks on the host, limiting potential damage to what is in your virtual machine. To do so, simply attach your CF writer to the VM and perform the installation as you would on the same OS on a physical machine. Refer to the VMware documentation for more information on USB redirection.

3.5 Installation Troubleshooting

The vast majority of the time, installations will finish with no problems. If issues pop up, the following sections describe the most common problems and the steps taken to resolve them.

3.5.1   Boot from Live CD Fails

Due to the wide array of hardware combinations in use, it is not uncommon for a CD to boot incorrectly (or not at all). The most common problems and solutions are:

Dirty CD-ROM Drive

Clean the drive with a cleaning disc or a can of compressed air, or try another drive.

Bad CD-R Media

Burn another disc and/or burn the disc at a lower speed. Perhaps try another brand of media.

BIOS Issues

Update to the most recent BIOS, and disable any unneeded peripherals such as Firewire, Floppy Drives, and Audio.

IDE Cable Issues

Try a different IDE cable between the CD-ROM drive and the IDE Controller or Motherboard

Boot Loader Issues

There have been cases where specific versions of FreeBSD's CD boot loader will not work on some systems. In this case, see the section above about performing the hard drive installation on a separate PC and then moving it to the target system.

There are more troubleshooting techniques listed on the pfSense documentation Wiki under Boot Troubleshooting.

3.5.2   Boot from hard drive after CD installation fails

After the CD installation completes and the system restarts, there are some conditions which may prevent pfSense from fully booting. The most common reasons are typically BIOS or hard drive controller related. Some of these may be worked around by choosing different options for the boot loader during the installation process, enabling/disabling Packet Mode, or by installing a third party boot loader such as GRUB[1]. Upgrading the BIOS to the latest version available may also help in this case.

Altering the SATA options in the BIOS has improved booting in some situations as well. If a SATA hard drive is being used, experiment with changing the SATA options in the BIOS for settings such as AHCI, Legacy, or IDE.

As in the previous section, there are more troubleshooting techniques listed in the online documentation under Boot Troubleshooting.

---

[1] GRUB is a featureful boot loader that supports various operating systems, boot media, and filesystems. Its website is at http://www.gnu.org/software/grub/.

3.5.3 Interface link up not detected

If the system complains that interface link up is not detected, first make sure that the cable is unplugged and that the interface does not have a link light prior to choosing the link detection option. You may also want to test or replace the cable in question. After selecting the option, plug the cable back into the interface and ensure it has a link light prior to pressing Enter.

If a network cable is being connected directly between two systems and not to a switch, ensure that a crossover cable is being used. Some newer adapters may support Auto-MDIX and will handle this internally, but many older adapters do not. Similarly, if connecting a pfSense system to a switch that does not support Auto-MDIX, use a straight-through patch cable.

If the interface is being properly connected but pfSense still does not detect the link up, the network interfaces being used may not properly detect link for some reason. In this case, manually assigning the interfaces is necessary.

3.5.3.1 Manually Assigning Interfaces

If the auto-detection feature didn't work, there is still hope of telling the difference between network cards prior to installation. One way is by MAC address, which should be shown next to the interface names on the assignment screen:

```
le0     08:00:27:26:a4:04
le1     08:00:27:32:ec:2f
```

The MAC address is sometimes printed on a sticker somewhere physically on the network card. MAC addresses also are assigned by manufacturer, and there are several online databases which will let you do a reverse lookup on a MAC address in order to find the company which made the card.[2]

Network cards of different makes, models, or sometimes chipsets may be detected with different drivers. It may be possible to tell an Intel-based card using the `fxp` driver apart from a Realtek card using the `rl` driver by looking at the cards themselves and comparing the names printed upon the circuitry.

Once it is determined which network card will be used for a given role, type it in at the interface assignment screen when prompted. In the above example, `le0` will be WAN and `le1` will be LAN. When prompted first for the LAN address, one would type **le1** and press enter. Then when prompted for WAN, type **le0**, and press enter. Since there are no optional interfaces, one more press of enter, then **y** will complete the assignment. On nearly all tower PCs, the highest PCI slot will be the first NIC, ordered sequentially in top down order. Where you have three Intel `fxp` cards in a system, the top NIC is normally `fxp0`, the one beneath that `fxp1`, and the lowest one `fxp2`. This is dependent on the motherboard, but almost always holds true. If you have an onboard NIC that is the same brand as an add-in NIC, be aware that some systems will list the onboard NIC first, and others will not.

3.5.4 Hardware Troubleshooting

If you run into problems with the hardware you are attempting to use, the following suggestions will help resolve them in many cases.

---

[2] `http://www.8086.net/tools/mac/,`   `http://www.coffer.com/mac_find/,`   and   `http://aruljohn.com/mac.pl,` among many others.

3.5.4.1   Remove unnecessary hardware

If the system contains any hardware that will not be used, remove it. For example, if you have rede-ployed an old desktop with a sound card, remove the sound card. This normally isn't an issue, but can cause problems and has the potential to reduce performance. If it's removable and you don't need it, take it out.

3.5.4.2   Disable PNP OS in your BIOS

This is the most common fix for hardware problems. Many BIOS configuration screens will have a setting for PNP OS or Plug and Play OS, which should be set to **disable** or **no**. A few have a setting for OS, which should usually be set to **other**.

3.5.4.3   Upgrade your BIOS

The second most common fix for hardware problems is upgrading your BIOS to the latest revision. People seem to have a hard time believing this one, but trust me, just do it. BIOS updates commonly fix bugs in your hardware. It isn't uncommon to hit problems induced by hardware bugs on systems that have stably run Windows for years. I presume either Windows doesn't trigger the bug, or has a work around, as I have personally seen this on multiple occasions. Things that BIOS updates can fix include failing to boot, time keeping problems, and general instability amongst others.

3.5.4.4   Reset BIOS settings to factory defaults

Some recycled systems may have an atypical BIOS configuration from its previous use. Most con-tain an option allowing you to reset all settings to the factory defaults. Try doing this. Also check Section 3.5.4.2 again after doing this.

3.5.4.5   Disable unused hardware in your BIOS

If your motherboard has any built in components that will not be used, try disabling them. Common examples include the parallel port, onboard modems, audio devices, firewire, possibly USB, and the serial ports unless you plan to use a serial console.

3.5.4.6   Other BIOS settings

If your BIOS allows power management configuration, try turning it off or on. Look for anything else that seems relevant and try changing some things. If you get to this point, your hardware is probably a lost cause and you should seek alternate hardware. Also check to see if your BIOS has an event log that may list hardware errors such as memory test failures.

3.5.4.7 Other Hardware Issues

There could also be some problem with the target hardware, which testing with diagnostic software may reveal. You should test the hard drive with the manufacturer's diagnostic software, and test the memory with a program such as memtest86+. These and more tools are available on the "Ultimate Boot CD", which is preloaded with many free hardware diagnostic tools.

Also ensure that all of the fans are spinning at speed, and that no components are overheating. If this is older reused hardware, some compressed/canned air cleaning of the fans and heat sinks can work wonders.

3.5.5 Embedded Boot Problems on ALIX Hardware

If an embedded system does not boot properly, connect a serial cable to the device and monitor the boot process for clues on how to proceed. The most common problem will be fore users of ALIX hardware. If you are using an ALIX board, you will need to ensure that the latest BIOS available at the time of this writing, 0.99h, is loaded on the board in order to properly boot NanoBSD images from both slices.

An ALIX in need of a BIOS update will typically exhibit the following symptoms on boot:

```
PC Engines ALIX.2 v0.99
640 KB Base Memory
261120 KB Extended Memory

01F0 Master 848A SanDisk SDCFH2-004G
Phys C/H/S 7964/16/63 Log C/H/S 995/128/63

1   FreeBSD
2   FreeBSD

Boot:   1 ############
```

The number of hash marks (#) will slowly grow over time as the boot attempts to continue. If this behavior is seen, follow the BIOS update procedures from your vendor to at least version 0.99h

In addition to needing BIOS version 0.99h, the BIOS must also be set for CHS mode (Cylinder/Head-/Sector mode for addressing data on a disk), as in the following example:

```
PC Engines ALIX.2 v0.99h
640 KB Base Memory
261120 KB Extended Memory

01F0 Master 848A SanDisk SDCFH2-004G
Phys C/H/S 7964/16/63 Log C/H/S 995/128/63

BIOS setup:

*9* 9600 baud (2) 19200 baud (3) 38400 baud (5) 57600 baud (1) 115200  ←
    baud
*C* CHS mode (L) LBA mode (W) HDD wait (V) HDD slave (U) UDMA enable
(M) MFGPT workaround
```

```
(P) late PCI init
*R* Serial console enable
(E) PXE boot enable
(X) Xmodem upload
(Q) Quit
```

To get to this screen, press **S** while the memory test is displayed over the serial console. Then press **C** to change to CHS mode, then press **Q** to quit.

At this point the ALIX should properly boot from either slice of a NanoBSD image.

3.6 Recovery Installation

There are two main scenarios for needing to reinstall the system. In the first case, a hard drive or mass storage device may have failed and a fast reinstall with a backup configuration is needed. In the second case, the configuration is still present on the hard drive but some contents of the filesystem may be corrupt. pfSense provides an easy and relatively painless process for recovering quickly from such problems, and if neither of these scenarios applies then there is always the traditional method of restoring a configuration from within the WebGUI.

3.6.1   Pre-Flight Installer Configuration Recovery

pfSense has, as part of the installation routine, a "Pre-Flight Install" or PFI. PFI will check for an existing configuration on a USB drive, and use it instead of prompting for a new configuration. When installing to a hard drive, the installation program will copy this configuration. When the process is complete, it will restart with the restored configuration file.

First, locate a USB drive that is FAT formatted. If it works in Windows, it is likely already FAT formatted.

Make a directory on the root of this USB drive called `conf`.

Place a configuration file in this folder. If the backup came from the pfSense WebGUI, it is likely named such as this: `config-routerhostname.example.com-20090520151000.xml`. Rename this file to `config.xml`. For more information on making backups, see Chapter 5.

The drive should now be ready to use. To double check that the config is in the right place, the file should be in `E:\conf\config.xml` if the USB drive is `E:`. Substitute the appropriate drive letter for the system being used.

Remove the USB drive from the workstation, and then plug it into the pfSense system being restored. Put the Live CD in its CD-ROM drive, and boot the system. It should be noticeable that the system used the configuration from the USB and did not prompt to configure interfaces. The only thing left to do is follow the steps described in Section 3.2.4 to perform a normal installation to a hard drive.

When the installation is finished, shut down the system, unplug the USB drive, and remove the installation CD. Turn the system back on, and it should boot normally and be fully operational. If any packages were in use, visit the WebGUI and after login they will be automatically reinstalled.

Note

Be careful when removing a USB drive from a pfSense system. It is always safest to do so when the power is turned off. If the USB drive is mounted by a running pfSense system and removed without dismounting, the system **will** crash and reboot with possibly unpredictable results. FreeBSD is incapable of losing currently mounted filesystems without inducing a panic. This will no longer be an issue in FreeBSD 8.0.

3.6.2 Installed Configuration Recovery

If portions of the installation on the hard drive are not working (as a result of a failed upgrade or other cause), the configuration may be retained while wiping out the rest of the installed files.

During the install process, before choosing Install pfSense there is a menu choice labeled Rescue config.xml. When this option is chosen, a configuration may be selected from any mass storage media connected to the system. The installation process will load this configuration, and once the reinstallation is complete, the system will be running with the rescued settings.

3.6.3 WebGUI Recovery

If all else fails, proceed to do a normal installation as described earlier in this chapter then restore the old configuration by visiting Diagnostics → Backup/Restore in the WebGUI once network connectivity has been restored. In the Restore Configuration section of the page, click Browse, find the configuration backup file. Once located, click Open, and then finally click Restore Configuration. The configuration will be restored and the system will automatically reboot. After rebooting, the full configuration should be present. This process is described in greater detail in Section 5.5.

3.7 Upgrading an Existing Installation

The supported means of upgrading from one pfSense release to another depend on the platform being used. In most cases, pfSense can be reliably upgraded to any other version while retaining the existing configuration.

By keeping a pfSense system updated with a current supported release, it will never be obsolete. New versions are released periodically that contain new features, updates, bug fixes, and various other changes. In most cases, updating a pfSense installation is very easy. If updating to a new release that is a only a point release (e.g 1.2.2 to 1.2.3), upgrading should be minimally invasive and unlikely to cause any problems. The most common problem is hardware-specific regressions from one FreeBSD version to another, though those are rare. Updated releases fix more hardware than they break, but regressions are always possible. Larger jumps, such as from 1.2.3 to 2.0 in the future should be handled with care, and ideally tested on identical hardware in a test environment prior to use in production.

3.7.1   Make a Backup ... and a Backup Plan

First things first, before making any modifications to a pfSense system, it is a good idea to make a backup. In the WebGUI, visit Diagnostics → Backup/Restore. In the Backup Configuration section of the page, ensure that Backup Area is set to **ALL**, then click Download Configuration. Save this file somewhere safe, and it wouldn't hurt to make multiple copies. Those with a pfSense Portal subscription should consider using the Auto Config Backup package, and making a manual backup noting the reason as prior to upgrade.

It may also be a good idea to have install media handy for the release currently being run, in case something goes awry and a reinstall is required. Should that happen, have the backup file on hand and refer to the earlier Section 3.6. Also refer to Chapter 5.

3.7.2   Upgrading an Embedded Install

Before version 1.2.3, the only 100% guaranteed reliable way to upgrade embedded was to re-flash the CF and restore a previous configuration backup afterward. That method may still be used, but thanks to the new NanoBSD-based embedded version in use from 1.2.3 forward, reliable upgrades can be performed just like a full install. Continue on into the Full Install upgrade instructions if you are already running pfSense version 1.2.3 or newer.

Note

If you are updating from an older version of pfSense up to version 1.2.3, you will still need to reflash the card with a new NanoBSD-based image. From then on you can update as usual.

3.7.3   Upgrading a Full Install

There are several methods available for updating a Full Installation of pfSense. Either the WebGUI or the console can be used, and either method has a means of supplying a downloaded update file or pulling one automatically from the Internet.

3.7.3.1   Upgrading using the WebGUI

There are two options for upgrading using the web interface, with the manual and automatic update. The following sections describe these update methods.

3.7.3.1.1   Manual Firmware Update

In order to perform a manual firmware update, first an update file will need to be downloaded. Browse to `http://www.pfsense.org` and click the Downloads link. On the Downloads page, click the link for Upgrades. This will lead to the mirror selection page. Pick a mirror geographically close to your location for best performance. Once a mirror has been selected, a directory listing will appear with update files for the current pfSense release. Download the `.tgz` file, (e.g. `pfSense-Full-Update-1.`

2.3.tgz) and the accompanying .md5 file to verify the download. See Section 3.1.1 on MD5 for details on how to use an .md5 file.

To install the update file, visit the pfSense WebGUI. Click System → Firmware. Click Enable Firmware Upload. Click the Browse button next to Firmware Image File. Locate the update file downloaded in the previous step, and click Open. Finally, click the Upgrade Firmware button. The update will take a few minutes to upload and apply, depending on the speed of the connection being used for the update and the speed of the target system. The firewall will reboot automatically when finished.

3.7.3.1.2 Automatic Update

Automatic Update is a new feature that will contact a pfSense.com server and determine if there is a newer released version than the one being run currently. This check is performed when you visit the Automatic Updates page found under System → Firmware, then click the Auto Update tab in the WebGUI. If a new update is available, it will be listed. Click the button to install the update. The update will take a few minutes to download and apply, depending on the speed of the Internet connection being used and the speed of the target system. The firewall will reboot automatically when finished.

By default, the update check only pertains to officially released versions of pfSense, but it is also possible to use this method to track snapshots as well. The update version can be changed by visiting the Updater Settings tab, located immediately to the right of the Auto Update tab. It is safest to use the released versions, as they see the most testing and should be reasonably safe and trouble-free. However, as with any upgrade, you should first visit the pfSense website and read the update notes for that release.

3.7.3.2 Upgrading using the Console

An update may also be run from the console. The console option is available from any means available for console access: Video/Keyboard, Serial Console, or SSH. Once connected to the console of the pfSense system to be upgraded, start the upgrade process by choosing menu option **13**.

3.7.3.2.1 Update from a URL

If the full URL to a pfSense update file is known, this is a good choice. It will avoid having to first download the update file only to upload it again, and unlike the Automatic Update feature in the WebGUI it also allows a custom update file location to be used.

From the console update menu, choose option **1** for Update from a URL. Enter the full URL to the update file, such as:

```
http://files.pfsense.org/mirror/updates/pfSense-Full-Update-1.2.3.tgz
```

Confirm that the update should be applied, and then it should be automatically downloaded and installed. After the installation is complete, the router will automatically reboot.

3.7.3.2.2 Update from a local file

An update file can be downloaded, as in the manual firmware update above, and then copied to the pfSense system via **scp** or Diagnostics → Command. To install such a file, from the console update menu, choose option **2** for Update From a Local File, and then enter the full path to the file that was uploaded, such as `/tmp/pfSense-Full-Update-1.2.3.tgz`. Confirm that the update should be applied, and then it should be automatically installed. After the installation is complete, the router will automatically reboot.

3.7.4 Upgrading a Live CD Install

On a separate system, download and burn a CD containing the latest release. Ensure that you have moved your configuration to removable media (USB or Floppy) from the console menu (see Section 4.6.15). Next, restart the pfSense router and boot with the new CD. When pfSense boots on the new CD, the existing storage media containing your configuration will be found and used.

Chapter 4

Configuration

After installation, the pfSense router is ready for configuration. The bulk of the configuration is done using the web-based GUI configurator (webConfigurator), or WebGUI for short. There are some tasks that may also be easily performed from the console, whether it be a monitor and keyboard, over a serial port, or via SSH. Some of these may be necessary before you will be able to access the WebGUI, such as if you want to bring up the LAN on an existing LAN network with a different IP address.

4.1   Connecting to the WebGUI

In order to reach the WebGUI, you must connect from another PC. This PC could be directly connected with a crossover cable, or connected to the same switch. By default, the LAN IP of a new pfSense system is 192.168.1.1 with a /24 mask (255.255.255.0), and there is also a DHCP server running. If the PC being used to connect is set to obtain its IP address by DHCP, it should only be a matter of pointing your favorite web browser to `http://192.168.1.1`.

If you need to change the LAN IP address or disable DHCP, this may be done from the console by choosing option 2, then enter the new LAN IP, subnet mask, and specify whether or not to enable DHCP. If you choose to enable DHCP, you will also be asked to enter the starting and ending address of the DHCP pool, which could be any range you like inside of the given subnet.

When you disable the DHCP server, you must statically assign an IP address in the pfSense system's LAN subnet on the PC being used for the configuration, such as *192.168.1.5*, with a subnet mask that matches the one given to pfSense, such as 255.255.255.0.

Once the PC is connected to the same LAN as the pfSense system, browse to the LAN IP address.

Note

Be careful when assigning a new LAN IP address. This IP address **cannot** be in the same subnet as the WAN or any other active interface.

4.2   Setup Wizard

When browsing to the WebGUI, you will first be greeted by a login prompt. For the username enter **admin** and for the password, enter **pfsense**.

Since this is the first time visiting the WebGUI, the Setup Wizard will begin automatically, and will look like Figure 4.1. Click Next to start the configuration process.

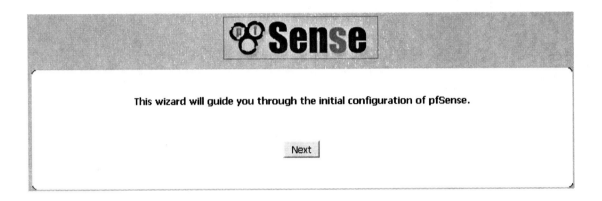

Figure 4.1: Setup Wizard Starting Screen

4.2.1   General Information Screen

The next screen (Figure 4.2) will ask for the name of this pfSense router, and the domain in which it resides. The Hostname can be anything you like, but must start with a letter, and then it may contain only letters, numbers, or a hyphen. After the hostname, enter a Domain, e.g. **example.com**. If you do not have a domain, you can use **<something>.local**, where *<something>* is anything you want: a company name, your last name, nick name, and so on. The hostname and domain name are combined to make up the fully qualified domain name of your router.

The Primary DNS Server and Secondary DNS Server may be filled in, if known. If you are using a dynamic WAN type such as DHCP, PPTP or PPPoE connections, these will usually be automatically assigned by your ISP and can be left blank. These WAN types are explained in more detail later in the Setup Wizard. Click Next when finished.

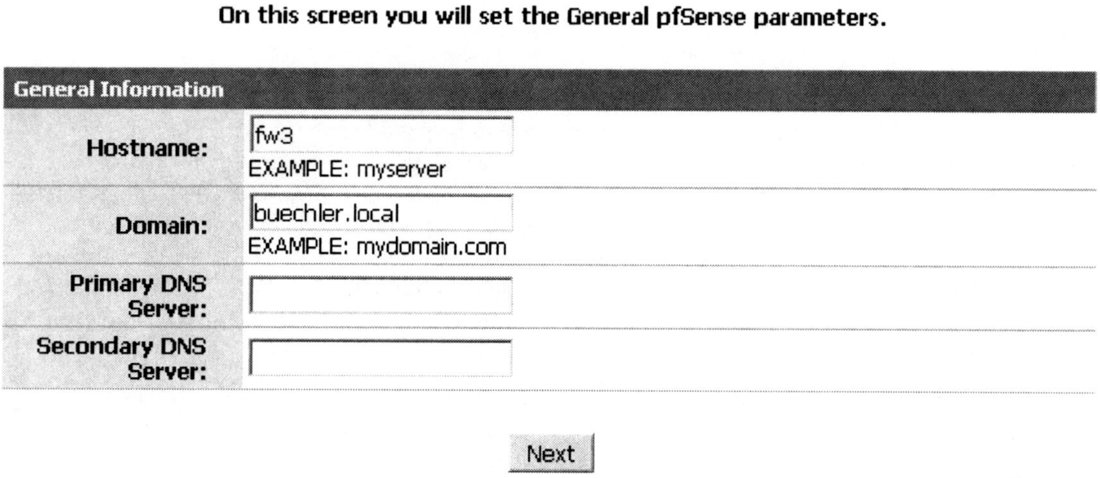

On this screen you will set the General pfSense parameters.

General Information	
Hostname:	fw3
	EXAMPLE: myserver
Domain:	buechler.local
	EXAMPLE: mydomain.com
Primary DNS Server:	
Secondary DNS Server:	

Next

Figure 4.2: General Information Screen

4.2.2 NTP and Time Zone Configuration

The next screen (Figure 4.3) has a place for a Network Time Protocol (NTP) server, and the time zone in which this server resides. Unless you have a specific preference for an NTP server such as one inside your LAN, it is best to leave the Time server hostname at the default **0.pfsense.pool.ntp.org**, which will pick random servers from a pool of known-good NTP hosts.

For the Timezone selection, choose a geographically named zone which best matches the pfSense system's location. Do not use the GMT (Greenwich Mean Time) offset style zones. For more information see Section 4.7.1 later in this chapter. When finished, click Next to continue.

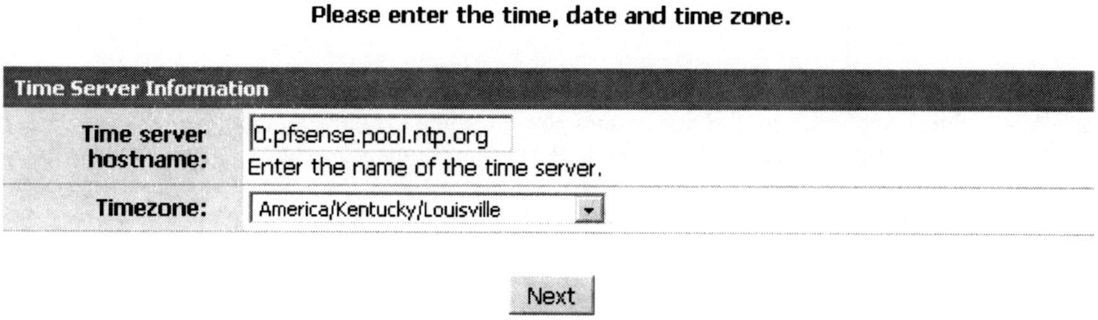

Please enter the time, date and time zone.

Time Server Information	
Time server hostname:	0.pfsense.pool.ntp.org
	Enter the name of the time server.
Timezone:	America/Kentucky/Louisville

Next

Figure 4.3: NTP and Time Zone Setup Screen

4.2.3   WAN Configuration

These next few paragraphs and their associated images will help guide you through setting up the WAN interface on the pfSense system. Since this is the side facing your ISP or upstream router, there are configuration choices to support several common ISP connection types. The first choice is for the WAN Type (Figure 4.4). This should match whatever your ISP supports, or whatever your previous router was configured to use. Possible choices are Static, DHCP, PPPoE, and PPTP. The default choice is DHCP since it is very common, and in most cases will allow a router to "Just Work" without additional configuration. If you are not sure which WAN type to use, or which fields to configure, you will need to obtain this information from your ISP.

Note

If you have a wireless interface for your WAN interface, some additional options may appear which are not covered during this walkthrough of the standard Setup Wizard. You may refer to Chapter 18, which has a section on Wireless WAN for additional information. You may need to skip the WAN setup for now, and then perform the wireless configuration afterward.

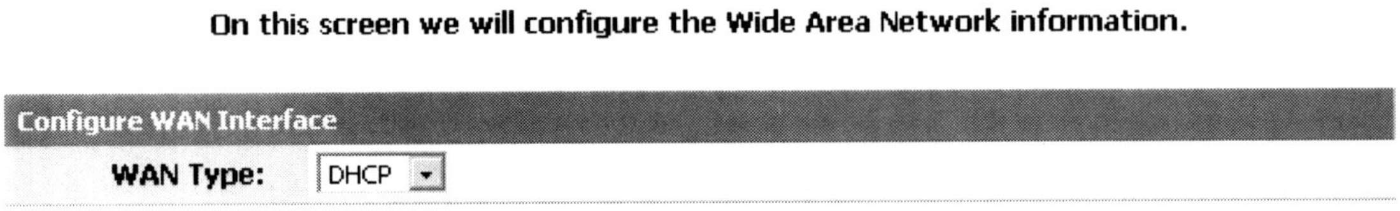

On this screen we will configure the Wide Area Network information.

Figure 4.4: WAN Configuration

The MAC Address field in the next section (Figure 4.5) is useful for replacing an existing router with minimal complications. Some ISPs, mainly those run by Cable providers, will not work properly if a new MAC address is encountered. Some require power cycling the modem, others require registering the new address with them over the phone. If this WAN connection is on a network segment with other systems that locate it via ARP, changing the MAC to match and older piece of equipment may also help ease the transition, rather than having to clear ARP caches or update static ARP entries.

The Maximum Transmission Unit (MTU) size field seen in Figure 4.5 can typically be left blank, but can be changed if desired. Some situations may call for a lower MTU to ensure packets are sized appropriately for your Internet connection. In most cases, the default assumed values for the WAN connection type will work properly.

General configuration	
MAC Address:	[ ] This field can be used to modify ("spoof") the MAC address of the WAN interface (may be required with some cable connections) Enter a MAC address in the following format: xx:xx:xx:xx:xx:xx or leave blank
MTU:	[ ] If you enter a value in this field, then MSS clamping for TCP connections to the value entered above minus 40 (TCP/IP header size) will be in effect. If you leave this field blank, an MTU of 1492 bytes for PPPoE and 1500 bytes for all other connection types will be assumed.

Figure 4.5: General WAN Configuration

If the "Static" choice for the WAN type is chosen, the IP address, CIDR Subnet mask, and Gateway must all be filled in (Figure 4.6). This information should be obtained from your ISP or whoever controls the network on the WAN side of your pfSense router. The IP Address and Gateway must both reside in the same Subnet.

Static IP Configuration	
IP Address:	[ ] / [24 ▾]
Gateway:	[ ]

Figure 4.6: Static IP Settings

Some ISPs require a certain DHCP hostname (Figure 4.7) to be sent along with the DHCP request to obtain a WAN IP. If you are unsure of what to put in this field, try leaving it blank unless directed otherwise by your ISP.

DHCP client configuration	
DHCP Hostname:	[ ] The value in this field is sent as the DHCP client identifier and hostname when requesting a DHCP lease. Some ISPs may require this (for client identification).

Figure 4.7: DHCP Hostname Setting

When using the PPPoE (Point-to-Point Protocol over Ethernet) WAN type (Figure 4.8), you must at least fill in the fields for PPPoE Username and PPPoE Password. These will be provided by your ISP, and typically are in the form of an e-mail address, such as **mycompany@ispexample.com**. The PPPoE Service name may be required by some ISPs, but is often left blank. If you are in doubt, leave it blank or contact your ISP and ask if it is necessary.

PPPoE Dial on demand will cause pfSense to leave the connection down/offline until data is requested that would need the connection to the Internet. PPPoE logins happen quite fast, so in most cases the delay while the connection is setup would be negligible. If you plan on running any services behind the pfSense box, **do not** check this, as you will want to maintain an online connection as much as possible in that case. Also note that this choice will not drop an existing connection.

The PPPoE Idle timeout specifies how much time pfSense will let the PPPoE connection go without transmitting data before disconnecting. This is really only useful when coupled with Dial on demand, and is typically left blank (disabled).

PPPoE configuration	
PPPoE Username:	
PPPoE Password:	
PPPoE Service name:	Hint: this field can usually be left empty
PPPoE Dial on demand:	☐ Enable Dial-On-Demand mode This option causes the interface to operate in dial-on-demand mode, allowing you to have a virtual full time connection. The interface is configured, but the actual connection of the link is delayed until qualifying outgoing traffic is detected.
PPPoE Idle timeout:	If no qualifying outgoing packets are transmitted for the specified number of seconds, the connection is brought down. An idle timeout of zero disables this feature.

Figure 4.8: PPPoE Configuration

The PPTP (Point-to-Point Tunneling Protocol) WAN type (Figure 4.9) is the source of some confusion. This option is for ISPs that require a PPTP login, and **not** for connecting to a remote PPTP VPN. These settings, much like the PPPoE settings, will be provided by your ISP. Unlike PPPoE, however, with a PPTP WAN you must also specify a Local IP address, CIDR subnet mask, and Remote IP Address to establish the connection.

PPTP configuration	
PPTP Username:	
PPTP Password:	
PPTP Local IP Address:	/ 1 ▾
PPTP Remote IP Address:	
PPTP Dial on demand:	☐ Enable Dial-On-Demand mode This option causes the interface to operate in dial-on-demand mode, allowing you to have a virtual full time connection. The interface is configured, but the actual connection of the link is delayed until qualifying outgoing traffic is detected.
PPTP Idle timeout:	If no qualifying outgoing packets are transmitted for the specified number of seconds, the connection is brought down. An idle timeout of zero disables this feature.

Figure 4.9: PPTP WAN Configuration

These last two options, seen in Figure 4.10, are useful for preventing invalid traffic from entering your network, also known as "Ingress Filtering". Enabling Block RFC 1918 Private Networks will block registered private networks such as 192.168.x.x and 10.x.x.x from making connections to your WAN address. A full list of these networks is in Section 1.7.1.1. The Block bogon networks option will stop traffic from coming in that is sourced from reserved or unassigned IP space that should not be in use. The list of bogon networks is updated periodically in the background, and requires no manual maintenance. Bogon networks are further explained in Section 6.5.1.4. Click Next to move on when finished.

RFC1918 Networks	
Block RFC1918 Private Networks:	☑ Block private networks from entering via WAN When set, this option blocks traffic from IP addresses that are reserved for private networks as per RFC 1918 (10/8, 172.16/12, 192.168/16) as well as loopback addresses (127/8). You should generally leave this option turned on, unless your WAN network lies in such a private address space, too.

Block bogon networks	
Block bogon networks:	☑ Block non-Internet routed networks from entering via WAN Block bogon networks when set, this option blocks traffic from IP addresses that are reserved (but not RFC 1918) or not yet assigned by IANA. Bogons are prefixes that should never appear in the Internet routing table, and obviously should not appear as the source address in any packets you receive.

Figure 4.10: Built-in Ingress Filtering Options

4.2.4   LAN Interface Configuration

Here you are given an opportunity to change the LAN IP Address and Subnet Mask (Figure 4.11). If you don't ever plan on connecting your network to any other network via VPN, the default is fine. If you want to be able to connect into your network using VPN from remote locations, you should choose a private IP address range much more obscure than the very common 192.168.1.0/24. Space within the 172.16.0.0/12 RFC 1918 private address block seems to be the least frequently used, so choose something between 172.16.x.x and 172.31.x.x for least likelihood of having VPN connectivity difficulties. If your LAN is 192.168.1.x and you are at a wireless hotspot using 192.168.1.x (very common), you won't be able to communicate across the VPN — 192.168.1.x is the local network, not your network over VPN.

If the LAN IP needs to be changed, enter it here along with a new subnet mask. Be aware that if you change these settings, you will also need to adjust your PC's IP address, release/renew its DHCP lease, or perform a "Repair" or "Diagnose" on the network interface when finished with the setup wizard.

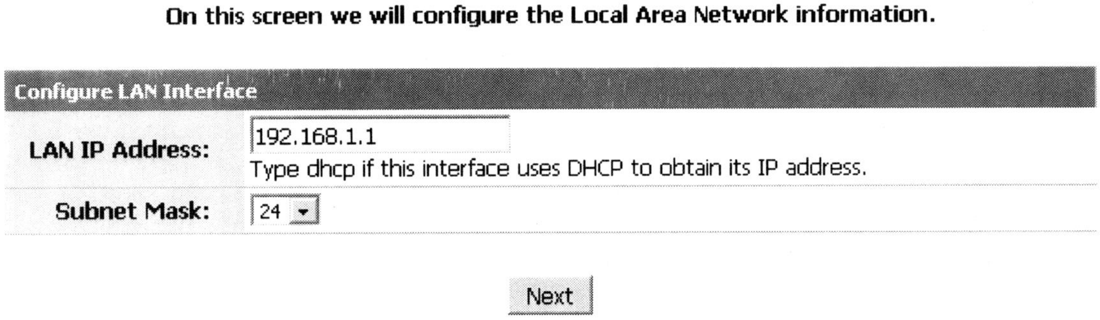

On this screen we will configure the Local Area Network information.

Configure LAN Interface	
LAN IP Address:	192.168.1.1 Type dhcp if this interface uses DHCP to obtain its IP address.
Subnet Mask:	24 ▾

Next

Figure 4.11: LAN Configuration

4.2.5   Set admin password

Next you must change the administrative password for the WebGUI as shown in Figure 4.12. This password should be something strong and secure, but no restrictions are automatically enforced. Enter the password twice to be sure that has been entered correctly, then click Next.

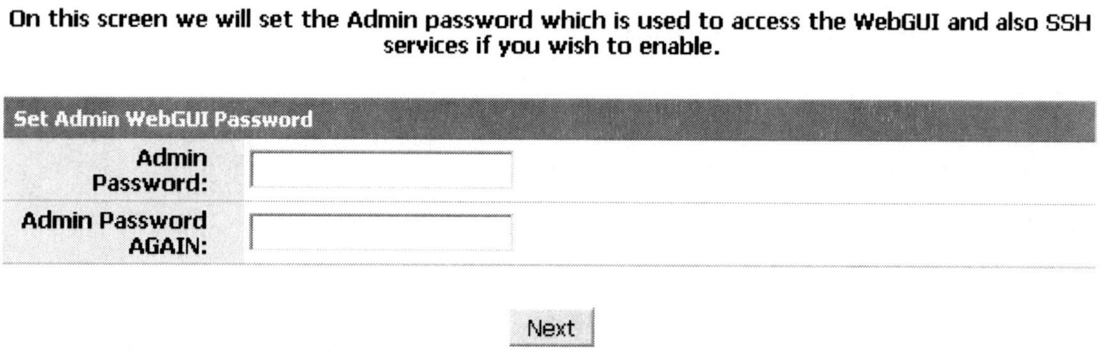

On this screen we will set the Admin password which is used to access the WebGUI and also SSH services if you wish to enable.

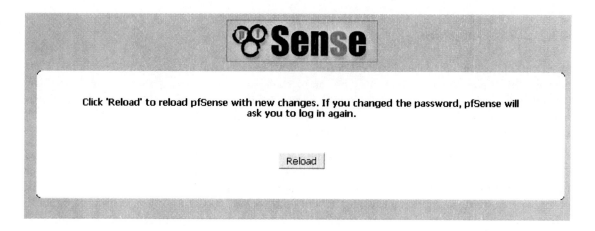

Figure 4.12: Change Administrative Password

4.2.6   Completing the Setup Wizard

That's the end of the setup wizard, click Reload (Figure 4.13) and the WebGUI will reload. If you changed the LAN IP, adjust your PC's IP address accordingly. You will also be prompted for the new password. The username is still **admin**.

Figure 4.13: Reload pfSense WebGUI

At this point you should have basic connectivity to the Internet, or the network on the WAN side. Clients on the LAN side should be able to reach sites through the pfSense router. If at any time you need to repeat this initial configuration, you may do so by going to System → Setup Wizard from within the WebGUI.

4.3   Interface Configuration

As you have seen, some interface configuration can be performed at the console and in the setup wizard to start things out, but changes may also be made after the initial setup by visiting the appropriate places under the Interfaces menu.

4.3.1   Assign interfaces

If additional interfaces are added post-setup, then they may be assigned roles by visiting Interfaces → (assign). There are two tabs here, Interface assignments and VLANs. (VLAN configuration is covered later in Chapter 10.) The Interface assignments tab shows a list of all currently assigned interfaces: WAN , LAN, and any OPTx that are configured. Next to each interface is a drop-down list of all network interfaces/ports found on the system, including real hardware interfaces as well as VLAN interfaces. The MAC address or VLAN tag will show along side the interface name to aid in identification.

You may change the currently assigned interfaces by picking a new network port, or add an additional OPTx interface by clicking 🔳. This will add another line, with a new OPT interface, numbered higher than any existing OPT interface, or if there are none, OPT1. By default, it will automatically choose the next available interface that is unassigned. For example, if the target system has fxp0, fxp1, and fxp2, and you have WAN set to fxp0, and LAN set for fxp1, choosing to add another interface will automatically assume OPT1 will be fxp2. If you have additional interfaces and this is not the intended setting, it may be altered. If any changes are made, be sure to click Save.

4.3.2   WAN Interface

Nearly all of the options found under Interfaces → WAN are identical to those mentioned in the WAN portion of the Setup Wizard. The WAN type can be changed, as well as assigning a static IP address, subnet mask, gateway, configuring DHCP, PPPoE, and PPTP. You can also enable or disable the blocking of private networks and bogon networks. A notable exception to this is wireless WAN, which will show the wireless configuration options along side the typical WAN options.

One option available here that is not shown during the setup wizard is the ability to Disable the userland FTP-Proxy application, also known as the FTP helper. If you are running a public FTP (File Transfer Protocol) server behind pfSense, you may want to enable the FTP helper so that FTP connections work properly. Be aware that by doing this all FTP connections will appear to originate from the pfSense router since will be acting as a proxy. See Section 7.8.1 for more in-depth information on the FTP proxy and related issues with FTP.

4.3.3   LAN Interface

Some additional options for the LAN side are available under Interfaces → LAN besides setting the IP address, which was covered in the Setup Wizard.

The Bridge with option will bridge the LAN interface to another interface on the system. Refer to Chapter 9 for more information on bridging.

As with the WAN interface configuration, there is also an option to Disable the userland FTP-Proxy application. You should almost always leave this enabled. When active on the LAN side, this will proxy FTP connections and make it so that clients on the LAN side may use the FTP protocol normally in active mode, and the proxy will open and forward the proper ports dynamically during an FTP session.

4.3.4 Optional Interfaces

Any additional optional (OPTx) interfaces will also show up in this menu, under OPT1, OPT2 ... OPTx, or custom names given to the interface. These interfaces have a few more options than the LAN interface, but less than WAN.

To enable an OPT interface, you must first check the Enable Optional *x* Interface checkbox, where *x* is the current number of the OPT interface you are configuring. For example, on OPT1, it would say Enable Optional 1 Interface. You may also rename this interface by entering in a short Description. This description (DMZ, Servers, Office, Engineering, etc.) will appear instead of "OPT1" in the menus and configuration. This makes it much easier to remember not only what an interface is for, but also to identify an interface for adding firewall rules or choosing other per-interface functionality.

OPT interfaces may be set for DHCP or Static IP, and as with the WAN you may alter the MAC address and MTU. Like the LAN interface, you may also bridge an OPT interface to another interface, joining them into the same broadcast domain. You could use this to add another port to your LAN, or create a bridged DMZ.

If this will be a WAN-type OPT interface, for a multi-WAN configuration, you should enter a Gateway IP address as well unless you are using DHCP. In pfSense 1.2.x you can only use a DHCP or Static IP connection for an additional WAN interface, not a PPPoE or PPTP type connection. This will be addressed in pfSense 2.0. For more details on configuring multiple WAN connections, see Chapter 11.

The FTP helper option is also available. Refer to Section 7.8.1 for more information.

4.4 General Configuration Options

Some general system options are found under System $\rightarrow$ General Setup; most of them will look familiar from the Setup Wizard.

The Hostname and Domain, DNS Servers, the administrative Username and Password, and the Time zone and NTP Time server can be changed if desired, as covered in the Setup Wizard.

Along with the ability to change the DNS Servers, there is another option: Allow DNS server list to be overridden by DHCP/PPP on WAN. This does essentially what it says; if checked, pfSense will use the DNS servers that are assigned dynamically by DHCP or PPP. They will be utilized by the system itself and as the upstream DNS servers for the DNS forwarder. These servers will not be passed on to the DHCP clients behind the pfSense system, however.

The WebGUI port and WebGUI Protocol may be set. Both HTTP and HTTPS are available. The best practice would be to use HTTPS so that the WebGUI traffic is encrypted, especially if the firewall will be managed remotely. Moving the WebGUI to an alternate port is also a good tactic for increased security, and it will free up the standard web ports for use with port forwards or other services such as a squid proxy. By default the WebGUI uses HTTP on port 80 for the best compatibility and ease of initial configuration.

Lastly, a Theme may also be chosen. Several are included in the base system, and they only make cosmetic — not functional — changes to the look and feel of the WebGUI.

4.5 Advanced Configuration Options

Under System → Advanced you will find a lot of options that are of a more advanced nature. None of these options should need adjustment for a basic routing/NAT setup, but you may find that some of the changes governed by these options will help in customizing your configuration in beneficial ways.

Some of these options may be covered in more detail in other sections of the book where their discussion would be more topical or relevant, but they are all mentioned here with a brief description.

4.5.1 Serial Console

If this pfSense system will be running "headless" (without keyboard, video, mouse attached) it may be desirable to enable this option, which will redirect the console input/output to the serial port. This will disable the onboard keyboard, video, and mouse but will allow you to attach a null modem cable to the serial port and manage it directly from another PC or serial device. After making any changes, be sure to click Save when finished.

For more information on connecting to a serial console, see Section 3.3.5.1 and Section 3.3.5.2.

4.5.2 Secure Shell (SSH)

The Secure Shell (SSH) server may be enabled which will allow remote console and file management. You may connect with any standard SSH client, such as the OpenSSH command line **ssh** client, PuTTY, SecureCRT, or iTerm. Either the WebGUI username (such as admin) or the root account may be used, and both accept the WebGUI password for login.

File transfers to and from the pfSense system are also possible by using a Secure Copy (SCP) client such as OpenSSH's command line **scp**, FileZilla, WinSCP or Fugu. To use SCP, you must connect as the root user, not admin.

To enable SSH, check the box next to Enable Secure Shell. It is also more secure to move the SSH server to an alternate port. As with moving the WebGUI to an alternate port, it provides a small security improvement, and frees up the port if you want to forward it to an internal system. To change the port, type the new port into the SSH Port box.

You can also set SSH to only allow key-based logins and not a password. To do this, check Disable Password login for Secure Shell (KEY only) and paste the allowed public keys into the Authorized Keys text field. Switching to only key-based login is a much more secure practice, though it does take a little more preparation to configure.

Should you find yourself in a situation that requires leaving SSH access unrestricted by firewall rules, which can be dangerous, it is highly recommended that in this situation you both move the SSH service to an alternate random port, and switch to key-based authentication. Moving to an alternate port will prevent log noise from brute-force SSH login attempts and casual scans. It can still be found with a port scan, so switching to key-based authentication should always be done on every publicly accessible SSH server to eliminate the possibility of successful brute force attacks.

4.5.3   Shared Physical Network

If you have two or more interfaces which share the same physical network, such as in a scenario where multiple interfaces are plugged into the same broadcast domain, the lone option in this section will hide the spurious ARP messages that would otherwise overload the logs with useless entries.

4.5.4   IPv6

Currently, pfSense does not support IPv6 filtering, though highly permissive rules could allow IPv6 traffic when most users do not expect IPv6 traffic to leave their network, as it isn't used. As such, IPv6 traffic is blocked by default. If you require IPv6 to pass the firewall, check the box for Allow IPv6 Traffic. You may also enable NAT encapsulated IPv6 packets (IP protocol 41/RFC 2893) by checking that box and entering an IPv4 address to which those packets should be forwarded.

4.5.5   Filtering Bridge

Before version 1.2.1 of pfSense, there was a choice of whether or not to filter traffic on bridged interfaces, retained from the older method of bridging used in m0n0wall. Newer FreeBSD releases use a different bridging methodology that made the former option obsolete. However a description is retained here to avoid confusion, as many users are accustomed to using it, and it is referred to in numerous places.

4.5.6   WebGUI SSL certificate/key

When using HTTPS mode for the WebGUI to encrypt access to the web interface, by default the system will use a self-signed certificate. That is not an ideal situation, but is better than no encryption at all. This option allows you to use an existing certificate to further enhance security and protect against man-in-the-middle attacks.

If you have an existing SSL certificate and key, you may paste them here. There is also a link labeled "Create certificates automatically" which will trigger an internal function in pfSense to generate a new self-signed certificate instead.

The main downside to using a custom self-generated certificate is the lack of assurance of the identity of the host, since the certificate is not signed by a Certificate Authority trusted by your browser. Additionally, because for the bulk of Internet users such an invalid certificate should be considered a risk, modern browsers have been cracking down on how they are handled. Firefox, for example, gives a warning screen and forces the user to import the certificate and allow a permanent exception. Internet Explorer will show a warning screen with a link to continue. Opera will show a warning dialog that also allows a permanent bypass.

4.5.7 Load Balancing

The text in the WebGUI best explains Sticky Connections option in this section: Successive connections will be redirected to the servers in a round-robin manner with connections from the same source being sent to the same web server. This "sticky connection" will exist as long as there are states that refer to this connection. Once the states expire, so will the sticky connection. Further connections from that host will be redirected to the next web server in the round robin.

"Sticky" connections are desirable for some applications that rely on the same IPs being maintained throughout a given session. This is used in combination with the server load balancing functionality, described further in Chapter 17.

4.5.8 Miscellaneous

A few options which did not fit into any other category may be found in here.

4.5.8.1 Device Polling

Device polling is a technique that lets the system periodically poll network devices for new data instead of relying on interrupts. This prevents your WebGUI, SSH, etc. from being inaccessible due to interrupt floods when under extreme load, at the cost of slightly higher latency (up to 1 ms). This is usually unnecessary, unless your hardware is undersized.

Polling also requires hardware support in your system's network cards. According to the polling(4) man page for FreeBSD 7.2 (upon which pfSense 1.2.3 is based), the `bge(4)`, `dc(4)`, `em(4)`, `fwe(4)`, `fwip(4)`, `fxp(4)`, `ixgb(4)`, `nfe(4)`, `nge(4)`, `re(4)`, `rl(4)`, `sf(4)`, `sis(4)`, `ste(4)`, `stge(4)`, `vge(4)`, `vr(4)`, and `xl(4)` devices are supported, with support for others pending in future FreeBSD releases.

4.5.8.2 Console Menu

Normally, the console menu is always showing on the system console, and will be available as long as you have physical access to the serial or video console. In some situations this is not desirable, so this option will allow the console to be password protected. You may login with the same username and password used for the WebGUI. After setting this option, you must reboot the pfSense system before it will take effect.

Note
While this will stop accidental keypresses, and keep out casual users, this is by no means a perfect security method. A knowledgeable person with physical access could still reset the passwords (see Section 4.10.2). You should consider other physical security methods if that is a requirement of your installation.

4.5.8.3 WebGUI anti-lockout

By default, access to the WebGUI on the LAN interface is always permitted, regardless of the user-defined filter rules. Enabling this feature will allow more fine-grained control over which LAN IP addresses may access the WebGUI, but be sure you have a filter rule in place to allow access before enabling this option!

Note

Resetting the LAN IP from the system console will also reset this option. If you find yourself locked out after enabling this, choose the console menu option to set the LAN IP, and enter in the exact same IP address and accompanying information.

4.5.8.4 Static Route Filtering

The Bypass firewall rules for traffic on the same interface option only applies if you have defined one or more static routes. If it is enabled, traffic that enters and leaves through the same interface will not be checked by the firewall. This may be desirable in some situations where multiple subnets are connected to the same interface.

4.5.8.5 IPsec SA Preferral

By default, if several IPsec Security Associations (SA) match, the newest one is preferred if it's at least 30 seconds old. Select this option to always prefer old SAs over new ones. This is rarely desirable. For more on Security Associations, refer to Section 13.1.1

4.5.9 Traffic Shaper and Firewall Advanced

These options govern some of the more advanced functionality and behavior of lower-level packet filtering performed by pf.

4.5.9.1 FTP RFC 959 data port violation workaround

Workaround for sites that violate RFC 959 which specifies that the data connection be sourced from one port less than the command port (typically port 20). This workaround doesn't expose you to much additional risk as the firewall will still only allow connections to a port upon which the FTP proxy is listening.

4.5.9.2 Clear DF bit instead of dropping

This is a workaround for operating systems that generate fragmented packets with the don't fragment (DF) bit set. Linux NFS (Network File System) is known to do this. This will cause the filter to not drop such packets but instead clear the don't fragment bit. The filter will also randomize the IP identification field of outgoing packets with this option on, to compensate for operating systems that set the DF bit but set a zero IP identification header field.

4.5.9.3 Firewall Optimization Options

There are a few choices here that control how the firewall expires states:

Normal
  The standard optimization algorithm.

High Latency
  Used for high latency links, such as satellite links. Expires idle connections later than default.

Aggressive
  Expires idle connections quicker. More efficient use of CPU and memory but can drop legitimate connections earlier than expected.

Conservative
  Tries to avoid dropping any legitimate connections at the expense of increased memory usage and CPU utilization.

4.5.9.4 Disable Firewall

If you choose to disable all packet filtering, it will turn your pfSense system into a routing-only platform. As a consequence, NAT will also be disabled.

4.5.9.5 Disable Firewall Scrub

Disables the PF scrubbing option which can sometimes interfere with NFS and PPTP traffic. By default, pfSense uses the random-id scrub option which randomizes the IP identification field of a packet for added security, and the fragment reassemble option which will reassemble fragmented packets before sending them on. More information on the Scrub feature can be found on the OpenBSD PF Scrub Documentation.

4.5.9.6 Firewall Maximum States

Sets the maximum number of connections to hold in the firewall state table. The default is 10,000 and should be sufficient for most installations, but can be adjusted higher or lower depending on the load and memory available. Each state consumes about 1 KB of RAM, or roughly 1 MB of RAM for every 1000 states, so ensure you have adequate free RAM before increasing this. Firewall states are discussed further in Section 6.1.2.

4.5.9.7 Disable Auto-added VPN rules

This disables automatically added rules for IPsec, PPTP, and OpenVPN. Normally, when you enable one of these VPNs, rules are automatically added to the appropriate interface which will allow traffic in to those ports. By disabling these automatic rules, you can have more control over which addresses are allowed to connect to the VPN.

4.5.10 Network Address Translation

The Disable NAT Reflection option will, when checked, disable the automatic creation of NAT redirect rules for access to your public IP addresses from within your internal networks. This option is checked by default, so NAT Reflection rules are not created unless you change this setting. NAT Reflection only works on port forward type items and does not work for large ranges of more than 500 ports. Refer to Section 7.5 for a discussion on the merits of NAT Reflection when compared to other techniques such as Split DNS.

4.5.11 Hardware Options

There are a few hardware-specific options that can be set. These options should usually be left alone, unless one of the mentioned cases applies to your hardware.

4.5.11.1 Hardware Checksum Offloading

Checking this option will disable hardware checksum offloading. Checksum offloading is broken in some hardware, particularly some Realtek cards. Rarely, drivers may have problems with checksum offloading and some specific NICs. Typical symptoms of broken checksum offloading include corrupted packets and poor throughput performance.

4.5.11.2 Disable glxsb loading

The AMD Geode LX Security Block (glxsb) driver is used mainly in ALIX and Soekris embedded systems. It is a cryptographic accelerator which can improve performance for certain ciphers, such as AES-128. This can improve VPN performance and other subsystems which may use AES-128, such as SSH. This driver can conflict with other cryptographic accelerator cards, such as those from Hifn, and take precedence over them when both are found. If you have a Hifn card, you should set this option so that the glxsb device is never loaded. If the driver is already in use, you must reboot after setting this option so it can be unloaded.

4.6 Console Menu Basics

Some configuration and maintenance tasks may also be performed from the system console. The console may be reached by using the keyboard and mouse, serial console if enabled or using embedded, or by using SSH. Below is an example of what the console menu will look like, but it may vary slightly depending on the version and platform.

```
*** Welcome to pfSense 1.2.3-pfSense on pfSense ***

LAN                    ->    fxp1    ->      192.168.1.1
WAN                    ->    fxp0    ->      1.2.3.4

pfSense console setup
```

```
* * * * * * * * * * * * * * * * * * * * * * *
  0)  Logout (SSH only)
  1)  Assign Interfaces
  2)  Set LAN IP address
  3)  Reset webConfigurator password
  4)  Reset to factory defaults
  5)  Reboot system
  6)  Halt system
  7)  Ping host
  8)  Shell
  9)  PFtop
 10)  Filter Logs
 11)  Restart webConfigurator
 12)  pfSense Developer Shell
 13)  Upgrade from console
 14)  Disable Secure Shell (sshd)
 98)  Move configuration file to removable device

Enter an option:
```

What follows is a general description of what is possible by using most of these options. As with other advanced options, some of these may be covered with more detail in other sections of the book where their discussion would be more topical or relevant.

4.6.1   Assign Interfaces

This will restart the Interface Assignment task, which was covered in detail in Section 3.2.3 and Section 3.5.3.1. You can create VLAN interfaces, reassign existing interfaces, or assign new ones.

4.6.2   Set LAN IP address

This option can be used in the obvious manner, to set the LAN IP address, but there are also some other useful tasks that happen when resetting the LAN IP. For starters, when this is set, you also get the option of turning DHCP on or off, and setting the DHCP IP range.

If you have disabled the WebGUI anti-lockout rule, you will be prompted to re-enable it. It will also prompt to revert to HTTP on the default port if using a non-standard port. This is done to help those who may find themselves locked out from using the WebGUI regain access.

4.6.3   Reset webConfigurator password

This option will reset the WebGUI username and password back to **admin** and **pfsense**, respectively.

4.6.4   Reset to factory defaults

This will restore the system configuration back to factory defaults. Be aware that this will not, however, make any changes to the filesystem or the packages installed on the OS. If you suspect that system files have been corrupted or altered in some undesirable way, the best practice is to make a backup, and reinstall from CD or other installation media. (Also possible in the WebGUI at Diagnostics → Factory defaults)

4.6.5   Reboot system

This will cleanly shutdown the pfSense system and restart the OS (Diagnostics → Reboot in the WebGUI).

4.6.6   Halt system

This will cleanly shutdown the system and either halt or power off, depending on hardware support. It is not recommended to ever pull the plug out of a running system, even embedded systems. Halting before removing power is always the safest choice should you ever need to turn off the system. On embedded systems, pulling the plug is less dangerous, but if the timing is bad it could also be harmful (Diagnostics → Halt System in the WebGUI).

4.6.7   Ping host

Prompts for an IP address, which will be sent three ICMP echo requests. The output from the **ping** will be shown, including the number of packets received, sequence numbers, response times, and packet loss percentage.

4.6.8   Shell

Starts a command line shell. Very useful, and very powerful, but also has the potential to be very dangerous. Some complex configuration tasks may require working in the shell, and some troubleshooting tasks are easier to accomplish from here, but there is always a chance of causing irreparable harm to the system if not handled with care. The majority of pfSense users may never touch the shell, or even know it exists.

Veteran FreeBSD users may feel slightly at home there, but there are many commands which are not present on a pfSense system, since unnecessary parts of the OS are removed for reasons of security and size constraints.

The shell started in this manner will be **tcsh**, and the only other shell available is **sh**. While it may be possible to install other shells (see Section 24.4) for the convenience of those who are very familiar with the OS, this is not recommended or supported.

4.6.9   PFtop

PFtop gives you a real-time view of the firewall states, and the amount of data they have sent and received. It can help pinpoint what IP addresses and sessions are currently using bandwidth, and may also help diagnose other network connection issues. See Section 22.6.2 for more details.

4.6.10   Filter Logs

Using the Filter Logs option, you will see any filter log entries appear in real-time, in their raw form. There is quite a bit more information shown per line than you will typically see in the firewall log view in the WebGUI (Status → System Logs, Firewall tab), but not all of this information is easy to read.

4.6.11   Restart webConfigurator

Restarting the webConfigurator will restart the system process that runs the WebGUI. On rare occasions there may be a change that might need this before it will take effect, or in extremely rare cases the process may have stopped for some reason, and restarting it will restore access.

4.6.12   pfSense Developer Shell (Formerly PHP shell)

The Developer shell, which used to be known as the pfSense PHP shell, is a very powerful utility that lets you execute PHP code in the context of the running system. As with the normal shell, is can also be very dangerous to use, and easy for things to go wrong. This is mainly used by developers and experienced users who are intimately familiar with both PHP and the pfSense code base.

4.6.13   Upgrade from console

Using this option, it is possible to upgrade by entering a full URL to a pfSense firmware image, or a full local path to an image uploaded in some other manner. This method of upgrading is covered in more detail in Section 3.7.3.2.

4.6.14   Enable/Disable Secure Shell (sshd)

This option will allow you to toggle the status of the Secure Shell daemon, sshd. It works similarly to the same option in the WebGUI covered earlier in this chapter, but is accessible from the console.

4.6.15   Move configuration file to removable device

If you wish to keep your system configuration on removable storage, such as a USB thumb drive, this option can be used to relocate the configuration file. Once used, be sure to make sure the media is accessible at boot time so that it may be reloaded. This is not a normal method of backing up the configuration. For information on making backups, see Chapter 5.

4.7 Time Synchronization

Time and clock issues are not that uncommon when configuring any system, but they can be important to get right on routers, especially if they are performing any kind of tasks involving validating certificates as part of a PKI infrastructure. Getting time synchronization to work properly is also an absolute necessity on embedded systems, some of which do not have a battery onboard to preserve their date and time settings when power is removed. There can be some quirks to getting not only a proper date and time into the system, and keeping it that way, but also in making sure that the time zone is properly reflected.

Not only will getting this all in line help with critical system tasks, but it also ensures that your log files are properly timestamped, which can greatly aid in troubleshooting, record keeping, and general system management.

4.7.1 Time Zones

You will see unexpected behavior if you select one of the GMT offset time zones.The offsets are the opposite of what you would expect them to be based on their names. For example the GMT-5 zone is actually GMT plus 5 hours. This comes from the TZ database that FreeBSD and many other Unix and Unix-like operating systems use.

Garrett Wollman described the reason for this in a FreeBSD PR database entry:

> These zones are included for compatibility with ancient UNIX systems. You are more likely to convince the TZ database developers to drop them altogether than you are to get them to change the definitions. In any case, FreeBSD will follow the practice of the TZ database.

We currently have a ticket open to review this confusing matter for pfSense 2.0. We may remove all these GMT offset zones from the web interface entirely. At this time, we recommend using only named time zones and not the GMT offset zones.

4.7.2 Time Keeping Problems

You may run into hardware that has significant problems keeping time. All PC clocks will drift to some extent, but you may find some hardware that will drift as much as one minute for every couple minutes that pass and get wildly out of sync quickly. NTP is designed to periodically update the system time to account for normal drift, it cannot reasonably correct clocks that drift significantly. This is very uncommon, but should you encounter it, the following will outline the things that usually fix this.

There are four things to check if you encounter hardware with significant time keeping problems.

4.7.2.1 Network Time Protocol

By default, pfSense is configured to synchronize its time using the ntp.org Network Time Protocol (NTP) server pool. This ensures an accurate date and time on your system, and will accommodate normal clock drift. If your system's date and time are incorrect, ensure NTP synchronization is functioning. The most common problem preventing synchronization is the lack of proper DNS configuration on the firewall. If the firewall cannot resolve hostnames, the NTP synchronization will fail. The results of synchronization are shown at boot time in the System log.

4.7.2.2 BIOS Updates

I have seen older hardware that ran fine for years on Windows encounter major timekeeping problems once redeployed on FreeBSD (and by consequence, pfSense). The systems were running a BIOS version several revisions out of date. One of the revisions addressed a timekeeping issue that apparently never affected Windows for some reason. Applying the BIOS update fixed the problem. The first thing you should check is to make sure you have the latest BIOS on your system.

4.7.2.3 PNP OS settings in BIOS

I have encountered other hardware that had time keeping difficulties in FreeBSD and pfSense unless PNP OS in the BIOS was set to "No". If your BIOS does not have a PNP OS configuration option, look for an "OS" setting and set it to "Other".

4.7.2.4 Disable ACPI

Some BIOS vendors have produced ACPI (Advanced Configuration and Power Interface) implementations which are buggy at best and dangerous at worst. On more than one occasion we have encountered systems that would not boot or run properly unless ACPI support was disabled in the BIOS and/or in the OS.

The best way to disable ACPI is in the BIOS. If there is no BIOS option to disable ACPI, then you can try to run without it in two different ways. The first, temporary method is to disable ACPI at the boot prompt. Early in the boot process, a menu appears with several choices, one of which is Boot pfSense with ACPI disabled. By choosing this, ACPI will be disabled for this single boot. If behavior improves, then you should disable ACPI permanently.

To permanently disable ACPI, you must add a setting to the /boot/device.hints file. You can do this by browsing to Diagnostics → Edit File, enter /boot/device.hints and then click Load. Add a new line at the end and then enter:

```
hint.acpi.0.disabled="1"
```

Then click Save.

For an alternate way to do this, from Diagnostics → Command or from a shell, type this:

```
# echo "hint.acpi.0.disabled=1" >> /boot/device.hints
```

Note

The /boot/device.hints file will be overwritten during an upgrade. Be aware that you will need to repeat this change after performing a firmware update.

4.7.2.5 Adjust Timecounter Hardware Setting

On very few systems, the kern.timecounter.hardware sysctl value may need to be changed to correct an inaccurate clock. To try this, browse to Diagnostics → Command and execute the following:

```
# sysctl -w kern.timecounter.hardware=i8254
```

This will make the system use the i8254 timecounter chip, which typically keeps good time but may not be as fast as other methods. The other timecounter choices will be explained below.

If the system keeps time properly after making this change, you need to make this change permanent. The previously made change will not survive a reboot. Browse to Diagnostics → Edit File, load /etc/sysctl.conf, and add this to the end:

```
kern.timecounter.hardware=i8254
```

Click Save, and then that setting should be read back in on the next boot. Alternately, you could add the line using a method similar to disabling ACPI above:

```
# echo "kern.timecounter.hardware=i8254" >> /etc/sysctl.conf
```

Note

The /etc/sysctl.conf file will be overwritten during an upgrade. Be aware that you will need to repeat this change after performing a firmware update.

Depending on your platform and hardware, there may also be other timecounters to try. For a list of available timecounters found on your system, execute the following command:

```
# sysctl kern.timecounter.choice
```

You should then see a list of available timecounters and their "quality" as reported by FreeBSD:

```
kern.timecounter.choice: TSC(-100) ACPI-safe(850) i8254(0) dummy ↩
    (-1000000)
```

You could then attempt to try any of those four values for the sysctl kern.timecounter.hardware setting. In terms of "quality" in this listing, the larger the number the better, but the actual usability varies from system to system. The TSC is a counter on the CPU, but is tied to the clock rate and is not readable by other CPUs. This makes its use in SMP systems impossible, and in those with variable-speed CPUs. The i8254 is a clock chip found in most hardware, which tends to be safe but can have some performance drawbacks. The ACPI-safe counter, if properly supported in the available hardware, is a good choice because it does not suffer from the performance limitations of i8254, but in practice its accuracy and speed vary widely depending on the implementation. This and more information on FreeBSD Timecounters can be found in the paper *Timecounters: Efficient and precise timekeeping in SMP kernels* by Poul-Henning Kamp of the FreeBSD Project.

4.7.2.6   Adjust the Kernel Timer Frequency

In some cases it may also be necessary to adjust the kernel timer frequency, or kern.hz kernel tunable. This is especially true on virtualized environments. The default is 1000, but in some cases 100, 50, or even 10 will be a better value depending on the system. When pfSense is installed in VMware, it detects it and automatically sets this to 100, which should work fine in nearly all cases with VMware products. As with the timecounter setting above, to adjust this setting you add a line to `/boot/loader.conf` with the new value:

```
kern.hz=100
```

4.8   Troubleshooting

The Setup Wizard and related configuration tasks will work for most, but there may be some issues getting packets to flow normally in their intended directions. Some of these issues may be unique to your particular setup, but can be worked through with some basic troubleshooting.

4.8.1   Cannot access WebGUI from LAN

The first thing to check if you cannot access the WebGUI from the LAN is the cabling. If you are directly connecting a client PC to a network interface on a pfSense system, you may need a crossover cable unless one or both network cards support Auto-MDIX.

Once you are sure there is a link light on both the client's network card and the pfSense LAN interface, the next thing to check is the TCP/IP configuration on the PC from which you are trying to connect. If the DHCP server is enabled on the pfSense system, as it will be by default, ensure that the client is also set for DHCP. If DHCP is disabled on the pfSense system, you will need to hard code an IP address on the client residing in the same subnet as the pfSense system's LAN IP address, with the same subnet mask, and use the pfSense LAN IP address as its gateway and DNS server.

If the cabling and network settings are correct, you should be able to ping the LAN IP of the pfSense system from the client PC. If you can ping, but you are still unable to access the WebGUI, there are still a few more things to try. First, if the error you receive on the client PC is a connection *reset* or *failure*, then either the server daemon that runs the WebGUI is not running, or you are trying to access it from the wrong port. If the error you receive is instead a connection *timeout*, that points more toward a firewall rule.

If you receive a connection reset, you may first try to restart the WebGUI server process from the system console, typically option 11. Should that not help, start a shell from the console (option 8), and type:

 # sockstat | grep lighttpd

That should return a list of all running lighttpd processes, and the port upon which they are listening, like so:

```
root      lighttpd   437    9   tcp4    *:80                    *:*
```

In that output, it shows that the process is listening on port 80 of each interface, but that may vary based on your configuration. Try connecting to the pfSense LAN IP by using that port directly, and with both http and https. For example, if your LAN IP was 192.168.1.1, and it was listening on port 82, try `http://192.168.1.1:82` and `https://192.168.1.1:82`.

If you receive a connection timeout, refer to Section 4.10. With a properly configured network connection, this shouldn't happen, and that section offers ways to work around firewall rule issues.

It is also a good idea to double check that WAN and LAN are not on the same subnet. If WAN is set for DHCP and is plugged in behind another NAT router, it may also be using 192.168.1.1. If the same subnet is present on WAN and LAN, unpredictable results may happen, including not being able to route traffic or access the WebGUI. When in doubt, unplug the WAN cable, reboot the pfSense router, and try again.

4.8.2 No Internet from LAN

If you are able to reach the WebGUI, but not the Internet, there are several things to consider. The WAN interface may not be properly configured, DNS resolution may not be working, there could be a problem with the firewall rules, NAT rules, or even something as simple as a local gateway issue.

4.8.2.1 WAN Interface Issues

First, check the WAN interface to be sure that pfSense sees it as operational. Browse to Status → Interfaces, and look at the WAN interface status there. The status should show as "up". If it shows down, double check your cabling and WAN settings under Interfaces → WAN. If you are using PPPoE or PPTP for the WAN type, there is an additional status line indicating if the PPP connection is active. If it is down, try pressing the Connect button. If that doesn't work, double check all of your settings on Interfaces → WAN, check or reboot your ISP equipment (cable/dsl modem, etc.), and perhaps consult with your ISP for help regarding the settings you should use there.

4.8.2.2 DNS Resolution Issues

Inside the WebGUI, go to Diagnostics → Ping, and enter in your ISP's gateway address if you know it. It will be listed on Status → Interfaces for the WAN interface. If you do not know the gateway, you may try some other known-valid address such as **4.2.2.2**. If you are able to ping that address, then repeat that same ping test from your client PC. Open a command prompt or terminal window, and ping that same IP address. If you can ping that IP address, then try to ping a site by name such as **www.google.com**. Try it from the pfSense WebGUI and from the client PC. If the IP ping test works, but you cannot ping by name, then there is a problem with DNS resolution. (See Figure 6.20 for an example.)

If DNS resolution does not work on the pfSense system, check your DNS server settings under System → General Setup, and under Status → Interfaces. Check with ping to be sure they are reachable. If you can reach the gateway address at your ISP, but not their DNS servers, it may be advisable to call your ISP and double check those values. If your DNS servers are obtained via DHCP or PPPoE and you cannot contact them, you may also need to contact your ISP regarding that issue. If all else fails, you may want to consider using OpenDNS (see Section 24.2) name servers on your pfSense router instead of those provided by your ISP.

If DNS works from the pfSense router, but not from a client PC, it could be the DNS Forwarder configuration on the pfSense system, the client configuration, or firewall rules. Out of the box, pfSense has a DNS forwarder which will handle DNS queries for clients behind the router. If your client PCs are configured with DHCP, they will be getting the IP address of the pfSense router interface to which they are connected as a DNS server, unless you specify an override. For example, if a PC is on the LAN side, and the pfSense system's LAN IP address is 192.168.1.1, then the client's DNS server should also be 192.168.1.1. If you have disabled the DNS Forwarder, you may also need to adjust the DNS servers which get assigned to DHCP clients under Services → DHCP Server. Normally when the DNS Forwarder is disabled, the system's DNS servers are assigned directly to the clients, but if that is not the case in practice for your setup, define them here. If the client PC is not configured for DHCP, be sure it has the proper DNS servers set: either the LAN IP address of the pfSense system or whatever internal or external DNS servers you would like for it to use.

Another possibility for DNS working from pfSense itself but not a local client is an overly strict firewall rule. Check Status → System Logs, on the Firewall tab. If you see blocked connections from your local client trying to reach a DNS server, then you should add a firewall rule at the top of the ruleset for that interface which will allow connections to the DNS servers on TCP and UDP port 53.

4.8.2.3   Client Gateway Issue

In order for the pfSense system to properly route Internet traffic for your client PCs, it must be their gateway. If the client PCs are configured using pfSense's DHCP server, this will be set automatically. However, if the clients receive DHCP information from an alternate DHCP server, or their IP addresses have been entered manually, double check that their gateway is set for the IP address of the interface to which they connect on the pfSense system. For example, if the clients are on the pfSense LAN side, and the IP address for pfSense's LAN interface is 192.168.1.1, then a client's gateway address must be set to 192.168.1.1.

4.8.2.4   Firewall Rule Issues

If the default "LAN to Any" rule has been changed or removed from the LAN interface, traffic attempting to reach the Internet from client PCs via the pfSense router may be blocked. This should be easily confirmed by browsing to Status → System Logs, and looking at the Firewall tab. If there are entries there that show blocked connections from LAN PCs trying to reach Internet hosts, revisit your LAN ruleset at Firewall → Rules, then the LAN tab and make the necessary adjustments to allow that traffic. Consult Chapter 6 for more detailed information on editing or creating additional rules.

If it works from the LAN side but not from an OPT interface, be sure you have rules in place to allow the traffic to leave. No rule is created by default on OPT interfaces.

4.8.2.5   NAT Rule Issues

If the outbound NAT rules have been changed from their defaults, it may also be possible that traffic attempting to reach the Internet does not have NAT properly applied. Navigate to Firewall → NAT, and go to the Outbound tab. Unless you are sure that you need it set to manual, change the setting to Automatic outbound NAT rule generation (IPsec passthrough) and then try to reach the Internet from a client PC again. If that did not help a PC on the LAN to get out, then the issue is likely elsewhere.

If you have this set to Manual Outbound NAT rule generation (Advanced Outbound NAT (AON)), and it works from LAN but not from an OPT interface, you will need to manually set a rule that matches traffic coming from there. Look at the existing rule for LAN and adjust it accordingly, or refer to the NAT chapter for more information on creating outbound NAT rules. The same applies for traffic coming from VPN users: PPTP, OpenVPN, IPsec, etc. If these users need to reach the Internet via this pfSense router, they will need outbound NAT rules for their subnets. See Section 7.6 for more information.

4.9 pfSense's XML Configuration File

pfSense stores all of its settings in an XML format configuration file. All system settings — including settings for packages — are held in this one file. All other configuration files for system services and behavior are generated dynamically at run time based on the settings held within the XML configuration file.

Some people who are familiar with FreeBSD and related operating systems have found this out the hard way, when their changes to some system configuration files were repeatedly overwritten by the system before they came to understand that pfSense handles everything automatically.

Most people will never need to know where the configuration file resides, but for reference it is in `/cf/conf/config.xml`. Typically, `/conf/` is a symlink to `/cf/conf`, so it may also be accessible directly from `/conf/config.xml`, but this varies by platform and filesystem layout.

4.9.1 Manually editing your configuration

A few configuration options are only available by manually editing your configuration file, though this isn't required in the vast majority of deployments. Some of these options are covered in other parts of this book.

The safest and easiest method of editing the configuration file is to make a backup from Diagnostics → Backup/Restore, save the file to your PC, edit the file and make any needed changes, then restore the altered configuration file to the system.

4.10 What to do if you get locked out of the WebGUI

Under certain circumstances you may find yourself locked out of the WebGUI, mostly due to pilot error. Don't be afraid if this happens to you; there are a number of ways to get back in. Some methods are a little tricky, but it should always be possible to regain access. The worst-case scenarios require physical access. As you'll remember from earlier this chapter we mentioned that anyone with physical access can bypass security measures and now you will see just how easy it is.

4.10.1   Forgotten Password

If you forgot the password for the system it can be reset easily with console access. Get to the physical console (Keyboard/Monitor, or Serial) and use option **3** to reset the WebGUI password.

4.10.2   Forgotten Password with a Locked Console

If the console is password protected and you do not know the password, all is not lost. It will take a couple reboots to accomplish, but it can be fixed with physical access to the console:

- Reboot the pfSense box

- Choose option 4 (Single User Mode) from the loader menu (the one with the ASCII pfSense logo)

- Press enter when prompted to start /bin/sh

- Remount all of the partitions as rewritable:

    `# /sbin/mount -a -t ufs`

- Run the built-in password reset command:

    `# /etc/rc.initial.password`

- Follow the prompts to reset the password

- Reboot

You should now be able to access the system with the default username and password of **admin** and **pfsense**, respectively.

4.10.3   HTTP vs HTTPS Confusion

Ensure you are connecting with the proper protocol, either HTTP or HTTPS. If one doesn't work, try the other. You may find that you need to try the opposite protocol on the others port, like so:

- `http://pfsensebox:443`

- `https://pfsensebox:80`

If you need to reset this from the console, reset the LAN IP, enter the same IP, and it will prompt to reset the WebGUI back to HTTP.

4.10.4 Blocked Access with Firewall Rules

If you blocked yourself out of the WebGUI remotely with a firewall rule, there may still be hope. This can't happen from the LAN unless you disable the anti-lockout rule that maintains access to the WebGUI from that interface.

Having to walk someone on-site through fixing the rule is better than losing everything!

4.10.5 Remotely Circumvent Firewall Lockout with Rules

You could (very temporarily) disable firewall rules by using the console. You can use the physical console, or if you are still able to get in via SSH, that will also work. From the console, use option 8 to start a shell, and then type:

```
# pfctl -d
```

That will disable the firewall. You should then be able to get into the WebGUI from anywhere, at least for a few minutes or until you save something in the WebGUI that causes the ruleset to be reloaded (which is almost every page). Once you have adjusted the rules and regained the necessary access, turn the firewall back on by typing:

```
# pfctl -e
```

Alternately, the loaded ruleset is retained in `/tmp/rules.debug`. If you are familiar with PF ruleset syntax, you can edit that to fix your connectivity issue and reload those rules like so:

```
# pfctl -f /tmp/rules.debug
```

After getting back into the WebGUI with that temporary fix, do whatever work you need to do in the WebGUI to make the fix permanent. When you save the rules in the WebGUI, that temporary ruleset will be overwritten.

4.10.6 Remotely Circumvent Firewall Lockout with SSH Tunneling

If you blocked access to the WebGUI remotely, but you still have access with SSH, then there is a relatively easy way to get in: SSH Tunneling.

If the WebGUI is on port 80, set your client to forward local port 80 (or 8080, or whatever) to remote port "localhost:80", then point your browser to **http://localhost:80** or whichever local port you chose. If your WebGUI is on another port, use that instead. If you are using HTTPS you will still need to use HTTPS to access the WebGUI this manner.

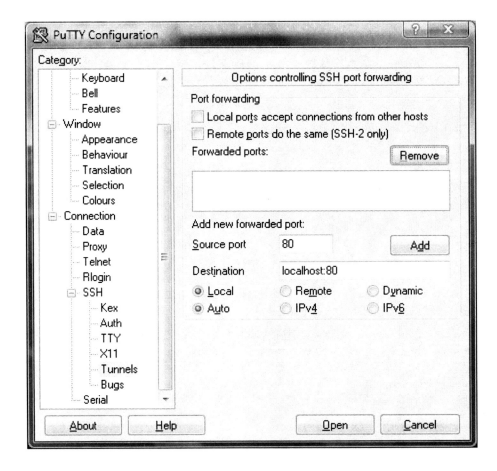

Figure 4.14: Setting up a port 80 SSH Tunnel in PuTTY

Fill out the options as shown in Figure 4.14, then click Add. Once you connect and enter your username/password, you can access the WebGUI using your redirected local port.

4.10.7   Locked Out Due to Squid Configuration Error

If you accidentally configure Squid to use the same port as the WebGUI, and then cannot get back in to fix the configuration, you may need to fix it using the following procedure.

- Connect to the pfSense system console with SSH or physical access

- Start a shell, option 8 from the console.

- Terminate the squid process like so:

  ```
  # /usr/local/etc/rc.d/squid.sh stop
  ```

  If that doesn't work, try it this way:

```
# killall -9 squid
```

or

```
# squid -k shutdown
```

Once the squid process is fully terminated, you should be able to regain access to the WebGUI. Be aware that you may need to work quickly, or repeat the shutdown command, as squid may be automatically restarted.

4.11 Final Configuration Thoughts

There are millions of ways to configure a pfSense system, and thus it is impossible to cover all aspects of each configuration and troubleshooting in this book. This chapter provided an overview of some of the general configuration options. The coming chapters go into detail on individual capabilities of the software. As we mentioned at the end of the introductory chapter, there are several other avenues for getting help. If you have tried all of the suggestions here and you still aren't able to make pfSense perform as you expect, there are forums, IRC, mailing lists, Google searches, and Commercial Support. You are free to take the DIY approach, or if you would like professionals to take care of the configuration for you, the Commercial Support team is more than capable. For links to the online support mediums, refer to Section 1.9.2.

Chapter 5

Backup and Recovery

Thanks to the XML-based configuration file used by pfSense, backups are a breeze. All of the settings for the system are held in one single file (see Section 4.9). In the vast majority of cases, this one file can be used to restore a system to a fully working state identical to what was running previously. There is no need to make an entire system backup, as the base system files are not modified by a normal, running, system. The one exception is the case of some packages, such as FreeSWITCH, which hold data outside of the configuration file.

5.1   Backup Strategies

The best practice is to make a backup after each minor change, and both before and after each major change (or series of changes). Typically, an initial backup is taken just in case the change being made has undesirable effects. An after-the-fact backup is taken after evaluating the change and ensuring it had the intended outcome. Periodic backups are also be helpful, regardless of changes, especially in cases where a manual backup may be missed for one reason or another.

pfSense makes an internal backup upon each change, and it's a good idea to download a manual one as well. The automatic backups made on each change are good for reverting to prior configurations after changes have proven detrimental, but are not good for disaster recovery as they are on the system itself and not kept externally. As it is a fairly simple and painless process, it should be easy to make a habit of downloading a backup now and then, and keeping it in a safe place. If you have a subscription on portal.pfsense.org, backups can be handled easily and automatically for you.

If you make any changes to the system files, such as custom patches or code alterations, you must remember to back these changes up by hand or with the backup package described in Section 5.6, as they will not be backed up or restored by the built-in backup system. This includes alterations to system files mentioned elsewhere in the book, such as `/boot/device.hints`, `/boot/loader.conf`, `/etc/sysctl.conf`, and others.

In addition to making backups, you should also test them. Before placing a system into production, you may want to backup the configuration, and then wipe the HDD, and then attempt some of the different restoration techniques in this chapter. Once you are familiar with how to both backup and restore a configuration, you may want to periodically test your backups on a non-production machine or virtual machine. The only thing worse than a missing backup is an unusable backup!

In pfSense 1.2.x, the RRD graph data, located in `/var/db/rrd`, is not backed up by any of the stock backup processes. This will be fixed in the next version, where the RRD data can be held in the XML configuration file backup, but this may still not be desirable for some people due to the size increase this brings. There are other ways to ensure this data is backed up, however. See Section 5.6 later in this chapter.

5.2   Making Backups in the WebGUI

Making a backup in the WebGUI is quite simple. Just visit Diagnostics → Backup/Restore. In the Backup Configuration section of the page, ensure that Backup Area is set to **ALL**, (the default choice) then click Download Configuration (Figure 5.1).

Diagnostics: Backup/restore

Config History	**Backup/Restore**

Backup configuration

Click this button to download the system configuration in XML format.

Backup area: ALL   ▾

☐ Do not backup package information.

Download configuration

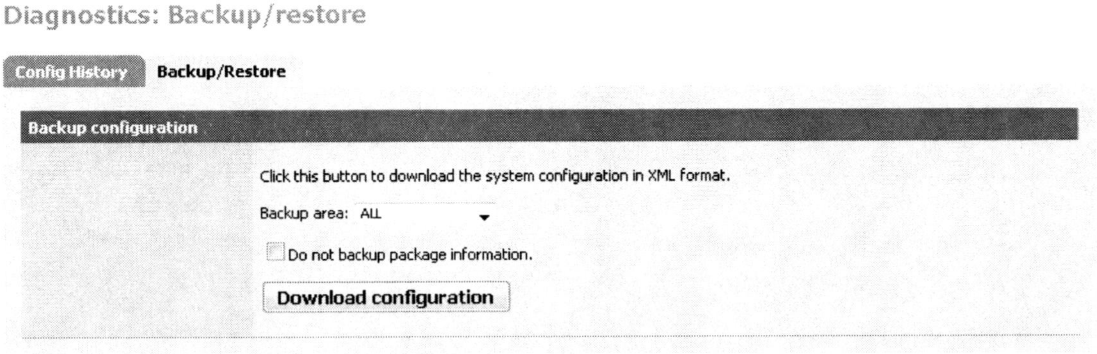

Figure 5.1: WebGUI Backup

Your web browser will then prompt you to save the file somewhere on the PC being used to view the WebGUI. It will be named `config-<hostname>-<timestamp>.xml`, but that may be changed before saving the file.

5.3   Using the AutoConfigBackup Package

Subscribers on portal.pfsense.org have access to our Automatic Configuration Backup Service, AutoConfigBackup. The most up to date information on AutoConfigBackup can be found on the pfSense documentation site.

5.3.1   Functionality and Benefits

When you make a change to your configuration, it is automatically encrypted with the passphrase entered in your configuration, and uploaded over HTTPS to our server. Only encrypted configurations are retained on our server. This gives you instant, secure offsite backup of your firewall with no user intervention.

5.3.2 pfSense Version Compatibility

The AutoConfigBackup package will work with pfSense 1.2-RELEASE and all subsequent releases including 2.0.

Note

There is one caveat to using this package on pfSense 1.2 — the only way we could tie the automatic backup into 1.2 release is to trigger it upon every filter reload. Most page saves will trigger a filter reload, but not all.

5.3.3 Installation and Configuration

To install the package, visit System → Packages and click the ⬚ next to the AutoConfigBackup package. It will download and install the package. Then click on the pfSense logo at the top of the page, which will return you to the front page, and refresh your menus. You will then find AutoConfigBackup under the Diagnostics menu.

5.3.3.1 Setting your hostname

Make sure you have a unique hostname and domain set on the System → General Setup page. The configurations are stored by FQDN (Fully Qualified Domain Name, i.e. hostname + domain), so you must make sure each firewall you are backing up has a unique FQDN, otherwise the system cannot differentiate between multiple installations.

5.3.3.2 Configuring AutoConfigBackup

The service is configured under Diagnostics → AutoConfigBackup. On the Settings tab, fill in your portal.pfsense.org username and password, and enter an encryption password. You should use a long, complex password to ensure your configuration is secure. For your security, we retain only encrypted configurations which are useless without your encryption password.

Note

It is very important to store this encryption key somewhere off of your firewall — if you lose it, it will be impossible to restore your configuration if you lose the hard drive in your firewall.

5.3.3.3   Testing Backup Functionality

Make a change to force a configuration backup, such as editing and saving a firewall or NAT rule, then click Apply Changes. Visit the Diagnostics → AutoConfigBackup screen, and you will be shown the Restore tab, which will list your available backups along with the page that made the change (where available).

5.3.3.4   Manually Backing Up

At times, you may want to force a backup of your configuration. You can do this on the Restore tab of the AutoConfigBackup page by clicking the Backup now button at the bottom. This will pop up a box where you can manually enter a description of your backup. You may wish to do this before making a series of significant changes, as it will leave you with a backup specifically showing the reason for the backup, which then makes it easy to revert to your configuration prior to initiating the changes. Since each configuration change triggers a backup, when you make a series of changes it can be difficult to know where you started if you should need to revert. Or you may wish to manually backup prior to upgrading to a new pfSense release, and name the backup so it's clear that is the reason you made the backup.

5.3.3.5   Restoring Your Configuration

To restore a configuration, click the ⊞ button to the right of the configuration as shown on the Diagnostics → AutoConfigBackup screen on the Restore tab. It will download the configuration specified from our server, decrypt it with your encryption password, and restore it. By default, it will not reboot. Depending on the configuration items restored, a reboot may not be necessary. For example, your firewall and NAT rules are automatically reloaded after restoring a configuration. After restoring, you are prompted if you want to reboot. If your restored configuration changes anything other than NAT and firewall rules, you should choose Yes.

5.3.4   Bare Metal Restoration

If you lose your hard drive, as of now you must do the following to recover on a new installation.

1. Install pfSense on the new hard drive.

2. Bring up LAN and WAN, and assign the hostname and domain exactly the same as it was previously configured.

3. Install the AutoConfigBackup package.

4. Configure the AutoConfigBackup package as described above, using your portal account and the same encryption password as used previously.

5. Visit the Restore tab and choose the configuration you wish to restore.

6. When prompted to reboot after the restoration, do so.

You will now be back to the state of your firewall as of the last configuration change.

5.3.5   Checking the AutoConfigBackup Status

You can check the success of an AutoConfigBackup run by reviewing the list of backups shown on the Restore tab. This list is pulled from our servers — if the backup is listed there, it was successfully created.

If a backup fails, an alert is logged, and you will see it scrolling across the top of the web interface.

5.4   Alternate Remote Backup Techniques

The following techniques may also be used to perform backups remotely, but each method has its own security issues which may rule out their use in many places. For starters, these techniques do not encrypt the configuration, which may contain sensitive information. This may result in the configuration being transmitted over an untrusted link in the clear. If you must use one of these techniques, it is best to do so from a non-WAN link (LAN, DMZ, etc.) or across a VPN. Access to the storage media holding the backup should also be controlled, if not encrypted. The AutoConfigBackup package is a much easier and more secure means of automating remote backups.

5.4.1   Pull with wget

The configuration may be retrieved from a remote system by using **wget**, and could be scripted with **cron** or by some other means. Even when using HTTPS, this is not a truly secure transport mode since certificate checking is disabled to accommodate self-signed certificates, enabling man in the middle attacks. When running backups with **wget** across untrusted networks, you should use HTTPS with a certificate that can be verified by **wget**.

For a router running HTTPS with a self-signed certificate, the command would be something such as this:

```
# wget -q --no-check-certificate --post-data 'Submit=download' \
    https://admin:pfsense@192.168.1.1/diag_backup.php \
    -O config-hostname-`date +%Y%m%d%H%M%S`.xml
```

For a router running regular HTTP, the command would be:

```
# wget -q --post-data 'Submit=download' \
    http://admin:pfsense@192.168.1.1/diag_backup.php \
    -O config-hostname-`date +%Y%m%d%H%M%S`.xml
```

In both of those cases, replace the username and password with your own, and the IP address would be whichever IP address is reachable from the system performing the backup. The system performing the backup will also need access to the WebGUI, so adjust your firewall rules accordingly. Performing this over the WAN is not recommended, at a minimum you should use HTTPS, and restrict access to the WebGUI to a trusted set of public IPs. It is preferable to do this over VPN.

5.4.2   Push with SCP

The configuration could also be pushed from the pfSense box to another UNIX system with **scp**. Using **scp** to push a one-time backup by hand can be useful, but using it in an automated fashion carries some risks. The command line for **scp** will vary greatly depending on your system configuration, but may look like:

```
# scp /cf/conf/config.xml \
      user@backuphost:backups/config-`hostname`-`date +%Y%m%d%H%M%S`.xml
```

In order to push the configuration in an automated manner you would need to generate an SSH key without a passphrase. Due to the insecure nature of a key without a passphrase, generating such a key is left as an exercise for the reader. This adds some risk due to the fact that anyone with access to that file has access to the designated account, though because the key is kept on the firewall where access is highly restricted, it isn't a considerable risk in most scenarios. If you do this, ensure the remote user is isolated and has little to no privileges on the destination system. A chrooted SCP environment may be desirable in this case. See the **scponly** shell available for most UNIX platforms which allows SCP file copies but denies interactive login capabilities. Some versions of OpenSSH have chroot support built in for **sftp** (Secure FTP). These steps greatly limit the risk of compromise with respect to the remote server, but still leave your backed up data at risk. Once access is configured, a **cron** entry could be added to the pfSense system to invoke **scp**. For more details visit the pfSense Documentation Wiki or search on the forums.

5.4.3   Basic SSH backup

Similar to the SCP backup, there is another method that will work from one UNIX system to another. This method does not invoke the SCP/SFTP layer, which in some cases may not function properly if a system is already in a failing state.

```
# ssh root@192.168.1.1 cat /cf/conf/config.xml > backup.xml
```

When executed, that command will yield a file called `backup.xml` in the current working directory that contains the remote pfSense system's configuration. Automating this method using **cron** is also possible, but this method requires a SSH key without as passphrase on the host performing the backup. This key will enable administrative access to your firewall, so it must be tightly controlled. (See Section 4.5.2 for SSH configuration details.)

5.5   Restoring from Backups

Backups won't do you much good without a means to restore them, and by extension, test them. pfSense offers several means for restoring configurations. Some are more involved than others, but each should have the same end result: a running system identical to what was there when the backup was made.

5.5.1 Restoring with the WebGUI

The easiest way for most people to restore a configuration is by using the WebGUI. Navigate to Diagnostics → Backup/Restore, and look at the Restore configuration section (Figure 5.2). To restore the backup, select the area to restore (typically **ALL**), then click Browse. Locate the backup file on your PC, and then click the Restore configuration button. The configuration will be applied, and the firewall will reboot with the settings obtained from the backup file.

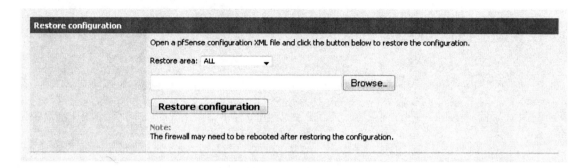

Figure 5.2: WebGUI Restore

While easy to work with, this method does have some prerequisites when dealing with a full restore to a new system. First, it would need to be done after the new target system is fully installed and running. Second, it requires an additional PC connected to a working network (or crossover cable) behind the pfSense system which is being restored.

5.5.2 Restoring from the Config History

For minor problems, one of pfSense's internal backups may be the easiest way to back out a change. From the Diagnostics → Backup/Restore page, click the Config History tab (Figure 5.3). The previous 30 configurations are stored, along with the current running configuration. To switch to one of these previous configurations, click the ⬇ beside its entry.

Diagnostics: Configuration History

Config History	Backup/Restore	

Date	Configuration Change	Current
6/24/09 20:04:13	/services_dhcp.php made unknown change	
6/24/09 19:56:30	/services_dhcp.php made unknown change	⬇ ✖
6/18/09 10:49:11	/firewall_rules_edit.php made unknown change	⬇ ✖
6/18/09 10:45:29	/vpn_ipsec_edit.php made unknown change	⬇ ✖
6/17/09 14:00:55	An OpenVPN server has been created/modified	⬇ ✖

Figure 5.3: Configuration History

The configuration will be switched, but a reboot is not automatic where required. Minor changes do not require a reboot, though reverting some major changes will. To be safe, you may want to reboot the router with the new configuration by going to Diagnostics → Reboot System and click Yes.

Previously saved configurations may be deleted by clicking 🗙, but you need not delete them by hand to save space; the old configuration backups are automatically deleted when new ones are created. You may want to remove a backup from a known-bad configuration change to ensure that it is not accidentally restored.

5.5.3   Restoring with PFI

Covered in Section 3.6, The Pre-Flight Installer (PFI) will take a configuration file which has been saved on a USB drive and restore it as the running configuration during the installation process. This is likely the fastest method for restoring a configuration, as it happens during the install process with no manual intervention on the pfSense box. It boots up the first time with the new configuration, and you do not need to worry about having a PC handy from which to perform the restore via the WebGUI.

5.5.4   Restoring by Mounting the CF/HDD

This method is popular with embedded users. If you attach the CF or HDD of the pfSense system to a computer running FreeBSD you can mount the drive and copy a new configuration directly onto an installed system, or even copy a config from a failed system.

Note

You can also perform this on a separate pfSense system in place of a computer running FreeBSD, but do not use an active production router for this purpose. Instead, use a spare system or test router.

The config file is kept in `/cf/conf/` for both embedded and full installs, but the difference is in the location where this directory resides. For embedded installs, this is on a separate slice, such as `ad0s3` if the drive is `ad0`. Thanks to GEOM (modular storage framework) labels on recent versions of FreeBSD and in use on NanoBSD-based embedded filesystems, this slice may also be accessed regardless of the device name by using the label `/dev/ufs/cf`. For full installs, it is part of the root slice (typically `ad0s1a`). The drive names will vary depending on type and position in the system.

5.5.4.1   Embedded Example

First, connect the CF to a USB card reader on a FreeBSD system or another inactive pfSense system (see the note in the previous section). For most, it will show up as `da0`. You should also see console messages reflecting the device name, and the newly available GEOM labels.

Now mount the config partition:

```
# mount -t ufs /def/ufs/cf /mnt
```

If for some reason you are unable to use the GEOM labels, use the device directly such as `/dev/da0s3`.

Now, copy a config onto the card:

```
# cp /usr/backups/pfSense/config-alix.example.com-20090606185703.xml \
     /mnt/conf/config.xml
```

Then be sure to unmount the config partition:

```
# umount /mnt
```

Unplug the card, reinsert it into the router, and turn it back on. The router should now be running with the previous configuration. If you want to copy the configuration *from* the card, the process is the same but the arguments to the **cp** command are reversed.

5.5.5 Rescue Config During Install

Also covered in Section 3.6, this process will reinstall pfSense onto a hard drive, but maintain the configuration that is present on that drive. This is used when the contents of the system are corrupted in some way, but the configuration file is intact.

5.6 Backup Files and Directories with the Backup Package

The Backup package will allow you to backup and restore any given set of files/folders on the system. For most, this is not necessary, but it can be useful for backing up RRD data or for packages like FreeSWITCH that may have files you want to keep (e.g. Voice Mail messages.) To install the package, browse to System → Packages, find Backup in the list, and click . Once installed, it is available from Diagnostics → Backup Files/Dir. It is fairly simple to use, as shown in the following example.

5.6.1 Backing up RRD Data

Using this Backup package it should be quite easy to make a backup of your RRD graph data (see Section 22.5) .

First, go to Diagnostics → Backup Files/Dir. Click to add a new location to the backup set. In the Name field, enter **RRD Data**. In the Path field, enter **/var/db/rrd**. Set Enabled to **True**, and for the Description, enter **RRD Graph Data**. Click Save.

From the main Backup screen, click the Backup button, and then you will be presented with a file to download which should contain your RRD data along with any other directories in the backup set. Save it somewhere safe, and consider keeping multiple copies if the data is very important to you.

5.6.2 Restoring RRD Data

From Diagnostics → Backup Files/Dir, click Browse, and find a backup file which was previously down-loaded. Click Upload, and the files should be restored. Because the RRD files are only touched when updated once every 60 seconds, you should not have to reboot or restart any services once the files are restored.

5.7   Caveats and Gotchas

While the configuration XML file kept by pfSense includes all of your settings, it does not include any changes that may have been made to the system by hand, such as manual modifications of source code. Additionally some packages require extra backup methods for their data.

The configuration file may contain sensitive information such as VPN keys or certificates, and pass-words (other than the admin password) in plain text in some cases. Some passwords must be available in plain text during run time, making secure hashing of those passwords impossible. Any obfuscation would be trivial to reverse for anyone with access to the source code — i.e. everyone. A conscious design decision was made in m0n0wall, and continued in pfSense, to leave those passwords in clear to make it exceedingly clear that the file contains sensitive content and should be protected as such. Hence you should protect backup copies of these files in some way. If you store them on removable media, take care with physical security of that media and/or encrypt the drive.

If you must use the WebGUI over the WAN without a VPN connection, you should at least use HTTPS. Otherwise, a backup is transmitted in the clear, including any sensitive information inside that backup file. It is highly recommended that you use a trusted link or encrypted connection.

Chapter 6

Firewall

One of the primary functions of pfSense regardless of the role in which it is deployed is filtering traffic. This chapter covers fundamentals of firewalling, best practices, and the information you need to configure your firewall rules as necessary for your environment.

6.1 Firewalling Fundamentals

This section deals primarily with introductory firewall concepts and lays the ground work for helping you to understand how best to appropriately configure firewall rules in pfSense.

6.1.1 Basic terminology

Rule and ruleset are two terms used throughout this chapter. Rule refers to a single entry on your Firewall → Rules screen. A rule is a configuration or action for how to look at or handle network traffic. Ruleset refers to all your firewall rules as a whole. This is the sum of all the user configured and automatically added rules, which are covered further throughout this chapter.

In pfSense, rulesets are evaluated in a first match basis. This means that if you read the ruleset for an interface from top to bottom, the first rule that matches will be the one used. Processing stops after reaching this match and then the action specified by that rule is taken. Always keep this in mind when creating new rules, especially when you are crafting rules to restrict traffic. The most permissive rules should always be toward the bottom of the list, so that restrictions or exceptions can be made above them.

6.1.2 Stateful Filtering

pfSense is a stateful firewall. This means you only permit traffic on the interface where the traffic is initiated. When a connection is initiated matching a pass rule on your firewall, an entry is created in the firewall's state table, where information on the active connections through the firewall is retained.

The reply traffic to connections initiated inside your network is automatically allowed back into your network by the state table. This includes any related traffic using a different protocol, such as ICMP control messages that may be provided in response to a TCP, UDP, or other connection.

See Section 4.5.9 and Section 6.6.10 about state options and types.

6.1.2.1 State table size

The firewall state table has a maximum size, to prevent memory exhaustion. Each state takes approximately 1 KB of RAM. (See Section 2.4.2.1 about large state tables.) The default state table size in pfSense is 10,000. This means if you have 10,000 active connections traversing your firewall, any additional connections will be dropped. This limit can be increased by browsing to the System → Advanced page, and scrolling down under Traffic Shaper and Firewall Advanced (Figure 6.1). Enter the desired number for Firewall Maximum States, or leave the box blank for the default 10,000. You can view your historical state usage under Status → RRD Graphs. On the System tab, choose **States** in the Graphs drop down.

Figure 6.1: Increased state table size to 50,000

6.1.3   Ingress Filtering

Ingress filtering refers to the firewalling of traffic coming into your network from the Internet. In deployments with multi-WAN you have multiple ingress points. The default ingress policy on pfSense is to block all traffic, as there are no allow rules on WAN by default. Replies to traffic initiated from inside your network are automatically allowed through by the state table.

6.1.4   Egress Filtering

Egress filtering refers to the filtering of traffic initiated inside your network destined for the Internet or any other interface on the firewall. pfSense, like nearly all similar commercial and open source solutions, comes with a LAN rule allowing everything from the LAN out to the Internet. This isn't the best way to operate, however. It has become the de facto default in most firewall solutions because it is simply what most people desire. The common misperception is anything on the internal network is "trustworthy", so why bother filtering?

6.1.4.1   Why should I employ egress filtering?

From my experience in working with countless firewalls from numerous vendors across many different organizations, most small companies and home networks do not employ egress filtering. It can increase the administrative burden, as each new application or service may require opening additional ports or protocols in the firewall. In some environments, it's difficult because the administrators don't really know what is happening on the network, and are hesitant to break things. In others, it's impossible for reasons of workplace politics. But you should strive to allow only the minimum required traffic to leave your network, where possible. Tight egress filtering is important for several reasons.

1. Limit the impact of a compromised system — malware commonly uses ports and protocols that are not required on many networks. Many bots rely on IRC connections to phone home and receive instructions. Some will use more common ports such as TCP port 80 (normally HTTP) to evade egress filtering, but many do not. If you do not permit TCP port 6667, the usual IRC port, you can cripple bots that rely on IRC to function.

   Another example I have seen is a case where the inside interface of a pfSense install was seeing 50-60 Mbps of traffic, while the WAN had less than 1 Mbps of throughput. There were no other interfaces on the firewall. Some investigation showed the cause as a compromised system on the LAN running a bot participating in a distributed denial of service (DDoS) attack against a Chinese gambling web site. It used UDP port 80, likely for a couple reasons. First, UDP allows you to send large packets without completing a TCP handshake. With stateful firewalls being the norm, large TCP packets will not pass until the handshake is successfully completed, and this limits the effectiveness of the DDoS. Second, those who do employ egress filtering are commonly too permissive, allowing TCP and UDP where only TCP is required, as in the case of HTTP. In this network, UDP port 80 was not permitted by the egress ruleset, so all the DDoS was accomplishing was pounding the inside interface of the firewall with traffic that was being dropped. I was looking at the firewall for an unrelated reason and found this; it was happily chugging along with no performance degradation and the network's administrator did not know it was happening.

   Outbound SMTP is another example. You should only allow SMTP, TCP port 25, to leave your network from your mail server. Or if your mail server is externally hosted, only allow your internal systems to talk to that specific outside system on TCP port 25. This prevents every other system in your network from being used as a spam zombie, since their SMTP traffic will be dropped. This has the obvious benefit of doing your part to limit spam, and also prevents your network from being added to numerous black lists across the Internet that will prevent you from sending legitimate email to many mail servers.

   The correct solution is to prevent these types of things from happening in the first place, but egress filtering provides another layer that can help limit the impact if your other measures fail.

2. Prevent a compromise — in some circumstances, egress filtering can prevent your systems from being compromised. Some exploits and worms require outbound access to succeed. An older but good example of this is the Code Red worm from 2001. The exploit caused affected systems to pull an executable file via TFTP (Trivial File Transfer Protocol) and then execute it. Your web server almost certainly does not need to use the TFTP protocol, and blocking TFTP via egress filtering prevented infection with Code Red even on unpatched servers. This is largely only useful for stopping completely automated attacks and worms, as a real human attacker will find any holes that exist in your egress filtering and use them to his advantage.

   Again, the correct solution to preventing compromise is to fix your network's vulnerabilities, however egress filtering can help.

3. Limit unauthorized application usage — many applications, such as VPN clients, peer-to-peer software, instant messengers and more rely on atypical ports or protocols to function. While a growing number of peer-to-peer and instant messengers will port hop until finding something allowed out of your network, many will be prevented from functioning by a restrictive egress ruleset, and this is an effective means of limiting many types of VPN connectivity.

4. Prevent IP spoofing — this is a commonly cited reason for employing egress filtering, but pf-Sense automatically blocks spoofed traffic via pf's *antispoof* functionality, so it isn't applicable here.

5. Prevent information leaks — certain protocols should never be allowed to leave your network. Specific examples will vary from one environment to another. Microsoft RPC (Remote Procedure Call) on TCP port 135, NetBIOS on TCP and UDP ports 137 through 139, and SMB/CIFS (Server Message Block/Common Internet File System) on TCP and UDP port 445 are all common examples of services that should not be allowed to leave your network. This can prevent information about your internal network from leaking onto the Internet, and will prevent your systems from initiating authentication attempts with Internet hosts. These protocols also fall under "limit the impact of a compromised system" as discussed previously, since many worms have relied upon these protocols to function in the past. Other protocols that may be relevant in your environment are syslog, SNMP, and SNMP traps. Restricting this traffic will prevent misconfigured network devices from sending logging and other potentially sensitive information out onto the Internet. Rather than worry about what protocols might leak information out of your network and need to be blocked, solely allow the traffic that is required.

6.1.4.2 Approaches for implementing egress filtering

On a network that has historically not employed egress filtering, it may be difficult to know what traffic is really required. This section describes some approaches for implementing egress filtering on your network.

6.1.4.2.1 Allow what you know about, block the rest, and work through the fallout

One approach is to add firewall rules for the traffic you know needs to be permitted. Start with making a list of things you know are required such as in Table 6.1.

Description	Source IP	Destination IP	Destination port
HTTP and HTTPS from all hosts	any	any	TCP 80 and 443
SMTP from mail server	mail server IP	any	TCP 25
Recursive DNS queries from internal DNS servers	DNS server IPs	any	TCP and UDP 53

Table 6.1: Egress traffic required

Then configure your firewall rules accordingly, and let everything else drop.

6.1.4.2.2 Log traffic and analyze logs

Another alternative is to enable logging on your pass rules, and send the logs to a syslog server, where you can analyze them to see what traffic is leaving your network. Two log analysis packages with support for PF's logging format are fwanalog[1] and Hatchet[2]. You may find it easier to parse the logs with a custom script if you have experience with parsing text files. This will help build the required ruleset with less fallout as you should have a better idea of what traffic is necessary on your network.

6.1.5 Block vs. Reject

There are two ways to disallow traffic in pfSense firewall rules — block and reject. The block setting silently drops traffic. This is the behavior of the default deny rule in pfSense, hence in a default configuration, all traffic initiated from the Internet will be silently dropped.

Reject sends a response to denied TCP and UDP traffic, letting the host that initiated the traffic know that the connection was refused. Rejected TCP traffic gets a TCP RST (reset) in response, and rejected UDP traffic gets an ICMP unreachable message in response. Though you can specify reject for any firewall rule, IP protocols other than TCP and UDP are not able to be rejected — these rules will silently drop other IP protocols. This is because there is no standard for rejecting other protocols.

6.1.5.1 Should I use block or reject?

There has been much debate amongst security professionals over the years as to the value of block vs. reject. Some argue that using block makes more sense, claiming it "slows down" attackers scanning the Internet. When you use reject, a response is sent back immediately that the port is closed, while block silently drops the traffic, causing the attacker's port scanner to wait for a response. That argument doesn't really hold water because every good port scanner can scan hundreds or thousands of hosts simultaneously, and isn't sitting there waiting for a response from your closed ports. There is a minimal difference in resource consumption and scanning speed, but so slight that it shouldn't be a consideration. If you block all traffic from the Internet, there is a notable difference between block and reject — nobody knows your system is actually online. If you have even a single port open, the value is minimal because the attacker knows you're online, and will also know what ports are open whether or not you reject blocked connections. While there isn't significant value in block over reject, I still recommend always using block on your WAN rules.

For rules on internal interfaces, I recommend using reject in most situations. When a host tries to access something that is not permitted in your firewall rules, the application accessing it may hang until the connection times out. With reject, since the connection is immediately refused, it avoids these hangs. This is usually nothing more than an annoyance, but I still generally recommend using reject to avoid potential application problems that silently dropping traffic inside your network could induce. There is one side effect to this that may be a factor in your choice of block or reject. If you use reject, it makes it easier for people inside your network to determine your egress filtering policies as the firewall will let them know what it is blocking. It is still possible for internal users to map your egress rules when using block, it just takes a little more time and effort.

---

[1] http://tud.at/programm/fwanalog/
[2] http://www.dixongroup.net/hatchet/

6.2   Introduction to the Firewall Rules screen

This section provides an introduction and overview of the Firewall Rules screen. First, browse to
Firewall → Rules. This will bring up the WAN ruleset, which by default has no entries other than those
for Block private networks and Block bogon networks if you enabled those, as shown in Figure 6.2. If
you click the to the right of the Block private networks or Block bogon networks rules, it will take
you to the WAN interface configuration page, where these options can be enabled or disabled. (See
Section 6.5.1.3 and Section 6.5.1.4 for more details about blocking private and bogon networks.)

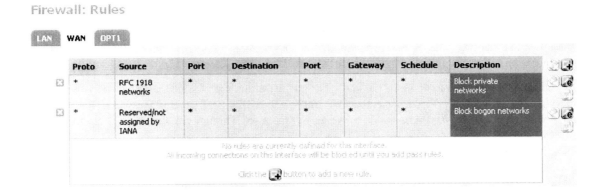

Figure 6.2: Default WAN rules

Click on the LAN tab to view the LAN rules. By default, this is only the **Default LAN -> any**
rule as seen in Figure 6.3.

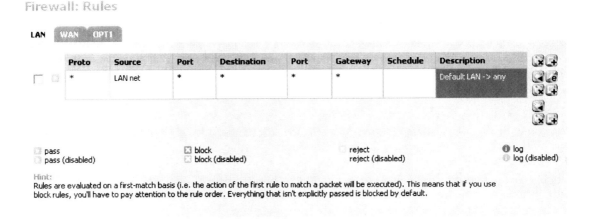

Figure 6.3: Default LAN rules

Rules for other interfaces may be viewed by clicking their respective tabs. OPT interfaces will appear with their descriptive names, so if you named your OPT1 interface DMZ, then the tab for its rules will also say DMZ.

To the left of each rule is an indicator icon showing the action of the rule — pass, block, or reject. If logging is enabled for the rule, the blue circle containing an i is shown there as well. The same icons are used for disabled rules, except the icon, like the rule, will be grayed out.

6.2.1 Adding a firewall rule

Click either of the 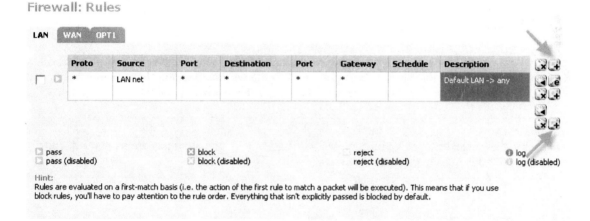 buttons on the Firewall: Rules screen to add a new rule. The top and bottom buttons, as shown in Figure 6.4, will add a new rule. The top ▣ adds a rule to the top of the ruleset, while the bottom ▣ adds the rule at the bottom.

Figure 6.4: Add LAN rule options

If you would like to make a new rule that is similar to an existing rule, click the ▣ at the end of the row. The edit screen will appear with the existing rule's settings pre-filled, ready to be adjusted. For more information about how to configure the rule that was just added, see Section 6.6.

6.2.2 Editing Firewall Rules

To edit a firewall rule, click the ▣ to the right of the rule, or double click anywhere on the line. You will then be taken to the edit screen for that rule, where you can make any needed adjustments. See Section 6.6 for more information on the options available when editing a rule.

6.2.3 Moving Firewall Rules

Rules may be reordered on their own or in groups. To move rules in the list, check the box next to the rules which should be moved, or single clicking the rule will also check the box, then click the ▣

button on the row which should be underneath the relocated rules. When you hover the mouse pointer over ⊡, a thick bar will appear to indicate where the rules will be inserted. After you click ⊡, the rules will then be inserted above the chosen row. You may also select rules to move by single clicking anywhere inside of the row you wish to select.

6.2.4   Deleting Firewall Rules

To delete a single rule, click the ⊡ to the right of the rule. You will be prompted to confirm the deletion, and if this is what you wanted to do, click OK to actually delete the rule.

To delete multiple rules, check the box at the start of the rows that should be removed, then click the ⊡ at the bottom of the list. Rules may also be selected by single clicking anywhere on their line.

6.3   Aliases

Aliases allow you to group ports, hosts, or networks and refer to them by name in your firewall rules, NAT configuration and traffic shaper configuration. This allows you to create significantly shorter and more manageable rulesets. Any box in the web interface with a red background is alias friendly.

Note
Aliases in this context should not be confused with interface IP aliases, which are a means of adding additional IP addresses to a network interface.

6.3.1   Configuring Aliases

To add an alias, go to the Firewall → Aliases screen and click the ⊡ button. The following sections describe each type of alias that can be used.

In pfSense 1.2.x, each alias is limited to 299 members.

To add new members to an alias, click the ⊡ at the bottom of the list of entries on the Firewall → Aliases → Edit screen.

6.3.1.1   Host Aliases

Host aliases allow you to create groups of IP addresses. Figure 6.5 shows an example usage of a hosts alias to contain a list of public web servers.

6.3.1.2   Network Aliases

Network aliases allow you to create groups of networks, or IP ranges via the use of CIDR summarization. Single hosts can also be included in network aliases by selecting a /32 network mask. Figure 6.6 shows an example of a network alias that is used later in this chapter.

Firewall: Aliases: Edit

Name	WebServers
	The name of the alias may only consist of the characters a-z, A-Z and 0-9.
Description	public web servers
	You may enter a description here for your reference (not parsed).
Type	Host(s) ▼
Host(s)	

Enter as many hosts as you would like. Hosts should be expressed in their ip address format.

IP		Description
192.168.2.10	▼	www1
192.168.2.11	32 ▼	www2
192.168.2.15	32 ▼	www3
192.168.2.18	32 ▼	www4

Figure 6.5: Example hosts alias

6.3.1.3 Port Aliases

Port aliases enable the grouping of ports and port ranges. The protocol is not specified in the alias, rather the firewall rule where you use the alias will define the protocol as TCP, UDP, or both. Figure 6.7 shows an example of a ports alias.

6.3.2 Using Aliases

Any box with a red background will accept an alias. When you type the first letter of an alias into any such input box, a list of matching aliases is displayed. You can select the desired alias, or type its name out completely.

Note

Alias autocompletion is case sensitive. If you have an alias named WebServers and type a lowercase "w", this alias will not appear. A capital "W" must be used. This will no longer be the case in 2.0.

Figure 6.8 shows how the WebServers alias configured as shown in Figure 6.5 can be used in the Destination field when adding or editing a firewall rule. Select "Single host or alias", then type the first letter of the desired alias. I just typed **W** and the alias appears as shown. Only aliases of the appropriate type are shown. For fields that require an IP address or subnet, only host and network aliases are shown.

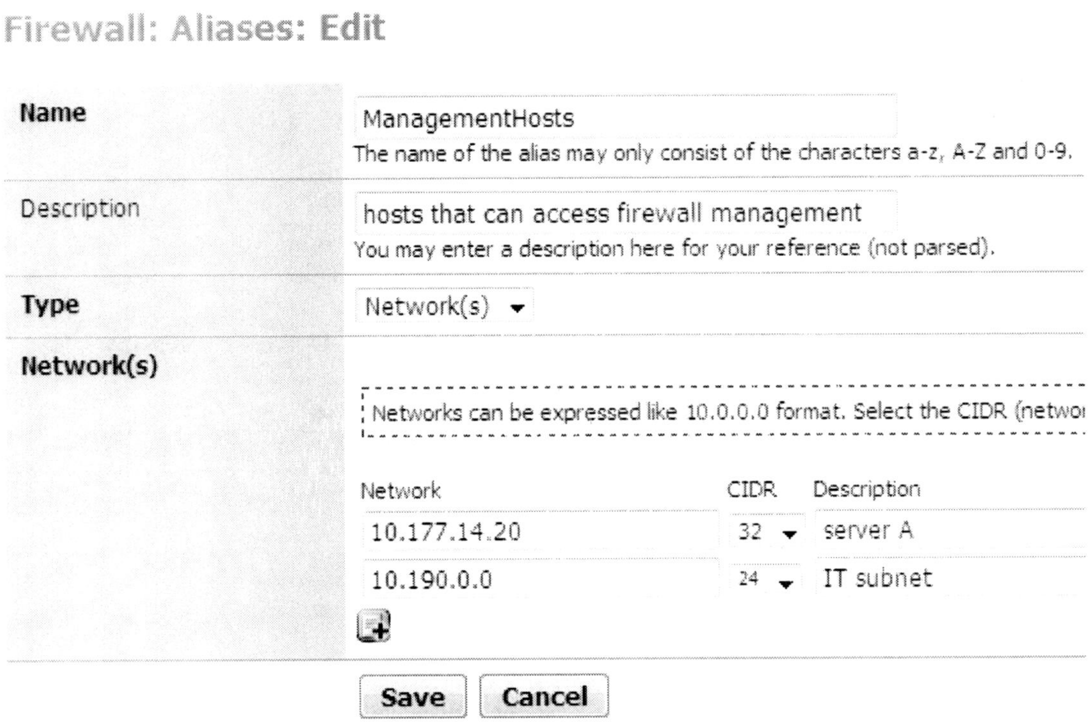

Firewall: Aliases: Edit

Name	ManagementHosts The name of the alias may only consist of the characters a-z, A-Z and 0-9.
Description	hosts that can access firewall management You may enter a description here for your reference (not parsed).
Type	Network(s) ▾
Network(s)	Networks can be expressed like 10.0.0.0 format. Select the CIDR (netwoɪ

Network	CIDR	Description
10.177.14.20	32 ▾	server A
10.190.0.0	24 ▾	IT subnet

Save   Cancel

Figure 6.6: Example network alias

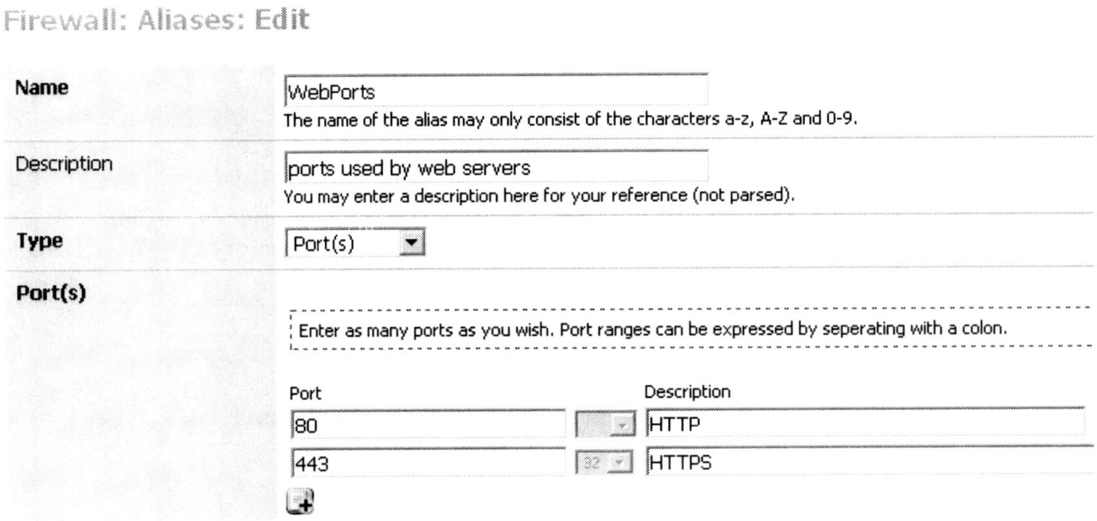

Firewall: Aliases: Edit

Name	WebPorts The name of the alias may only consist of the characters a-z, A-Z and 0-9.
Description	ports used by web servers You may enter a description here for your reference (not parsed).
Type	Port(s) ▾
Port(s)	Enter as many ports as you wish. Port ranges can be expressed by seperating with a colon.

Port		Description
80	▾	HTTP
443	32 ▾	HTTPS

Figure 6.7: Example ports alias

For fields that require ports, only ports aliases are shown. If there were multiple aliases beginning with "W", the drop down list that appears would show all the matching aliases.

Figure 6.8: Autocompletion of hosts alias

Figure 6.9 shows the autocompletion of the ports alias configured as shown in Figure 6.7. Again if multiple aliases match the letter entered, all matching aliases would be listed. You can click on the desired alias to select it.

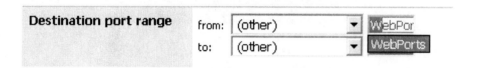

Figure 6.9: Autocompletion of ports alias

Figure 6.10 shows the rule I created using the WebServers and WebPorts aliases. This rule is on WAN, and allows any source to the IP addresses defined in the WebServers alias when using the ports defined in the WebPorts alias.

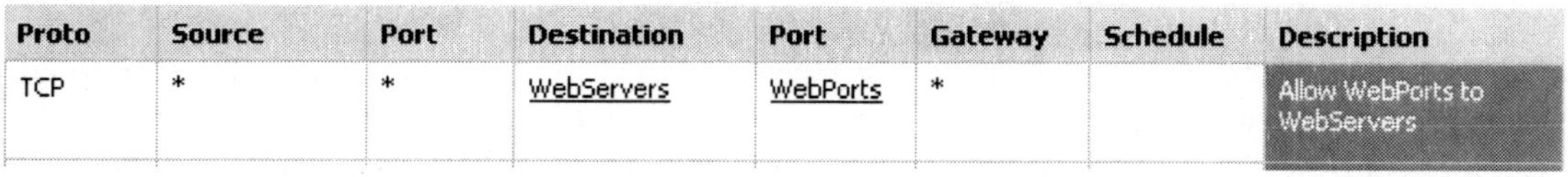

Proto	Source	Port	Destination	Port	Gateway	Schedule	Description
TCP	*	*	WebServers	WebPorts	*		Allow WebPorts to WebServers

Figure 6.10: Example Rule Using Aliases

If you hover your mouse over an alias on the Firewall → Rules screen, a box appears showing the contents of the alias with the descriptions included in the alias. Figure 6.11 shows this for the WebServers alias and Figure 6.12 for the ports alias.

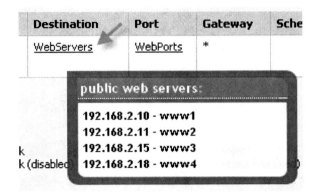

Figure 6.11: Hovering shows Hosts contents

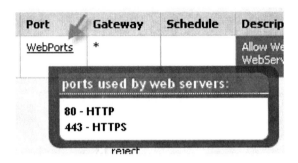

Figure 6.12: Hovering shows Ports contents

6.3.3   Alias Enhancements in 2.0

pfSense 2.0 will allow you to nest aliases within other aliases, and will include the ability to enter a URL location of an alias for download.

pfSense 2.0 also includes a user manager for OpenVPN, and the ability to create aliases grouping OpenVPN users. For example, your IT users may need access to your entire internal network, but other users only need access to a small subset of your network. OpenVPN user aliases will make this easy to accomplish. OpenVPN is covered in more detail in Chapter 15.

6.4   Firewall Rule Best Practices

This section covers some general best practices to take into consideration when configuring your firewall.

6.4.1 Default Deny

There are two basic philosophies in computer security related to access control — default allow and default deny. You should always follow a default deny strategy with your firewall rules. Configure your rules to permit only the bare minimum required traffic for the needs of your network, and let the rest drop with pfSense's built in default deny rule. In following this methodology, the number of deny rules in your ruleset should be minimal. They still have a place for some uses, but will be minimized in most environments by following a default deny strategy.

In a default two interface LAN and WAN configuration, pfSense uses a default deny philosophy on the WAN and a default allow on the LAN. Everything inbound from the Internet is denied, and everything out to the Internet from the LAN is permitted. All home grade routers use this methodology, as do all similar open source projects and most similar commercial offerings. It's what most people want — hence is the default configuration. However it is not the recommended means of operation.

pfSense users often ask "what bad things do I need to block?" That's the wrong question, as it applies to a default permit methodology. Noted security professional Marcus Ranum includes default permit in his *"Six Dumbest Ideas in Computer Security"* paper, which is recommended reading for any security professional.[3] Permit only what you require, and avoid leaving the default allow all rule on the LAN and adding block rules for "bad things" above the permit rule.

6.4.2 Keep it short

The shorter your ruleset, the easier it is to manage. Long rulesets are difficult to work with, increase the chances of human error, tend to become overly permissive, and significantly more difficult to audit. Utilize aliases to help keep your ruleset as short as possible.

6.4.3 Review your Rules

You should manually review your firewall rules and NAT configuration on a periodic basis to ensure they still match the minimum requirements of your current network environment. The recommended frequency of such review will vary from one environment to another. In networks that do not change frequently, with a small number of firewall administrators and good change control procedures, quarterly or semi-annually is usually adequate. For fast changing environments or those with poor change control and several people with firewall access, the configuration should be reviewed at least on a monthly basis.

6.4.4 Document your Configuration

In all but the smallest networks, it can be hard to recall what is configured where and why. Use of the Description field in firewall and NAT rules is always recommended. In larger or more complex deployments, you should also maintain a more detailed configuration document describing your entire pfSense configuration. When reviewing your configuration in the future, this should help you determine which rules are necessary and why they are there. This also applies to any other area of the configuration.

---

[3] http://ranum.com/security/computer_security/editorials/dumb/index.html

It is also important to keep this document up to date. When performing your periodic configuration reviews, it is a good idea to also review this document to ensure it remains up to date with your current configuration. You should ensure this document is updated whenever configuration changes are made.

6.4.5   Reducing Log Noise

Logging is enabled on the default deny rule in pfSense by default. This means all the noise getting blocked from the Internet is going to get logged. Sometimes you won't see much noise, but in many environments you will find something incessantly spamming your logs. With connections using large broadcast domains — a practice commonly employed by cable ISPs — this is most often NetBIOS broadcasts from clue-deficient individuals who connect Windows machines directly to their broadband connections. These machines will constantly pump out broadcast requests for network browsing, among other things. You may also see your ISP's routing protocol, or router redundancy protocols such as VRRP or HSRP. In co-location environments such as data centers, you sometimes see a combination of all of those things.

Because there is no value in knowing your firewall blocked 14 million NetBIOS broadcasts in the past day, and that noise could be covering up logs that are important, it's a good idea to add a block rule on the WAN interface for repeated noise traffic. By adding a block rule without logging enabled on the WAN interface, this traffic will still be blocked, but no longer fill your logs.

The rule shown in Figure 6.13 is one I have configured on one of my test systems, where the "WAN" is on a LAN. To get rid of the log noise so I can see the things of interest, I added this rule to block but not log anything with the destination of the broadcast address of that subnet.

WAN

	Proto	Source	Port	Destination	Port	Gateway	Schedule	Description
	*	*	*	10.0.64.255	*	*		don't log broadcasts

Figure 6.13: Firewall Rule to Prevent Logging Broadcasts

You should add similar rules, matching the specifics of any log noise you are seeing in your environment. Check the firewall logs under Status → System Logs → Firewall tab to see what kind of traffic you are blocking and review its frequency. If any particular traffic is consistently being logged more than 5 times a minute, you should probably add a block rule for it to reduce your log noise.

6.4.6   Logging Practices

Out of the box, pfSense does not log any passed traffic and logs all dropped traffic. This is the typical default behavior of almost every open source and commercial firewall. It is the most practical, as logging all passed traffic should rarely be done due to the load and log levels generated. But this methodology is really a bit backwards. Blocked traffic cannot harm you so its log value is limited, while traffic that gets passed could be very important log information to have if a system is compromised.

After eliminating any useless block noise as described in the previous section, the remainder is of some value for trend analysis purposes. If you are seeing significantly more or less log volume than usual, it's probably good to investigate why that is. OSSEC, an open source host-based intrusion detection system (IDS), is one system that can gather logs from pfSense via syslog and alert you to log volume abnormalities.[4]

6.5 Rule Methodology

Rules in pfSense are applied on a per-interface basis, always in the inbound direction on that interface. This means traffic initiated from the LAN is filtered using the LAN interface rules. Traffic initiated from the Internet is filtered with the WAN interface rules. Because all rules in pfSense are stateful by default, a state table entry is created when traffic matches an allow rule. All reply traffic is automatically permitted by this state table entry.

At this time, there is no way to accommodate for outbound rules on any interface. Outbound rules are never required, because filtering is applied on the inbound direction of every interface. In some limited circumstances, such as a firewall with numerous internal interfaces, having them available can significantly reduce the number of required firewall rules. In such a case, you could apply your egress rules for Internet traffic as outbound rules on the WAN to avoid having to duplicate them for every internal interface. The use of inbound and outbound filtering makes things more complex and more prone to user error, but we understand it can be desirable and hope to accommodate this in some fashion in the future.

6.5.1 Automatically Added Firewall Rules

pfSense automatically adds some firewall rules, for a variety of reasons. This section describes every automatically added rule and their purpose.

6.5.1.1 Anti-lockout Rule

To prevent locking yourself out of the web interface, pfSense enables an anti-lockout rule by default. This is configurable on the System → Advanced page under webGUI Anti-lockout. This automatically added rule allows traffic from any source inside your network to any protocol listening on the LAN IP.

In security-conscious environments, you should disable this rule, and configure your LAN rules so only an alias of trusted hosts can access the administrative interfaces of the firewall.

6.5.1.1.1 Restricting access to the administrative interface from LAN

First you need to configure the firewall rules as desired to restrict access to the management interfaces. I will walk through an example of how I usually configure this. I use both SSH and HTTPS for management, so I create a ManagementPorts alias containing these ports (Figure 6.14).

Then I create an alias for hosts and/or networks that will have access to the management interfaces (Figure 6.15).

---

[4] http://www.ossec.net

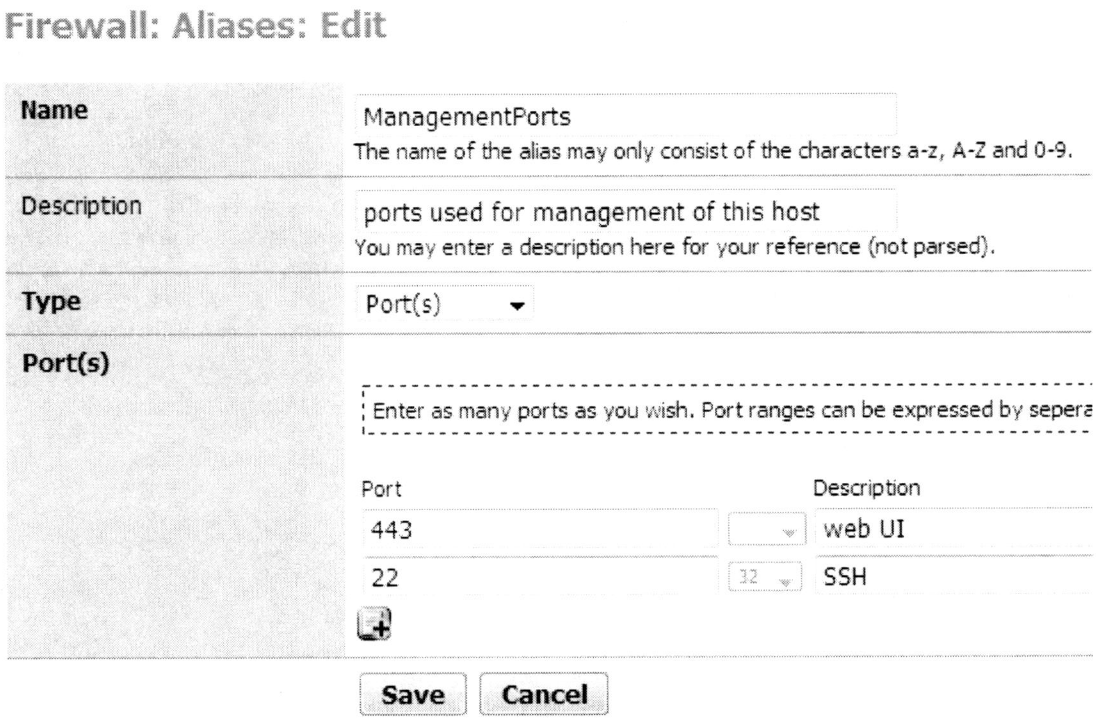

Firewall: Aliases: Edit

Name	ManagementPorts
	The name of the alias may only consist of the characters a-z, A-Z and 0-9.
Description	ports used for management of this host
	You may enter a description here for your reference (not parsed).
Type	Port(s) ▼
Port(s)	

Enter as many ports as you wish. Port ranges can be expressed by sepera

Port		Description
443	▾	web UI
22	32 ▾	SSH
⊞		

Save   **Cancel**

Figure 6.14: Alias for management ports

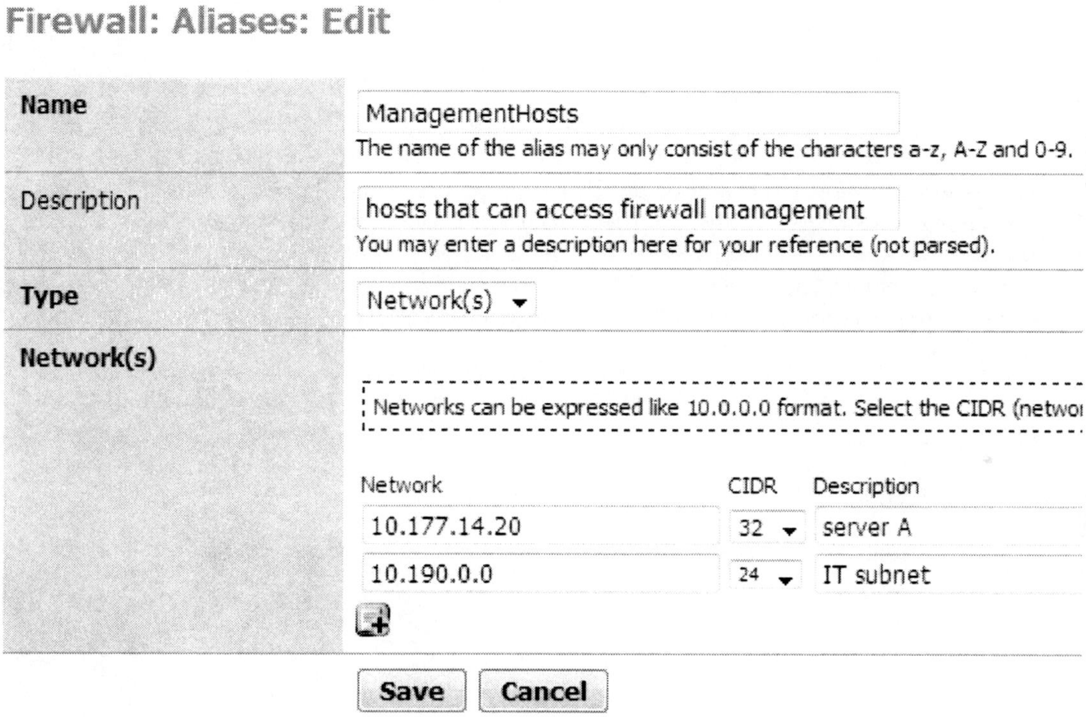

Firewall: Aliases: Edit

Name	ManagementHosts
	The name of the alias may only consist of the characters a-z, A-Z and 0-9.
Description	hosts that can access firewall management
	You may enter a description here for your reference (not parsed).
Type	Network(s) ▾
Network(s)	

Networks can be expressed like 10.0.0.0 format. Select the CIDR (networ

Network	CIDR	Description
10.177.14.20	32 ▾	server A
10.190.0.0	24 ▾	IT subnet

Save   **Cancel**

Figure 6.15: Alias for management hosts

The resulting aliases are shown in Figure 6.16.

Firewall: Aliases

Name	Values	Description
ManagementHosts	10.177.14.20/32, 10.190.0.0/24	hosts that can access firewall management
ManagementPorts	443, 22	ports used for management of this host

Figure 6.16: Alias list

Then the LAN firewall rules must be configured to allow access to the previously defined hosts, and deny access to all else. There are numerous ways you can accomplish this, depending on specifics of your environment and how you handle egress filtering. Figure 6.17 and Figure 6.18 show two examples. The first allows DNS queries to the LAN IP, which is needed if you are using the DNS forwarder, and also allows LAN hosts to ping the LAN IP. It then rejects all other traffic. The second example allows access from the management hosts to the management ports, then rejects all other traffic to the management ports. Choose the methodology that works best for your environment. Remember that the source port is not the same as the destination port.

Firewall: Rules

LAN WAN OPT1

	Proto	Source	Port	Destination	Port	Gateway	Schedule	Description
	TCP/UDP	10.0.0.0/8	*	LAN address	53 (DNS)	*		Allow internal network to DNS forwarder
	ICMP	10.0.0.0/8	*	LAN address	*	*		Allow internal network to ping LAN IP
	TCP	ManagementHosts	*	LAN address	ManagementPorts	*		Allow access to firewall management
	*	*	*	LAN address	*	*		Reject all else to LAN IP
	*	10.0.0.0/8	*	*	*	*		Default LAN -> any

Figure 6.17: Example restricted management LAN rules

Once the firewall rules are configured, you need to disable the webGUI anti-lockout rule on the System → Advanced page (Figure 6.19). Check the box and click Save.

Firewall: Rules

Proto	Source	Port	Destination	Port	Gateway	Schedule	Description
TCP	ManagementHosts	*	LAN address	ManagementPorts	*		Allow access to firewall management
TCP	*	*	LAN address	ManagementPorts	*		Reject all other hosts to management ports
*	10.0.0.0/8	*	*	*	*		Default LAN -> any

Figure 6.18: Restricted management LAN rules — alternate example

Note

If you can no longer access the management interface after disabling the anti-lockout rule, you did not configure your firewall rules appropriately. You can re-enable the anti-lockout rule by using the Set LAN IP option at the console menu. Just set it to its current IP, and the rule will automatically be re-enabled.

Figure 6.19: Anti-lockout rule disabled

6.5.1.2 Anti-spoofing Rules

pfSense uses PF's antispoof feature to block spoofed traffic. This provides Unicast Reverse Path Forwarding (uRPF) functionality as defined in RFC 3704. The firewall checks each packet against its routing table, and if a connection attempt comes from a source IP on an interface where the firewall knows that network does not reside, it is dropped. For example, something coming in WAN with a source IP of an internal network is dropped. Anything initiated on the internal network with a source IP that does not reside on the internal network is dropped.

6.5.1.3 Block Private Networks

The Block private networks option on the WAN interface automatically puts in a block rule for RFC 1918 subnets. Unless you have private IP space on your WAN, you should enable this. This only applies to traffic initiated on the WAN side. You can still access hosts on private networks from the inside. This option is not available for OPT WAN interfaces in pfSense 1.2.x, but is in 2.0. You can manually add a rule to block private networks on your OPT WAN interfaces by creating an alias containing the RFC 1918 subnets and adding a firewall rule to the top of your OPT WAN interface rules to block traffic with a source matching that alias. (See Section 1.7.1.1 for more information about private IP addresses.)

6.5.1.4   Block Bogon Networks

Bogon networks are those which should never be seen on the Internet, including reserved and unassigned IP address space. These networks should never be seen as source IPs on the Internet, and indicate either spoofed traffic, or an unused subnet that has been hijacked for malicious use. pfSense provides a bogons list that is updated as needed. If you have Block bogon networks enabled, your firewall will fetch an updated bogons list on the first day of each month from files.pfsense.org. The script runs at 3:00 a.m. local time, and sleeps a random amount of time up to 12 hours before performing the update. This list does not change very frequently, and new IP assignments are removed from the bogons list months before they are actually used, so the monthly update is adequate. Make sure your firewall can resolve DNS host names, otherwise the update will fail. To ensure you can resolve DNS, browse to Diagnostics → Ping, and try to ping **files.pfsense.org** as demonstrated in Figure 6.20.

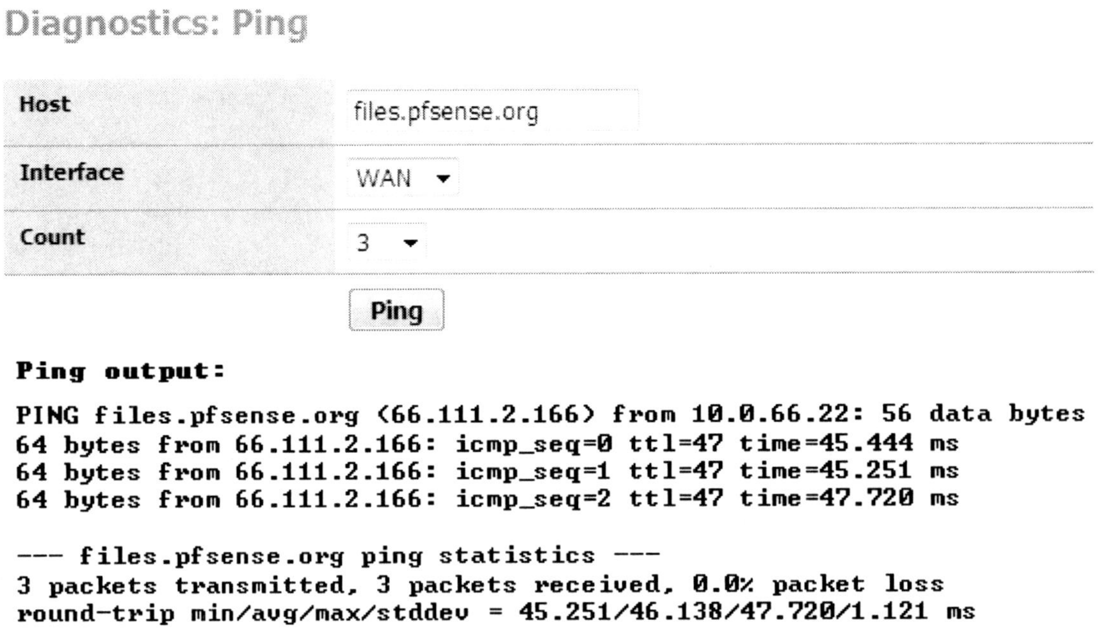

Diagnostics: Ping

Host	files.pfsense.org
Interface	WAN ▾
Count	3 ▾

                        [Ping]

```
Ping output:

PING files.pfsense.org (66.111.2.166) from 10.0.66.22: 56 data bytes
64 bytes from 66.111.2.166: icmp_seq=0 ttl=47 time=45.444 ms
64 bytes from 66.111.2.166: icmp_seq=1 ttl=47 time=45.251 ms
64 bytes from 66.111.2.166: icmp_seq=2 ttl=47 time=47.720 ms

--- files.pfsense.org ping statistics ---
3 packets transmitted, 3 packets received, 0.0% packet loss
round-trip min/avg/max/stddev = 45.251/46.138/47.720/1.121 ms
```

Figure 6.20: Testing name resolution for bogon updates

6.5.1.4.1 Forcing a bogons update

With the relatively infrequent changes to the bogons list, and advance notice of new public IP assignments, the monthly bogons update is adequate. However there may be scenarios where you want to manually force a bogon update, such as if your bogon updates have been failing because of an incorrect DNS configuration. You can execute an update via the web interface's Diagnostics → Command screen, by running **/etc/rc.update_bogons.sh now**. The **now** argument following the script is important because it tells the script to run immediately and not sleep.

6.5.1.5 IPsec

When you enable a site to site IPsec connection, rules are automatically added allowing the remote tunnel endpoint IP address access to UDP port 500 and the ESP protocol on the WAN IP address used for the connection. When mobile clients IPsec is enabled, UDP port 500 and ESP traffic is allowed from any source.

Because of the way policy routing works, any traffic that matches a rule specifying a gateway will be forced out to the Internet and will bypass IPsec processing. When you have an allow rule specifying a gateway on the inside interface containing the subnet used by the IPsec connection, and the destination of the rule is "any", a rule is automatically added to negate policy routing for traffic destined to the remote VPN subnet.

Automatically added IPsec rules are discussed in further depth in Chapter 13.

6.5.1.6 PPTP

When you enable the PPTP server, hidden rules are automatically added allowing TCP port 1723 and the GRE (Generic Routing Encapsulation) protocol to your WAN IP address from any source IP address. More information about these rules can be found in Section 12.3.

6.5.1.7 Default Deny Rule

Rules that don't match any user defined rules nor any of the other automatically added rules are silently blocked by the default deny rule (as discussed in Section 6.4.1).

6.6 Configuring firewall rules

This section covers each individual option available on the Firewall → Rules → Edit screen when configuring firewall rules.

6.6.1 Action

This is where you specify whether the rule will pass, block, or reject traffic. Each of these is covered earlier in this chapter.

6.6.2   Disabled

If you wish to disable a rule without removing it from the rule list, check this box. It will still show in your firewall rules screen, but will be grayed out to indicate its disabled state.

6.6.3   Interface

The Interface drop down specifies the interface on which the rule will be applied. Remember that traffic is only filtered on the interface where the traffic is initiated. Traffic initiated from your LAN destined to the Internet or any other interface on your firewall is filtered by the LAN ruleset.

6.6.4   Protocol

This is where you specify the protocol this rule will match. Most of these options are self-explanatory. TCP/UDP will match both TCP and UDP traffic. Specifying ICMP will make another drop down box appear where you can select the ICMP type. Several other common protocols are also available.

6.6.5   Source

This is where you specify the source IP address, subnet, or alias that will match this rule. You may also check the not box to negate the match.

For the Type you may specify: Any, which will match any address; Single host or alias, which will match a single IP address/hostname or alias name; or Network, which will take both an IP address and subnet mask to match a range of addresses. Lastly, there are several available presets that can be quite useful instead of entering these addresses by hand: WAN address, LAN address, LAN subnet, PPTP clients, and PPPoE users.

For rules using TCP and/or UDP, you can also specify the source port here by clicking the Advanced button. The source port is hidden behind the Advanced button because you will normally want to leave the source port set to "any", as TCP and UDP connections are sourced from a random port in the ephemeral port range (between 1024 through 65535, the exact range used varying depending on the OS and OS version that is initiating the connection). The source port is almost never the same as the destination port, and you should never configure it as such unless you know the application you are using employs this atypical behavior. It is also safe to define your source port as a range from 1024 to 65535.

6.6.6   Source OS

One of the more unique features of pf and hence pfSense is the ability to filter by the operating system initiating the connection. For TCP rules, pf enables passive operating system fingerprinting that allows you to create rules based on the operating system initiating the TCP connection. The p0f feature of pf determines the OS in use by comparing characteristics of the TCP SYN packet that initiates TCP connections with a fingerprints file. Note that it is possible to change the fingerprint of your operating system to look like another OS, especially with open source operating systems such as the BSDs and

Linux. This isn't easy, but if you have technically proficient users with administrator or root level access to systems, it is possible.

6.6.7 Destination

This is where you specify the destination IP address, subnet, or alias that will match this rule. See the description of the Source option in Section 6.6.5 for more details. As with the Source address setting, you may check not to negate the match.

For rules specifying TCP and/or UDP, the destination port, port range, or alias is also specified here.

6.6.8 Log

This box determines whether packets that match this rule will be logged to the firewall log. Logging is discussed in more detail in Section 6.4.6.

6.6.9 Advanced Options

This section lets you configure pf's powerful abilities to limit firewall states on a per-rule basis. By default, there are no limits set for any of these parameters.

6.6.9.1 Simultaneous client connection limit

This option specifies how many total state entries may exist for this rule. If this is set to 10, and there are 10 connections that match the rule, the 11th will be dropped. It could be 10 different hosts, or 9 connections on one host and 1 on another, it's the total that matters.

6.6.9.2 Maximum state entries per host

If you prefer to limit based on connections per host, this setting is what you want. Using this setting, you may limit a rule to 10 connections per source host, instead of 10 connections total.

6.6.9.3 Maximum new connections / per second

This method of rate limiting can help to ensure that a high connection rate will not overload a server or your state table. For example, limits can be placed on incoming connections to a mail server to reduce the burden of being overloaded by spambots. It can also be used on outbound traffic rules to set limits that would prevent any single machine from loading up your state table or making too many rapid connections, behaviors which are common with viruses. You can set both a connection amount and a number of seconds for the time period. Any IP address exceeding that number of connections within the given time frame will be blocked for one hour. Behind the scenes, this is handled by the virusprot table, named for its typical purpose of virus protection.

6.6.9.4   State timeout in seconds

Here you can define a state timeout for traffic matching this rule, overriding the system's default state timeout. Any inactive connections will be closed when the connection has been idle for this amount of time. The default state timeout depends on the firewall optimization algorithm in use. The optimization choices are covered in Section 4.5.9.3

6.6.10   State Type

There are three options for state tracking in pfSense that can be specified on a per-rule basis.

6.6.10.1   keep state

This is the default, and what you should almost always use.

6.6.10.2   synproxy state

This option causes pfSense to proxy incoming TCP connections. TCP connections start with a three way handshake. The first packet of a TCP connection is a SYN from source, which elicits a SYN ACK response from the destination. This helps protect against one type of Denial of Service attack, SYN floods. This is typically only used with rules on WAN interfaces. This type of attack is not very common today, and every major modern operating system includes capabilities of handling this on its own. It could be useful when opening TCP ports to hosts that do not handle network abuse well.

6.6.10.3   none

This option will not keep state on this rule. This is only necessary in some highly specialized advanced scenarios, none of which are covered in this book because they are exceedingly rare. You should never have a need for using this option.

6.6.11   No XML-RPC Sync

Checking this box prevents this rule from synchronizing to other CARP members. This is covered in Chapter 20.

6.6.12   Schedule

Here you can select a schedule specifying the days and times this rule will be in effect. Selecting "none" means the rule will always be enabled. For more information, see Section 6.9 later in this chapter.

6.6.13 Gateway

Gateway allows you to specify a WAN interface or load balancer pool for traffic matching this rule to use. This is covered in Chapter 11.

6.6.14 Description

Enter a description here for your reference. This is optional, and does not affect functionality of the rule. You should enter something here describing the purpose of the rule. The maximum length is 52 characters.

6.7 Methods of Using Additional Public IPs

If you only have a single public IP address, you can skip to the next section. The methods of deploying additional public IP addresses will vary depending on how they are assigned, how many you have assigned, and the goals for your network environment. To use additional public IPs with NAT, you need to configure Virtual IPs. You also have two options for directly assigning public IPs to hosts with routing public IP subnets and bridging.

6.7.1 Choosing between routing, bridging, and NAT

You can either use your additional public IPs by directly assigning them on the systems that will use them, or by using NAT.

6.7.1.1 Additional IPs via DHCP

Some ISPs force you to obtain additional IP addresses via DHCP. This offers limited flexibility in what you can do with these addresses, leaving you with two feasible options.

6.7.1.1.1 Bridging

If you want the additional IPs directly assigned to the systems that will use them, bridging is your only option. Use an OPT interface bridged with WAN for these systems.

6.7.1.1.2 Pseudo multi-WAN

Your only option for having the firewall pull these addresses as leases is a pseudo multi-WAN deployment. Install one network interface per public IP, and configure them for DHCP. Plug all the interfaces into a switch between your firewall and your modem or router. Since you will have multiple interfaces sharing a single broadcast domain, you will want to check the box next to "This will suppress ARP messages when interfaces share the same physical network" on the System → Advanced page to eliminate ARP warnings in your logs that are normal in this type of deployment.

The only use of multiple public IPs assigned in this fashion is for port forwarding. You can configure port forwards on each WAN interface that will use the IP assigned to that interface by your ISP's DHCP server. Outbound NAT to your OPT WANs will not work because of the limitation that each WAN must have a unique gateway IP to properly direct traffic out of that WAN. This is discussed further in Chapter 11.

6.7.1.2   Additional static IPs

Methods of using additional static public IPs will vary depending on the type of assignment. Each of the common scenarios is described here.

6.7.1.2.1   Single IP subnet

With a single public IP subnet, one of the public IPs will be on the upstream router, commonly belonging to your ISP, with one of the IPs assigned as the WAN IP on pfSense. The remaining IPs can be used with either NAT, bridging or a combination of the two. To use them with NAT, add Proxy ARP or CARP VIPs. To assign public IPs directly to hosts behind your firewall, you will need a dedicated interface for those hosts that is bridged to WAN. When used with bridging, the hosts with the public IPs directly assigned must use the same default gateway as the WAN of the firewall, the upstream ISP router. This will create difficulties if the hosts with public IPs need to initiate connections to hosts behind other interfaces of your firewall, since the ISP gateway will not route traffic for your internal subnets back to your firewall. Figure 6.21 shows an example of using multiple public IPs in a single block with a combination of NAT and bridging. For information on configuration, NAT is discussed further in Chapter 7, and bridging in Chapter 9.

6.7.1.2.2   Small WAN IP subnet with larger LAN IP subnet

Some ISPs will give you a small IP subnet as the "WAN side" assignment, and route a larger "inside" subnet to your end of the WAN subnet. Commonly this is a /30 on the WAN side, and a /29 or larger for the inside. The provider's router is assigned one end of the /30, typically the lowest IP, and your firewall is assigned the higher IP. The provider then routes the LAN subnet to your WAN IP. You can use those additional IPs on a routed interface with public IPs directly assigned to hosts, or with NAT using Other VIPs, or a combination of the two. Since the IPs are routed to you, ARP is not needed, and you don't need any VIP entries for use with 1:1 NAT. Because pfSense is the gateway on the OPT1 segment, routing from OPT1 hosts to LAN is much easier than in the bridged scenario required when using a single public IP block. Figure 6.22 shows an example that combines a routed IP block and NAT. Routing public IPs is covered in Section 8.2, and NAT in Chapter 7.

If you are using CARP, the WAN side subnet will need to be a /29, so each firewall has its own WAN IP, and you have a CARP IP where the provider will route the larger inside block. The inside IP subnet must be routed to an IP that is always available regardless of which firewall is up, and the smallest subnet usable with CARP is a /29. Such a setup with CARP is the same as illustrated above, with the OPT1 gateway being a CARP IP, and the provider routing to a CARP IP rather than the WAN IP. CARP is covered in Chapter 20.

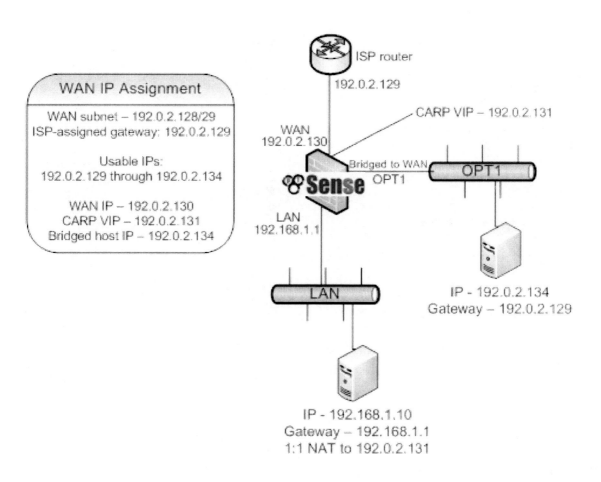

Figure 6.21: Multiple public IPs in use — single IP block

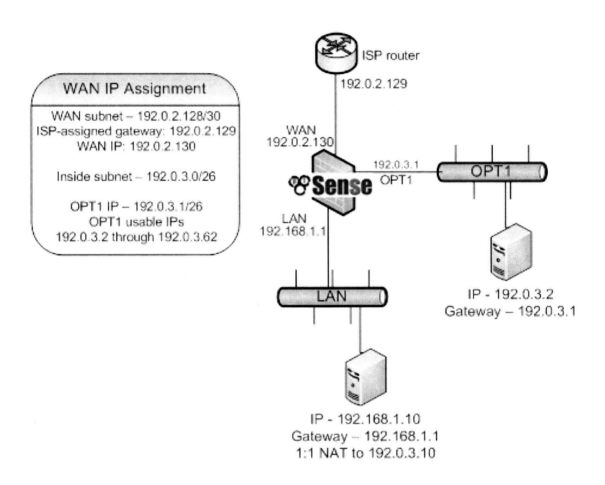

Figure 6.22: Multiple public IPs in use — two IP blocks

6.7.1.2.3 Multiple IP subnets

In other cases, you may have multiple IP subnets from your ISP. Usually you start with one of the two previously described arrangements, and later when requesting additional IPs you are provided with an additional IP subnet. This additional subnet should be routed to you by your ISP, either to your WAN IP in the case of a single firewall, or to a CARP IP when using CARP. If your provider refuses to route the IP subnet to you, but rather routes it to their router and uses one of the IPs from the subnet as a gateway IP, you will need to use Proxy ARP VIPs for the additional subnet. If at all possible, your provider should route the IP subnet to you, as it makes it easier to work with regardless of your firewall of choice.

Where the IP subnet is routed to you, the scenario described in Section 6.7.1.2.2 applies, just for an additional inside subnet. You can assign it to a new OPT interface, use it with NAT, or a combination of the two.

6.8 Virtual IPs

pfSense enables the use of multiple public IP addresses in conjunction with NAT through Virtual IPs (VIPs).

There are three types of Virtual IPs available in pfSense: Proxy ARP, CARP, and Other. Each is useful in different situations. In most circumstances, pfSense will need to provide ARP on your VIPs so you must use Proxy ARP or CARP. In situations where ARP is not required, such as when additional public IPs are routed by your provider to your WAN IP, use Other type VIPs.

6.8.1 Proxy ARP

Proxy ARP functions strictly at layer 2, simply providing ARP replies for the specified IP address or CIDR range of IP addresses. This allows pfSense to forward traffic destined to that address according to your NAT configuration. The address or range of addresses are not assigned to any interface on pfSense, because they don't need to be. This means no services on pfSense itself can respond on these IPs. This is generally considered a benefit, as your additional public IPs should only be used for NAT purposes.

6.8.2 CARP

CARP VIPs are mostly used with redundant deployments utilizing CARP. For information on using CARP VIPs, see Chapter 20 about hardware redundancy.

Some people prefer to use CARP VIPs even when using only a single firewall. This is usually because pfSense will respond to pings on CARP VIPs if your firewall rules permit this traffic (the default rules do not, for VIPs on WAN). Another situation where CARP VIPs must be used is for any VIPs that will host a FTP server. The FTP proxy in pfSense must be able to bind to the VIP to function, and only CARP VIPs allow that.

pfSense will not respond to pings destined to Proxy ARP and Other VIPs regardless of your firewall rule configuration. With Proxy ARP and Other VIPs, you must configure NAT to an internal host for ping to function. See Chapter 7 for more information.

6.8.3   Other

"Other" VIPs allow you to define additional IP addresses for use when ARP replies for the IP address are not required. The only function of adding an Other VIP is making that address available in the NAT configuration screens. This is useful when you have a public IP block routed to your WAN IP address or a CARP VIP.

6.9   Time Based Rules

Time based rules allow you to apply firewall rules only on specified days and/or time ranges. Time based rules are implemented in 1.2.x using the ipfw filter, because difficulties with state keeping at the time this functionality was written meant this was the only possibility to properly disconnect active sessions when the schedule expired. New functionality in pfSense 2.0 allowed this to be integrated with the pf filter, allowing time based rules to function the same as any other rule. In the mean time, there are some caveats to using time based rules, and the logic for these rules is a bit different. This section will discuss how to use time based rules, and the differences between them and other firewall rules.

6.9.1   Time Based Rules Logic

When dealing with time-based rules, the schedule determines when to apply the action specified in the firewall rule. When the current time or date is not covered by the schedule, the action of the rule is reversed. For example, a rule that passes traffic on Saturdays will block it every other day, regardless of any later rules defined on the firewall. The rules are processed from the top-down, the same as other firewall rules. The first match is used, and once a match is found, that action is taken and no other rules are evaluated. If you are working with a pass rule on a certain schedule, say Saturday and Sunday, and that does not have the intended effect then you might instead try a block rule for Monday through Friday.

It is important to always remember when using schedules that the rule will have some effect whether it is within the scheduled time or not. The rule will not just be skipped because the current time is not within the scheduled time. Keep this in mind to ensure that you do not accidentally allow more access than intended with a scheduled rule. Take this other example: If you have a restrictive egress policy for HTTP traffic, and you want to schedule HTTP traffic rules, then you will need to schedule the restrictive rules, and not just have a scheduled block rule for HTTP traffic. In this instance the scheduled block rule, when out of the scheduled time, will turn into a blanket HTTP pass rule and ignore the more restrictive HTTP egress rules.

6.9.2   Time Based Rules Caveats

Because time based rules use ipfw rather than PF, they are incompatible with captive portal. For the same reason, multi-WAN and some of the other advanced firewall rule capabilities are also unavailable with time based rules.

6.9.3 Configuring Schedules for Time Based Rules

Schedules are defined under Firewall → Schedules, and each schedule can contain multiple time ranges. Once a schedule is defined, it may then be used for a firewall rule. In the following example, a company wants to deny access to HTTP during business hours, and allow it all other times.

6.9.3.1 Defining Times for a Schedule

To add a schedule from Firewall → Schedules, click [+]. That should bring up the schedule editing screen, as seen in Figure 6.23. The first field on this screen is for the Schedule Name. This setting is the name that will appear in the selection list for use in firewall rules. Much like alias names, this name must only contain letters and digits, and no spaces. For this example, we'll put in **BusinessHours**. Next in the Description box, enter a longer free-form description of this schedule, such as **Normal Business Hours**. Since a schedule is made up of one or more time range definitions, you must next define a time range before you can save the schedule.

A schedule can apply to specific days, such as September 2, 2009, or to days of the week, such as Monday-Wednesday. To select any given day within the next year, choose the Month from the drop-down list, then click on the specific day or days on the calendar. To select a day of the week, click its name in the column headers. For our example, click on Mon, Tue, Wed, Thu, and Fri. This will make the schedule active for any Monday-Friday, regardless of the month. Now select the time in which this schedule should be active, in 24-hour format. Our business hours will be **9:00** to **17:00** (5pm). All times are given in the local time zone. Now enter a Time Range Description, like **Work Week**, then click Add Time.

Once the time range has been defined, it will appear in the list at the bottom of the schedule editing screen, as in Figure 6.24.

If there are more times to define, repeat that process until you are satisfied with the results. For example, to expand on this setup, there may be a half day on Saturday to define, or maybe the shop opens late on Mondays. In that case, define a time range for the identical days, and then another range for each day with different times. This collection of time ranges will be the full schedule. When all of the necessary time ranges have been defined, click Save. You will then return to the schedule list, and the new schedule will appear, as in Figure 6.25. This schedule will now be available for use in firewall rules.

Name	Time Range(s)		Description	
BusinessHours	Mon - Fri	9:00-17:00 Work Week	Normal Business Hours	

Figure 6.25: Schedule List after Adding

6.9.3.2 Using the Schedule in a Firewall Rule

To create a firewall rule employing this schedule, you must add a rule on the desired interface. See Section 6.2.1 and Section 6.6 for more information about adding and editing rules. For our example, add

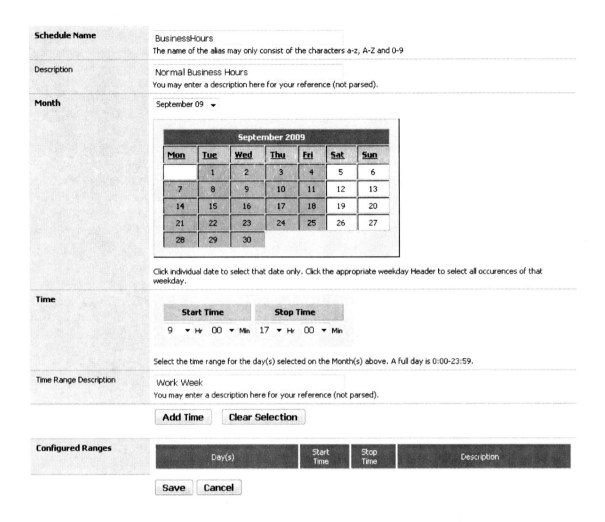

Figure 6.23: Adding a Time Range

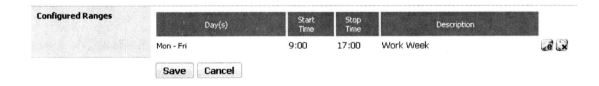

Figure 6.24: Added Time Range

a rule to block TCP traffic on the LAN interface from the LAN subnet, to any destination on the HTTP port. When you get to the Schedule setting choose the schedule we just defined, **BusinessHours**, as in Figure 6.26.

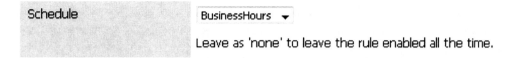

Figure 6.26: Choosing a Schedule for a Firewall Rule

After saving the rule, the schedule will appear in the firewall rule list, along with an indication of the schedule's active state. As you can see in Figure 6.27, this is a block rule, but the schedule column is indicating that the rule is currently not in its active blocking state because it is being viewed at a time that is outside of the scheduled range. If you hover over the schedule name, it will show the times defined for that schedule. If you hover over the schedule state indicator, it will tell you descriptively how the rule is behaving at that point in time. Since this is being viewed outside of the times defined in our BusinessHours schedule, this will say "Traffic matching this rule is currently being allowed". Had we used a pass rule, the opposite would be true.

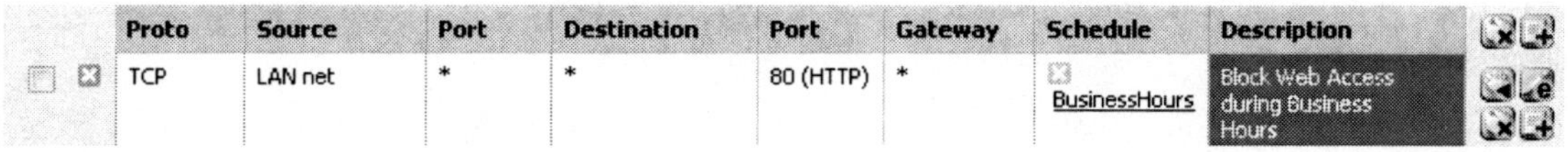

		Proto	Source	Port	Destination	Port	Gateway	Schedule	Description		
	☒	TCP	LAN net	*	*	80 (HTTP)	*	☒ BusinessHours	Block Web Access during Business Hours		

Figure 6.27: Firewall Rule List with Schedule

Now that the rule is defined, be sure to test it both inside and outside of the scheduled times to ensure that the desired behavior is enacted. Also keep the time based rule caveats (Section 6.9.2) in mind when crafting these rules.

6.10 Viewing the Firewall Logs

For each rule that is set to log, and the default deny rule, a log entry is made. There are several ways to view these log entries, with varying levels of detail, and there is no clear "best" method.

Like other logs in pfSense, the firewall logs only keep a certain number of records. If the needs of your organization require that you maintain a permanent record of firewall logs for a longer period of time, see Section 22.1 for information on copying these log entries to a syslog server as they happen.

6.10.1 Viewing in the WebGUI

The firewall logs are visible from the WebGUI, and may be found under Status → System Logs, on the Firewall tab. You can view either parsed logs, which are easier to read, or the raw logs, which have more detail if you understand PF's logging format. There is also a setting for the system logs which will show these entries in forward or reverse order. If you are unsure in which order the log entries are displayed, check the timestamp of the first and last lines, or check Section 22.1 for information on how to view and change these settings.

The parsed WebGUI logs, seen in Figure 6.28, are in 6 columns: Action, Time, Interface, Source, Destination, and Protocol. Action shows what happened to the packet which generated the log entry, either pass, block, or reject. Time is the time that the packet arrived. Interface is where the packet entered pfSense. Source is the source IP address and port. Destination is the destination IP address and port. Protocol is the protocol of the packet, be it ICMP, TCP, UDP, etc.

Act	Time	If	Source	Destination	Proto
☒	Jul 16 20:54:05	WAN	0.0.0.0:68	255.255.255.255:67	UDP
☒	Jul 16 20:56:05	WAN	0.0.0.0:68	255.255.255.255:67	UDP
☒	Jul 16 21:05:05	WAN	0.0.0.0:68	255.255.255.255:67	UDP
☒	Jul 16 21:06:05	WAN	0.0.0.0:68	255.255.255.255:67	UDP

Figure 6.28: Example Log Entries viewed from the WebGUI

The action icon is a link which will lookup and display the rule which caused the log entry. More often than not, this simply says "Default Deny", but when troubleshooting rule issues it can help narrow down the suspects.

If the protocol is TCP, you will also see extra fields here that represent TCP flags present in the packet. These indicate various connection states or packet attributes. Some of the more common ones are:

S — SYN

Synchronize sequence numbers. Indicates a new connection attempt when only SYN is set.

A — ACK

Indicates ACKnowledgment of data. As discussed earlier, these are replies to let the sender know data was received OK.

F — FIN

Indicates there is no more data from the sender, closing a connection.

R — RST

Connection reset. This flag is set when replying to a request to open a connection on a port which has no listening daemon. Can also be set by firewall software to turn away undesirable connections.

There are several other flags, and their meaning is outlined in many materials on the TCP protocol. As usual, the Wikipedia article on TCP has more information.

6.10.2   Viewing from the Console Menu

The raw logs may be viewed directly in real time from pf's logging interface by using option **10** from the console menu. An easy example is a log entry like that seen above in Figure 6.28:

```
000000 rule 54/0(match): block in on vr1: 0.0.0.0.68 >  ↵
   255.255.255.255.67: BOOTP/DHCP, Request [|bootp]
```

This shows that rule 54 was matched, which resulted in a block action on the `vr1` interface. The source and destination IP addresses are shown next. Packets from other protocols may show significantly more data.

6.10.3 Viewing from the Shell

When using the shell either from SSH or from the console, there are numerous options available to view the filter logs.

When directly viewing the contents of the clog file, the log entries may be quite complex and verbose. It should be relatively easy to pick out the various fields, but depending on the context of the match, it may be more difficult.

6.10.3.1 Viewing the current contents of the log file

The filter log, as discussed in the opening on this chapter, is contained in a binary circular log so you cannot use traditional tools like **cat**, **grep**, etc. on the file directly. The log must be read back with the **clog** program, and may then be piped through whatever program you like.

To view the current contents of the log file, run the following command:

```
# clog /var/log/filter.log
```

The entire contents of the log file will be displayed. If you are only interested in the last few lines, you can pipe it through **tail** like so:

```
# clog /var/log/filter.log | tail
```

6.10.3.2 Following the log output in real time

To "follow" the output of the clog file, you must use the `-f` parameter to **clog**. This is the equivalent of **tail -f** for those used to working with normal log files on UNIX systems.

```
# clog -f /var/log/filter.log
```

This will output the entire contents of the log file but does not quit afterward. It will instead wait for more entries and print them as they happen.

6.10.3.3   Viewing parsed log output in the shell

There is a simple log parser written in PHP which can be used from the shell to produce reduced output instead of the full raw log. To view the parsed contents of the current log, run:

```
# clog /var/log/filter.log | php /usr/local/www/filterparser.php
```

You will see the log entries output one per line, with simplified output like so:

```
Jul 17 00:06:05 block vr1 UDP 0.0.0.0:68 255.255.255.255:67
```

6.10.3.4   Finding the rule which caused a log entry

When viewing one of the raw log formats, the rule number for an entry is displayed. You can use this rule number to find the rule which caused the match. In the following example, we are trying to find out what rule is numbered *54*.

```
# pfctl -vvsr | grep '^@54 '
@54 block drop in log quick all label "Default deny rule"
```

As you can see, this was the default deny rule.

6.10.4   Why do I sometimes see blocked log entries for legitimate connections?

Sometimes you will see log entries that, while labeled with the "Default deny" rule, look like they belong to legitimate traffic. The most common example is seeing a connection blocked involving a web server.

This is likely to happen when a TCP FIN packet, which would normally close the connection, arrives after the connection's state has been removed. This happens because on occasion a packet will be lost, and the retransmits will be blocked because the firewall has already closed the connection.

It is harmless, and does not indicate an actual blocked connection. All stateful firewalls do this, though some don't generate log messages for this blocked traffic even if you log all blocked traffic.

You will see this on occasion even if you have allow all rules on all your interfaces, as allow all for TCP connections only allows TCP SYN packets. All other TCP traffic will either be part of an existing state in the state table, or will be packets with spoofed TCP flags.

6.11   Troubleshooting Firewall Rules

This section provides guidance on what to do if your firewall rules are not behaving as you desire or expect.

6.11.1   Check your logs

Your first step when troubleshooting suspected blocked traffic should be to check your firewall logs (Status → System Logs, on the Firewall tab). Remember that by default pfSense will log all dropped traffic and will not log any passed traffic. Unless you add block or reject rules that do not use logging, all blocked traffic will always be logged. If you do not see the traffic with a red X next to it in your firewall logs, pfSense is not dropping the traffic.

6.11.2   Review rule parameters

Edit the rule in question and review the parameters you have specified for each field. For TCP and UDP traffic, remember the source port is almost never the same as the destination port, and should usually be set to any. If the default deny rule is to blame, you may need to craft a new pass rule that will match the traffic that needs to be allowed.

6.11.3   Review rule ordering

Remember the first matching rule wins — no further rules are evaluated.

6.11.4   Rules and interfaces

Ensure your rules are on the correct interface to function as intended. Remember traffic is filtered only by the ruleset configured on the interface where the traffic is initiated. Traffic coming from a system on your LAN destined for a system on any other interface is filtered by only the LAN rules. The same is true for all other interfaces.

6.11.5   Enable rule logging

It can be helpful to determine which rule is matching the traffic in question. By enabling logging on your pass rules, you can view the firewall logs and click on an individual entry to determine which rule passed the traffic.

6.11.6   Troubleshooting with packet captures

Packet captures can be invaluable for troubleshooting and debugging traffic issues. You can tell if the traffic is reaching the outside interface at all, or leaving the inside interface, among many other uses. See Chapter 25 for more details on troubleshooting with packet captures and **tcpdump**.

Chapter 7

Network Address Translation

In its most common usage, Network Address Translation (NAT) allows you to connect multiple computers to the Internet using a single public IP address. pfSense enables these simple deployments, but also accommodates much more advanced and complex NAT configurations required in networks with multiple public IP addresses.

NAT is configured in two directions — inbound and outbound. Outbound NAT defines how traffic leaving your network destined for the Internet is translated. Inbound NAT refers to traffic entering your network from the Internet. The most common type of inbound NAT and the one most are familiar with is port forwards.

7.1 Default NAT Configuration

This section describes the default NAT configuration of pfSense. The most commonly suitable NAT configuration is generated automatically. In some environments you will want to modify this configuration, and pfSense fully enables you to do so — entirely from the web interface. This is a contrast from many other open source firewall distributions, which do not allow the capabilities commonly required in all but small, simple networks.

7.1.1 Default Outbound NAT Configuration

The default NAT configuration in pfSense with a two interface LAN and WAN deployment automatically translates Internet-bound traffic to the WAN IP address. When multiple WAN interfaces are configured, traffic leaving any WAN interface is automatically translated to the address of the WAN interface being used.

Static port is automatically configured for IKE (part of IPsec) and SIP (VoIP) traffic. Static port is covered in more detail in Section 7.6 about Outbound NAT.

7.1.2   Default Inbound NAT Configuration

By default, nothing is allowed in from the Internet. If you need to allow traffic initiated on the Internet to a host on your internal network, you must configure port forwards or 1:1 NAT. This is covered in the coming sections.

7.2   Port Forwards

Port forwards allow you to open a specific port, port range or protocol to a privately addressed device on your internal network. The name "port forward" was chosen because it is what most people understand, and it was renamed from the more technically appropriate "Inbound NAT" after countless complaints from confused users. However it is a bit of a misnomer, as you can redirect the GRE and ESP protocols in addition to TCP and UDP ports. This is most commonly used when hosting servers, or using applications that require inbound connections from the Internet.

7.2.1   Risks of Port Forwarding

In a default configuration, pfSense does not let in any traffic initiated on the Internet. This provides protection from anyone scanning the Internet looking for systems to attack. When you add a port forward, pfSense will allow any traffic matching the corresponding firewall rule. It doesn't know the difference from a packet with a malicious payload and one that is benign. If it matches the firewall rule, it's allowed. You need to rely on host based controls to secure any services allowed through the firewall.

7.2.2   Port Forwarding and Local Services

Port forwards take precedence over any services running locally on the firewall, such as the web interface, SSH, and any other services you may be running. For example this means if you allow remote web interface access from the WAN using HTTPS on TCP port 443, if you add a port forward on WAN for TCP 443 that port forward will work and your web interface access from WAN will no longer function. This does not affect access on other interfaces, just the interface containing the port forward.

7.2.3   Adding Port Forwards

Port Forwards are managed at Firewall → NAT, on the Port Forward tab. The rules on this screen are managed in the same manner as firewall rules (see Section 6.2).

To begin adding a port forward entry, click the ⊞ button at the very top or bottom of the list, as indicated by Figure 7.1.

Firewall: NAT: Port Forward

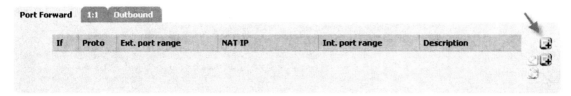

Figure 7.1: Add Port Forward

You will now be looking at the Port Forward editing screen, shown in Figure 7.2, with the default options chosen. First, select the Interface on which the port to be forwarded resides. In most cases this will be WAN, but if you have an OPT WAN link, or if this will be a local redirect, it may be another interface.

The External Address in most cases should be set to **Interface Address** or an available Virtual IP (see Section 6.8), unless this is a local redirect.

The Protocol and External Port Range must be set accordingly for the service being forwarded. For example, to forward VNC[1] you would set Protocol to **TCP** and the External Port Range to **5900**. (Since this is a commonly forwarded port, it is also available in the drop-down list for port selection.)

The NAT IP should be the local IP address to which this external port will forward, and the Local port is where the forwarded port range will begin. If you are forwarding a range of ports, say 19000-19100, you need only specify a local starting point since the ports must match up one to one. This field allows you to open a different port on the outside than the host on the inside is listening on, for example external port 8888 may forward to local port 80 for HTTP on an internal server.

The description field, as in other parts of pfSense, is available for a short sentence about what the port forward does or why it exists.

If you are not using a CARP failover cluster, skip over the No XML-RPC Sync option. If you are, then checking this box will prevent this rule from being synchronized to the other members of a failover cluster (see Chapter 20), which is usually undesirable.

The final option is very important. If you check Auto-add a firewall rule to permit traffic through this NAT rule, then a firewall rule will automatically be created for you that will allow traffic to reach the target port. It is usually best to leave this checked, and then alter the firewall rule afterward if needed. Click Save when finished, then Apply Changes.

In Figure 7.2 there is an example of the port forward editing screen filled in with the proper settings to forward VNC to a local system.

---

[1] Virtual Network Computing, a multi-platform desktop sharing protocol with many free/open source implementations such as UltraVNC (http://www.uvnc.com/)

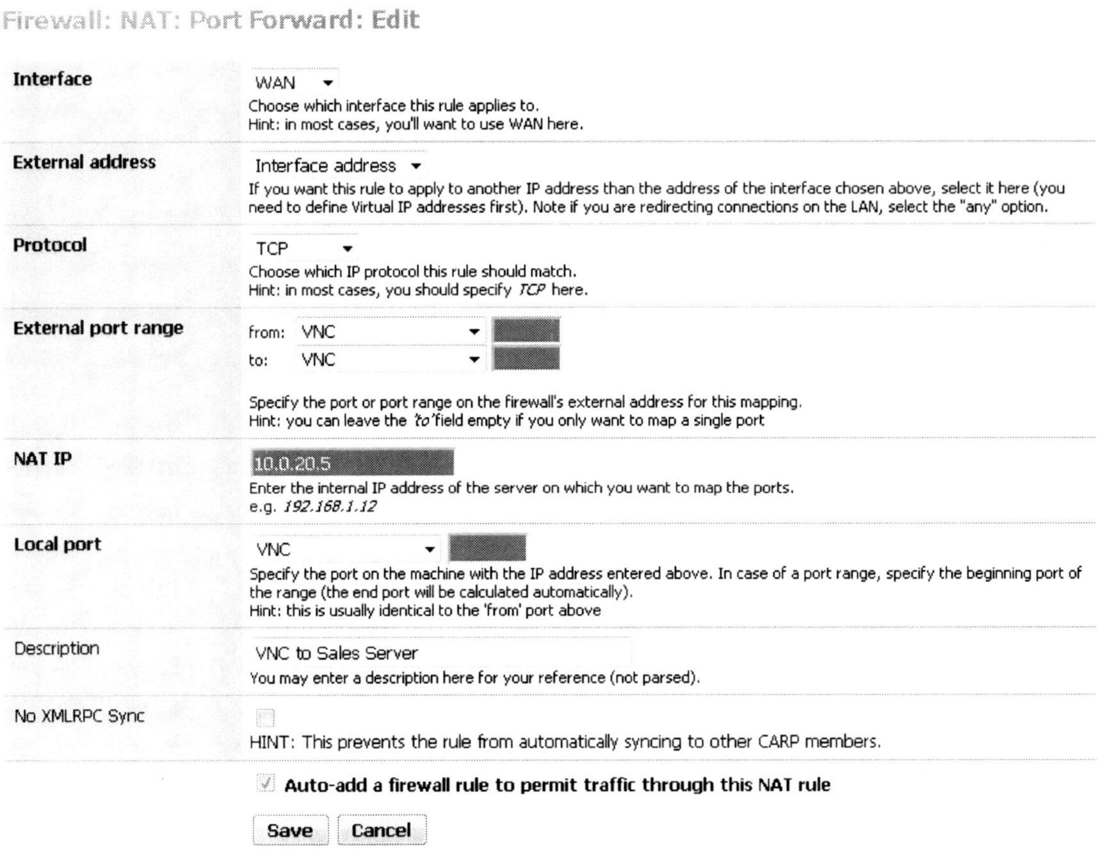

Firewall: NAT: Port Forward: Edit

Interface	WAN ▾ Choose which interface this rule applies to. Hint: in most cases, you'll want to use WAN here.
External address	Interface address ▾ If you want this rule to apply to another IP address than the address of the interface chosen above, select it here (you need to define Virtual IP addresses first). Note if you are redirecting connections on the LAN, select the "any" option.
Protocol	TCP ▾ Choose which IP protocol this rule should match. Hint: in most cases, you should specify *TCP* here.
External port range	from: VNC ▾ ▮▮ to: VNC ▾ ▮▮ Specify the port or port range on the firewall's external address for this mapping. Hint: you can leave the *'to'* field empty if you only want to map a single port
NAT IP	10.0.20.5 Enter the internal IP address of the server on which you want to map the ports. e.g. *192.168.1.12*
Local port	VNC ▾ ▮▮ Specify the port on the machine with the IP address entered above. In case of a port range, specify the beginning port of the range (the end port will be calculated automatically). Hint: this is usually identical to the 'from' port above
Description	VNC to Sales Server You may enter a description here for your reference (not parsed).
No XMLRPC Sync	☐ HINT: This prevents the rule from automatically syncing to other CARP members.

☑ **Auto-add a firewall rule to permit traffic through this NAT rule**

[Save] [Cancel]

Figure 7.2: Port Forward Example

After clicking Save, you will be taken back to the port forward list, and you will see the newly created entry as in Figure 7.3.

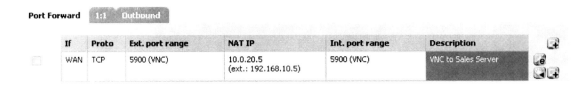

Port Forward 1:1 Outbound

	If	Proto	Ext. port range	NAT IP	Int. port range	Description	
☐	WAN	TCP	5900 (VNC)	10.0.20.5 (ext.: 192.168.10.5)	5900 (VNC)	VNC to Sales Server	

Figure 7.3: Port Forward List

You may want to double check the firewall rule, as seen under Firewall → Rules on the tab for the interface upon which the port forward was created. It will show that traffic will be allowed into the NAT IP on the proper port, as shown in Figure 7.4.

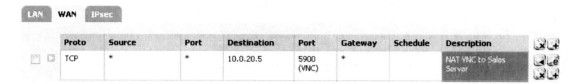

Figure 7.4: Port Forward Firewall Rule

You will want to restrict the **Source** of the automatically generated rule where possible. For things such as mail servers that need to be widely accessible, this isn't practical, but for the VNC example it is likely there are only a small number of hosts that should be able to connect using VNC into a server from across the Internet. Creating an alias of authorized hosts, and changing the source from **any** to the alias is far more secure than leaving the source wide open to the entire Internet. You may want to test first with the unrestricted source, and after verifying it works as desired, restrict the source as desired.

If everything looks right, the port forward should work when tested from outside your network. If something went wrong, see Section 7.9.1 later in this chapter.

7.2.4   Port Forward Limitations

You can only forward a single port to one internal host for each public IP address you have available. For instance, you if you only have one public IP address, you can only have one internal web server that uses TCP port 80 to serve web traffic. Any additional servers would need to use alternate ports such as 8080. If you have five available public IP addresses configured as Virtual IPs, you could then have five internal web servers using port 80. See Section 6.8 for more about Virtual IP addresses.

In order for port forwards on WAN addresses to be accessible by using their respective WAN IP address from internal-facing interfaces, you will need to setup NAT reflection which is described in Section 7.5. You should always test your port forwards from a system on a different Internet connection, and not from inside your network.

7.2.5   Service Self-Configuration With UPnP

Some programs now support Universal Plug-and-Play (UPnP) to automatically configure NAT port forwards and firewall rules. Even more security concerns apply there, but in home use the benefits often outweigh any potential concerns. See Section 21.6 for more information on configuring and using UPnP.

7.2.6   Traffic Redirection with Port Forwards

Another use of port forwards is for transparently redirecting traffic from your internal network. Port forwards specifying the LAN interface or another internal interface will redirect traffic matching the forward to the specified destination. This is most commonly used for transparently proxying HTTP traffic to a proxy server, or redirecting all outbound SMTP to one server.

Note

The system you are directing this traffic to must reside on a different interface of the firewall. Otherwise its own network traffic will be redirected back to itself. In the case of a HTTP proxy server with a redirection port forward on LAN, its own requests will never be able to leave the network unless the server resides on an OPT interface. There is no way to negate a port forward on an internal interface in pfSense 1.2.x, though there is a feature request open on that and it may be included in 2.0.

The NAT entry shown in Figure 7.5 is an example of a configuration that will redirect all HTTP traffic coming into the LAN interface to Squid (port 3129) on the host 172.30.50.10.

Firewall: NAT: Port Forward: Edit

Interface	LAN ▼ Choose which interface this rule applies to. Hint: in most cases, you'll want to use WAN here.
External address	any ▼ If you want this rule to apply to another IP address than the address of the interface chosen a need to define Virtual IP addresses first). Note if you are redirecting connections on the LAN, s
Protocol	TCP ▼ Choose which IP protocol this rule should match. Hint: in most cases, you should specify *TCP* here.
External port range	from: HTTP ▼ to: HTTP ▼ Specify the port or port range on the firewall's external address for this mapping. Hint: you can leave the *'to'* field empty if you only want to map a single port
NAT IP	172.30.50.10 Enter the internal IP address of the server on which you want to map the ports. e.g. *192.168.1.12*
Local port	(other) ▼ 3129 Specify the port on the machine with the IP address entered above. In case of a port range, s the range (the end port will be calculated automatically). Hint: this is usually identical to the 'from' port above
Description	Redirect HTTP to Squid You may enter a description here for your reference (not parsed).
No XMLRPC Sync	☐ HINT: This prevents the rule from automatically syncing to other CARP members.

Figure 7.5: Example redirect port forward

Remember the server you are redirecting to must reside on a different interface than the one used in the port forward, as previously described.

7.3   1:1 NAT

1:1 (pronounced one to one) NAT maps one public IP to one private IP. All traffic from that private IP to the Internet will be mapped to the public IP defined in the 1:1 NAT mapping, overriding your Outbound NAT configuration. All traffic initiated on the Internet destined for the specified public IP will be translated to the private IP, then evaluated by your WAN firewall ruleset. If the traffic is permitted by your firewall rules, it will be passed to the internal host.

7.3.1   Risks of 1:1 NAT

The risks of 1:1 NAT are largely the same as port forwards, if you allow traffic to that host in your WAN firewall rules. Any time you allow traffic, you are permitting potentially harmful traffic into your network. There is a slight added risk when using 1:1 NAT in that firewall rule mistakes can have more dire consequences. With port forward entries, you are limiting the traffic that will be allowed within the NAT rule, as well as the firewall rule. If you port forward TCP port 80, then add an allow all rule on your WAN, only TCP 80 on that internal host will be accessible. If you are using 1:1 NAT and add an allow all rule on WAN, everything on that internal host will be accessible from the Internet. Misconfigurations are always a potential hazard, and this usually should not be considered a reason to avoid 1:1 NAT. Just keep this fact in mind when configuring your firewall rules, and as always, avoid permitting anything that is not required.

7.3.2   Configuring 1:1 NAT

To configure 1:1 NAT, first add a Virtual IP for the public IP to be used for the 1:1 NAT entry as described in Section 6.8. Then browse to Firewall → NAT and click the 1:1 tab. Click ⊞ to add a 1:1 entry.

7.3.2.1   1:1 NAT Entry Fields

Figure 7.6 shows the 1:1 NAT Edit screen, then each field will be detailed.

Firewall: NAT: 1:1: Edit

Interface	WAN ▾
	Choose which interface this rule applies to. Hint: in most cases, you'll want to use WAN here.
External subnet	⬚ / 32 ▾
	Enter the external (WAN) subnet for the 1:1 mapping. You may map single IP addresses by specifying a /32 subnet.
Internal subnet	⬚
	Enter the internal (LAN) subnet for the 1:1 mapping. The subnet size specified for the external subnet also applies to the internal subnet (they have to be the same).
Description	⬚
	You may enter a description here for your reference (not parsed).

Figure 7.6: 1:1 NAT Edit screen

7.3.2.1.1 Interface

The interface box is where you select the location of the external subnet. This is almost always your WAN, or an OPT WAN interface in multi-WAN deployments.

7.3.2.1.2 External subnet

The external subnet is where you define the public IP address or IP address range for the 1:1 mapping. This can be a single IP address by specifying a /32 mask, or a CIDR range by selecting another mask.

7.3.2.1.3 Internal subnet

The internal subnet is where you specify the internal IP address or IP address range for the 1:1 mapping. This IP address or range must be reachable on one of your internal interfaces, whether on a directly attached subnet, or one reachable via static route.

7.3.2.1.4 Description

This is an optional field that does not affect the behavior of the 1:1 NAT entry. Fill in something that will allow you to easily identify this entry when working with your firewall in the future.

7.3.2.2 Example single IP 1:1 configuration

This section will show how to configure a 1:1 NAT entry with a single internal and external IP. In this example, 10.0.0.5 is a Virtual IP on the WAN. In most deployments this will be substituted with one of your public IP addresses. The mail server being configured for this mapping resides on a DMZ segment using internal IP 192.168.2.5. The 1:1 NAT entry to map 10.0.0.5 to 192.168.2.5 is shown in Figure 7.7. A diagram depicting this configuration is in Figure 7.8.

Firewall: NAT: 1:1: Edit

Interface	WAN ▾
	Choose which interface this rule applies to.
	Hint: in most cases, you'll want to use WAN here.
External subnet	10.0.0.5 / 32 ▾
	Enter the external (WAN) subnet for the 1:1 mapping. You may map single IP addresses by specifying a /32 subnet.
Internal subnet	192.168.2.5
	Enter the internal (LAN) subnet for the 1:1 mapping. The subnet size specified for the external subnet also applies to the internal subnet (they have to be the same).
Description	mail server
	You may enter a description here for your reference (not parsed).

Figure 7.7: 1:1 NAT Entry

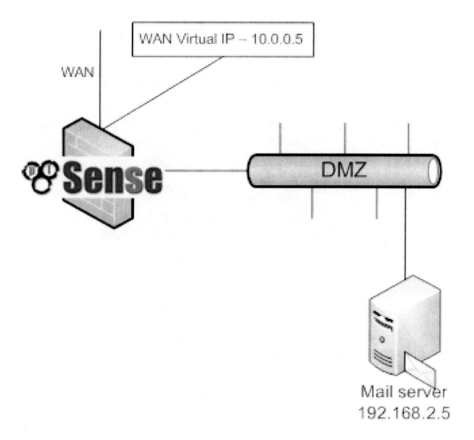

Figure 7.8: 1:1 NAT Example — Single inside and outside IP

7.3.2.3 Example IP range 1:1 configuration

1:1 NAT can be configured for multiple public IPs by using CIDR ranges. CIDR summarization is covered in Section 1.7.5. This section covers configuration of 1:1 NAT for a /30 CIDR range of IPs.

External IPs	Internal IPs
10.0.0.64/30	**192.168.2.64/30**
10.0.0.64	192.168.2.64
10.0.0.65	192.168.2.65
10.0.0.66	192.168.2.66
10.0.0.67	192.168.2.67

Table 7.1: /30 CIDR mapping — matching final octet

The last octet of the IP addresses need not be the same on the inside and outside, but I recommend doing so whenever possible. For example, Table 7.2 would also be valid.

External IPs	Internal IPs
10.0.0.64/30	**192.168.2.200/30**
10.0.0.64	192.168.2.200
10.0.0.65	192.168.2.201
10.0.0.66	192.168.2.202
10.0.0.67	192.168.2.203

Table 7.2: /30 CIDR mapping — non-matching final octet

I recommend choosing an addressing scheme where the last octet matches, because it makes your network easier to understand and hence maintain. Figure 7.9 shows how to configure 1:1 NAT to achieve the mapping listed in Table 7.1.

Firewall: NAT: 1:1: Edit

Interface	WAN ▾
	Choose which interface this rule applies to.
	Hint: in most cases, you'll want to use WAN here.
External subnet	10.0.0.64 / 30 ▾
	Enter the external (WAN) subnet for the 1:1 mapping. You may map single IP addresses by specifying a /32 subnet.
Internal subnet	192.168.2.64
	Enter the internal (LAN) subnet for the 1:1 mapping. The subnet size specified for the external subnet also applies to the internal subnet (they have to be the same).
Description	.64 through .67 range
	You may enter a description here for your reference (not parsed).

Figure 7.9: 1:1 NAT entry for /30 CIDR range

7.3.3   1:1 NAT on the WAN IP, aka "DMZ" on Linksys

Some consumer routers like those from Linksys have what they call a "DMZ" feature that will forward all ports and protocols destined to the WAN IP address to a system on the LAN. In effect, this is 1:1 NAT between the WAN IP address and the IP address of the internal system. "DMZ" in that context, however, has nothing to do with what an actual DMZ network is in real networking terminology. In fact, it's almost quite the opposite. A host in a true DMZ is in an isolated network away from the other LAN hosts, secured away from the Internet and LAN hosts alike. In contrast, a "DMZ" host in the Linksys meaning is not only on the same network as the LAN hosts, but completely exposed to incoming traffic with no protection.

In pfSense, you cannot have 1:1 NAT active on the WAN IP. The WebGUI will not permit such a configuration, as it would break connectivity for other hosts on your network. Instead, you should only forward the protocols and ports required by your server or application, and restrict their use by firewall rules where possible. You can technically achieve the same thing by forwarding TCP and UDP ports 1 through 65535 and the GRE and ESP protocols, but this is very strongly discouraged as it has serious security consequences.

7.4   Ordering of NAT and Firewall Processing

Understanding the order in which firewalling and NAT occurs is important when configuring NAT and firewall rules. The Figure 7.10 illustrates this ordering. It also depicts where **tcpdump** ties in, since its use as a troubleshooting tool will be described later in this book (see Chapter 25).

Each layer is not always hit. Figure 7.11 and Figure 7.12 illustrate which layers apply for traffic initiated from the LAN going to the WAN, and also for traffic initiated on the WAN going to LAN (when such traffic is permitted).

For traffic from LAN to WAN, first the firewall rules are evaluated, then the outbound NAT is applied if the traffic is permitted. The WAN NAT and firewall rules do not apply to traffic initiated on the LAN.

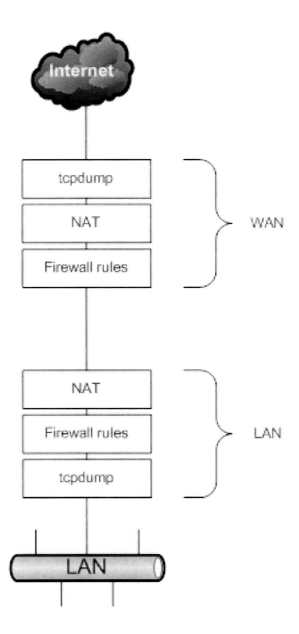

Figure 7.10: Ordering of NAT and Firewall Processing

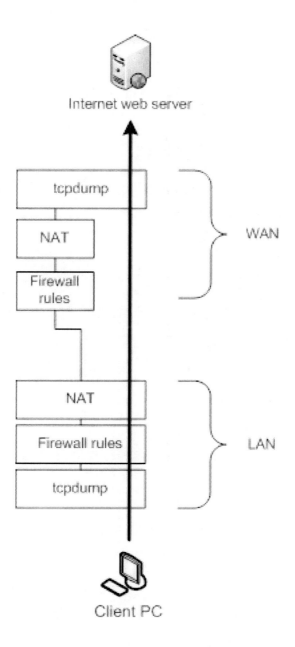

Figure 7.11: LAN to WAN Processing

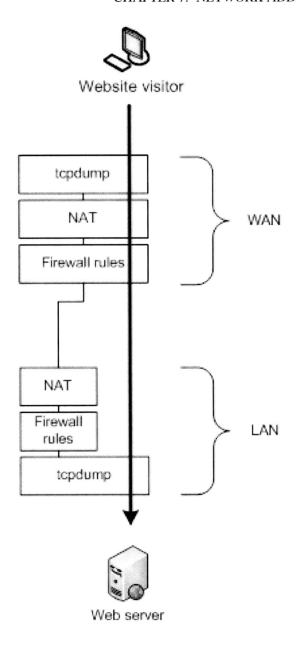

Figure 7.12: WAN to LAN Processing

For traffic initiated on the WAN, NAT applies first, then the firewall rules.

Note that **tcpdump** is always the first and last thing to see traffic — first on the incoming interface, before any NAT and firewall processing, and last on the outbound interface. It shows what is on the wire. (See Chapter 25)

7.4.1   Extrapolating to additional interfaces

The previous diagrams only illustrate a basic two interface LAN and WAN deployment. When working with firewalls with OPT and OPT WAN interfaces, the same rules apply. All OPT interfaces behave the same as LAN, and all OPT WAN interfaces behave the same as WAN. Traffic between two internal interfaces behaves the same as LAN to WAN traffic, though the default NAT rules will not translate traffic between internal interfaces so the NAT layer does not do anything in those cases. If you define Outbound NAT rules that match traffic between internal interfaces, it will apply as shown.

7.4.2   Rules for NAT

For rules on WAN or OPT WAN interfaces, because NAT translates the destination IP of the traffic before the firewall rules evaluate it, your WAN firewall rules must always specify the private IP address as the destination. For example, when you add a port forward for TCP port 80 on WAN, and check the Auto-add firewall rule box, this is the resulting firewall rule on WAN. The internal IP on the port forward is 192.168.1.5. Whether using port forwards or 1:1 NAT, firewall rules on all WAN interfaces must use the internal IP as the destination address. Refer to Figure 7.13 for an example of how such a rule should appear.

Figure 7.13: Firewall Rule for Port Forward to LAN Host

7.5   NAT Reflection

NAT reflection refers to the ability to access your external services from the internal network by public IP, the same as you would if you were on the Internet. Many commercial and open source firewalls do not support this functionality at all. pfSense has somewhat limited support for NAT reflection, though some environments will require a split DNS infrastructure to accommodate this functionality. Split DNS is covered in Section 7.5.2.

7.5.1   Configuring and Using NAT Reflection

To enable NAT reflection, browse to the System → Advanced page. Scroll down under Network Address Translation and uncheck the Disable NAT Reflection box as shown in Figure 7.14. Click Save, and NAT reflection will be enabled. No further configuration is needed, it will immediately work.

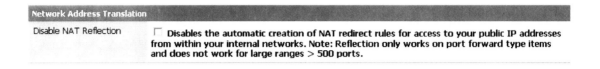

Network Address Translation

Disable NAT Reflection   ☐ **Disables the automatic creation of NAT redirect rules for access to your public IP addresses from within your internal networks. Note: Reflection only works on port forward type items and does not work for large ranges > 500 ports.**

Figure 7.14: Enable NAT Reflection

7.5.1.1 NAT Reflection Caveats

NAT reflection is always a bit of a hack as it loops traffic through the firewall. Because of the limited options pf allows for accommodating these scenarios, there are some limitations in the pfSense NAT reflection implementation. Port ranges larger than 500 ports do not have NAT reflection enabled, and 1:1 NAT is not supported. Split DNS is the only means of accommodating large port ranges and 1:1 NAT. I would love to tell you this situation will improve in pfSense 2.0, but that is unlikely due to the challenges of handling this given the limits of the underlying software. Maintaining a split DNS infrastructure is required by many commercial firewalls even, and typically isn't a problem.

7.5.2 Split DNS

A preferable alternative to NAT reflection is deploying a split DNS infrastructure. Split DNS refers to a DNS configuration where your public Internet DNS resolves to your public IPs, and DNS on your internal network resolves to the internal, private IPs. The means of accommodating this will vary depending on the specifics of your DNS infrastructure, but the end result is the same. You bypass the need for NAT reflection by resolving hostnames to the private IPs inside your network.

7.5.2.1 DNS Forwarder Overrides

If you use pfSense as your DNS server for internal hosts, you can use DNS forwarder overrides to accomplish a split DNS deployment. To add an override to the DNS forwarder, browse to Services → DNS Forwarder, and click the ⊞ under "You may enter records that override the results from the forwarders below", as indicated by Figure 7.15.

You may enter records that override the results from the forwarders below.

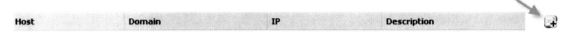

Host	Domain	IP	Description	

Figure 7.15: Add DNS Forwarder Override

This brings up the DNS forwarder: Edit host screen. The Figure 7.16 and Figure 7.17 show examples of DNS overrides for example.com and www.example.com.

You will need to add an override for each hostname in use behind your firewall.

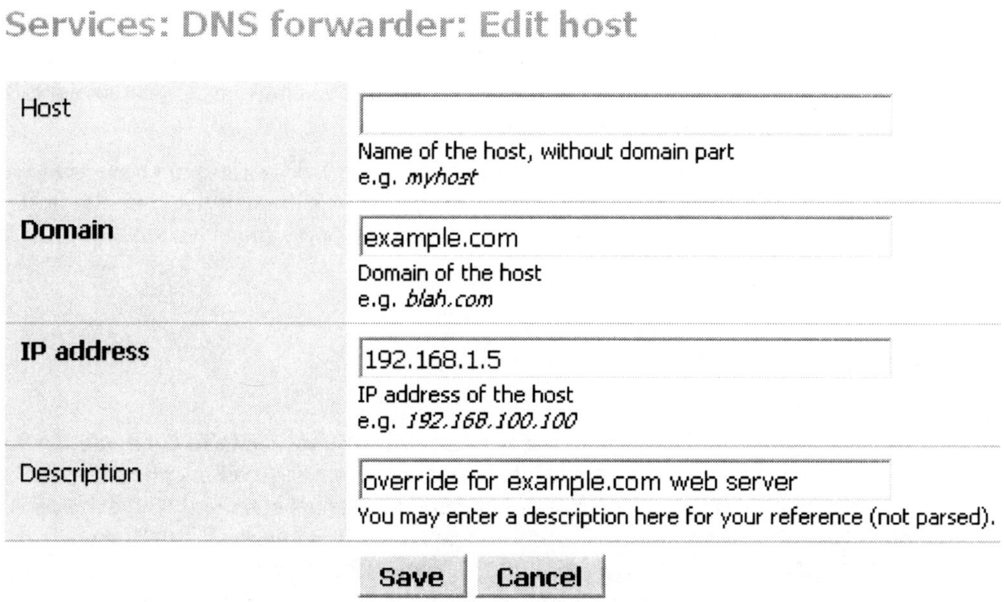

Services: DNS forwarder: Edit host

Host	
	Name of the host, without domain part e.g. *myhost*
Domain	example.com
	Domain of the host e.g. *blah.com*
IP address	192.168.1.5
	IP address of the host e.g. *192.168.100.100*
Description	override for example.com web server
	You may enter a description here for your reference (not parsed).

Save   Cancel

Figure 7.16: Add DNS Forwarder Override for example.com

Services: DNS forwarder: Edit host

Host	www
	Name of the host, without domain part e.g. *myhost*
Domain	example.com
	Domain of the host e.g. *blah.com*
IP address	192.168.1.5
	IP address of the host e.g. *192.168.100.100*
Description	override for www.example.com web server
	You may enter a description here for your reference (not parsed).

Save   Cancel

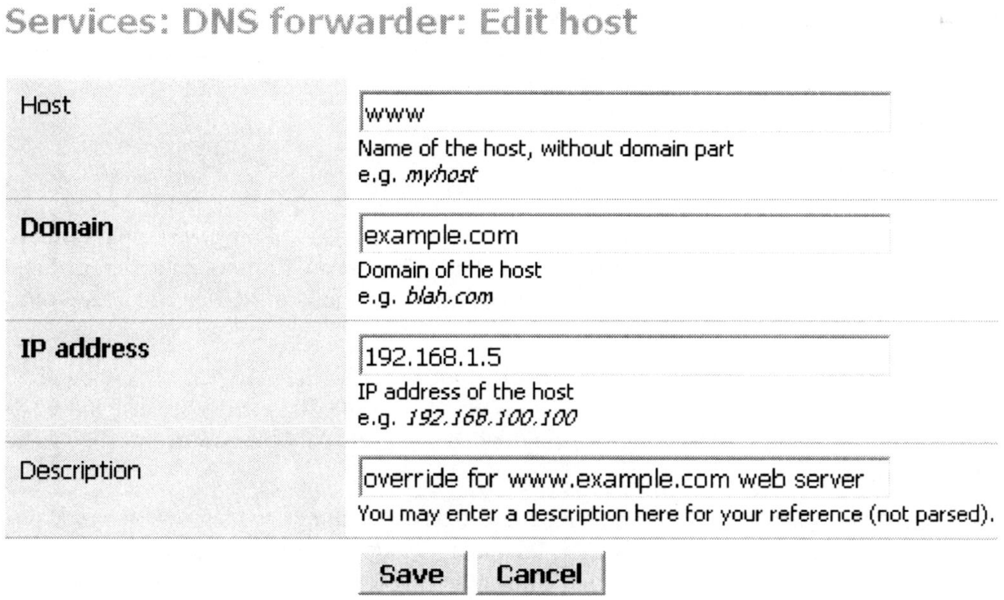

Figure 7.17: DNS Forwarder Override for www.example.com

7.5.2.2   Internal DNS servers

If you use other DNS servers on your internal network, such as is common when using Microsoft Active Directory, you will need to create zones for all the domains you host inside your network, along with all other records for those domains (A, CNAME, MX, etc.).

In environments running the BIND DNS server where the public DNS is hosted on the same server as the private DNS, BIND's views feature is used to resolve DNS differently for internal hosts than external ones. If you are using a different DNS server, it may support similar functionality. Check its documentation for information.

7.6   Outbound NAT

Outbound NAT controls how traffic leaving your network will be translated. To configure it, visit the Firewall → NAT page and choose the Outbound tab. There are two configuration options for Outbound NAT in pfSense, Automatic outbound NAT rule generation and Manual outbound NAT generation (Advanced Outbound NAT (AON)). In networks with a single public IP address per WAN, there is usually no reason to enable AON. In environments with multiple public IP addresses, this may be desirable. For environments using CARP, it is important to NAT outbound traffic to a CARP IP address, as discussed in Chapter 20.

7.6.1   Default Outbound NAT Rules

When using the default Automatic outbound NAT, pfSense will automatically create NAT rules translating traffic leaving any internal network to the IP address of the WAN interface which the traffic leaves.

7.6.2   Static Port

By default, pfSense rewrites the source port on all outgoing packets. Many operating systems do a poor job of source port randomization, if they do it at all. This makes IP spoofing easier, and makes it possible to fingerprint hosts behind your firewall from their outbound traffic. Rewriting the source port eliminates these potential (but unlikely) security vulnerabilities.

However, this breaks some applications. There are built in rules when Advanced Outbound NAT is disabled that don't do this for UDP 500 (IKE for VPN traffic) and 5060 (SIP) because these types of traffic will almost always be broken by rewriting the source port. All other traffic has the source port rewritten by default.

You may use other protocols, like some games amongst other things, which do not work properly when the source port gets rewritten. To disable this functionality, you need to use the static port option. Click Firewall → NAT, and the Outbound tab. Click Manual Outbound NAT rule generation (Advanced Outbound NAT (AON)) and click Save. You will then see a rule at the bottom of the page labeled Auto created rule for LAN. Click the 🖉 button to the right of that rule to edit it. Check the Static Port box on that page, and click Save. Apply Changes. After making that change, the source port on outgoing traffic will be preserved.

7.6.3 Disabling Outbound NAT

If you are using public IP addresses on local interfaces, and thus do not need to apply NAT to traffic passing through the firewall, you should disable NAT for that interface. In order to do this, you must first change the Outbound NAT setting to Manual Outbound NAT, and then Save. After making that change, one or more rules will appear in the list on the Outbound NAT screen. Delete the rule or rules for the public IP subnets by clicking each line once (or check the box at the start of the line) and then click the ⊠ button at the bottom of the list. Click Apply Changes to complete the process.

Once all of the rules have been deleted, outbound NAT will no longer be active for those addresses, and pfSense will then route public IP addresses without translation.

To completely disable outbound NAT, delete all of the rules that are present when using Manual Outbound NAT.

7.7 Choosing a NAT Configuration

Your choice of NAT configuration will depend primarily on the number of public IPs you have and number of systems that require inbound access from the Internet.

7.7.1 Single Public IP per WAN

When you have only a single public IP per WAN, your NAT options are limited. You can only use 1:1 NAT with Virtual IPs, not with any WAN IPs. In this case, you may only use port forwards.

7.7.2 Multiple Public IPs per WAN

With multiple public IPs per WAN, you have numerous options for your inbound and outbound NAT configuration. Port forwards, 1:1 NAT, and Advanced Outbound NAT may all be desirable in some circumstances.

7.8 NAT and Protocol Compatibility

Some protocols do not work well and some not at all with NAT. Some protocols embed IP addresses within packets, some do not work properly if the source port is rewritten, and some are difficult because of limitations of pf. This section covers the protocols that have difficulties with NAT in pfSense, and how to work around these issues where possible.

7.8.1 FTP

FTP poses problems with both NAT and firewalls because of the design of the protocol. FTP was initially designed in the 1970s, and the current standard defining the specifications of the protocol was written in 1985. Since FTP was created more than a decade prior to NAT, and long before firewalls were common, it does some things that are very NAT and firewall unfriendly. pfSense uses two different FTP proxy applications, pftpx and ftpsesame. pftpx is used for all NAT scenarios, while ftpsesame accommodates bridging and routing of public IPs.

7.8.1.1   FTP Limitations

Because pf lacks the ability to properly handle FTP traffic without a proxy, and the pfSense FTP proxy implementation is somewhat lacking, there are some restrictions on the usage of FTP.[2]

7.8.1.1.1   FTP client connections to the Internet

FTP client connections will always use the primary WAN interface and cannot use any OPT WAN interfaces. More information on this can be found in Chapter 11

7.8.1.1.2   FTP servers behind NAT

FTP servers behind NAT must use port 21, as the FTP proxy will only launch when port 21 is specified.

7.8.1.2   FTP modes

7.8.1.2.1   Active Mode

With Active Mode FTP, when a file transfer is requested, the *client* listens on a local port, and then tells the server the client IP address and port. The server will then connect back to that IP address and port in order to transfer the data. This is a problem for firewalls because the port is typically random, though modern clients allow for limiting the range that is used. As you may have guessed, in the case of a client behind NAT, the IP address given would be a local address, unreachable from the server. Not only that, but a firewall rule would need to be added and a port forward allowing traffic into this port.

When the FTP proxy is in use, it attempts to do three major things. First, it will rewrite the FTP PORT command so that the IP address is the WAN IP address of the firewall, and a randomly chosen port on that IP address. Next, it adds a port forward that connects the translated IP address and port to the original IP address and port specified by the FTP client. Finally, it allows traffic from the FTP server to connect to that "public" port.

When everything is working as it should, this all happens transparently. The server never knows it's talking to a client behind NAT, and the client never knows that the server isn't connecting directly.

In the case of a server behind NAT, this is not usually a problem since the server will only be listening for connections on the standard FTP ports and then making outbound connections back to the clients.

---

[2] In pfSense 2.0, the ftp proxy and related helpers have been eliminated and all of this functionality is handled seamlessly in a more robust way inside of the kernel.

7.8.1.2.2 Passive Mode

Passive Mode (PASV) acts somewhat in reverse. For clients, it is more NAT and firewall friendly because the *server* listens on a port when a file transfer is requested, not the client. Typically, PASV mode will work for FTP clients behind NAT without using any proxy or special handling at all.

If a server is behind NAT, however, then the traffic must be proxied in reverse when its clients attempt to use PASV mode. The FTP proxy can handle this scenario, but all incoming FTP requests will appear to come from the pfSense system instead of from clients. Similar to the situation in the previous section, when a client requests PASV mode the server will have to give its IP address and a random port to which the client can attempt to connect. Since the server is on a private network, that IP address and port will need to be translated and allowed through the firewall.

7.8.1.2.3 Extended Passive Mode

Extended Passive Mode (EPSV) works similar to PASV mode but makes allowances for use on IPv6. When a client requests a transfer, the server will reply with the port to which the client should connect. The same caveats for servers in PASV mode apply here.

7.8.1.3 FTP Servers and Port Forwards

To ensure the FTP proxy works properly for port forwards

- Public IP must be the WAN interface's IP or a CARP type VIP because the FTP proxy must be able to listen on the public IP, and Proxy ARP and Other type VIPs do not allow this.

- FTP helper must be enabled on the WAN interface where the port forward resides.

- Server must be using port 21.

7.8.1.4 FTP Servers and 1:1 NAT

When hosting a FTP server using 1:1 NAT, you must do three things to ensure the FTP proxy will function, allowing FTP to work properly.

- Use CARP type VIPs

  Because the FTP proxy must be able to listen on the VIP, and Proxy ARP and Other type VIPs do not allow this, you must use CARP VIPs with any 1:1 NAT entries hosting FTP servers.

- Enable the FTP helper on the WAN where the 1:1 entry is configured

  Browse to the interface where the 1:1 external subnet resides, under the Interfaces menu. In a single WAN deployment, this is Interfaces → WAN. Under FTP Helper, ensure Disable the userland FTP proxy application is unchecked.

- Add a port forward entry for TCP 21

  This isn't exactly straight forward, but the way you trigger the FTP helper to listen on a 1:1 NAT IP is by adding a port forward entry using the same internal and external IPs and TCP port 21. This does not actually add the specified NAT configuration, as the system recognizes your 1:1 NAT entry, and simply launches the FTP proxy on that IP. This may become more straight forward in pfSense 2.0, but the existing behavior will be retained for backwards compatibility.

7.8.2   TFTP

Standard TCP and UDP traffic initiate connections to remote hosts using a random source port in the ephemeral port range (range varies by operating system, but falls within 1024-65535), and the destination port of the protocol in use. Replies from server to client reverse that — the source port is the client's destination port, and the destination port is the client's source port. This is how pf associates the reply traffic with connections initiated from inside your network.

TFTP (Trivial File Transfer Protocol) does not follow this, however. The standard defining TFTP, RFC 1350, specifies the reply from the TFTP server to client will be sourced from a pseudo-random port number. Your TFTP client may choose a source port of 10325 (as an example) and use the destination port for TFTP, port 69. The server for other protocols would then send the reply using source port 69 and destination port 10325. Since TFTP instead uses a pseudo-random source port, the reply traffic will not match the state pf has created for this traffic. Hence the replies will be blocked because they appear to be unsolicited traffic from the Internet.

TFTP is not a commonly used protocol across the Internet. The only situation that occasionally comes up where this is an issue is with some IP phones that connect to outside VoIP providers on the Internet using TFTP to pull configuration and other information. Most VoIP providers do not require this.

There is no work around for this limitation at this time — TFTP will not work through pfSense 1.2. pfSense 2.0 includes a TFTP proxy that eliminates this limitation.

7.8.3   PPTP / GRE

The limitations with PPTP in pfSense are caused by limitations in pf's ability to NAT the GRE protocol. As such, the limitations apply to any use of the GRE protocol, however PPTP is the most common use of GRE in most networks today.

The state tracking code in pf for the GRE protocol can only track a single session per public IP per external server. This means if you use PPTP VPN connections, only one internal machine can connect simultaneously to a PPTP server on the Internet. A thousand machines can connect simultaneously to a thousand different PPTP servers, but only one simultaneously to a single server. A single client can also connect to an unlimited number of outside PPTP servers.

The only available work around is to use multiple public IPs on your firewall, one per client via Outbound or 1:1 NAT, or to use multiple public IPs on the external PPTP server. This is not a problem with other types of VPN connections.

Due to the same GRE limitations mentioned above, if you enable the PPTP Server on pfSense, you cannot connect to any PPTP server on the Internet from clients NATed to the WAN IP on pfSense. The work around for this also requires the use of more than one public IP address. You can NAT internal clients to another public IP, and only be subject to the same per-public IP restrictions mentioned above.

Since we largely rely on the functionality of the underlying system, and simply wrap a GUI around that functionality, this is a difficult problem for us to solve. At the time of this writing we are investigating potential solutions for this problem in pfSense 2.0, but do not yet have a solution.

7.8.4   Online Games

Games typically are NAT friendly aside from a couple caveats. This section refers to PC games with online capabilities as well as console gaming systems with online capabilities. This section provides an overview of the experiences of numerous pfSense users. I recommend visiting the Gaming board on the pfSense forum to find more information.

7.8.4.1   Static Port

Some games do not work properly unless you enable static port. If you are having problems with a game, the best thing to try first is enabling static port. See the static port section earlier in this chapter for more information.

7.8.4.2   Multiple players or devices behind one NAT device

Some games have issues where multiple players or devices are behind a single NAT device. These issues appear to be specific to NAT, not pfSense, as users who have tried other firewalls experience the same problems with them as well. Search the Gaming board on the pfSense forum for the game or system you are using and you are likely to find information from others with similar experiences in the past.

7.8.4.3   Overcome NAT issues with UPnP

Many modern game systems support Universal Plug-and-Play (UPnP) to automatically configure any special needs in terms of NAT port forwards and firewall rules. You may find that enabling UPnP on your pfSense system will easily allow games to work with little or no intervention. See Section 21.6 for more information on configuring and using UPnP.

7.9   Troubleshooting

NAT can be a complex animal, and in all but the most basic environments, there are bound to be some issues getting a good working configuration. This section will go over a few common problems and some suggestions on how they might be solved.

7.9.1   Port Forward Troubleshooting

Port forwards in particular can be tricky, since there are many things to go wrong, many of which could be in the client configuration and not pfSense. Most issues encountered by our users have been solved by one or more of the following suggestions.

7.9.1.1   Port forward entry incorrect

Before any other troubleshooting task, ensure that your settings for the port forward are correct. Go over the process in Section 7.2.3 again, and double check that the values are correct. Remember, if you change the NAT IP or the Ports, you will also need to adjust the matching firewall rule. Common things to check for:

- Correct interface (usually WAN, or wherever traffic will be entering the pfSense box).

- Correct NAT IP, which must be reachable from an interface on the pfSense router.

- Correct port range, which must correspond to the service you are trying to forward.

7.9.1.2   Missing or incorrect firewall rule

After checking the port forward settings, double check that the firewall rule has the proper settings. An incorrect firewall rule would also be apparent by viewing the firewall logs (Section 6.10). Remember, that the destination for the firewall rule should be the *internal* IP address of the *target system* and not the address of the interface containing the port forward. See Section 7.4.2 for more details.

7.9.1.3   Firewall is enabled on the target machine

Another thing to consider is that pfSense may be forwarding the port properly, but a firewall on the target machine may be blocking the traffic. If there is a firewall on the target system, you will need to check its logs and settings to confirm whether or not the traffic is being blocked at that point.

7.9.1.4   pfSense is not the target system's gateway

In order for pfSense to properly forward a port for a local system, pfSense must be the default gateway for the target system. If pfSense is not the gateway, the target system will attempt to send replies to port forward traffic out whatever system *is* the gateway, and then one of two things will happen: It will be dropped at that point since there would be no matching connection state on that router — or — it would have NAT applied by that router and then be dropped by the system originating the request since the reply is from a different IP address than the one to which the request was initially sent.

7.9.1.5 Target machine is not listening on the forwarded port

If, when the connection is tested, the request is rejected instead of timing out, in all likelihood pfSense is forwarding the connection properly and the connection is rejected by the target system. This can happen when the target system has no service listening on the port in question, or if the port being forwarded does not match the port on which the target system is listening.

For example, if the target system is supposed to be listening for SSH connections, but the port forward was entered for port 23 instead of 22, the request would most likely be rejected. You can usually tell the difference by trying to connect to the port in question using **telnet**. A message such as **Connection refused** indicates something, frequently the inside host, is actively refusing the connection.

7.9.1.6 ISP is blocking the port you are trying to forward

In some cases, ISPs will filter incoming traffic to well-known ports. Check your ISP's Terms of Service (ToS), and see if there is a clause about running servers. Such restrictions are more common on residential connections than commercial connections. When in doubt, a call to the ISP may clear the matter up.

If ports are being filtered by your ISP, you may need to move your services to a different port in order to work around the filtering. For example, if your ISP disallows servers on port 80, try 8080 or 8888.

Before attempting to work around a filter, consult your ISP's ToS to ensure you are not violating their rules.

7.9.1.7 Testing from inside your network instead of outside

By default, port forwards will only work when connections are made from outside of your network. This is a very common mistake when testing port forwards.

If you require port forwards to work internally, see Section 7.5. However, Split DNS (Section 7.5.2) is a more proper and elegant solution to this problem without needing to rely on NAT reflection or port forwards, and it would be worth your time to implement that instead.

7.9.1.8 Incorrect or missing Virtual IP address

When using IP addresses that are not the actual IP addresses assigned to an interface, you must use Virtual IPs (VIPs, see Section 6.8). If a port forward on an alternate IP address is not working, you may need to switch to a different type of VIP. For example, you may need to use a Proxy ARP type instead of an "Other" type VIP.

When testing, also make sure that you are connecting to the proper VIP.

7.9.1.9 pfSense is not the border/edge router

In some scenarios, pfSense is an internal router, and there are other routers between it and the Internet also performing NAT. In such a case, a port forward would need to be entered on the edge router forwarding the port to pfSense, which will then use another port forward to get it to the local system.

7.9.1.10   Further testing needed

If none of these solutions helped you obtain a working port forward, consult Chapter 25 for information on using packet captures to diagnose port forwarding issues.

7.9.2   NAT Reflection Troubleshooting

NAT Reflection (Section 7.5) is more of a kludge than a solution, and as such it is prone to not work as expected. We cannot recommend enough that you use Split DNS instead (see Section 7.5.2). If NAT Reflection is not working properly, ensure that it was enabled the right way, and make sure you are not forwarding a large range of ports.

NAT Reflection rules are also duplicated for each interface present in the system, so if you have a lot of port forwards and interfaces, the number of reflectors can easily surpass the limits of the system. If this happens, an entry is printed in the system logs.

7.9.2.1   Web Access is Broken with NAT Reflection Enabled

If you have an improperly specified NAT Port Forward, it can cause problems when NAT Reflection is enabled. The most common way this problem arises is when you have a local web server, and port 80 is forwarded there with an improperly specified External Address.

If NAT Reflection is enabled and the External Address is set to **any**, any connection you make comes up as your own web site. To fix this, edit your NAT Port Forward for the offending port, and change External Address to **Interface Address** instead.

If you really require an external address of **any**, then NAT Reflection will not work for you, and you'll need to employ Split DNS instead.

7.9.3   Outbound NAT Troubleshooting

When you have manual outbound NAT enabled, and there are multiple local subnets, an outbound NAT entry will be needed for each. This applies especially if you intend to have traffic exit with NAT after coming into the pfSense router via a VPN connection such as PPTP or OpenVPN.

One indication of a missing outbound NAT rule would be seeing packets leave the WAN interface with a source address of a private network. See Chapter 25 for more details on obtaining and interpreting packet captures.

Chapter 8

Routing

One of the primary functions of a firewall is routing traffic, in addition to filtering and performing NAT. This chapter covers several routing related topics, including static routes, routing protocols, routing of public IPs, and displaying routing information.

8.1   Static Routes

Static routes are used when you have hosts or networks reachable via a router other than your default gateway. Your firewall or router knows about the networks directly attached to it, and reaches all other networks as directed by its routing table. In networks where you have an internal router connecting additional internal subnets, you must define a static route for that network to be reachable.

8.1.1   Example static route

Figure 8.1 illustrates a scenario where a static route is required.

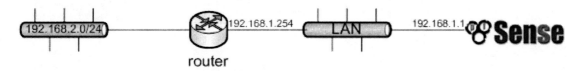

Figure 8.1: Static Route

Because the 192.168.2.0/24 network in Figure 8.1 is not on a directly connected interface of pfSense, you need a static route so it knows how to reach that network. Figure 8.2 shows the appropriate static route for the above diagram.

System: Static Routes: Edit route

Interface	LAN ▼ Choose which interface this route applies to.
Destination network	192.168.2.0 / 24 ▼ Destination network for this static route
Gateway	192.168.1.254 Gateway to be used to reach the destination network
Description	 You may enter a description here for your reference (not parsed).

Figure 8.2: Static route configuration

The Interface box defines the interface where the specified Gateway is reachable. The Destination network specifies the subnet reachable via this route. Gateway specifies the IP address of the router where this network is reachable. This must be an IP address within the IP subnet of the Interface chosen. Firewall rule adjustments may also be required. The default LAN rule only allows traffic sourced from the LAN subnet, so if you maintained that rule, you will have to open up the source network to also include the networks reachable via static routes on LAN. The next section describes a common scenario with static routes that you also should review.

8.1.2 Bypass Firewall Rules for Traffic on Same Interface

In many situations when using static routes you end up with asymmetric routing. This means the traffic in one direction will take a different path from the traffic in the opposite direction. Take Figure 8.3 for example.

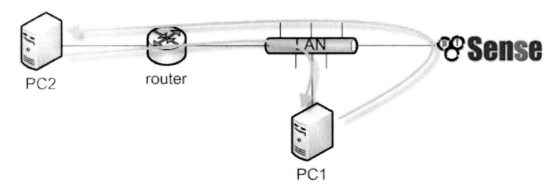

Figure 8.3: Asymmetric routing

Traffic from PC1 to PC2 will go through pfSense since it is PC1's default gateway, but traffic in the opposite direction will go directly from the router to PC1. Since pfSense is a stateful firewall, it must see all of the connection to be able to filter traffic properly. With asymmetric routing like this, any stateful firewall will end up dropping legit traffic because it cannot properly keep state without seeing traffic in both directions. Always check the Bypass firewall rules for traffic on the same interface box on the System → Advanced page in asymmetric routing scenarios to prevent legitimate traffic from being dropped. This adds firewall rules allowing all traffic between networks defined in static routes using PF's no state option. Alternatively, you can add firewall rules yourself specifying **none** as the State Type, matching traffic between the local and remote subnets, but that is usually not recommended due to the complexity it can introduce and the increased likelihood of mistakes. Should you need to filter traffic between statically routed subnets, it must be done on the router and not the firewall since the firewall is not in a position on the network where it can effectively control that traffic.

8.1.3 ICMP Redirects

When a device sends a packet to its default gateway, and the gateway knows the sender can reach the destination network via a more direct route, it will send an ICMP redirect message in response and forward the packet as configured. The ICMP redirect causes a route for that destination to be added to the routing table of the sending device, and the device will subsequently use that more direct route to reach that network. This will not work if your OS is configured to not permit ICMP redirects, which is typically not the case by default.

ICMP redirects are common when you have a static route pointing to a router on the same interface as client PCs and other network devices. The asymmetric routing diagram from the previous section is an example of this.

ICMP redirects have mostly undeservedly gotten a bad reputation from some in the security community because they allow modification of a system's routing table. However they are not the risk that some imply, as to be accepted, the ICMP redirect message must include the first 8 bytes of the original datagram's data. A host in a position to see that data and hence be able to successfully forge illicit ICMP redirects is in a position to accomplish the same end result in multiple other ways.

8.2 Routing Public IPs

This section covers the routing of public IPs, where you have a public IP subnet assigned to an internal interface, and single firewall deployments. If you are using CARP, see Section 20.7.

8.2.1 IP Assignments

You need at least two public IP subnets assigned to you by your ISP. One is for the WAN of your firewall, and one is for the inside interface. This is commonly a /30 subnet for the WAN, with a second subnet assigned for the internal interface. This example will use a /30 on WAN as shown in Table 8.1 and a /29 public subnet on an internal OPT interface as shown in Table 8.2.

| 11.50.75.64/30 ||
IP Address	Assigned To
11.50.75.65	ISP router (pfSense's default gateway IP)
11.50.75.66	pfSense WAN interface IP

Table 8.1: WAN IP Block

| 192.0.2.128/29 ||
IP Address	Assigned To
192.0.2.129	pfSense OPT interface
192.0.2.130	
192.0.2.131	
192.0.2.132	Internal hosts
192.0.2.133	
192.0.2.134	

Table 8.2: Inside IP Block

8.2.2   Interface Configuration

First configure the WAN and OPT interfaces. The LAN interface can also be used for public IPs if you desire. In this example, LAN is a private IP subnet and OPT1 is the public IP subnet.

8.2.2.1   Configure WAN

Add the IP address and gateway accordingly. Figure 8.4 shows the WAN configured as shown in Table 8.1.

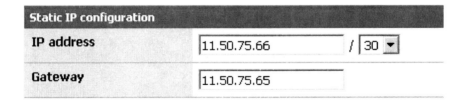

Figure 8.4: WAN IP and gateway configuration

8.2.2.2   Configure OPT1

Now enable OPT1, optionally change its name, and configure the IP address and mask. Figure 8.5 shows OPT1 configured as shown in Table 8.2.

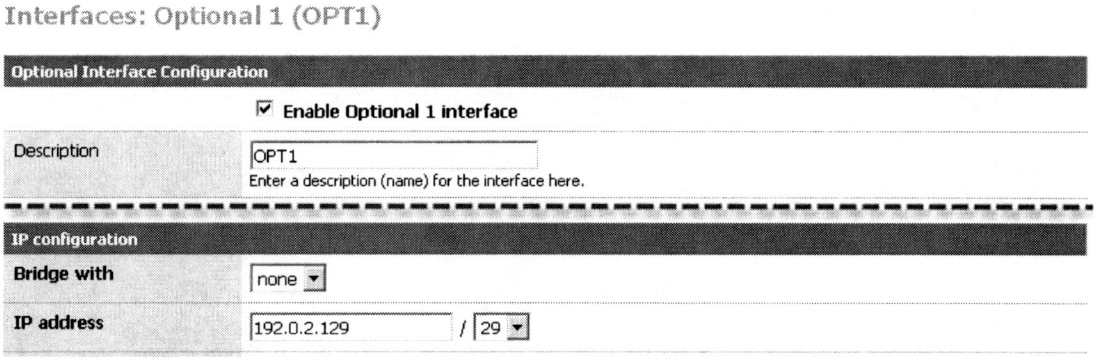

Interfaces: Optional 1 (OPT1)

Optional Interface Configuration

☑ **Enable Optional 1 interface**

Description   OPT1

Enter a description (name) for the interface here.

IP configuration

Bridge with   none ▾

IP address   192.0.2.129 / 29 ▾

Figure 8.5: Routing OPT1 configuration

8.2.3   NAT Configuration

The default of translating internal traffic to the WAN IP must be overridden when using public IPs on an internal interface. Browse to Firewall → NAT, and click the Outbound tab. Select Manual Outbound NAT rule generation and click Save. This will generate a default rule translating all traffic from the LAN subnet leaving the WAN interface to the WAN IP, the default behavior of pfSense. If your LAN contains a private subnet as in this example, this is the exact desired configuration. Traffic sourced from the OPT1 network's 192.0.2.128/29 is not translated because the source is limited to 192.168.1.0/24. This configuration is shown in Figure 8.6. If you use public IPs on your LAN, delete this automatically added entry. Then click Apply Changes.

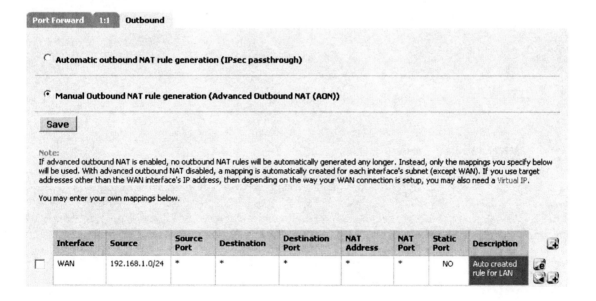

Figure 8.6: Outbound NAT configuration

8.2.4   Firewall Rule Configuration

The NAT and IP configuration is now complete. Firewall rules will need to be added to permit outbound and inbound traffic. Figure 8.7 shows a DMZ-like configuration, where all traffic destined for the LAN subnet is rejected, DNS and pings to the OPT1 interface IP are permitted, and HTTP is allowed outbound.

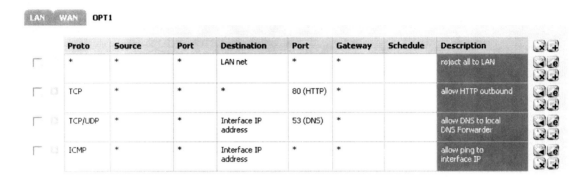

Figure 8.7: OPT1 firewall rules

To allow traffic from the Internet to the public IPs on an internal interface, you need to add rules on the WAN using the public IPs as the destination. Figure 8.8 shows a rule that allows HTTP to 192.0.2.130, one of the public IPs on the internal interface as shown in Table 8.2.

Figure 8.8: WAN firewall rules

After configuring the firewall rules as desired, your setup is complete.

8.3   Routing Protocols

At the time of this writing, two routing protocols are supported with pfSense, RIP (Routing Information Protocol) and BGP (Border Gateway Protocol). OSPF (Open Shortest Path First) will likely be added as a package at some point. This section is light on details, and presumes understanding of the routing protocols as a prerequisite. An in depth discussion of routing protocols is outside the scope of this book.

8.3.1   RIP

RIP can be configured under Services → RIP. To use it:

1. Check the Enable RIP box

2. Choose the interfaces RIP will listen and send routing updates on

3. Select your RIP version

4. When using RIPv2, enter a RIPv2 password if one is used on your network.

5. Click Save

RIP will immediately launch and start sending and receiving routing updates on the specified interfaces.

8.3.2 BGP

A BGP package using OpenBSD's OpenBGPD is available. To install it, visit System → Packages, and click the plus to the right of OpenBGPD. Click OK to install the package. Then click on the pfSense logo at the top left, to take you to the home page and refresh the menus. You will find OpenBGPD under the Services menu.

BGP is a complex beast, and describing it in detail is outside the scope of this book. Configuration of pfSense's OpenBGPD is straight forward if you understand BGP. During development of this package, we relied on *O'Reilly's BGP* book and recommend it for anyone looking to deploy BGP.

8.4 Route Troubleshooting

When diagnosing traffic flow issues, one of the first thing to check is the routes known to pfSense.

8.4.1 Viewing Routes

There are two ways to view the routes: Via the WebGUI, and via the command line.

To view the routes in the WebGUI, visit Diagnostics → Routes and you will see the output like that shown in Figure 8.9.

IPv4							
Destination	Gateway	Flags	Refs	Use	Mtu	Netif	Expire
default	10.0.2.2	UGS	0	53	1500	le0	
10.0.2.0/24	link#1	UC	0	0	1500	le0	
10.0.2.2	52:54:00:12:35:02	UHLW	2	30	1500	le0	850
10.0.2.15	127.0.0.1	UGHS	0	0	16384	lo0	
127.0.0.1	127.0.0.1	UH	1	0	16384	lo0	
192.168.56.0/24	link#2	UC	0	0	1500	le1	
192.168.56.101	08:00:27:00:d4:84	UHLW	1	521	1500	le1	1160

Figure 8.9: Route Display

The output from the command line is similar to that seen in the WebGUI:

```
# netstat -rn
Routing tables

Internet:
Destination        Gateway              Flags  Refs    Use  Netif Expire
default            10.0.2.2             UGS       0     53   le0
10.0.2.0/24        link#1               UC        0      0   le0
10.0.2.2           52:54:00:12:35:02    UHLW      2     35   le0    796
10.0.2.15          127.0.0.1            UGHS      0      0   lo0
127.0.0.1          127.0.0.1            UH        1      0   lo0
192.168.56.0/24    link#2               UC        0      0   le1
192.168.56.101     08:00:27:00:d4:84    UHLW      1    590   le1   1197
```

The columns shown on these screens indicate various properties of the routes, and are explained next.

8.4.1.1   Destination

The destination host or network. The default route for the system is simply listed as "default". Otherwise, hosts are listed as by IP address, and networks are listed with an IP address and CIDR subnet mask.

8.4.1.2   Gateway

A gateway is the router by which packets going to a specific destination need to be sent. If this column shows a link, such as link#1, then that network is directly reachable by that interface and no special routing is necessary. If a host is visible with a MAC address, then it is a locally reachable host with an entry in the ARP table, and packets are sent there directly.

8.4.1.3   Flags

There are quite a few flags, all of which are covered in the FreeBSD man page for netstat(1), reproduced in Table 8.3 with some modifications.

For example, a route flagged as UGS is a usable route, packets are sent via the gateway listed, and it is a static route.

8.4.1.4   Refs

This column counts the current number of active uses of a given route.

8.4.1.5   Use

This counter is the total number of packets sent via this route. This is helpful for determining if a route is actually being used, as it will continually increment as packets flow if this route was used.

Letter	Flag	Meaning
1	RTF_PROTO1	Protocol specific routing flag #1
2	RTF_PROTO2	Protocol specific routing flag #2
3	RTF_PROTO3	Protocol specific routing flag #3
B	RTF_BLACKHOLE	Discard packets during updates
b	RTF_BROADCAST	Represents a broadcast address
C	RTF_CLONING	Generate new routes on use
c	RTF_PRCLONING	Protocol-specified generate new routes on use
D	RTF_DYNAMIC	Created dynamically by redirect
G	RTF_GATEWAY	Destination requires forwarding by intermediary
H	RTF_HOST	Host entry (net otherwise)
L	RTF_LLINFO	Valid protocol to link address translation
M	RTF_MODIFIED	Modified dynamically (by redirect)
R	RTF_REJECT	Host or net unreachable
S	RTF_STATIC	Manually added
U	RTF_UP	Route usable
W	RTF_WASCLONED	Route was generated as a result of cloning
X	RTF_XRESOLVE	External daemon translates proto to link address

Table 8.3: Route Table Flags and Meanings

8.4.1.6 Netif

The network interface used for this route.

8.4.1.7 Expire

For dynamic entries, this field shows how long until this route expires if it is not used again.

8.4.2 Using traceroute

Traceroute is a useful tool for testing and verifying routes and multi-WAN functionality, among other uses. It will allow you to view each "hop" along a packet's path as it travels from one end to the other, along with the latency encountered in reaching that intermediate point. On pfSense, you can perform a traceroute by going to Diagnostics → Traceroute, or by using **traceroute** at the command line. From clients running Windows, the program is available under the name **tracert**.

Every IP packet contains a time-to-live (TTL) value. When a router passes a packet, it decrements the TTL by one. When a router receives a packet with a TTL of 1 and the destination is not a locally attached network, the router returns an ICMP error message — Time-to-live exceeded — and drops the packet. This is to limit the impact of routing loops, which otherwise would cause each packet to loop indefinitely.

Traceroute uses this TTL to its advantage to map the path to a specific network destination. It starts by sending the first packet with a TTL of 1. The first router (usually the system's default gateway) will send back the ICMP time-to-live exceeded error. The time between sending the packet and receiving the ICMP error is the time displayed, listed along with the IP that sent the error and its reverse DNS, if any. After sending three packets with a TTL of 1 and displaying their response times, it will increment the TTL to 2 and send three more packets, noting the same information for the second hop. It keeps incrementing the TTL until it reaches the specified destination, or exceeds the maximum number of hops.

Traceroute functions slightly differently on Windows and Unix-like operating systems (BSD, Linux, Mac OS X, Unix, etc.). Windows uses ICMP echo request packets (pings) while Unix-like systems use UDP packets. ICMP and UDP are layer 4 protocols, and traceroute is done at layer 3, so the protocol used is largely irrelevant except when considering your policy routing configuration. Traceroute from Windows clients will be policy routed based on which rule permits ICMP echo requests, while Unix-like clients will be routed by the rule matching the UDP ports in use.

In this example, we will try to find the route to www.google.com:

```
# traceroute www.google.com
traceroute: Warning: www.google.com has multiple addresses; using  ↵
    74.125.95.99
traceroute to www.l.google.com (74.125.95.99), 64 hops max, 40 byte  ↵
    packets
 1   core (172.17.23.1)  1.450 ms  1.901 ms  2.213 ms
 2   172.17.25.21 (172.17.25.21)  4.852 ms  3.698 ms  3.120 ms
 3   bb1-g4-0-2.ipltin.ameritech.net (151.164.42.156)  3.275 ms  3.210 ms  ↵
       3.215 ms
 4   151.164.93.49 (151.164.93.49)  8.791 ms  8.593 ms  8.891 ms
 5   74.125.48.117 (74.125.48.117)  8.460 ms  39.941 ms  8.551 ms
 6   209.85.254.120 (209.85.254.120)  10.376 ms  8.904 ms  8.765 ms
 7   209.85.241.22 (209.85.241.22)  19.479 ms  20.058 ms  19.550 ms
 8   209.85.241.29 (209.85.241.29)  20.547 ms  19.761 ms
     209.85.241.27 (209.85.241.27)  20.131 ms
 9   209.85.240.49 (209.85.240.49)  30.184 ms
     72.14.239.189 (72.14.239.189)  21.337 ms  21.756 ms
10   iw-in-f99.google.com (74.125.95.99)  19.793 ms  19.665 ms  20.603 ms
```

As you can see, it took 10 hops to get there, and the latency generally increases with each hop.

8.4.3 Routes and VPNs

Depending on the VPN being used, you may or may not see a route showing in the table for the far side. IPsec does not use the routing table, it is instead handled internally in the kernel using the IPsec SPD. Static routes will never cause traffic to be directed across an IPsec connection. OpenVPN uses the system routing table and as such you will see entries for networks reachable via an OpenVPN tunnel, as in the following example:

```
# netstat -rn
Routing tables

Internet:
Destination        Gateway         Flags   Refs      Use  Netif Expire
default            10.34.29.1      UGS        0 19693837   ng0
```

10.34.29.1	72.69.77.6	UH	1	205590	ng0
72.69.77.6	lo0	UHS	0	0	lo0
172.17.212.0/22	192.168.100.1	UGS	0	617	tun0
127.0.0.1	127.0.0.1	UH	0	0	lo0
192.168.10.0/24	link#2	UC	0	0	em0
192.168.100.1	192.168.100.2	UH	3	0	tun0
192.168.130.0/24	192.168.100.1	UGS	0	144143	tun0
192.168.140.0/24	192.168.100.1	UGS	0	0	tun0

The OpenVPN interface is 192.168.100.2, with a gateway of 192.168.100.1 and the interface is tun0. There are three networks with OpenVPN pushed routes in that example: 192.168.130.0/24, 192.168.140.0/24, and 172.17.212.0/22.

With IPsec, **traceroute** is not as useful as with routed setups like OpenVPN, because the IPsec tunnel itself does not have IPs. When running **traceroute** to a destination across IPsec, you will see a timeout for the hop that is the IPsec tunnel for this reason.

Chapter 9

Bridging

Normally each interface on pfSense represents its own broadcast domain with a unique IP subnet, acting the same as separate switches. In some circumstances it is desirable or necessary to combine multiple interfaces onto a single broadcast domain, where two ports on the firewall will act as if they are on the same switch, except traffic between the interfaces can be controlled with firewall rules. This is commonly referred to as a transparent firewall.

9.1   Bridging and Layer 2 Loops

When bridging, you need to be careful to avoid layer 2 loops, or have a switch configuration in place that handles them as you desire. A layer 2 loop is when you create the same effect as if you plugged both ends of a patch cable into the same switch. If you have a pfSense install with two interfaces, bridge those interfaces together, then plug both interfaces into the same switch you have created a layer 2 loop. Connecting two patch cables between two switches also does this. Managed switches employ Spanning Tree Protocol (STP) to handle situations like this, because it is often desirable to have multiple links between switches, and you don't want your network to be exposed to complete meltdown by someone plugging one network port into another network port. STP is not enabled by default on all managed switches though, and is almost never available with unmanaged switches. Without STP, the result of a layer 2 loop is frames on the network will circle endlessly and the network will completely cease to function until the loop is removed.

In a nutshell — bridging has the potential to completely melt down the network you are plugging into if you don't watch what you're plugging in where.

9.2   Bridging and firewalling

Filtering with bridged interfaces functions no differently than with routed interfaces. Firewall rules are applied on each member interface of the bridge on an inbound basis. Those who have been using pfSense for quite some time will recall an Enable filtering bridge check box on the System → Advanced page. There is outdated information in numerous places referencing this check box. It was inherited

from m0n0wall, which did bridging in a different way. Since pfSense uses a different bridging methodology this box is unnecessary, and with the way the bridging methodology in newer FreeBSD versions
works it is impossible to have a non-filtering bridge unless you disable pf entirely.

9.3   Bridging two internal networks

You can bridge two internal interfaces to combine them on the same broadcast domain and enable
filtering on traffic between the two interfaces. This is commonly done with wireless interfaces configured as an access point, to connect the wired and wireless segments on the same broadcast domain.
Occasionally a firewall with a LAN and OPT interface will be used in lieu of a switch in networks
where only two internal systems are needed. You may encounter scenarios where two interfaces of the
firewall need to be on the same broadcast domain for another reason.

Note

There are additional requirements and restrictions when bridging wireless interfaces because of the
way 802.11 functions. See Section 18.3 for more information.

9.3.1   DHCP and Internal Bridges

If you bridge one internal network to another, two things need to be done. First, ensure that DHCP is
only running on the main interface (the one with the IP address) and not the one being bridged. Second,
you will need an additional firewall rule at the top of your rules on this OPT interface to allow DHCP
traffic.

Normally, when creating a rule to allow traffic on an interface, the source is specified similar to "OPT1
Subnet", so that only traffic from that subnet is allowed out of that segment. With DHCP, that is not
enough. Because a client does not yet have an IP address, a DHCP request is performed as a broadcast.
To accommodate these requests, you must create a rule on the bridged interface with the Protocol set
to **UDP**, the Source is **0.0.0.0**, source port **68**, Destination **255.255.255.255**, destination port
67. Add a Description stating this will **Allow DHCP**, then click Save and Apply Changes. You will
end up with a rule that looks like Figure 9.1.

		Proto	Source	Port	Destination	Port	Gateway	Schedule	Description		
		UDP	0.0.0.0	68	255.255.255.255	67	*		Allow DHCP		
		*	LAN net	*	*	*	*		Default LAN net -> Any		

Figure 9.1: Firewall Rule to Allow DHCP

After adding that rule, clients in the bridged segment should be able to successfully make requests to
the DHCP daemon listening on the interface to which it is bridged.

9.4   Bridging OPT to WAN

Bridging an OPT interface with WAN allows you to use public IPs on your internal network that have a gateway IP residing on your WAN network. One situation where this is common is for DHCP assigned public IP addresses. You can use pfSense to protect systems that obtain public IPs directly from your ISP's DHCP server by using a bridged interface. This is also useful in scenarios with a single public IP block where you need public IPs directly assigned to hosts, as described in Section 6.7.1.2.1.

9.5   Bridging interoperability

Since bridged interfaces behave differently than normal interfaces in some regards, there are a few things that are incompatible with bridging, and others where additional considerations must be made to accommodate bridging. This section covers features that work differently with bridging than with non-bridged interfaces.

9.5.1   Captive portal

Captive portal (Chapter 19) is not compatible with bridging because it requires an IP on the interface being bridged, used to serve the portal contents. Bridged interfaces do not have an IP assigned.

9.5.2   CARP

CARP (Chapter 20) is not compatible with bridging at this time — but, there are some manual hacks. Using CARP with networks that involve bridging is not generally recommended, but this kind of setup has worked for a number of individuals. Great care must be taken to handle layer 2 loops, which are unavoidable in a CARP+Bridge scenario. When two network segments are bridged, they are in effect merged into one larger network, as discussed earlier in this chapter. When CARP is added into the mix, that means there will be two paths between the switches for each respective interface, creating a loop.

Managed switches can handle this with Spanning Tree Protocol (STP) but unmanaged switches have no defenses against looping. Left unchecked, a loop can bring a network to its knees and make it impossible to pass any traffic. If STP is not available, there are two other approaches for handling a bridge in this scenario, similar but not as elegant as STP. Both of these methods require changing files on the pfSense system, and would not survive a backup/restore without special consideration. These techniques are a **cron** script to manage the bridge, or a **devd** hook to manage the bridge. Both of these methods are described in a sticky post on the CARP/VIP forum.[1]

9.5.2.1   Configure your primary and backup firewalls

Configure your primary and backup firewalls as you would with any CARP deployment, as covered in Chapter 20. Configure the bridge interface on both the primary and secondary, using the same interface description. If the bridge is OPT1 on the primary, make it OPT1 on the secondary. Do not plug in both

---

[1] http://forum.pfsense.org/index.php/topic,4984.0.html

bridges simultaneously until the end. You will need to be able to access the pfSense WebGUI from a firewall interface other than the bridge interface. You will need to perform all of these steps for both your primary and secondary firewalls.

9.5.2.2 Configuring STP

Even with STP active, some configuration will be needed on the switch in order to nudge STP into making the right choice about which port should be kept open and which should be blocked. Otherwise you could end up with a situation where the traffic is actually flowing through your backup router's bridge instead of the primary router, leading to unpredictable behavior. Port blocking in this situation is controlled by setting port priorities and path costs.

On a Cisco switch, the configuration would look something like this:

```
interface FastEthernet0/1
  description Firewall - Primary - DMZ Port
  switchport access vlan 20
  spanning-tree vlan 20 port-priority 64
  no cdp enable

interface FastEthernet0/2
  description Firewall - Backup - DMZ Port
  switchport access vlan 20
  spanning-tree vlan 20 cost 500
  no cdp enable
```

By giving the primary's port a lower than normal priority (64 vs. the default 128), it will be more likely to be used, especially given the higher path cost (500 vs. the default 19) of the other port. These values can be checked as follows (on the switch):

```
# show spanning-tree interface FastEthernet0/1
Interface FastEthernet0/1 (port 13) in Spanning tree 20 is FORWARDING
Port path cost 19, Port priority 64
Designated root has priority 32768, address 0002.4b6e.xxxx
Designated bridge has priority 32768, address 0002.b324.xxxx
Designated port is 3, path cost 131
Timers: message age 6, forward delay 0, hold 0
BPDU: sent 18411032, received 16199798

# show spanning-tree interface FastEthernet0/2
Interface FastEthernet0/2 (port 14) in Spanning tree 20 is BLOCKING
Port path cost 500, Port priority 128
Designated root has priority 32768, address 0002.4b6e.xxxx
Designated bridge has priority 32768, address 0002.b324.xxxx
Designated port is 4, path cost 131
Timers: message age 6, forward delay 0, hold 0
BPDU: sent 434174, received 15750118
```

As you can see, the primary system's switch port is forwarding is it should be, and the backup port is blocking. If traffic stops flowing through the primary port, the backup should switch to a forwarding state.

Switches from other vendors support similar functionality. Refer to your switch's documentation for information on STP configuration.

In pfSense 2.0, STP can be configured and handled directly on a bridged interface.

9.5.2.3 CARP check script for cron

In this method, a script runs from **cron** every minute and checks to see if the system is MASTER or BACKUP in the CARP cluster. If the system is MASTER, the bridge is brought up, if the system is BACKUP, the bridge is taken down. It prevents the loop by only having one bridge active at any given time, but as you can probably tell by how often the **cron** script runs, there may be as much as a minute of downtime for bridged systems before the script detects the switch and activates the backup bridge.

9.5.2.3.1 Add the Script

First you need to add a script to check your CARP status and modify your bridge status accordingly. The following provides an example that can be used. It is also available for download.

```
#!/bin/sh
#
# CARP check script for bridging
#
# from eblevins on the forum
#
if ifconfig carp0 | grep BACKUP > /dev/null 2>&1 ; then
        /sbin/ifconfig bridge0 down
else
        /sbin/ifconfig bridge0 up
fi
```

Copy that script somewhere, for example, `/usr/bin/bridgecheck.sh`. The following command will download this file from files.pfsense.org and save it as `/usr/bin/bridgecheck.sh`.

```
# fetch -o /usr/bin/bridgecheck.sh \
    http://files.pfsense.org/misc/bridgecheck.sh
```

Then you need to make the script executable by running the following command.

```
# chmod +x /usr/bin/bridgecheck.sh
```

9.5.2.3.2 Schedule the script

Now you need to schedule the script to run. Download a backup of your configuration on the Diagnostics → Backup/Restore screen. Open the configuration in a text editor, and search for **<cron>**. You will find the section of the configuration containing all the scheduled tasks that **cron** runs.

```
<cron>
  <item>
    <minute>0</minute>
    <hour>*</hour>
    <mday>*</mday>
    <month>*</month>
    <wday>*</wday>
    <who>root</who>
    <command>/usr/bin/nice -n20 newsyslog</command>
  </item>
  <item>
    <minute>1,31</minute>
    <hour>0-5</hour>
    <mday>*</mday>
    <month>*</month>
    <wday>*</wday>
    <who>root</who>
    <command>/usr/bin/nice -n20 adjkerntz -a</command>
  </item>
```

Add **bridgecheck.sh** as a **cron** entry. Adding the following will run the script every minute.

```
<item>
  <minute>*/1</minute>
  <hour>*</hour>
  <mday>*</mday>
  <month>*</month>
  <wday>*</wday>
  <who>root</who>
  <command>/usr/bin/bridgecheck.sh</command>
</item>
```

Make sure to change both the primary and the secondary.

9.5.2.3.3   Disable bridge at boot

You will want to add a command to the configuration to down the bridge at boot time. This will help prevent layer 2 loops, as **bridgecheck.sh** will bring the CARP master's bridge online within 1 minute. Above the line that reads `</system>`, add the following line.

`<shellcmd>/sbin/ifconfig bridge0 down</shellcmd>`

Save your changes to both configuration files. Now restore the modified configurations to both the primary and the secondary. The firewalls will reboot after restoring the configuration, and when they boot back up they should be fully functional.

9.5.2.4   devd Hooks

This solution is only possible in pfSense 1.2.3 or later, and involves using **devd** to catch the actual CARP state transition as it happens. Edit `/etc/devd.conf` on the backup and master, and add these lines:

```
notify 100 {
          match "system"          "IFNET";
          match "type"            "LINK_UP";
          match "subsystem"   "carp";
          action "/usr/local/bin/carpup";
};
notify 100 {
          match "system"          "IFNET";
          match "type"            "LINK_DOWN";
          match "subsystem"   "carp";
          action "/usr/local/bin/carpdown";
};
```

Then create two new files: `/usr/local/bin/carpup`

```
#!/bin/sh
/sbin/ifconfig bridge0 up
```

And: `/usr/local/bin/carpdown`

```
#!/bin/sh
/sbin/ifconfig bridge0 down
```

Then make those scripts executable:

```
# chmod a+x /usr/local/bin/carpup
# chmod a+x /usr/local/bin/carpdown
```

That will automatically bring the bridge up and down any time a CARP state change is detected.

9.5.2.5 Troubleshooting failover bridging

If something is not working as intended, check the Status → Interfaces page on both systems to review the `bridge0` interface, and the CARP status page to verify CARP's master or backup status. You can run **bridgecheck.sh** from the command line, as well as checking interface status using **ifconfig**. An understanding of the underlying FreeBSD OS may be necessary to successfully troubleshoot any problems with this type of deployment.

Many problems with CARP and Bridging will arise from switch loops and STP issues. Go over Section 9.5.2 again, and also check your switch configuration to see the port status for your bridged interfaces. If your ports are blocking when they should be forwarding, you will probably need to adjust STP settings or employ one of the alternate techniques to shut down a backup bridge.

9.5.3 Multi-WAN

Bridging by its nature is incompatible with multi-WAN in many of its uses. When using bridging, commonly something other than pfSense will be the default gateway for the hosts on the bridged interface, and that router is the only thing that can direct traffic from those hosts. This doesn't prevent you from using multi-WAN with other interfaces on the same firewall that are not bridged, it only impacts the hosts on bridged interfaces where they use something other than pfSense as their default gateway. If you bridge multiple internal interfaces together and pfSense is the default gateway for your hosts on a bridged interface, then you can use multi-WAN the same as with non-bridged interfaces.

Chapter 10

Virtual LANs (VLANs)

VLANs provide a means of segmenting a single switch into multiple broadcast domains, allowing a single switch to function the same as multiple switches. This is commonly used for network segmentation in the same way that multiple switches could be used, to place hosts on a specific segment as configured on the switch. Where trunking is employed between switches, devices on the same segment need not reside on the same switch. The concepts, terminology and configuration of VLANs are all covered in this chapter.

10.1 Requirements

There are two requirements, both of which must be met to deploy VLANs.

1. 802.1Q VLAN capable switch — every decent managed switch manufactured since about the year 2000 supports 802.1Q VLAN trunking. You cannot use VLANs with an unmanaged switch.

2. Network adapter capable of VLAN tagging — you will need a NIC that supports hardware VLAN tagging or has long frame support. Because each frame has a 4 byte 802.1Q tag added in the header, the frame size can be up to 1522 bytes. A NIC supporting hardware VLAN tagging or long frames is required because other adapters will not function with frames larger than the normal 1518 byte maximum with 1500 MTU Ethernet. This will cause large frames to be dropped, which causes performance problems and connection stalling.

Note

Just because an adapter is listed as having long frame support does not guarantee your NIC's specific implementation of that chipset properly supports long frames. Realtek `rl(4)` NICs are the biggest offenders. Many will work fine, but some do not properly support long frames, and some will not accept 802.1Q tagged frames at all. If you encounter problems using one of the NICs listed under long frame support, trying an interface with VLAN hardware tagging support is recommended. We are not aware of any similar problems with NICs listed under VLAN hardware support.

Ethernet interfaces with VLAN hardware support:

bce(4), bge(4), cxgb(4), em(4), ixgb(4), msk(4), nge(4), re(4), stge(4), ti(4), txp(4), vge(4).

Ethernet interfaces with long frame support:

bfe(4), dc(4), fxp(4), gem(4), hme(4), le(4), nfe(4), nve(4), rl(4), sis(4), sk(4), ste(4), tl(4), tx(4), vr(4), xl(4)

10.2 Terminology

This section covers the terminology you will need to understand to successfully deploy VLANs.

10.2.1 Trunking

Trunking refers to a means of carrying multiple VLANs on the same switch port. The frames leaving a trunk port are marked with an 802.1Q tag in the header, enabling the connected device to differentiate between multiple VLANs. Trunk ports are used to connect multiple switches, and for connecting any devices that are capable of 802.1Q tagging and require access to multiple VLANs. This is commonly limited to only the router providing connectivity between the VLANs, in this case, pfSense, as well as any connections to other switches containing multiple VLANs.

10.2.2 VLAN ID

Each VLAN has an ID associated with it that is used for identification of tagged traffic. This is a number between 1 and 4094. The default VLAN on switches is VLAN 1, and this VLAN should not be used when deploying VLAN trunking. This is discussed further in Section 10.3. Aside from avoiding the use of VLAN 1, you can choose which VLAN numbers you wish to use. Some will start with VLAN 2 and increment by one until the required number of VLANs is reached. Another common practice is using the third octet in the IP subnet of the VLAN as the VLAN ID. For example, if you use 10.0.10.0/24, 10.0.20.0/24 and 10.0.30.0/24, it is logical to use VLANs 10, 20, and 30 respectively. Choose a VLAN ID assignment scheme that makes sense to you.

10.2.3 Parent interface

The parent interface refers to the physical interface where the VLANs reside, such as em0 or bge0. When you configure VLANs on pfSense or FreeBSD, each is assigned a virtual interface, starting with vlan0 and incrementing by one for each additional VLAN configured. In pfSense 1.2.x, the number of the VLAN interface has no correlation to the VLAN ID. You *should not* assign your parent interface to any interface on pfSense — its sole function should be as the parent for the defined VLANs. In some situations this will work, but can cause difficulties with switch configuration, can cause problems with using Captive Portal, and forces you to use the trunk port's default VLAN, which should be avoided as discussed further in Section 10.3.

10.2.4 Access Port

An access port refers to a switch port providing access to a single VLAN, where the frames are not tagged with an 802.1Q header. You connect every device residing on a single VLAN to an access port. Most of your switch ports will be configured as access ports. Devices on access ports are unaware of any VLANs in your network. They see each VLAN the same as they would a switch without VLANs.

10.2.5 Double tagging (QinQ)

It is also possible to double tag traffic, using both an outer and inner 802.1Q tag. This is referred to as *QinQ*. This can be useful in large ISP environments and some other very large networks. Triple tagging is also possible. pfSense does not support QinQ at this time, but will in 2.0. These types of environments generally need the kind of routing power that only a high end ASIC-based router can support, and QinQ adds a level of complexity that is unnecessary in most environments.

10.2.6 Private VLAN (PVLAN)

PVLAN refers to capabilities of some switches to segment hosts within a single VLAN. Normally hosts within a single VLAN function the same as hosts on a single switch without VLANs configured. PVLAN provides a means of preventing hosts on a VLAN from talking to any other host on that VLAN, only permitting communication between that host and its default gateway. This isn't directly relevant to pfSense, but is a common question users have. Switch functionality such as this is the only way to prevent communication between hosts in the same subnet. Without a function like PVLAN, no network firewall can control traffic within a subnet because it never touches the default gateway.

10.3 VLANs and Security

VLANs offer a great means to segment your network and isolate subnetworks, but there are some security issues which need to be taken into account when designing and implementing a solution involving VLANs. VLANs are not inherently insecure, but misconfiguration can leave your network vulnerable. There have also been security problems in switch vendors' implementations of VLANs in the past.

10.3.1 Segregating Trust Zones

Because of the possibility of misconfiguration, you should segregate networks of considerably different trust levels onto their own physical switches. For example, while you could technically use the same switch with VLANs for all your internal networks as well as the network outside your firewalls, that should be avoided as a simple misconfiguration of the switch could lead to unfiltered Internet traffic entering your internal network. At a minimum, you should use two switches in such scenarios, one for outside the firewall and one inside. In many environments, DMZ segments are also treated separately, on a third switch in addition to the WAN and LAN switches. In others, the WAN side is on its own switch, while all the networks behind the firewall are on the same switches using VLANs. Which scenario is most appropriate for your network depends on your specific circumstances, and level of risk and paranoia.

10.3.2   Using the default VLAN1

Because VLAN1 is the default, or "native", VLAN, it may be used in unexpected ways by the switch. It is similar to using a default-allow policy on firewall rules instead of default deny and selecting what you need. It is always better to use a different VLAN, and ensure that you only select the ports you want on your switch group to be on that VLAN, to better limit access. Switches will send internal protocols such as STP (Spanning Tree Protocol), VTP (VLAN Trunking Protocol), and CDP (Cisco Discover Protocol) untagged over the native VLAN, where your switches use these protocols. It is generally best to keep that internal traffic isolated from your data traffic.

If you must use VLAN1, you must take great care to assign every single port on every switch to a different VLAN except those you want in VLAN1, and do not create a management interface for the switch on VLAN1. You should also change the native VLAN of the switch group to a different, unused, VLAN. Some switches may not support any of these workarounds, and so it is typically easier to move your data to a different VLAN instead of fussing with making VLAN1 available. With VLAN ID 2 through 4094 to choose from, it is undoubtedly better to just ignore VLAN1 when designing your VLAN scheme.

10.3.3   Using a trunk port's default VLAN

When VLAN tagged traffic is sent over a trunk on the native VLAN, tags in the packets that match the native VLAN may be stripped by the switch to preserve compatibility with older networks. Worse yet, packets that are double tagged with the native VLAN and a different VLAN will only have the native VLAN tag removed when trunking in this way and when processed later, that traffic can end up on a different VLAN. This is also called "VLAN hopping".

As mentioned in the previous section, any untagged traffic on a trunk port will be assumed to be the native VLAN, which could also overlap with an assigned VLAN interface. Depending on how the switch handles such traffic and how it is seen by pfSense, using the interface directly could lead to two interfaces being on the same VLAN.

10.3.4   Limiting access to trunk ports

Because a trunk port can talk to any VLAN in a group of trunked switches, possibly even ones not present on the current switch depending on your switch configurations, it is important to physically secure trunk ports. Also make sure there are no ports configured for trunking that are left unplugged where someone could hook into one, accidentally or otherwise. Depending on your switch, it may support dynamic negotiation of trunking. You should ensure this functionality is disabled or properly restricted.

10.3.5   Other Issues with Switches

There have been reports that some VLAN based switches will leak traffic across VLANs when they come under heavy loads, or if a MAC address of a PC on one VLAN is seen on another VLAN. These issues tend to be in older switches with outdated firmware, or extremely low-quality managed switches. These types of issues were largely resolved many years ago, when such security problems were common. No matter what switch from what brand you have, do some research online to see if it has undergone any kind of security testing, and ensure you are using the latest firmware. While these issues are a problem with the switch, and not pfSense, they are part of your overall security.

Many of the things here are specific to particular makes and models of switches. There may be different security considerations specific to the switch you are using. Refer to its documentation for recommendations on VLAN security.

10.4   pfSense Configuration

This section covers the configuration of VLANs on the pfSense side.

10.4.1   Console VLAN configuration

You can configure VLANs at the console using the Assign Interfaces function. The following example shows how to configure two VLANs, ID 10 and 20, with `le2` as the parent interface. The VLAN interfaces are assigned as OPT1 and OPT2.

```
pfSense console setup
*********************
0)   Logout (SSH only)
1)   Assign Interfaces
2)   Set LAN IP address
3)   Reset webConfigurator password
4)   Reset to factory defaults
5)   Reboot system
6)   Halt system
7)   Ping host
8)   Shell
9)   PFtop
10)  Filter Logs
11)  Restart webConfigurator
12)  pfSense Developer Shell
13)  Upgrade from console
14)  Disable Secure Shell (sshd)
98)  Move configuration file to removable device

Enter an option: 1

Valid interfaces are:

le0    00:0c:29:d6:e7:dc    (up)
le1    00:0c:29:d6:e7:e6    (up)
le2    00:0c:29:d6:e7:f0    (up)
plip0  0

Do you want to set up VLANs first?
If you are not going to use VLANs, or only for optional interfaces, you  ↵
    should
```

```
say no here and use the webConfigurator to configure VLANs later, if ←
    required.

Do you want to set up VLANs now [y|n]? y

VLAN Capable interfaces:

le0     00:0c:29:d6:e7:dc     (up)
le1     00:0c:29:d6:e7:e6     (up)
le2     00:0c:29:d6:e7:f0     (up)

Enter the parent interface name for the new VLAN (or nothing if finished ←
    ): le2
Enter the VLAN tag (1-4094): 10

VLAN Capable interfaces:

le0     00:0c:29:d6:e7:dc     (up)
le1     00:0c:29:d6:e7:e6     (up)
le2     00:0c:29:d6:e7:f0     (up)

Enter the parent interface name for the new VLAN (or nothing if finished ←
    ): le2
Enter the VLAN tag (1-4094): 20

VLAN Capable interfaces:

le0     00:0c:29:d6:e7:dc     (up)
le1     00:0c:29:d6:e7:e6     (up)
le2     00:0c:29:d6:e7:f0     (up)

Enter the parent interface name for the new VLAN (or nothing if finished ←
    ): <enter>


VLAN interfaces:

vlan0   VLAN tag 10, interface le2
vlan1   VLAN tag 20, interface le2

If you do not know the names of your interfaces, you may choose to use
auto-detection. In that case, disconnect all interfaces now before
hitting 'a' to initiate auto detection.

Enter the LAN interface name or 'a' for auto-detection: le1

Enter the WAN interface name or 'a' for auto-detection: le0

Enter the Optional 1 interface name or 'a' for auto-detection
(or nothing if finished): vlan0
```

```
Enter the Optional 2 interface name or 'a' for auto-detection
(or nothing if finished): vlan1

Enter the Optional 3 interface name or 'a' for auto-detection
(or nothing if finished): <enter>

The interfaces will be assigned as follows:

LAN  -> le1
WAN  -> le0
OPT1 -> vlan0
OPT2 -> vlan1

Do you want to proceed [y|n]? y

One moment while we reload the settings...
```

After a few seconds, your settings will reload and you will be returned to the console menu. When configuring VLAN interfaces at the console, it doesn't warn you about the reboot that may be needed before VLANs will function. Some network adapters or drivers will not work properly with VLANs until the system is rebooted. This isn't always necessary, but we have not been able to find a means of detecting when this is needed. To be on the safe side, rebooting after your initial VLAN setup is recommended. For future VLAN additions once VLANs are already configured, a reboot is not required.

10.4.2 Web interface VLAN configuration

Browse to Interfaces → Assign. Figure 10.1 shows the system being used for this example. WAN and LAN are assigned as `le0` and `le1` respectively. There is also a `le2` interface that will be used as the VLAN parent interface.

Interfaces: Assign

Interface assignments [VLANs]

Interface	Network port
LAN	le1 (08:00:27:ea:d6:75) ▾
WAN	le0 (08:00:27:6d:54:4b) ▾

Figure 10.1: Interfaces: Assign

Click the VLANs tab. Then click ⊞ to add a new VLAN, as shown in Figure 10.2.

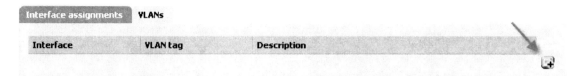

Figure 10.2: VLAN List

The VLAN editing screen should now be shown, like Figure 10.3. From here, pick a Parent Interface, **le2**. Then enter a VLAN tag, **10**, and enter a Description, such as what network is on that VLAN (DMZ, Databases, testing, etc.).

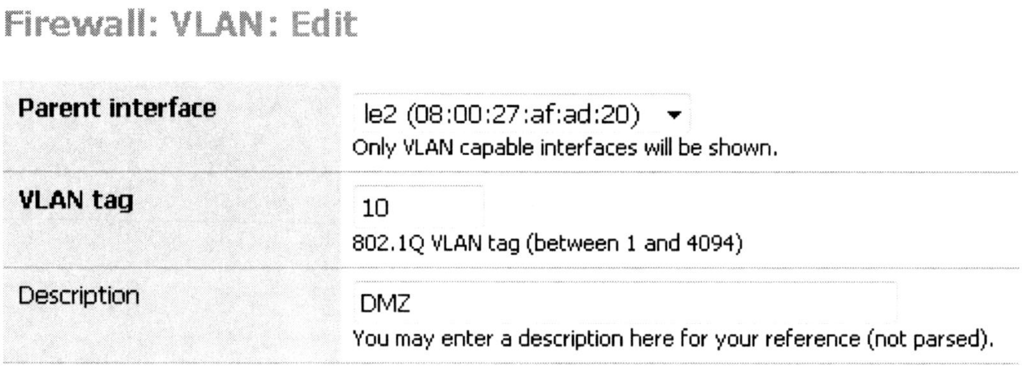

Firewall: VLAN: Edit

Parent interface	le2 (08:00:27:af:ad:20) ▾
	Only VLAN capable interfaces will be shown.
VLAN tag	10
	802.1Q VLAN tag (between 1 and 4094)
Description	DMZ
	You may enter a description here for your reference (not parsed).

Figure 10.3: Edit VLAN

Once Save is clicked, you will return to the list of available VLANs, which should now include the newly added VLAN 10. Repeat that process to add additional VLANs, such as VLAN 20. These can be seen in Figure 10.4

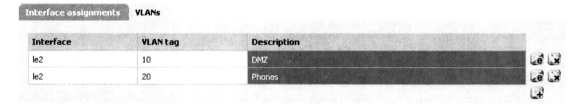

Figure 10.4: VLAN List

Now, to assign the VLANs to interfaces, click the Interface Assignments tab, then click 🔲, and in the drop-down list of available interface assignments, you should see the new VLANs. For OPT1, pick the interface with VLAN ID 10. Click ⊞ again, and for OPT2, pick the interface with VLAN ID 20. When finished, it will look something like Figure 10.5

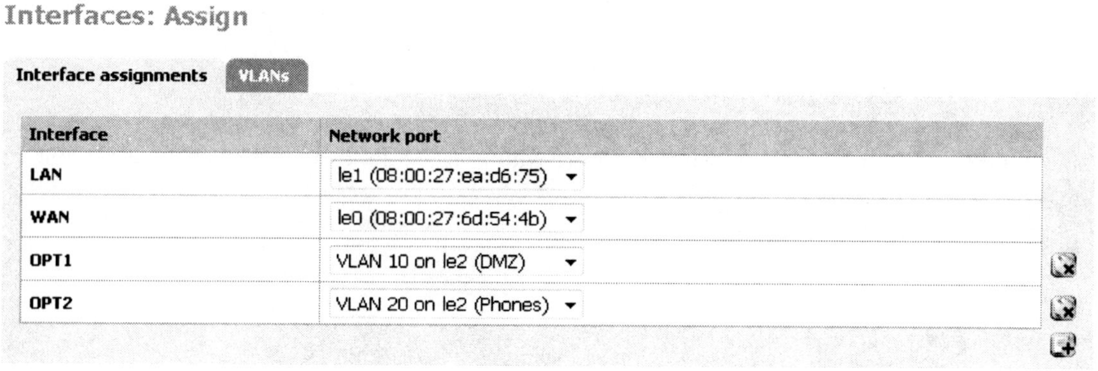

Interfaces: Assign

Interface assignments **VLANs**

Interface	Network port	
LAN	le1 (08:00:27:ea:d6:75) ▾	
WAN	le0 (08:00:27:6d:54:4b) ▾	
OPT1	VLAN 10 on le2 (DMZ) ▾	⊠
OPT2	VLAN 20 on le2 (Phones) ▾	⊠
		⊞

Figure 10.5: Interface list with VLANs

The VLAN-based OPT interfaces behave as any other OPT interfaces do, which means they must be enabled, configured, firewall rules added, and services like the DHCP Server will need to be configured if needed. See Section 4.3.4 for more information on configuring optional interfaces.

10.5 Switch Configuration

This section provides guidance on configuring your switch. This offers generic guidance that will apply to most if not all 802.1Q capable switches, then goes on to cover configuration on specific switches from Cisco, HP, Netgear, and Dell. Note this is the bare minimum configuration you will need for VLANs to function, and it does not necessarily show the ideal secure switch configuration for your environment. An in depth discussion of switch security is outside the scope of this book.

10.5.1 Switch configuration overview

Generally you will need to configure three or four things on VLAN capable switches.

1. Add/define the VLANs — most switches have a means of adding VLANs, and they must be added before they can be configured on any ports.

2. Configure the trunk port — configure the port pfSense will be connected to as a trunk port, tagging all your VLANs on the interface.

3. Configure the access ports — configure the ports your internal hosts will be using as access ports on the desired VLANs, with untagged VLANs.

4. Configure the Port VLAN ID (PVID) — some switches require configuring the PVID for a port. This specifies which VLAN to use for the traffic entering that switch port. For some switches this is a one step process, by configuring the port as an access port on a particular VLAN, it automatically tags traffic coming in on that port. Other switches require you to configure this in two places. Check your switch's documentation for details if it is not one detailed in this chapter.

10.5.2   Cisco IOS based switches

Configuring and using VLANs on Cisco switches with IOS is a fairly simple process, taking only a few commands to create and use VLANs, trunk ports, and assigning ports to VLANs. Many switches from other vendors behave similarly to IOS, and will use nearly the same if not identical syntax for configuration.

10.5.2.1   Create VLANs

VLANs can be created in a standalone fashion, or using VLAN Trunk Protocol (VTP). Using VTP may be more convenient, as it will automatically propagate the VLAN configuration to all switches on a VTP domain, though it also can create its own security problems and open up possibilities for inadvertently wiping out your VLAN configuration. With VTP, if you decide you need another VLAN it only needs added to a single switch, and then all other trunked switches in the group can assign ports to that VLAN. If VLANs are configured independently, you must add them to each switch by hand. Refer to Cisco's documentation on VTP to ensure you have a secure configuration not prone to accidental destruction. In a network with only a few switches where VLANs do not change frequently, you are usually better off not using VTP to avoid its potential downfalls.

10.5.2.1.1   Standalone VLANs

To create standalone VLANs:

```
sw# vlan database
sw(vlan)# vlan 10 name "DMZ Servers"
sw(vlan)# vlan 20 name "Phones"
sw(vlan)# exit
```

10.5.2.1.2   VTP VLANs

To setup your switch for VTP and VLANs, create a VTP database on the master switch and then create two VLANs:

```
sw# vlan database
sw(vlan)# vtp server
sw(vlan)# vtp domain example.com
sw(vlan)# vtp password SuperSecret
sw(vlan)# vlan 10 name "DMZ Servers"
sw(vlan)# vlan 20 name "Phones"
sw(vlan)# exit
```

10.5.2.2   Configure Trunk Port

For pfSense, a switch port not only has to be in trunk mode, but also must be using 802.1q tagging. This can be done like so:

```
sw# configure terminal
sw(config)# interface FastEthernet 0/24
sw(config-if)# switchport mode trunk
sw(config-if)# switchport trunk encapsulation dot1q
```

Note

On some newer Cisco IOS switches, the Cisco-proprietary ISL VLAN encapsulation method is deprecated and no longer supported. If your switch does not allow the `encapsulation dot1q` configuration option, it only supports 802.1Q and you need not worry about specifying the encapsulation.

10.5.2.3   Add Ports to the VLAN

To add ports to these VLANs, you need to assign them as follows:

```
sw# configure terminal
sw(config)# interface FastEthernet 0/12
sw(config-if)# switchport mode access
sw(config-if)# switchport access vlan 10
```

10.5.3   Cisco CatOS based switches

Creating VLANs on CatOS is a little different, though the terminology is the same as using VLANs under IOS. You still have the option of using standalone VLANs or VTP or to maintain the VLAN database:

```
# set vtp domain example mode server
# set vtp passwd SuperSecret
# set vlan 10 name dmz
# set vlan 20 name phones
```

And configure a trunk port to automatically handle every VLAN:

```
# set trunk 5/24 on dot1q 1-4094
```

Then add ports to the VLAN:

```
# set vlan 10 5/1-8
# set vlan 20 5/9-15
```

10.5.4   HP ProCurve switches

HP ProCurve switches only support 802.1q trunking, so no consideration is needed there. First, telnet into the switch and bring up the management menu.

10.5.4.1   Enable VLAN Support

First, VLAN support needs to be enabled on the switch if it is not already.

1. Choose Switch configuration

2. Choose Advanced Features

3. Choose VLAN Menu...

4. Choose VLAN Support

5. Set Enable VLANs to Yes if it is not already, and choose a number of VLANs. Each time this value is changed the switch must be restarted, so ensure it is large enough to support as many VLANs as you envision needing.

6. Restart the switch to apply the changes.

10.5.4.2   Create VLANs

Before the VLANs can be assigned to ports, you need to create the VLANs. At the switch configuration menu:

1. Choose Switch configuration

2. Choose Advanced Features

3. Choose VLAN Menu...

4. Choose VLAN Names

5. Choose Add

6. Enter the VLAN ID, *10*

7. Enter the name, *LAN*

8. Choose Save

9. Repeat the steps from Add to Save for any remaining VLANs

10.5.4.3 Assigning Trunk Ports to VLANs

Next, configure the trunk port for the firewall, as well as any trunk ports going to other switches containing multiple VLANs.

1. Choose Switch configuration

2. Choose VLAN Menu...

3. Choose VLAN Port Assignment

4. Choose Edit

5. Find the port you want to assign

6. Press **space** on Default VLAN until it says No

7. Move over to the column for each of the VLANs on this trunk port, and Press **space** until it says Tagged. Every VLAN in use must be tagged on the trunk port.

10.5.4.4 Assigning Access Ports to VLANs

1. Choose Switch configuration

2. Choose VLAN Menu...

3. Choose VLAN Port Assignment

4. Choose Edit

5. Find the port you want to assign

6. Press **space** on Default VLAN until it says No

7. Move over to the column for the VLAN to which this port will be assigned

8. Press **space** until it says Untagged.

10.5.5 Netgear managed switches

This example is on a GS108T, but other Netgear models we have seen are all very similar if not identical. There are also several other vendors including Zyxel who sell switches made by the same manufacturer, using the same web interface with a different logo. Log into your switch's web interface to start.

10.5.5.1 Planning the VLAN configuration

Before configuring the switch, you need to know how many VLANs you will configure, what IDs you will use, and how each switch port needs to be configured. For this example, we are using an 8 port GS108T, and will be configuring it as shown in Table 10.1.

Switch port	VLAN mode	VLAN assigned
1	trunk	`10` and `20`, tagged
2	access	`10` untagged
3	access	`10` untagged
4	access	`10` untagged
5	access	`20` untagged
6	access	`20` untagged
7	access	`20` untagged
8	access	`20` untagged

Table 10.1: Netgear GS108T VLAN Configuration

10.5.5.2 Enable 802.1Q VLANs

In the System menu on the left side of the page, click VLAN Group Setting, as indicated in Figure 10.6.

VLAN
VLAN Group Setting
Management VLAN

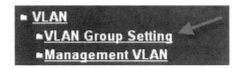

Figure 10.6: VLAN Group Setting

Select IEEE 802.1Q VLAN (Figure 10.7).

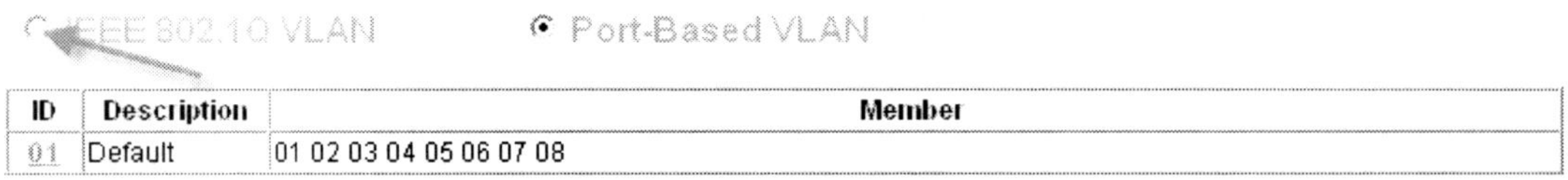
IEEE 802.1Q VLAN
Port-Based VLAN
ID
Description
Member
01
Default
01 02 03 04 05 06 07 08

Figure 10.7: Enable 802.1Q VLANs

This will prompt you with a pop up asking if you really want to change, and listing some of the consequences, as shown in Figure 10.8. If you want to trunk VLANs, you must use 802.1Q. Click OK.

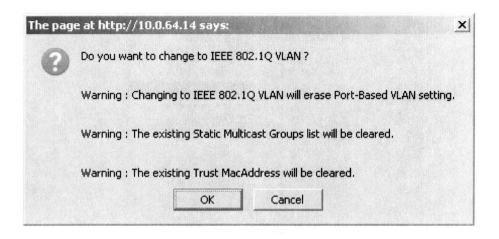

Figure 10.8: Confirm change to 802.1Q VLAN

After clicking OK, the page will refresh with your 802.1Q VLAN configuration as shown in Figure 10.9.

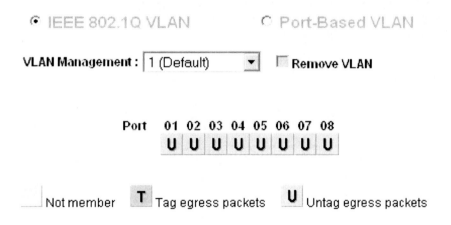

Figure 10.9: Default 802.1Q configuration

10.5.5.3 Add VLANs

For this example, I will add two VLANs with IDs *10* and *20*. To add a VLAN, click the VLAN Management drop down and click Add new VLAN as shown in Figure 10.10.

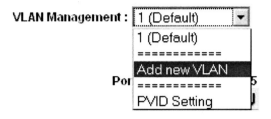

Figure 10.10: Add new VLAN

Enter the VLAN ID for this new VLAN, then click Apply. The VLAN screen will now let you configure VLAN *10* (Figure 10.11). Before configuring it, I will again click Add new VLAN as shown in
Figure 10.10 to add VLAN *20* (Figure 10.12).

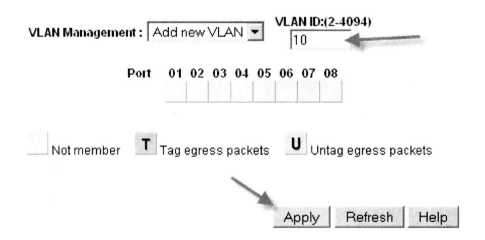

Figure 10.11: Add VLAN 10

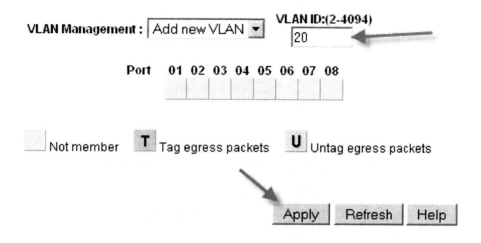

Figure 10.12: Add VLAN 20

Add as many VLANs as you need, then continue to the next section.

10.5.5.4   Configure VLAN tagging

When you select a VLAN from the VLAN Management drop down, it shows you how that VLAN is configured on each port. A blank box means the port is not a member of the selected VLAN. A box containing **T** means the VLAN is sent on that port with the 802.1Q tag. **U** indicates the port is a member of that VLAN and it leaves the port untagged. The trunk port will need to have both VLANs added and tagged.

Note

Do not change the configuration of the port you are using to access the switch's web interface. You would lock yourself out, with the only means of recovery on the GS108T is hitting the reset to factory defaults button — it doesn't have a serial console. For the switches that have serial consoles, have a null modem cable handy in case you disconnect yourself from network connectivity with the switch. Configuring the management VLAN is covered later in this section.

Click in the boxes beneath the port number as shown in Figure 10.13 to toggle between the three VLAN options.

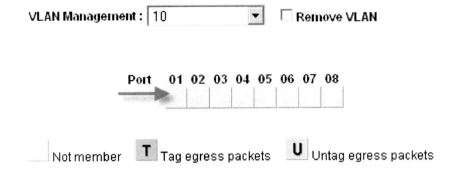

Figure 10.13: Toggle VLAN membership

10.5.5.4.1   Configure VLAN 10 membership

Figure 10.14 shows VLAN *10* configured as outlined in Table 10.1. The access ports on this VLAN are set to untagged while the trunk port is set to tagged.

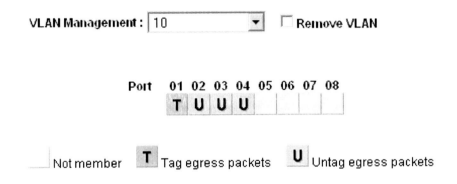

Figure 10.14: Configure VLAN 10 membership

10.5.5.4.2   Configure VLAN 20 membership

Select *20* from the VLAN Management drop down to configure the port memberships for VLAN *20*.

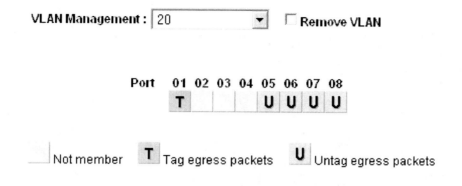

Figure 10.15: Configure VLAN 20 membership

10.5.5.4.3 Change PVID

On Netgear switches, in addition to the previously configured tagging settings, you must also configure the PVID to specify the VLAN used for frames entering that port. In the VLAN Management drop down, click PVID Setting as shown in Figure 10.16.

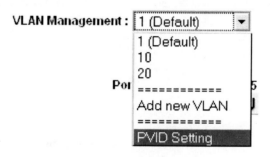

Figure 10.16: PVID Setting

The default PVID setting is VLAN 1 for all ports as shown in Figure 10.17.

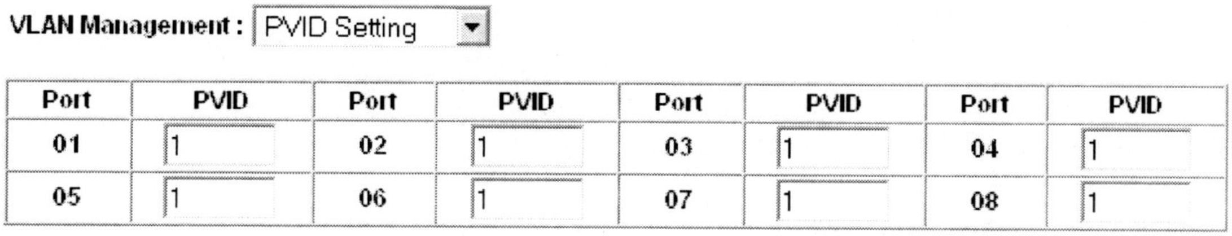

VLAN Management : | PVID Setting ▼ |

Port	PVID	Port	PVID	Port	PVID	Port	PVID
01	1	02	1	03	1	04	1
05	1	06	1	07	1	08	1

Figure 10.17: Default PVID Configuration

Change the PVID for each access port, but leave the trunk port and port you are using to access the switch's management interface set to **1**. Figure 10.18 shows the PVID configuration matching the port assignments shown in Table 10.1, with port 8 being used to access the switch's management interface. Apply your changes when finished.

VLAN Management : PVID Setting ▼

Port	PVID	Port	PVID	Port	PVID	Port	PVID
01	1	02	10	03	10	04	10
05	20	06	20	07	20	08	1

Figure 10.18: VLAN 10 and 20 PVID Configuration

10.5.5.4.4   Remove VLAN 1 configuration

By default, all ports are members of VLAN 1 with untagged egress frames. Select **1 (Default)** from the VLAN Management drop down. Remove VLAN 1 from all ports *except* the one you are using to manage the switch and the trunk port, so you don't get disconnected. I am using port 8 to manage the switch. When finished, your screen should look like Figure 10.19.

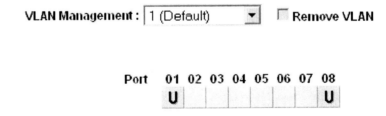

VLAN Management : 1 (Default) ▼   ☐ **Remove VLAN**

Port	01	02	03	04	05	06	07	08
	U							U

Figure 10.19: Remove VLAN 1 membership

Apply your changes when finished.

10.5.5.4.5   Verify VLAN functionality

Configure your VLANs on pfSense, including the DHCP server on the VLAN interfaces if you will be using DHCP. Plug systems into the configured access ports and test connectivity. If everything works as desired, continue to the next step. If things do not work as intended, review your tagging and PVID configuration on the switch, and your VLAN configuration and interface assignments on pfSense.

10.5.6 Dell PowerConnect managed switches

The management interface of Dell switches varies slightly between models, but the following procedure will accommodate most models. The configuration is quite similar in style to Cisco IOS.

First, create the VLANs:

```
console# config
console(config)# vlan database
console(config-vlan)# vlan 10 name dmz media ethernet
console(config-vlan)# vlan 20 name phones media ethernet
console(config-vlan)# exit
```

Next, setup a trunk port:

```
console(config)# interface ethernet 1/1
console(config-if)# switchport mode trunk
console(config-if)# switchport allowed vlan add 1-4094 tagged
console(config-if)# exit
```

Finally, add ports to the VLANs:

```
console(config)# interface ethernet 1/15
console(config-if)# switchport allowed vlan add 10 untagged
console(config-if)# exit
```

Chapter 11

Multiple WAN Connections

The multiple WAN (multi-WAN) capabilities of pfSense allow you to utilize multiple Internet connections to achieve higher uptime and greater throughput capacity. Before proceeding with a multi-WAN configuration, you need a working two interface (LAN and WAN) configuration. pfSense is capable of handling many WAN interfaces, with multiple deployments using 10-12 WANs in production. It should scale even higher than that, though we aren't aware of any installations using more than 12 WANs.

Any additional WAN interfaces are referred to as OPT WAN interfaces. References to WAN refer to the primary WAN interface, and OPT WAN to any additional WAN interfaces. There are important differences between the two types in pfSense 1.2 that are covered throughout this chapter.

This chapter starts by covering things you should consider when implementing any multi-WAN solution, then covers multi-WAN configuration with pfSense.

11.1 Choosing your Internet Connectivity

The ideal choice of Internet connectivity will depend largely upon the options available at your location, but there are some additional factors to take into consideration.

11.1.1 Cable Paths

Speaking from the experience of those who have seen first hand the effects of multiple cable seeking backhoes, as well as nefarious copper thieves, it is very important to make sure your connectivity choices for a multi-WAN deployment utilize disparate cabling paths. In many locations, all T1 and DSL connections as well as any others utilizing copper pairs are carried on a single cable subject to the same cable cut.

If you have one connection coming in over copper pair (T1, DSL, etc.), choose a secondary connection utilizing a different type and path of cabling. Cable connections are typically the most widely available option not subject to the same outage as copper services. Other options include fixed wireless, and fiber services coming in on a different cable path from your copper services.

You cannot rely upon two connections of the same type to provide redundancy in most cases. An ISP outage or cable cut will commonly take down all connections of the same type. Some pfSense users do use multiple DSL lines or multiple cable modems, though the only redundancy that typically offers is isolating you from modem or other CPE (Customer Premise Equipment) failure. You should consider multiple connections from the same provider as only a solution for additional bandwidth, as the redundancy such a deployment offers is minimal.

11.1.2   Paths to the Internet

Another consideration when selecting your Internet connectivity is the path from your connection to the Internet. For redundancy purposes, multiple Internet connections from the same provider, especially of the same type should not be relied upon.

With larger providers, two different types of connections such as a DSL modem and T1 line will usually traverse significantly different networks until reaching core parts of the network. These core network components are generally designed with high redundancy and any problems are addressed quickly since they have widespread effects. Hence such connectivity is isolated from most ISP issues, but since they commonly utilize the same cable path, it still leaves you vulnerable to extended outages from cable cuts.

11.1.3   Better Redundancy, More Bandwidth, Less Money

For many years, T1 service has been the choice for any environment with high availability requirements. Generally the Service Level Agreements (SLA) offered on T1 connections are better than other types of connectivity, and T1s are generally seen as more reliable. But with pfSense's multi-WAN capabilities, you can have more bandwidth and better redundancy for less money in many cases.

Most organizations requiring high availability Internet connections do not want to rely upon DSL, cable or other "lesser class" broadband Internet connections. While they're usually significantly faster and cheaper, the lesser SLA is enough to make many companies stick with T1 connectivity. In areas where multiple lower cost broadband options are available, such as DSL and cable, the combination of pfSense and two low cost Internet connections provides more bandwidth and better redundancy at a lower cost. The chance of two different broadband connections going down simultaneously is significantly less than the chance of a T1 failure or outage of any single service.

11.2   Multi-WAN Terminology and Concepts

This section covers the terminology and concepts you will need to understand to deploy multi-WAN with pfSense.

11.2.1   Policy routing

Policy routing refers to a means of routing traffic by more than the destination IP address of the traffic, as is done with the routing table in most operating systems and routers. This is accomplished by the use of a policy of some sort, usually firewall rules or an access control list. In pfSense, the Gateway field available when editing or adding firewall rules enables the use of policy routing. The Gateway field contains all your WAN interfaces, plus any failover or load balancing pools you have defined.

Policy routing provides a powerful means of directing traffic to the appropriate WAN interface, since it allows matching anything a firewall rule can match. Specific hosts, subnets, protocols and more can be used to direct traffic.

Note

Remember that all firewall rules including policy routing rules are processed in top down order, and the first match wins.

11.2.2 Gateway Pools

Gateway pools are what provide the failover and load balancing functionality in pfSense. They are configured under Services → Load Balancer, on the Pool tab.

11.2.3 Failover

Failover refers to the ability to use only one WAN interface, but fail over to another WAN if the preferred WAN fails.

11.2.4 Load Balancing

Load balancing refers to the ability to distribute load between multiple WAN interfaces. Note that load balancing and failover are not mutually exclusive. Load balancing automatically also provides failover capabilities, as any interface that is down is removed from the load balancing pool.

11.2.5 Monitor IPs

When configuring failover or load balancing, each WAN interface is associated with a monitor IP. pfSense will ping this IP, and if it stops responding, the interface is marked as down. If this monitor IP is on an OPT WAN interface, pfSense will automatically add a static route for this destination to direct the traffic out the correct WAN interface. This means each WAN must have a unique monitor IP. You can use the same monitor IP in multiple pools as long as it is used in association with only one WAN.

11.2.5.1 So what constitutes failure?

As you may have guessed, it's a little more complex than "if pings to the monitor IP fail, the interface is marked as down." Specifically, the following **ping** command is used for this monitoring.

```
# ping -t 5 -oqc 5 -i 0.7 <ip address>
```

Command line option	Function
-t 5	Wait 5 seconds
-o	Exit successfully after receiving one reply packet
-q	Quiet output. Only summary output at start and finish.
-c 5	Send 5 packets
-i 0.7	Wait 0.7 seconds between sending each packet

Table 11.1: Dissecting the ping monitoring

Unless you're exceptionally well versed in **ping**, that doesn't tell you much. The options are detailed in Table 11.1.

So this means it sends 5 pings to your monitor IP, waiting 0.7 seconds between each ping. It waits up to 5 seconds for a response, and exits successfully if one reply is received. This has been tweaked and tuned multiple times over the years to reach this point. It detects nearly all failures, and isn't overly sensitive. Since it is successful with 80% packet loss, it is theoretically possible that your connection could be experiencing so much packet loss that it is unusable, but is not marked as down. This used to be more strict, but we found that false positives and flapping were common with less strict settings, and this is the best combination for detecting outages and preventing unnecessary flapping. Some of these options will be user configurable in pfSense 2.0.

11.3 Multi-WAN Caveats and Considerations

This section contains the caveats and considerations specific to multi-WAN in pfSense.

11.3.1 Multiple WANs sharing a single gateway IP

Because of the way pf handles multi-WAN traffic, it can only direct it by the gateway IP of the connection. This is fine in most scenarios. If you have multiple connections on the same network using the same gateway IP, as is common if you have multiple cable modems, you must use an intermediate NAT device so pfSense sees each WAN gateway as a unique IP.

11.3.2 Multiple PPPoE or PPTP WANs

pfSense 1.2 only supports a single PPPoE or PPTP WAN interface, on the primary WAN. OPT WANs must be DHCP or statically assigned. You can accommodate multiple PPPoE WANs by configuring the PPPoE on your modem and passing through the public IP to pfSense. pfSense 2.0 supports PPPoE and PPTP on an unlimited number of WANs.

11.3.3 Local Services and Multi-WAN

There are some considerations with local services and multi-WAN, since any traffic initiated from the firewall itself will not be affected by any policy routing you have configured, but rather follows the system's routing table. Hence static routes are required under some circumstances when using OPT WAN interfaces, otherwise only the WAN interface would be used. We hope to offer the ability to policy route traffic initiated by the firewall in pfSense 2.0 to allow more flexibility. This only applies to traffic that is initiated by the firewall. In the case of traffic initiated on the Internet destined for an OPT WAN interface, pfSense automatically uses pf's `reply-to` directive in all WAN and OPT WAN rules, which ensures the reply traffic is routed back out the correct WAN interface.

Note

The following presumes you are running pfSense 1.2.1 or newer. If you are running an earlier release, in some circumstances you may encounter problems caused by a bug fixed after 1.2 was released.

11.3.3.1 DNS Forwarder

The DNS servers used by the DNS forwarder must have static routes defined if they use an OPT WAN interface, as described later in this chapter. There are no other caveats to DNS forwarder in multi-WAN environments.

11.3.3.2 IPsec

IPsec is fully compatible with multi-WAN. For site to site connections using OPT WAN interfaces, a static route is automatically added for the remote tunnel endpoint pointing to the OPT WAN's gateway to ensure the firewall sends traffic out the correct interface when it is initiating the connection. For mobile connections, the client always initiates the connection, and the reply traffic is correctly routed by the state table.

11.3.3.3 OpenVPN

OpenVPN multi-WAN capabilities are described in Section 15.7.

11.3.3.4 PPTP Server

The PPTP server is not multi-WAN compatible. It can only be used on the primary WAN interface.

11.3.3.5 CARP and multi-WAN

CARP is multi-WAN capable as long as all WAN interfaces use static IPs and you have at least three public IPs per WAN. This is covered in Section 20.5.

11.4 Interface and DNS Configuration

First you need to configure your WAN interfaces and DNS servers.

11.4.1   Interface Configuration

The WAN interfaces first need to be configured. Setup the primary WAN as previously described in Section 4.2. Then for the OPT WAN interfaces, select DHCP or static, depending on your Internet connection type. For static IP connections, fill in the IP address and gateway.

11.4.2   DNS Server Configuration

You will want to configure pfSense with DNS servers from each WAN connection to ensure it is always able to resolve DNS. This is especially important if your internal network uses pfSense's DNS forwarder for DNS resolution. If you only use one ISP's DNS servers, an outage of that WAN connection will result in a complete Internet outage regardless of your policy routing configuration since DNS will no longer function.

11.4.2.1   DNS Servers and Static Routes

pfSense uses its routing table to reach the configured DNS servers. This means without any static routes configured, it will only use the primary WAN connection to reach DNS servers. Static routes must be configured for any DNS server on an OPT WAN interface, so pfSense uses the correct WAN interface to reach that DNS server.

This is required for two reasons. One, most all ISPs prohibit recursive queries from hosts outside their network, hence you must use the correct WAN interface to access that ISP's DNS server. Secondly, if you lose your primary WAN and do not have a static route defined for one of your other DNS servers, you will lose all DNS resolution ability from pfSense itself as all DNS servers will be unreachable when the system's default gateway is unreachable. If you are using pfSense as your DNS server, this will result in a complete failure of DNS for your network.

The means of accommodating this vary depending on the type of WANs in use.

11.4.2.2   All Static IP WANs

This is the easiest scenario to handle, as each WAN has a gateway IP that will not change. No additional considerations are necessary here.

11.4.2.3   All Dynamic IP WANs

Dynamic IP WAN interfaces pose difficulties because their gateway is subject to change and static routes in pfSense 1.2 must point to a static IP address. This commonly isn't a major problem because only the IP address changes while the gateway remains the same. If your OPT WAN public IP changes subnets and hence gateways frequently, use of the DNS forwarder on pfSense is not a suitable solution for redundant DNS services as you will have no reliable means of reaching a DNS server over anything other than the WAN interface.

In scenarios where you cannot configure a static route to reach one of your DNS servers over an OPT WAN, you have two alternatives. Because traffic from the inside networks is policy routed by your firewall rules, it isn't subject to this limitation. You can either use DNS servers on the Internet on all your internal systems, such as OpenDNS, or use a DNS server or forwarder on your internal network. As long as DNS requests are initiated from inside your network, and not on the firewall itself as in the case of the DNS forwarder, static routes are not required (and have no effect on traffic initiated inside your network when using policy routing).

Another option to consider is using one of your DNS server IPs from each Internet connection as the monitor IP for that connection. This will automatically add the appropriate static routes for each DNS server.

11.4.2.4 Mix of Static and Dynamic IP WANs

If you have a mix of statically and dynamically addressed WAN interfaces, the primary WAN should be one of your dynamic IP WANs since static routes are not required for DNS servers on the primary WAN interface.

11.4.2.5 Example Static Route Configuration

This example illustrates using OpenDNS's DNS servers 208.67.220.220 and 208.67.222.222, one on WAN and one on WAN2. In this example, the gateway of WAN is 10.0.0.1 and the gateway of WAN2 is 192.168.0.1. The static route for WAN is not required, as the system's default route always resides on the WAN interface, but adding it will not hurt anything and makes it clear which DNS server uses which WAN. The routes from this example should appear like Figure 11.1

Interface	Network	Gateway	Description
WAN2	208.67.220.220/32	192.168.0.1	OpenDNS #2 out WAN2
WAN	208.67.222.222/32	10.0.0.1	OpenDNS #1 out WAN

Figure 11.1: Example static route configuration for Multi-WAN DNS services

11.4.3 Scaling to Large Numbers of WAN Interfaces

There are numerous pfSense users deploying 6-12 Internet connections on a single installation. One pfSense user has 10 DSL lines because in his country it is significantly cheaper to get ten 256 Kb connections than it is one 2.5 Mb connection. He uses pfSense to load balance a large number of internal machines out 10 different connections. For more information on this scale of deployment, see Section 11.11 about "Multi-WAN on a stick" later in this chapter.

11.5 Multi-WAN Special Cases

Some multi-WAN deployments require workarounds due to limitations in pfSense 1.2. This section covers those cases and how to accommodate them.

11.5.1   Multiple Connections with Same Gateway IP

Because of the way pfSense distributes traffic over multiple Internet connections, if you have multiple Internet connections using the same gateway IP, you will need to insert a NAT device between all but one of those connections. This isn't a great solution, but it is workable. We would like to accommodate this in a future release, but it's very difficult because of the way the underlying software directs traffic when doing policy routing.

11.5.2   Multiple PPPoE or PPTP Type Connections

pfSense can only accommodate one PPPoE or PPTP WAN connection. OPT WAN interfaces cannot use PPPoE or PPTP WAN types. The best work around is to use PPPoE or PPTP on your modem, or another firewall outside of pfSense.

For PPPoE, most DSL modems can handle the PPPoE and either directly assign your public IP to pfSense, or give it a private IP and provide NAT. Public IP passthrough is possible on many modems and is the preferred means of accomplishing this.

11.6   Multi-WAN and NAT

The default NAT rules generated by pfSense will translate any traffic leaving the WAN or an OPT WAN interface to that interface's IP address. In a default two interface LAN and WAN configuration, pfSense will NAT all traffic leaving the WAN interface to the WAN IP address. The addition of OPT WAN interfaces extends this to NAT any traffic leaving an OPT WAN interface to that interface's IP address. This is all handled automatically unless Advanced Outbound NAT is enabled.

The policy routing rules direct the traffic to the WAN interface used, and the Outbound and 1:1 NAT rules specify how the traffic will be translated.

11.6.1   Multi-WAN and Advanced Outbound NAT

If you require Advanced Outbound NAT with multi-WAN, you need to ensure you configure NAT rules for all your WAN interfaces.

11.6.2   Multi-WAN and Port Forwarding

Each port forward applies to a single WAN interface. A given port can be opened on multiple WAN interfaces by using multiple port forward entries, one per WAN interface. The easiest way to accomplish this is to add the port forward on the first WAN connection, then click the ⊞ to the right of that entry to add another port forward based on that one. Change the interface to the desired WAN, and click Save.

11.6.3 Multi-WAN and 1:1 NAT

1:1 NAT entries are specific to a single WAN interface. Internal systems can be configured with a 1:1 NAT entry on each WAN interface, or a 1:1 entry on one or more WAN interfaces and use the default outbound NAT on others. Where 1:1 entries are configured, they always override any other Outbound NAT configuration for the specific interface where the 1:1 entry is configured.

11.7 Load Balancing

The load balancing functionality in pfSense allows you to distribute traffic over multiple WAN connections in a round robin fashion. This is done on a per-connection basis.

A monitoring IP is configured for each connection, which pfSense will ping. If the pings fail, the interface is marked as down and removed from all pools until the pings succeed again.

11.7.1 Configuring a Load Balancing Pool

In the pfSense WebGUI, browse to Services → Load Balancer. On the Pools tab, click ⬚. This will bring you to the Load Balancer Pool Edit screen. The following sections describe each field on this page.

11.7.1.1 Name

In the Name field, fill in a name for the failover pool up to 16 characters in length. This will be the name used to refer to this pool in the Gateway field in firewall rules. This field is required.

11.7.1.2 Description

You may enter a description here for your reference. This field is shown on the Load Balancer Pools screen, and does not affect functionality of the pool. It is optional.

11.7.1.3 Type

Select Gateway in this drop down box.

11.7.1.4 Behavior

Select Load Balancing here.

11.7.1.5 Port

This field is grayed out when using Gateway load balancing.

11.7.1.6   Monitor

This field is grayed out when using Gateway load balancing because only ICMP can be used to monitor gateways.

11.7.1.7   Monitor IP

This is the IP address that will determine whether the chosen interface (selected next) is available. If pings to this address fail, this interface is marked as down and no longer used until it is accessible again, as covered in Section 11.2.5.

11.7.1.8   Interface Name

Here you define the interface to be used along with the preceding monitor IP. Since this is a load balancing pool, each added interface will be used equally as long as its monitor IP is responding. If any interface in the list fails, it is removed from the pool and the load is distributed amongst the remaining interface(s).

11.7.1.9   Add to pool

After selecting an interface and choosing a monitor IP, click the Add to pool button to add the interface.

After adding the first interface to the pool, select the second interface, select its monitor IP, and click Add to pool again. When finished adding interfaces to the pool, click Save, then Apply Changes.

11.7.2   Problems with Load Balancing

Some websites store session information including your IP address, and if a subsequent connection to that site is routed out a different WAN interface using a different public IP, the website will not function properly. This is pretty rare and only includes a few banks in my experience. The suggested means of working around this is to create a failover pool and direct traffic destined to these sites to the failover pool rather than the load balancing pool.

The sticky connections feature of pf is supposed to resolve this problem, but has had issues in the past. This should be resolved in 1.2.3 and beyond.

11.8   Failover

Failover refers to the ability to use only one WAN connection, but switch to another WAN if the preferred connection fails. This is useful for situations where you want certain traffic, or all your traffic to utilize one specific WAN connection unless it is unavailable.

11.8.1 Configuring a Failover Pool

In the pfSense WebGUI, browse to Services → Load Balancer. On the Pools tab, click 🔳. This will bring you to the Load Balancer Pool Edit screen. The following sections describe each field on this page. These fields are largely the same as those for the load balancing pool configuration.

11.8.1.1 Name

In the Name field, fill in a name for the failover pool up to 16 characters in length. This will be the name used to refer to this pool in the Gateway field in firewall rules. This field is required.

11.8.1.2 Description

You may enter a description here for your reference. This field is shown on the Load Balancer Pools screen, and does not affect functionality. It is optional, but recommended to enter something descriptive here.

11.8.1.3 Type

Select Gateway in this drop down box. All load balancing for multi-WAN uses the Gateway type.

11.8.1.4 Behavior

Select Failover here.

11.8.1.5 Port

This field is grayed out when using Gateway load balancing.

11.8.1.6 Monitor

This field is grayed out when using Gateway load balancing because only ICMP can be used to monitor gateways.

11.8.1.7 Monitor IP

This is the IP address that will determine whether the chosen interface (selected next) is available. If pings to this address fail, this interface is marked as down and no longer used until it is accessible again.

11.8.1.8   Interface Name

Here you define the interface to be used along with the preceding monitor IP. Since this is a failover pool, the first interface added will be used as long as its monitor IP is responding to pings. If the first interface added to the pool fails, the second interface in the pool will be used.

Make sure you add the interfaces to the pool in order of preference. The first in the list will always be used unless it fails, at which point the remaining interfaces in the list are fallen back on in top down order.

11.8.1.9   Add to pool

After selecting an interface and choosing a monitor IP, click the Add to pool button to add the interface.

After adding the first interface to the pool, select the second interface, select its monitor IP, and click Add to pool again. When finished adding interfaces to the pool, click Save, then Apply Changes.

11.9   Verifying Functionality

Once configuring your multi-WAN setup you will want to verify its functionality. The following sections describe how to test each portion of your multi-WAN configuration.

11.9.1   Testing Failover

If you have configured failover, you will want to test it after completing your configuration to ensure it functions as you desire. Don't make the mistake of waiting until one of your Internet connections fails to first try out your failover configuration.

Browse to Status → Load Balancer and ensure all your WAN connections show as "Online" under Status. If they do not, verify your monitoring IP configuration as discussed earlier in this chapter.

11.9.1.1   Creating a WAN Failure

There are a number of ways you can simulate a WAN failure, differing depending on the type of Internet connection being used. For any type, first try unplugging the target WAN interface's Ethernet cable from the firewall.

For cable and DSL connections, you will also want to try powering off your modem, and just unplugging the coax or phone line from the modem. For T1 and other types of connections with a router outside of pfSense, try unplugging the Internet connection from the router, and also turning off the router itself.

All of the described testing scenarios will likely end with the same result. However there are some circumstances where trying all these things individually will find a fault you would not have otherwise noticed until an actual failure. One of the most common is using a monitor IP assigned to your DSL or cable modem (in some circumstances you may not be aware where your gateway IP resides). Hence when the coax or phone line is disconnected, simulating a provider failure rather than an Ethernet or modem failure, the monitor ping still succeeds since it is pinging the modem. From what you told pfSense to monitor, the connection is still up, so it will not fail over even if the connection is actually down. There are other types of failure that can similarly only be detected by testing all the individual possibilities for failure.

11.9.1.2   Verifying Interface Status

After creating a WAN failure, refresh the Status → Load Balancer screen to check the current status.

11.9.2   Verifying Load Balancing Functionality

This section describes how to verify the functionality of your load balancing configuration.

11.9.2.1   Verifying HTTP Load Balancing

The easiest way to verify a HTTP load balancing configuration is to visit one of the websites that displays the public IP address you are coming from. A page on the pfSense site is available for this purpose, and there are also countless other sites that serve the same purpose. Search for "what is my IP address" and you will find numerous websites that will show you what public IP address the HTTP request is coming from. Most of those sites tend to be full of spammy ads, so we provide several sites that simply tell you your IP address.

HTTP sites for finding your public IP

- `http://www.pfsense.org/ip.php`

- `http://files.pfsense.org/ip.php`

- `http://cvs.pfsense.org/ip.php`

- `http://www.bsdperimeter.com/ip.php`

HTTPS site for finding your public IP

- `https://portal.pfsense.org/ip.php`

If you load one of these sites, and refresh your browser a number of times, you should see your IP address changing if your load balancing configuration is correct. Note if you have any other traffic on your network, you likely will not see your IP address change on every page refresh. Refresh the page 20 or 30 times and you should see the IP change at least a few times. If the IP never changes, try several different sites, and make sure your browser really is requesting the page again, and not returning something from its cache or using a persistent connection to the server. Manually deleting the cache and trying multiple web browsers are good things to attempt before troubleshooting your load balancer configuration further. Using **curl**, as described in Section 17.2.6 is a better alternative as it ensures cache and persistent connections will have no impact on the results.

11.9.2.2   Testing load balancing with traceroute

The **traceroute** utility (or **tracert** in Windows) allows you to see the network path taken to a given destination. See Section 8.4.2 for details on using **traceroute**.

11.9.2.3   Using Traffic Graphs

The real time traffic graphs, under Status → Traffic Graph, are useful for showing the real time throughput on your WAN interfaces. You can only show one graph at a time per browser window, but you can open additional windows or tabs in your browser and show all your WAN interfaces simultaneously. The Dashboard feature in pfSense 2.0 (also available as a beta package in 1.2) enables the simultaneous display of multiple traffic graphs on a single page.

The RRD traffic graphs under Status → RRD Graphs are useful for longer-term and historical evaluation of your individual WAN utilization.

Note
Your bandwidth usage may not be exactly equally distributed, since connections are simply directed on a round robin basis without regard for bandwidth usage.

11.10   Policy Routing, Load Balancing and Failover Strategies

You will need to determine the multi-WAN configuration that best suits the needs of your environment. This section provides some guidance on common goals, and how they are achieved with pfSense.

11.10.1   Bandwidth Aggregation

One of the primary desires with multi-WAN is bandwidth aggregation. With load balancing, pfSense can help you accomplish this. There is, however, one caveat. If you have two 5 Mbps WAN circuits, you cannot get 10 Mbps of throughput with a single client connection. Each individual connection must be tied to only one specific WAN. This is true of any multi-WAN solution, you cannot aggregate the bandwidth of two Internet connections into a single large "pipe" without involvement from the ISP. With load balancing, since individual connections are balanced in a round robin fashion, you can achieve 10 Mbps of throughput using two 5 Mbps circuits, just not with a single connection. Applications that utilize multiple connections, such as many download accelerators, will be able to achieve the combined throughput capacity of the two or more connections.

In networks with numerous internal machines accessing the Internet, load balancing will enable you to achieve near the aggregate throughput by balancing the many internal connections out all of the WAN interfaces.

11.10.2 Segregation of Priority Services

In some situations, you may have a reliable, high quality Internet connection that offers low bandwidth, or high costs for excessive transfers, and another connection that is fast but of lesser quality (higher latency, more jitter, or less reliable). In these situations, you can segregate services between the two Internet connections by their priority. High priority services may include VoIP, traffic destined to a specific network such as an outsourced application provider, some specific protocols used by critical applications, amongst other options. Low priority traffic commonly includes any permitted traffic that doesn't match the list of high priority traffic. You can setup your policy routing rules in such a way as to direct the high priority traffic out the high quality Internet connection, and the lower priority traffic out the lesser quality connection.

Another example of a similar scenario is getting a dedicated Internet connection for quality critical services such as VoIP, and only using that connection for those services.

11.10.3 Failover Only

There are some scenarios where you may want to only use failover. Some pfSense users have a secondary backup Internet connection with a low bandwidth limit, and only want to use that connection if their primary connection fails, and only while it is down. Failover pools allow you to achieve this.

Another usage for failover pools is when you want to ensure a certain protocol or destination always uses only one WAN.

11.10.4 Unequal Cost Load Balancing

In pfSense 1.2, you cannot configure a weight or preference value to WANs. However this does not mean unequal cost load balancing cannot be achieved. This is a bit of a hack, but it works well. If you have WAN and WAN2, and add WAN to the pool twice, and WAN2 once, WAN will get two thirds of the total traffic and WAN2 will get a third. The following table depicts some possible combinations and the percentage distribution on each WAN.

WAN instances	WAN2 instances	WAN load	WAN2 load
3	2	60%	40%
2	1	67%	33%
3	1	75%	25%
4	1	80%	20%

Table 11.2: Unequal cost load balancing

Figure 11.2 depicts a balance of 67% on WAN and 33% on an OPT WAN named DSL.

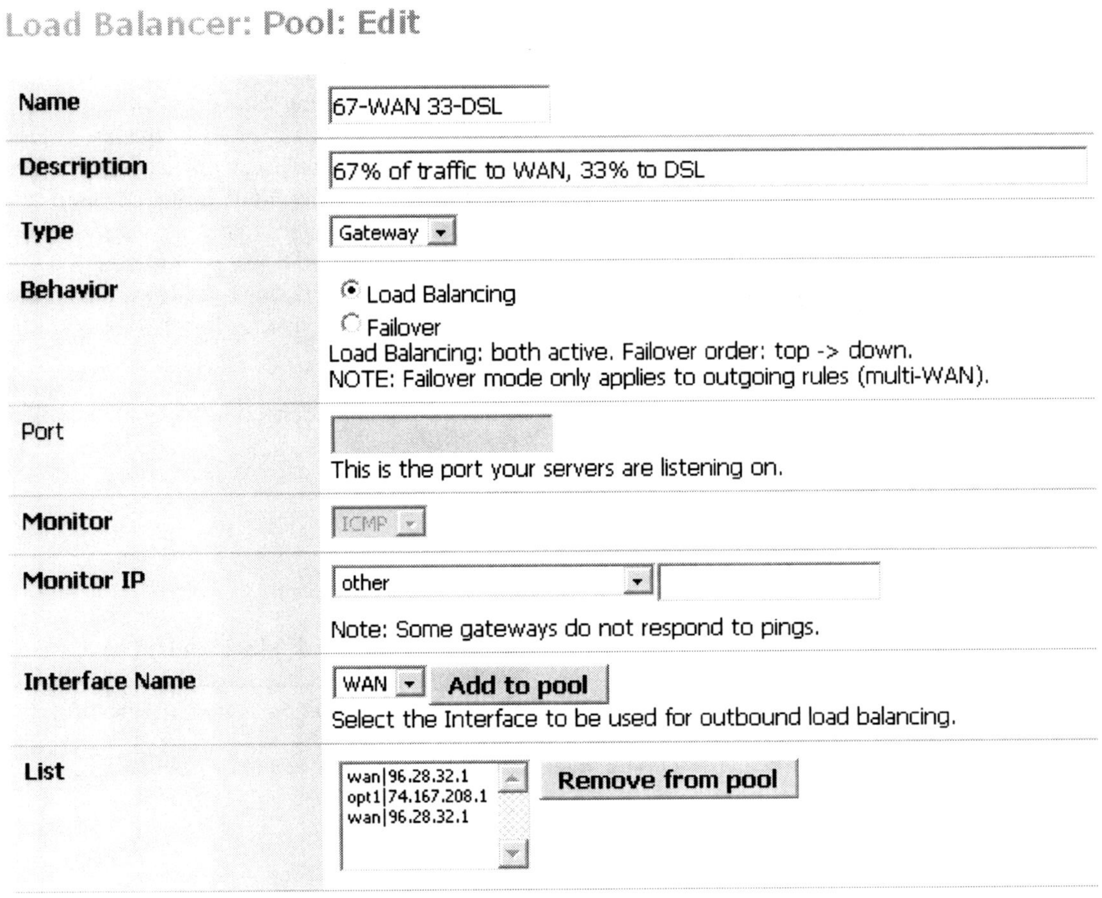

Load Balancer: Pool: Edit

Name	67-WAN 33-DSL
Description	67% of traffic to WAN, 33% to DSL
Type	Gateway ▾
Behavior	⦿ Load Balancing ○ Failover Load Balancing: both active. Failover order: top -> down. NOTE: Failover mode only applies to outgoing rules (multi-WAN).
Port	 This is the port your servers are listening on.
Monitor	ICMP ▾
Monitor IP	other ▾ Note: Some gateways do not respond to pings.
Interface Name	WAN ▾ **Add to pool** Select the Interface to be used for outbound load balancing.
List	wan|96.28.32.1 opt1|74.167.208.1 wan|96.28.32.1 **Remove from pool**

Figure 11.2: Unequal cost load balancing configuration

Note that this distribution is strictly balancing the number of connections, it does not take interface throughput into account. This means your bandwidth usage will not necessary be distributed equally, though in most environments it works out to be roughly distributed as configured over time. This also means if an interface is loaded to its capacity with a single high throughput connection, additional connections will still be directed to that interface. Ideally you would want it to distribute connections based on interface weights and the current throughput of the interface. We are looking into options for this ideal scenario for future pfSense releases, though the existing means of load balancing works very well for most all environments.

11.11   Multi-WAN on a Stick

In the router world, Cisco and others refer to a VLAN router as a "router on a stick" since it can be a functioning router with only one physical network connection. Expanding upon this, we can have multi-WAN on a stick using VLANs and a managed switch capable of 802.1q trunking. Most of the deployments running more than 5 WANs use this methodology to limit the number of physical interfaces required on the firewall. In such a deployment, the WANs all reside on one physical interface on the firewall, with the internal network(s) on additional physical interfaces. Figure 11.3 illustrates this type of deployment.

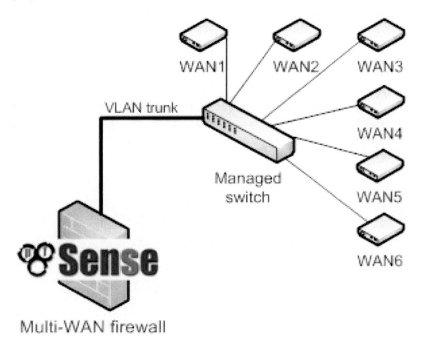

Figure 11.3: Multi-WAN on a stick

11.12 Troubleshooting

This section describes some of the most common problems with multi-WAN and how to troubleshoot them.

11.12.1 Verify your rule configuration

The most common error when configuring multi-WAN is improper firewall rule configuration. Remember the first matching rule wins — any further rules are ignored. If you add a policy routing rule below the default LAN rule, no traffic will ever match that rule because it will match the default LAN rule first.

If your rule ordering and configuration appears correct, it may help to enable logging on the rules. See the troubleshooting section in the firewall chapter for more information. Ensure the appropriate policy routing rule is passing the traffic.

11.12.2   Load balancing not working

First, ensure the firewall rule being matched directs traffic to the load balancing pool. If the rules are correct, and the traffic is matching a rule with the load balancer pool specified, verify that all of the connections show as Online under Status → Load Balancer. Connections marked as Offline will not be used. Lastly, this may be a problem not with the configuration, but with the testing methodology. Rather than testing with a web browser, try testing with **curl** as described in Section 17.2.6.

11.12.3   Failover not working

If problems occur when an Internet connection fails, typically it's because the monitor IP is still answering so the firewall thinks the connection is still available. Check Status → Load Balancer to verify. You may be using your modem's IP address as a monitor IP, which will typically still be accessible even if the Internet connection is down.

Chapter 12

Virtual Private Networks

VPNs provide a means of tunneling traffic through an encrypted connection, preventing it from being seen or modified in transit. pfSense offers three VPN options with IPsec, OpenVPN and PPTP. This chapter provides an overview of VPN usage, the pros and cons of each type of VPN in pfSense, and how to decide which is the best fit for your environment. Subsequent chapters go on to discuss each VPN option in detail.

12.1   Common deployments

There are four common uses of the VPN capabilities of pfSense, each covered in this section.

12.1.1   Site to site connectivity

Site to site connectivity is primarily used to connect networks in multiple physical locations, where a dedicated, always-on connection between the locations is required. This is frequently used to connect branch offices to a main office, connect the networks of business partners, or connect your network to another location such as a co-location environment. Before the proliferation of VPN technology, private WAN circuits were the only solution to connect multiple locations. These technologies include point to point dedicated circuits, packet switching technologies such as frame relay and ATM, and more recently, MPLS (Multiprotocol Label Switching) and fiber and copper based metropolitan Ethernet services. While these types of private WAN connectivity provide reliable, low latency connections, they are also very costly with recurring monthly fees. VPN technology has grown in popularity because it provides the same secure site to site connectivity using Internet connections that are generally much less costly.

12.1.1.1   Limitations of VPN connectivity

In some networks, only a private WAN circuit can meet the requirements for bandwidth or latency. Latency is usually the biggest factor. A point to point T1 circuit has end to end latency of about 3-5 ms, while the latency to the first hop on your ISP's network will generally be at least that much if not higher. Metro Ethernet services have end to end latency of about 1-3 ms, usually less than the latency to the first hop of your ISP's network. That will vary some based on geographical distance between the sites. The stated numbers are typical for sites within a couple hundred miles of each other. VPNs usually see latency of around 30-60 ms depending on the Internet connections in use and the geographical distance between the locations. You can minimize latency and maximize VPN performance by using the same ISP for all your VPN locations, but this isn't always feasible.

Certain protocols perform very poorly with the latency inherent in connections over the Internet. Microsoft file sharing (SMB) is a common example. At sub-10 ms latency, it performs well. At 30 ms or higher, it's sluggish, and at more than 50 ms it's painfully slow, causing frequent hangs when browsing folders, saving files, etc. Getting a simple directory listing requires numerous round trip connections between the client and server, which significantly exacerbates the increased delay of the connection. In Windows Vista and Server 2008, Microsoft introduced SMB 2.0 which includes new capabilities to address the issue described here. SMB 2.0 enables the sending of multiple actions in a single request, as well as the ability to pipeline requests, meaning the client can send additional requests without waiting for the response from prior requests. If your network uses exclusively Vista and Server 2008 or newer operating systems this won't be a concern, but given the rarity of such environments, this will usually be a consideration.

Two more examples of latency sensitive protocols are Microsoft Remote Desktop Protocol (RDP) and Citrix ICA. There is a clear performance and responsiveness difference with these protocols between sub-20 ms response times typically found in a private WAN, and the 50-60+ ms response times common to VPN connections. If your remote users work on published desktops using thin client devices, there will be a notable performance difference between a private WAN and VPN. Whether that performance difference is significant enough to justify the expense of a private WAN will vary from one environment to another. I have worked in thin client environments that accepted the performance hit, and in others where it was considered unacceptable.

There may be other network applications in your environment that are latency sensitive, where the reduced performance of a VPN is unacceptable. Or you may have all your locations within a relatively small geographical area using the same ISP, where the performance of your VPN rivals that of private WAN connections. Performance is an important consideration when planning a VPN solution.

12.1.2   Remote access

Remote access VPNs enable users to securely connect into your network from any location where an Internet connection is available. This is most frequently used for mobile workers (often referred to as "Road Warriors") whose job requires frequent travel and little time in the office, and to give employees the ability to work from home. It can also allow contractors or vendors temporary access to your network.

12.1.3   Protection for wireless networks

A VPN can provide an additional layer of protection for your wireless networks. This protection is twofold, in that it provides an additional layer of encryption for traffic traversing your wireless network, and it can be deployed in such a way that it requires additional authentication before access to network resources is permitted. This is deployed mostly the same as remote access VPNs. This is covered in Section 18.6.

12.1.4 Secure relay

Remote access VPNs can be configured in a way that passes all traffic from the client system over the VPN. This is nice to have when using untrusted networks, such as wireless hotspots as it lets you push all your Internet traffic over the VPN, and out to the Internet from your VPN server. This protects you from a number of attacks that people might be attempting on untrusted networks, though it does have a performance impact since it adds additional hops and latency to all your connections. That impact is usually minimal with high speed connectivity when you are geographically relatively close.

12.2 Choosing a VPN solution for your environment

Each VPN solution has its pros and cons. This section will cover the primary considerations in choosing a VPN solution, providing the information you will need to make a choice for your environment.

12.2.1 Interoperability

If you need a solution to interoperate with a firewall or router product from another vendor, IPsec will usually be the best choice since it is included with every VPN-capable device. It also keeps you from being locked into any particular firewall or VPN solution. For interoperable site to site connectivity, IPsec is usually the only choice. OpenVPN is interoperable with a few other packaged firewall/VPN solutions, but not many. Interoperability in this sense isn't applicable with PPTP since it can't be used for site to site connections.

12.2.2 Authentication considerations

Of the available VPN options in pfSense 1.2.x, only PPTP supports username and password authentication. IPsec and OpenVPN rely solely on shared keys or certificates. OpenVPN certificates can be password protected, in which case a compromised certificate alone isn't adequate for connecting to your VPN. The lack of additional authentication can be a security risk in that a lost, stolen, or compromised system containing a key or certificate means whoever has access to the device can connect to your VPN. However while not ideal, it isn't as great a risk as it may seem. A compromised system can easily have a key logger installed to capture the username and password information and easily defeat that protection. In the case of lost or stolen systems containing keys, if the hard drive isn't encrypted, the keys can be used to connect. However adding password authentication isn't of great help there either, as usually the same username and password will be used to log into the computer, and most passwords are crackable within minutes using modern hardware when you have access to an unencrypted drive. Password security is also frequently compromised by users with notes on their laptop or in their laptop case with their password written down.

In pfSense 2.0, all available VPN options support username and password authentication in addition to shared keys and certificates.

12.2.3   Ease of configuration

None of the available VPN options are extremely difficult to configure, but there are differences between the options. PPTP is very simple to configure and is the fastest and easiest to get working, but has considerable drawbacks in other areas. IPsec has numerous configuration options and can be difficult for the uninitiated. OpenVPN requires the use of certificates for remote access in most environments, which comes with its own learning curve and can be a bit arduous to manage. IPsec and OpenVPN are preferable options in many scenarios for other reasons discussed in this chapter, but ease of configuration isn't one of their strengths.

12.2.4   Multi-WAN capable

If you want your users to have the ability to connect to multiple WAN connections, PPTP is not an option because of the way GRE functions in combination with how pfSense's multi-WAN functions. Both IPsec and OpenVPN can be used with multi-WAN.

12.2.5   Client availability

For remote access VPNs, the availability of client software is a primary consideration. PPTP is the only option with client support built into most operating systems, but all three options are cross platform compatible.

12.2.5.1   IPsec

IPsec clients are available for Windows, Mac OS X, BSD and Linux though they are not included in the OS except for some Linux distributions. A good free option for Windows is the Shrew Soft client. Mac OS X includes IPsec support, but no user friendly interface for using it. There are free and commercial options available with a user-friendly GUI.

The Cisco IPsec client included with the iPhone and iPod Touch is not compatible with pfSense IPsec.

12.2.5.2   OpenVPN

OpenVPN has clients available for Windows, Mac OS X, all the BSDs, Linux, Solaris, and Windows Mobile, but the client does not come pre-installed in any of these operating systems.

12.2.5.3   PPTP

PPTP clients are included in every Windows version since Windows 95 OSR 2, every Mac OS X release, Apple iPhone and iPod Touch, and clients are available for all the BSDs and every major Linux distribution.

12.2.6 Firewall friendliness

VPN protocols can cause difficulties for many firewalls and NAT devices. This is primarily relevant to remote access connectivity, where your users will be behind a myriad of firewalls mostly outside of your control with varying configurations and capabilities.

12.2.6.1 IPsec

IPsec uses both UDP port 500 and the ESP protocol to function. Some firewalls don't handle ESP traffic well where NAT is involved, because the protocol does not have port numbers like TCP and UDP that make it easily trackable by NAT devices. IPsec clients behind NAT may require NAT-T to function, which encapsulates the ESP traffic over UDP port 4500. Currently, pfSense does not support NAT-T, so clients behind NAT may not function in some cases. There is one caveat to the lack of NAT-T support, discussed in Section 13.7.

12.2.6.2 OpenVPN

OpenVPN is the most firewall friendly of the VPN options. Since it uses TCP or UDP and is not affected by any common NAT functions such as rewriting of source ports, it is rare to find a firewall which will not work with OpenVPN. The only possible difficulty is if the protocol and port in use is blocked. You may want to use a common port like UDP 53 (usually DNS), or TCP 80 (usually HTTP) or 443 (usually HTTPS) or to evade most egress filtering.

12.2.6.3 PPTP

PPTP relies on a control channel running on TCP port 1723 and uses the GRE protocol to transmit data. GRE is frequently blocked or broken by firewalls and NAT devices. It is also subject to NAT limitations on many firewalls including pfSense (described in Section 14.4). PPTP works in many environments, but your users will likely encounter locations where it does not work. In some cases this can be a significant problem preventing the use of PPTP. As one example, some 3G wireless data providers assign private IPs to customers, and do not properly NAT GRE traffic, making the use of PPTP over 3G impossible on some networks.

12.2.7 Cryptographically secure

One of the critical functions of a VPN is to ensure the confidentiality of the data transmitted. PPTP has suffered from multiple security issues in the past, and has some design flaws that make it a weak VPN solution. The situation is not as dire as some make it out to be, though the security of PPTP is dependent upon users choosing strong passwords. Since most users do not employ strong passwords, or follow poor practices such as writing down passwords, PPTP is more subject to compromise than the other options. PPTP is still widely used, though whether it should be is a matter of debate. Strong passwords should always be employed, which limits the risk. Where ever possible, I recommend not using PPTP. Some deploy it regardless because of the convenience factor.

IPsec using pre-shared keys can be broken if a weak key is used. Use a strong key, at least 10 characters in length containing a mix of upper and lowercase letters, numbers and symbols.

OpenVPN's encryption is compromised if your PKI or shared keys are disclosed.

12.2.8 Recap

Table 12.1 shows an overview of the considerations provided in this section.

VPN Type	Client included in most OSes	Widely inter-operable	Multi-WAN	Crypto-graphically secure	Firewall friendly
IPsec	no	yes	yes	yes	no (without NAT-T)
OpenVPN	no	no	yes	yes	yes
PPTP	yes	n/a	no	no	most

Table 12.1: Features and Characteristics by VPN Type

12.3   VPNs and Firewall Rules

VPNs and firewall rules are handled somewhat inconsistently in pfSense 1.2.x. This section describes how firewall rules are handled for each of the individual VPN options. For the automatically added rules discussed here, you can disable the addition of those rules by checking Disable all auto-added VPN rules under System → Advanced .

12.3.1   IPsec

Rules for IPsec traffic coming in to the specified WAN interface is automatically allowed as described in Section 6.5.1.5. Traffic encapsulated within an active IPsec connection is controlled via user defined rules on the IPsec tab under Firewall → Rules .

12.3.2   OpenVPN

OpenVPN does not automatically add rules to WAN interfaces, but it does automatically add rules permitting traffic from authenticated clients, opposite of the behavior of IPsec and PPTP.

12.3.3   PPTP

PPTP automatically adds rules permitting TCP 1723 and GRE traffic into the WAN IP. Traffic from connected PPTP clients is controlled via user defined rules on the PPTP tab under Firewall → Rules , similar to IPsec.

Chapter 13

IPsec

IPsec provides a standards-based VPN implementation that is compatible with a wide range of clients for mobile connectivity, and other firewalls and routers for site to site connectivity. It supports numerous third party devices and is being used in production with devices ranging from consumer grade Linksys routers all the way up to IBM z/OS mainframes, and everything imaginable in between. This chapter describes the configuration options available, and how to configure various common scenarios.

For general discussion of the various types of VPNs available in pfSense and their pros and cons, see Chapter 12.

13.1   IPsec Terminology

Before delving too deeply into configuration, there are some terms that are used throughout the chapter that need some prior explanation. Other terms are explained in more detail upon their use in configuration options.

13.1.1   Security Association

A Security Association (SA) is a one-way tunnel through which encrypted traffic will travel. Each active IPsec tunnel will have two security associations, one for each direction. The Security Associations are setup between the *public* IP addresses for each endpoint. Knowledge of these active security associations is kept in the Security Association Database (SAD).

13.1.2   Security Policy

A Security Policy manges the complete specifications of the IPsec tunnel. As with Security Associations, these are one-way, so for each tunnel there will be one in each direction. These entries are kept in the Security Policy Database (SPD). The SPD is populated with two entries for each tunnel connection as soon as a tunnel is added. By contrast, SAD entries only exist upon successful negotiation of the connection.

13.1.3   Phase 1

There are two phases of negotiation for an IPsec tunnel. During Phase 1, the two endpoints of a tunnel setup a secure channel between the endpoints using Internet Security Association and Key Management Protocol (ISAKMP) to negotiate the SA entries and exchange keys. This also includes authentication, checking identifiers, and checking the pre-shared keys (PSK) or certificates. When Phase 1 is complete the two ends can exchange information securely, but have not yet decided what traffic will traverse the tunnel or how it will be encrypted.

13.1.4   Phase 2

In Phase 2, the two endpoints negotiate how to encrypt and send the data for the private hosts based on Security Policies. This is the part that builds the actual tunnel to be used for transferring data between the endpoints and clients whose traffic is handled by those routers. If Phase 2 has been successfully established, the tunnel will be up and ready for use.

13.2   Choosing configuration options

IPsec offers numerous configuration options, affecting the performance and security of your IPsec connections. Realistically, it matters little which options you choose here as long as you don't use DES, and use a strong pre-shared key, unless you're protecting something so valuable that an adversary with many millions of dollars worth of processing power is willing to devote it to breaking your IPsec. Even in that case, there is likely an easier and much cheaper way to break into your network and achieve the same end result (social engineering, for one).

13.2.1   Interface Selection

In many cases, the Interface option for an IPsec tunnel will be WAN, since the tunnels are connecting to remote sites. However, there are plenty of exceptions, the most common of which are outlined below.

13.2.1.1   CARP Environments

In CARP environments (Chapter 20), any CARP virtual IP addresses are also available in the Interface drop-down menu. You should choose the appropriate CARP address for your WAN or wherever the IPsec tunnel will terminate on the pfSense system. By using the CARP IP address, it ensures that the IPsec tunnel will be handled by the MASTER member of the CARP cluster, so even if the main firewall is down, the tunnel will connect to whichever CARP cluster member has taken over.

13.2.1.2   Multi-WAN Environments

When using Multi-WAN (Chapter 11), you should pick the appropriate Interface choice for the WAN-type interface to which the tunnel will connect. If you expect the connection to enter via WAN, pick WAN. If the tunnel should use a different WAN, choose whichever OPT WAN interface is needed.

13.2.1.3 Wireless Internal Protection

If you are configuring IPsec to add encryption to a wireless network, as described in Section 18.6.2, you should choose the OPT interface which corresponds to your wireless card. If you are using an external wireless access point, pick the interface pfSense can use to connect to the wireless access point.

13.2.2 Encryption algorithms

There are six options for encryption algorithms on both phase 1 and phase 2. DES (Data Encryption Standard) is considered insecure due to its small 56 bit key size, and should never be used unless you are forced to connect with a remote device that only supports DES. The remaining options are all considered cryptographically secure. Which to choose depends on what device you're connecting to, and the hardware available in your system. When connecting to third party devices, 3DES (also called "Triple DES") is commonly the best choice as it may be the only option the other end supports. For systems without a hardware cryptography accelerator, Blowfish and CAST are the fastest options. When using systems with `glxsb` accelerators, such as ALIX, choose Rijndael (AES) for best performance. For systems with `hifn` accelerators, chose 3DES or AES for best performance.

13.2.3 Lifetimes

The lifetimes specify how often the connection must be rekeyed, specified in seconds. 28800 seconds on phase 1 and 3600 seconds on phase 2 is a pretty standard configuration and is appropriate for most scenarios.

13.2.4 Protocol

With IPsec you have the option of choosing AH (Authenticated Header) or ESP (Encapsulating Security Payload). In nearly all circumstances, you should use ESP, as it is the only option that encrypts traffic. AH only provides assurance the traffic came from the trusted source and is rarely used.

13.2.5 Hash algorithms

Hash algorithms are used with IPsec to verify the authenticity of packet data. MD5 and SHA1 are the available hash algorithms on phase 1 and phase 2. Both are considered cryptographically secure, though SHA1 (Secure Hash Algorithm, Revision 1) is considered the stronger of the two. SHA1 does require more CPU cycles. These hash algorithms may also be referred to with HMAC (Hash Message Authentication Code) in the name in some contexts, but that usage varies depending on the hardware or software in use.

13.2.6 DH key group

All of the DH (Diffie-Hellman, named after its authors) key group options are considered cryptographically secure, though the higher numbers are slightly more secure at the cost of increased CPU usage.

13.2.7   PFS key group

Perfect Forward Secrecy (PFS) provides keying material with greater entropy, hence improving the cryptographic security of the connection, at the cost of higher CPU usage when rekeying occurs.

13.2.8   Dead Peer Detection (DPD)

Dead Peer Detection (DPD) is a periodic check that the host on the other end of the IPsec tunnel is still alive. If a DPD check fails, the tunnel is torn down by removing its associated SAD entries and renegotiation is attempted.

13.3   IPsec and firewall rules

When you configure an IPsec tunnel connection, pfSense automatically adds hidden firewall rules to allow UDP port 500 and the ESP protocol from the Remote gateway IP destined to the Interface IP specified in the configuration. When Allow mobile clients is enabled, the same firewall rules are added, except with the source set to any. To override the automatic addition of these rules, check Disable all auto-added VPN rules under System → Advanced. If you check that box, you must manually add firewall rules for UDP 500 and ESP to the appropriate WAN interface.

Traffic initiated from the remote end of an IPsec connection is filtered with the rules configured under Firewall → Rules, IPsec tab. Here you can restrict what resources can be accessed by remote IPsec users. To control what traffic can be passed from local networks to the remote IPsec VPN connected devices or networks, the rules on the local interface where the host resides control the traffic (e.g. connectivity from hosts on LAN are controlled with LAN rules).

13.4   Site to Site

A site to site IPsec tunnel allows you to interconnect two networks as if they were directly connected by a router. Systems at Site A can reach servers or other systems at Site B, and vice versa. This traffic may also be regulated via firewall rules, just as with any other network interface. If more than one client will be connecting to another site from the same controlled location, a site to site tunnel will likely be more efficient, not to mention more convenient and easier to support.

With a site to site tunnel, the systems on either network need not have any knowledge that a VPN even exists. No client software is needed, and all of the tunnel work is handled by the routers on either end of the connection. This is also a good solution for devices that have network support but do not handle VPN connections such as printers, cameras, HVAC systems, and other embedded hardware.

13.4.1   Site to site example configuration

The key to making a working IPsec tunnel is to make sure that both sides have matching settings for authentication, encryption, and so on. Before starting, make a note of the local and remote WAN IP addresses, as well as the local and remote internal subnets that you will be connecting. An IP from the remote subnet to ping is optional, but recommended to keep the tunnel alive. The system doesn't check for replies, as any traffic initiated to an IP on the remote network will trigger IPsec negotiation, so it doesn't matter if the host actually responds or not as long as it is an IP on the other side of the connection. Aside from the cosmetic tunnel Description and these pieces of information, the other connection settings will be identical.

In this example and some of the subsequent examples in this chapter, the following settings will be assumed:

Site A		Site B	
Name	Louisville Office	Name	London Office
WAN IP	172.23.1.3	WAN IP	172.16.1.3
LAN Subnet	192.168.1.0/24	LAN Subnet	10.0.10.0/24
LAN IP	192.168.1.1	LAN IP	10.0.10.1

Table 13.1: IPsec Endpoint Settings

We will start with Site A. First, we must enable IPsec on the router. Navigate to VPN → IPsec, check Enable IPsec, then click Save (Figure 13.1).

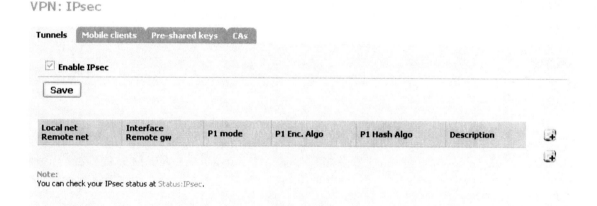

Figure 13.1: Enable IPsec

Now, create the tunnel by pressing the 🖫 button. You will now see a large page that has every setting needed for the tunnel to function. Don't be too discouraged, as many of these settings may be left at their default values.

To get started, fill in the top section that holds the general tunnel information and network settings, shown in Figure 13.2. Items in bold are required. Make sure that the Disable this tunnel box is unchecked. The interface setting should likely be **WAN**, but see the note earlier in the chapter on selecting the proper interface if you are unsure. Fill in the Dead Peer Detection (DPD) value with something reasonable, such as **60** seconds. Depending on your needs a lower value may be better, more like **10** or **20** seconds, but a problematic WAN connection on either side might make that too low. For the Local

Subnet, is probably best to leave this as **LAN Subnet**. You could also change this to **Network** and fill in the proper values, in this case **192.168.1.0/24**, but leaving it as **LAN Subnet** will ensure that should the network ever be renumbered, this end of the tunnel will follow. Note the other end must be changed manually. The Remote Subnet will be the network at Site B, in this case **10.0.10.0/24**. The Remote Gateway is the WAN address at Site B, **172.16.1.3**. Finally, enter a Description for the tunnel. It is a good idea to put the name of Site B in this box, and some detail about the tunnel's purpose may also help future administration. We'll put "**ExampleCo London Office**" in the description so we have some idea where the tunnel terminates.

VPN: IPsec: Edit tunnel

Mode	Tunnel
Disabled	☐ **Disable this tunnel** Set this option to disable this tunnel without removing it from the list.
Interface	WAN ▾ Select the interface for the local endpoint of this tunnel.
DPD interval	60 seconds Enter a value here to enable Dead Peer Detection (e.g. 60 seconds).
Local subnet	Type: LAN subnet ▾ Address: [ ] / 0 ▾
Remote subnet	10.0.10.0 / 24 ▾
Remote gateway	172.16.1.3 Enter the public IP address or hostname of the remote gateway
Description	ExampleCo London Office You may enter a description here for your reference (not parsed).

Figure 13.2: Site A VPN Tunnel Settings

The next section controls IPsec Phase 1, or Authentication. It is shown in Figure 13.3. The defaults are desirable for most of these settings, and simplifies the process. The most important setting to get right is the Pre-Shared Key. As mentioned in the VPN overview, IPsec using pre-shared keys can be broken if a weak key is used. Use a strong key, at least 10 characters in length containing a mix of upper and lowercase letters, numbers and symbols. The *same exact key* will need to be entered into the tunnel configuration for Site B later, so you may want to write it down, or copy and paste it elsewhere. Copy and paste may come in handy, especially with a complex key like **aBc123%XyZ9$7qwErty99**. A Lifetime setting may also be specified, otherwise the default value of **86400** will be used. As we are using a Pre-Shared Key and not certificates, leave all of the certificate boxes empty.

As for Phase 2 (Figure 13.4), there can be a little more variability. The Protocol choice could be **AH** for only authenticated packets, or **ESP** for encryption. ESP is the right choice in all but a few unusual situations. The Encryption algorithms and Hash algorithms can both be set to allow multiple options, and both sides will negotiate and agree upon the settings. In some cases that may be a good thing, but it is usually better to restrict this to the options that you know will be in use. For this example, the only Encryption algorithm selected is 3DES, and the only Hash algorithm selected is SHA1. PFS, or Perfect Forward Secrecy, can help protect against certain key attacks, but is optional. A Lifetime setting may also be specified, otherwise the default value of **3600** will be used.

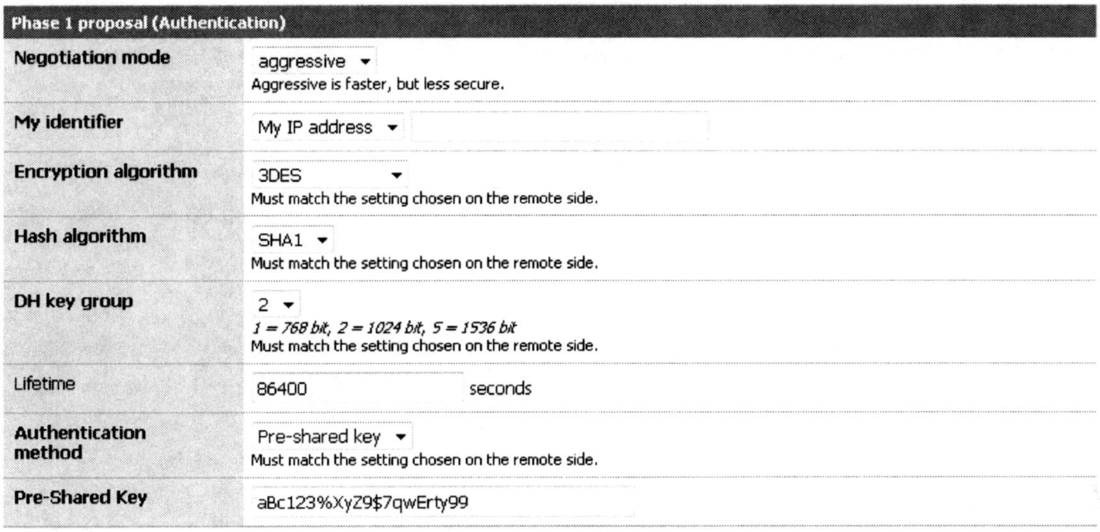

Phase 1 proposal (Authentication)	
Negotiation mode	aggressive ▼ Aggressive is faster, but less secure.
My identifier	My IP address ▼
Encryption algorithm	3DES ▼ Must match the setting chosen on the remote side.
Hash algorithm	SHA1 ▼ Must match the setting chosen on the remote side.
DH key group	2 ▼ *1 = 768 bit, 2 = 1024 bit, 5 = 1536 bit* Must match the setting chosen on the remote side.
Lifetime	86400 seconds
Authentication method	Pre-shared key ▼ Must match the setting chosen on the remote side.
Pre-Shared Key	aBc123%XyZ9$7qwErty99

Figure 13.3: Site A Phase 1 Settings

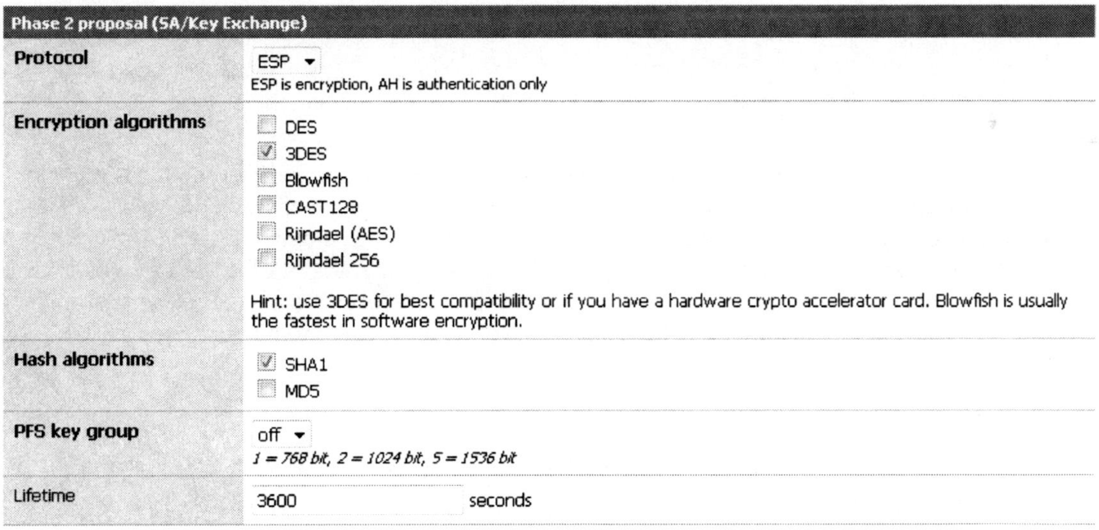

Phase 2 proposal (SA/Key Exchange)	
Protocol	ESP ▼ ESP is encryption, AH is authentication only
Encryption algorithms	☐ DES ☑ 3DES ☐ Blowfish ☐ CAST128 ☐ Rijndael (AES) ☐ Rijndael 256 Hint: use 3DES for best compatibility or if you have a hardware crypto accelerator card. Blowfish is usually the fastest in software encryption.
Hash algorithms	☑ SHA1 ☐ MD5
PFS key group	off ▼ *1 = 768 bit, 2 = 1024 bit, 5 = 1536 bit*
Lifetime	3600 seconds

Figure 13.4: Site A Phase 2 Settings

Lastly, you can enter an IP address for a system on the remote LAN that should periodically be sent an ICMP ping, as in Figure 13.5. The return value of the ping is not checked, this will only ensure that some traffic is sent on the tunnel so that it will stay established. In this setup, we can use the LAN IP address of the pfSense router at Site B, `10.0.10.1`.

Figure 13.5: Site A Keep Alive

Click the Save button, and then you will need to click Apply changes on the IPsec Tunnels screen, as seen in Figure 13.6.

Figure 13.6: Apply IPsec Settings

The tunnel for Site A is finished, but now firewall rules are needed to allow traffic from Site B's network to come in via the IPsec tunnel. These rules must be added to the IPsec tab under Firewall → Rules. See the chapter on Firewall rules for specifics on adding the rules. You may be as permissive as you like, (allow any protocol from anywhere to anywhere), or restrictive (allow TCP from a certain host on Site B to a certain host at Site A on a certain port). In each case, make sure the Source address(es) are Site B addresses, such as **10.0.10.0/24**. The destination addresses should be the Site A network, **192.168.1.0/24**.

Now that Site A is configured, it is time to tackle Site B. Repeat the process on Site B's router to enable IPsec and add a tunnel.

Only two parts of this setup will differ from Site A. Those are the general settings and the Keep Alive setting, as you can see in Figure 13.7. Make sure that the Disable this tunnel box is unchecked. The interface setting should be **WAN**. Fill in the Dead Peer Detection (DPD) value with the same setting as Site A.. For the Local Subnet, it is probably best to leave this as **LAN Subnet**. You could also change this to **Network** and fill in the proper values, in this case **10.0.10.0/24**. The Remote Subnet will be the network at Site A, in this case **192.168.1.0/24**. The Remote Gateway is the WAN address at Site A, **172.23.1.3**. A Description for the tunnel is still a good idea. We'll put "**ExampleCo Louisville Office**" on this side.

VPN: IPsec: Edit tunnel

Mode	Tunnel
Disabled	☐ **Disable this tunnel** Set this option to disable this tunnel without removing it from the list.
Interface	WAN ▾ Select the interface for the local endpoint of this tunnel.
DPD interval	60 seconds Enter a value here to enable Dead Peer Detection (e.g. 60 seconds).
Local subnet	Type: LAN subnet ▾ Address: [ ] / [0 ▾]
Remote subnet	192.168.1.0 / 24 ▾
Remote gateway	172.23.1.3 Enter the public IP address or hostname of the remote gateway
Description	ExampleCo Louisville Office You may enter a description here for your reference (not parsed).

Figure 13.7: Site B VPN Tunnel Settings

The Phase 1 and Phase 2 settings must match Site A exactly. Review that section of this example for the details and figures.

The last change is the Keep Alive setting (Figure 13.8). In this setup, we can use the LAN IP address of the pfSense router at Site A, **192.168.1.1**.

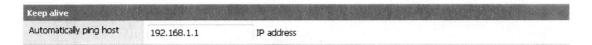

Keep alive		
Automatically ping host	192.168.1.1	IP address

Figure 13.8: Site B Keep Alive

Now click the Save button, and then click Apply changes on the IPsec Tunnels screen.

As with Site A, you must also add firewall rules to allow traffic on the tunnel to cross from Site A to Site B. Add these rules to the IPsec tab under Firewall → Rules. For more details, see Section 13.3. This time, the source of the traffic would be Site A, destination Site B.

Both tunnels are now configured and should be active. Check the IPsec status by visiting Status → IPsec. You should see a description of the tunnel along with an indicator icon for its status.

If you do not see a ☐ icon, there may be a problem establishing the tunnel. This soon, the most likely reason is that no traffic has attempted to cross the tunnel. Try to ping a system in the remote subnet at Site B from Site A (or vice versa) and see if the tunnel establishes. Look at Section 13.6 for other means of testing a tunnel.

Failing that, the IPsec logs will offer an explanation. They are located under Status → System Logs on the IPsec VPN tab. Be sure to check the status and logs at both sites. For more troubleshooting information, check the Section 13.8 section later in this chapter.

13.4.2   Routing and gateway considerations

When the VPN endpoint, in this case a pfSense router, is the default gateway for a network there should be no problems with routing. As a client PC sends traffic, it will go to the pfSense box, over the tunnel, and out the other end. However, if the pfSense router is *not* the default gateway for a given network, then other routing measures will need to be taken.

As an example, imagine that the pfSense router is the gateway at Site B, but not Site A, as illustrated in Figure 13.9. A client, PC1 at Site B sends a ping to PC2 at Site A. The packet leaves PC1, then through Site B's router, across the tunnel, out the pfSense router at Site A, and on to PC2. But what happens on the way back? PC2's gateway is another router entirely. The reply to the ping will be sent to the gateway system and most likely be tossed out, or even worse, it may be sent out the Internet link and be lost that way.

There are several ways around this problem, and any one may be better depending on the circumstances of a given case. First, a static route could be entered into the gateway router that will redirect traffic destined for the far side of the tunnel to the pfSense router. Even with this route, additional complexities are introduced because this scenario results in asymmetric routing as covered in Section 8.1.2. Should that not work, a static route could be added to the client systems individually so that they know to send that traffic directly to the pfSense box and not via their default gateway. Unless there are only a very small number of hosts that need to access the VPN, this is a management headache and should be avoided. Last but not least, in some situations it may be easier to make the pfSense box the gateway and let it handle your Internet connection.

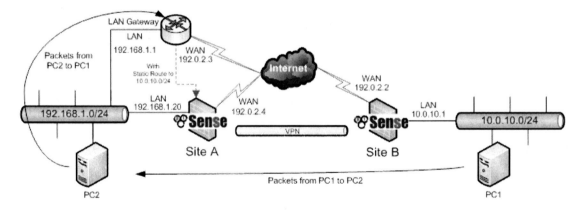

Figure 13.9: Site to Site IPsec Where pfSense is not the Gateway

13.4.3   Routing multiple subnets over IPsec

If you need to route multiple IP subnets over IPsec, you have two options — CIDR summarization and parallel IPsec tunnels. pfSense 2.0 allows the definition of multiple subnets per IPsec connection, but for 1.2 you must do one of the following.

Note

Traffic will traverse an IPsec tunnel only if it matches an existing SAD entry. Static routes will *not* route traffic over an IPsec connection, never configure static routes for any IPsec traffic except in the case of traffic initiated from pfSense itself (which will be discussed later).

13.4.3.1   CIDR Summarization

If the subnets are contiguous, you can route multiple subnets on one tunnel using a larger subnet which includes all the smaller subnets. For example if one site includes the subnets 192.168.0.0/24 and 192.168.1.0/24, that can be summarized as 192.168.0.0/23. See Section 1.7.5 for more information.

13.4.3.2   Parallel IPsec Tunnels

The only option if the subnets are not summarized is to create parallel IPsec tunnels, one for each subnet.

Click the 🖼 to the right of the first connection to add another based on this one. Change only the remote subnet (to the second subnet you wish to connect) and set the PSK to something different from the first connection. Save your changes.

13.4.4   pfSense-initiated Traffic and IPsec

To access the remote end of IPsec connections from pfSense itself, you will need to "fake" the system by adding a static route pointing the remote network to the system's LAN IP. Note this example presumes the VPN is connecting the LAN interface on both sides. If your IPsec connection is connecting an OPT interface, replace Interface and IP address of the interface accordingly. Because of the way IPsec is tied into the FreeBSD kernel, without the static route the traffic will follow the system's routing table, which will likely send this traffic out your WAN interface rather than over the IPsec tunnel. Take Figure 13.10, for example.

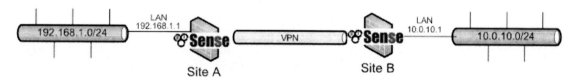

Figure 13.10: Site to Site IPsec

You need to add a static route on each firewall. Figure 13.11 and Figure 13.12 show the route to be added on each side.

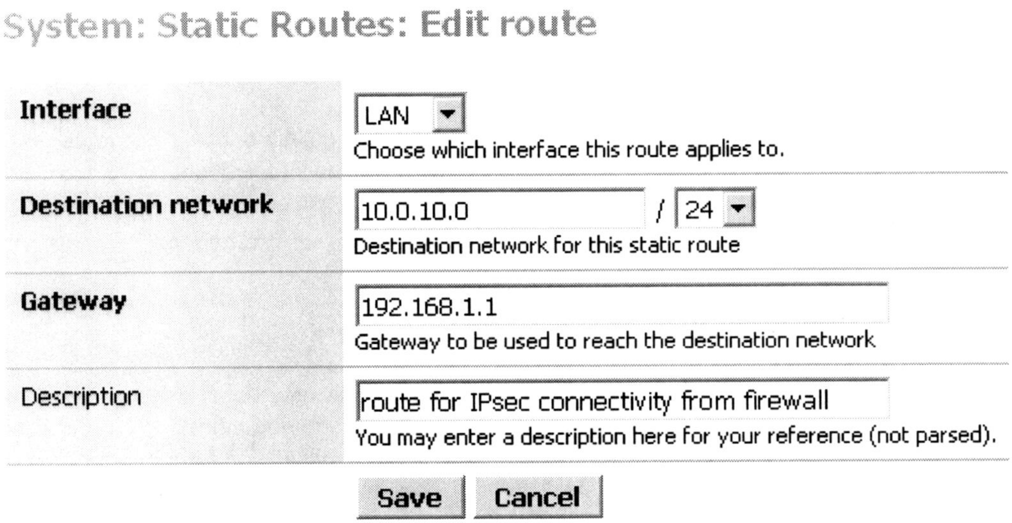

System: Static Routes: Edit route

Interface	LAN ▼
	Choose which interface this route applies to.
Destination network	10.0.10.0 / 24 ▼
	Destination network for this static route
Gateway	192.168.1.1
	Gateway to be used to reach the destination network
Description	route for IPsec connectivity from firewall
	You may enter a description here for your reference (not parsed).

Save | Cancel

Figure 13.11: Site A — Static route to remote subnet

System: Static Routes: Edit route

Interface	LAN ▼
	Choose which interface this route applies to.
Destination network	192.168.1.0 / 24 ▼
	Destination network for this static route
Gateway	10.0.10.1
	Gateway to be used to reach the destination network
Description	route for IPsec connectivity from firewall
	You may enter a description here for your reference (not parsed).

Save | Cancel

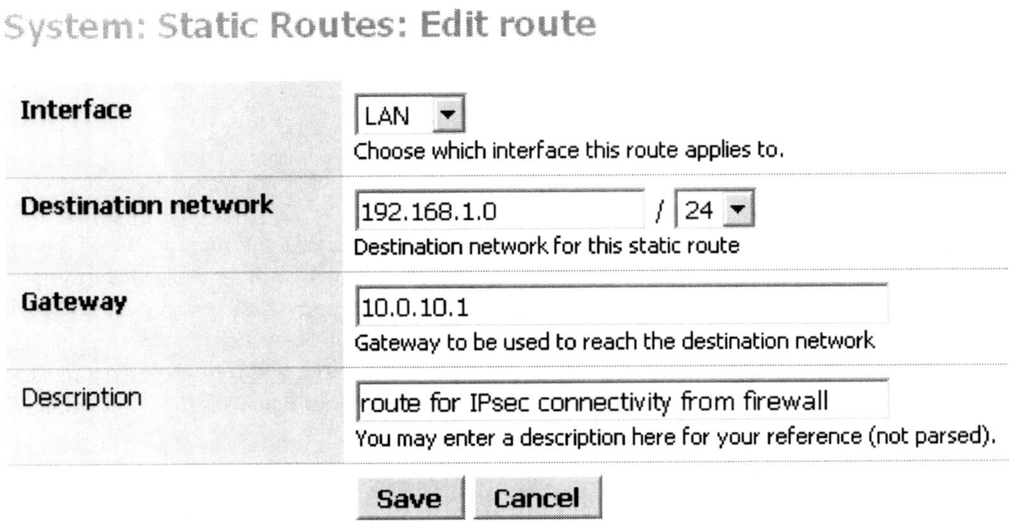

Figure 13.12: Site B — Static route to remote subnet

13.5   Mobile IPsec

Mobile IPsec will allow you to make a so-called "Road Warrior" style connection, named after the variable nature of anyone who is not in the office that needs to connect back to the main network. It may be a sales person using Wi-Fi on a business trip, the boss from his limo via 3G modem, or a programmer working from their broadband line at home. Most of these will be forced to deal with dynamic IP addresses, and often will not even know the IP address they have. Without a router or firewall supporting IPsec, a traditional IPsec tunnel will not work. In telecommuting scenarios, it's usually undesirable and unnecessary to connect the user's entire home network to your network, and will introduce routing complications. This is where IPsec Mobile Clients come in.

There is only one definition for Mobile IPsec on pfSense, so you may be wondering how to setup multiple clients. Instead of relying on a fixed address for the remote end of the tunnel, a unique Identifier/Pre-Shared Key pair is used, much like a username and password. This allows the clients to be authenticated and distinguished from one another.

Before you begin configuring clients, you may want to choose an IP address range they will be using. This is not controlled on the server side, so some care will be needed to ensure that IP addresses do not overlap when setting up client software. The IP addresses must differ from those in use at the site hosting the mobile tunnel. In this example, *192.168.111.0/24* will be used, but it can be any unused subnet that you desire. Alternatively, you aren't required to specify an IP address. The clients can be configured so they pass through the local IP address of the connecting client. This will be a private IP where the client is behind NAT, and a public IP where one is directly assigned to the client. If you will be filtering based on the source IP on the IPsec interface, you will want to specify an IP for each client so you always know the source IP and it will not change. Not specifying the source IP may also create routing difficulties, where the client is on a local network conflicting with one of your internal networks.

13.5.1 Example Server Configuration

There are two components to the server configuration for mobile clients: Creating the tunnel, and creating the Pre-Shared Keys.

13.5.1.1 Mobile Client Tunnel Creation

First, we must enable IPsec on the router if you haven't done so already. Navigate to VPN → IPsec, check Enable IPsec, then click Save. With IPsec enabled, mobile client support must also be turned on. From VPN → IPsec, click on the Mobile clients tab (Figure 13.13). Check the Allow mobile clients box, and then continue on to the next set of options.

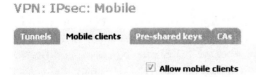

Figure 13.13: Enable Mobile IPsec Clients

Phase 1 proposal (Authentication)	
Negotiation mode	aggressive ▾ Aggressive is faster, but less secure.
My identifier	My IP address ▾
Encryption algorithm	3DES ▾ Must match the setting chosen on the remote side.
Hash algorithm	SHA1 ▾ Must match the setting chosen on the remote side.
DH key group	2 ▾ 1 = 768 bit, 2 = 1024 bit, 5 = 1536 bit Must match the setting chosen on the remote side.
DPD Interval	120 Dead Peer Detection interval in seconds. Leave this empty to only respond to DPD requests and not send any requests.
Lifetime	86400 seconds
Authentication method	Pre-shared key ▾ Must match the setting chosen on the remote side.

Figure 13.14: Mobile Clients Phase 1

A Phase 1 proposal must now be configured for Authentication, as shown in Figure 13.14. When dealing with mobile clients, it is best to use safe, widely-compatible settings. Using **aggressive** for the Negotiation mode will allow for using a wider range of identifier types, such as the e-mail address style that are used in this example setup. Since this side should have a static address, using **My IP address** for the My identifier option should be safe. The Encryption algorithm, **3DES** and the Hash algorithm **SHA1** are secure and well-supported. A DH key group of **2** is a good, safe, middle ground as well. Due to the large variance in connection types that will be dealt with, a higher DPD value of around **120** seconds is more likely to ensure that connections are not dropped prematurely. The Lifetime can be set much lower if you'd like, but **86400** should still be acceptable. We will be using **Pre-Shared Key** for the Authentication method, since in this example we want everyone to have individual Identifiers and Pre-Shared Keys.

Figure 13.15 shows the Phase 2 options for the mobile tunnels. Since encrypted traffic is important in this case, the Protocol should be set for **ESP**. The Encryption algorithms for Phase 2 can be set for as many as needed. You may find that certain software clients behave better than others using different algorithms. A safe choice is to at least check **3DES**, but others may be used. For Hash algorithms, you can choose both **SHA1** and **MD5**, or just one of the two. PFS is optional, and depending on the client software involved it may be best to leave this **off**. The default Lifetime of **3600** is probably still a good idea here. Now click Save and move on.

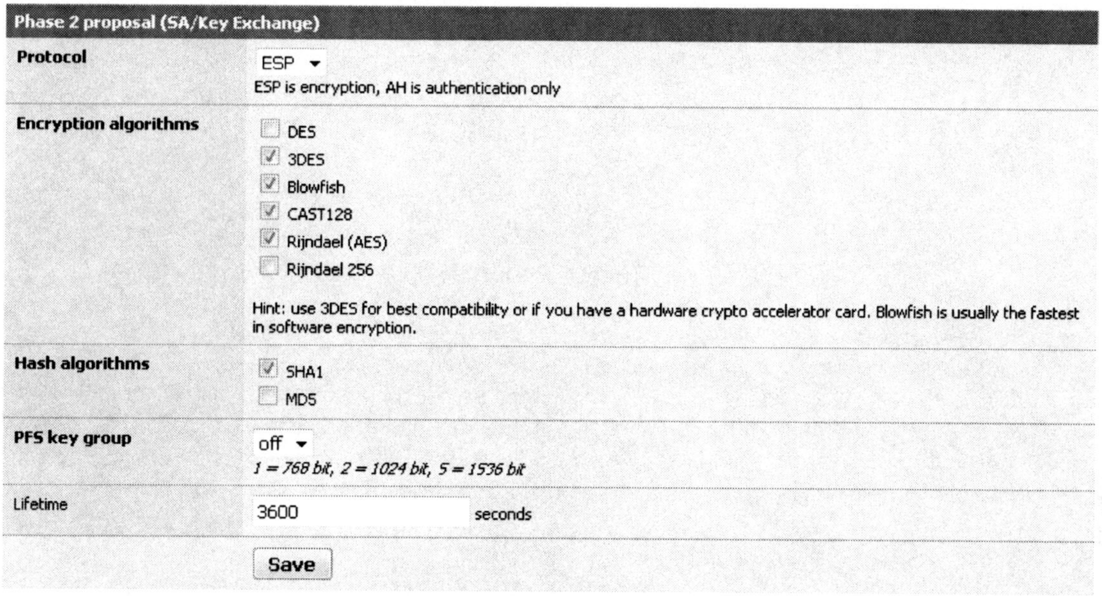

Phase 2 proposal (SA/Key Exchange)

Protocol	ESP ▾ ESP is encryption, AH is authentication only
Encryption algorithms	☐ DES ☑ 3DES ☑ Blowfish ☑ CAST128 ☑ Rijndael (AES) ☐ Rijndael 256 Hint: use 3DES for best compatibility or if you have a hardware crypto accelerator card. Blowfish is usually the fastest in software encryption.
Hash algorithms	☑ SHA1 ☐ MD5
PFS key group	off ▾ *1 = 768 bit, 2 = 1024 bit, 5 = 1536 bit*
Lifetime	3600 seconds

Save

Figure 13.15: Mobile Clients Phase 2

After clicking Save, the settings must be applied before they will take effect. Click Apply changes (Figure 13.16) and then the tunnel setup for mobile clients is complete.

VPN: IPsec: Mobile

❗ The IPsec tunnel configuration has been changed.
You must apply the changes in order for them to take effect.   **Apply changes**

Figure 13.16: Apply Mobile Tunnel Settings

13.5.1.2 Mobile Client Pre-Shared Key Creation

The next part of the mobile client setup is to enter Identifiers and Pre-Shared Keys for the individual clients. From VPN → IPsec, click on the Pre-shared keys tab. This will list all of the currently created Identifier/PSK pairs, as seen in Figure 13.17. Since we just started, this is likely empty. To create a new pair, click the ⊞ button.

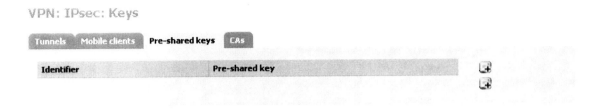

Figure 13.17: IPsec Pre-shared Key "User" List

A screen with two fields will appear. One for the Identifier, and one for the Pre-shared key (Figure 13.18). In the first box, enter an e-mail address for this client. It does not have to be a real, valid, address, it need only resemble one. As mentioned in the VPN overview, IPsec using pre-shared keys can be broken if a weak key is used. Use a strong key, at least 10 characters in length containing a mix of upper and lowercase letters, numbers and symbols. Click Save when finished.

VPN: IPsec: Edit pre-shared key

Identifier	fieldtech@lvx.example.com
	This can be either an IP address, fully qualified domain name or an e-mail address.
Pre-shared key	PSk33##44$$55%%789

Save

Figure 13.18: Adding an Identifier/Pre-Shared Key Pair

As with the tunnel settings, after altering key settings, the changes will need to be applied. The Identifier and Pre-shared key just created should also be listed on this screen. If there are more Identifier/PSK pairs to add, click and repeat the above step. Otherwise, click Apply changes to complete the IPsec setup (Figure 13.19).

VPN: IPsec: Keys

The IPsec tunnel configuration has been changed. You must apply the changes in order for them to take effect.   Apply changes

| Identifier | Pre-shared key |
| fieldtech@lvx.example.com | PSk33##44$$55%%789 |

Figure 13.19: Applying Changes; PSK List

13.5.1.3 Firewall Rules

As with the static site-to-site tunnels, mobile tunnels will also need firewall rules added to the IPsec tab under Firewall → Rules. In this instance the source of the traffic would be the subnet you chose for the mobile clients (or the addresses of their remote networks), and the destination will be your LAN network. For more details, Section 13.3.

13.5.2 Example Client Configuration

Each mobile client computer will need to run some kind of IPsec client software. There are many different IPsec clients available for use, some free, and some commercial applications. Typically IPsec is a fairly interoperable protocol when it comes to router-to-router tunnels, but client programs have proven more fickle, or at times incorporate proprietary extensions that are not compatible with standards-based IPsec implementations. As mentioned before, the Cisco IPsec client included with the iPhone and iPod Touch is not compatible with pfSense IPsec, and the client provided for connecting to Watchguard Fireboxes has seen mixed results as well.

13.5.2.1 Shrew Soft Client for Windows

The Shrew Soft VPN Client is a solid choice for using IPsec on Windows. Not only is it easy to use and reliable, but it is also available completely free. Visit `http://www.shrew.net` and download the latest version of the Shrew Soft client for your platform. Run the installer, and click Next or Continue through all the prompts.

Start the Shrew Soft Client by clicking the Access Manager icon. The main screen should appear, and look like Figure 13.20. Next, click the Add button to start configuring a new connection.

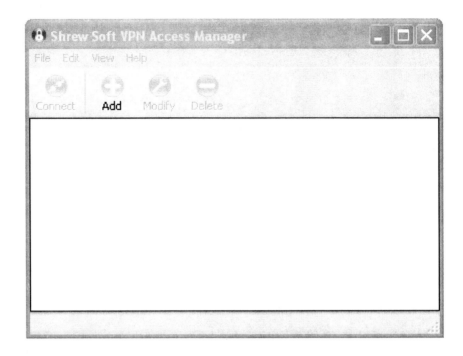

Figure 13.20: Shrew Soft VPN Access Manager — No Connections Yet

The VPN Site Configuration window should open, with several tabs as in Figure 13.21. It should start on the General tab. Here, enter the Host as the pfSense Box WAN IP, or the IP address of the pfSense interface chosen previously for IPsec use. In our example, **172.23.1.3**. The Port should be **500**. Auto Configuration should be **Disabled**. For the Address Method, change that to **Use virtual adapter and assigned address**. In the Address field, pick an IP out of the range you decided upon earlier. We'll use *192.168.111.5*, with a Netmask of *255.255.255.0*. Alternatively if you just want to pass through the IP of the client without specifying one specific to IPsec, in the Address Method box, choose **Use an existing adapter and current address**.

Changes may not be needed on the Client tab. The default values should be fine, but you can compare them with Figure 13.22 to be sure they match up with the defaults at the time this was being written.

On the Name Resolution tab, uncheck Enable WINS (Windows Internet Name Service) and uncheck Enable DNS. You may experiment with these options as they relate to your own setup, but in this example we will leave them off. See Figure 13.23 for examples. In environments where a WINS server might be present, you can enter the IP address here for a server reachable over this tunnel, to aid in resolving NetBIOS names and browsing the remote network. Adding DNS servers here may not work as expected with many ISPs. Typically, the DNS servers for IPsec clients are used as a last resort. If a name is not resolved over the client's normal DNS servers, these additional servers may be used. Unfortunately, many ISPs are "helpfully" providing services which resolve any non-existing domains to a landing page full of advertising. In this scenario, unresolvable names will never happen and thus additional servers will not be used. Use this option with caution, and test it first before using it on clients in the wild.

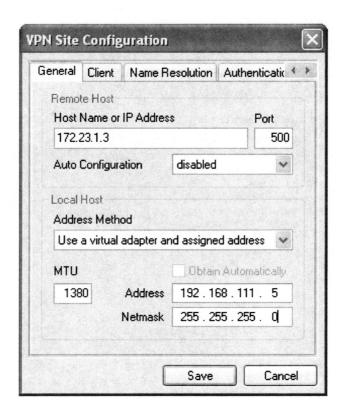

Figure 13.21: Client Setup: General Tab

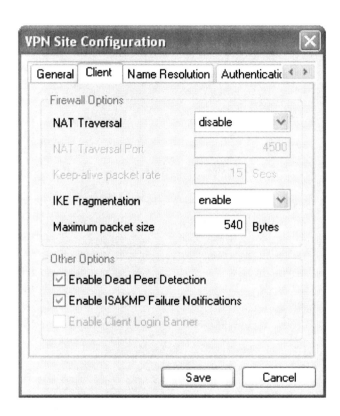

Figure 13.22: Client Setup: Client Tab

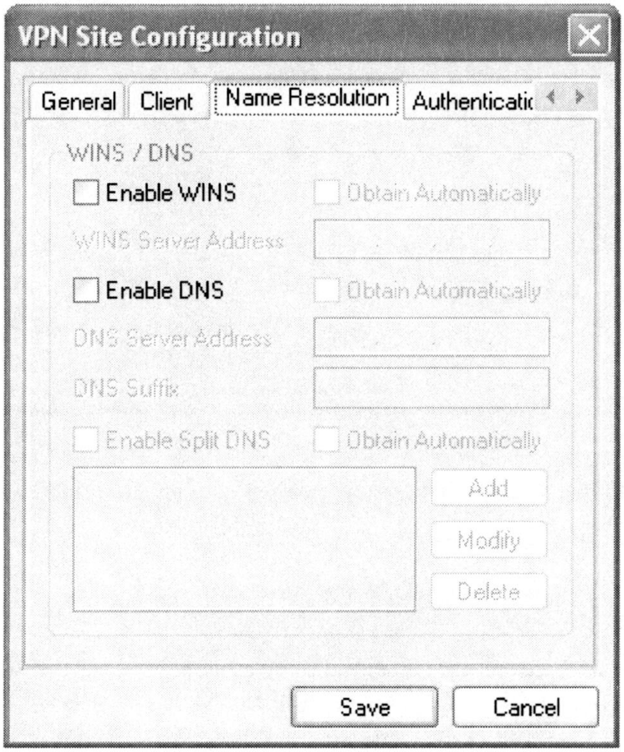

Figure 13.23: Client Setup: Name Resolution Tab

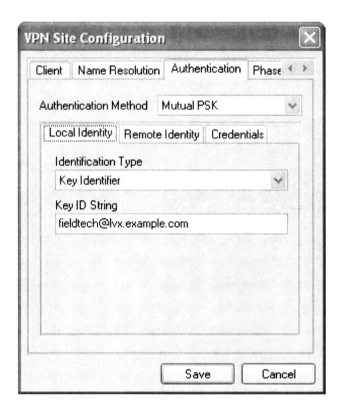

Figure 13.24: Client Setup: Authentication, Local Identity

The Authentication tab has three sub-tabs that need setup as well. First, set the Authentication Method to **Mutual PSK** at the top, then continue on to the Local Identity tab underneath, shown in Figure 13.24. Set the Identification type to **Key Identifier**, and the Key ID String to one of the e-mail style identifiers that was created earlier for a mobile client.

Click the Remote Identity tab (Figure 13.25). Set the Identification Type to **IP Address**, and check Use a discovered remote host address.

On the Credentials tab, shown in Figure 13.26, fill in the Pre-Shared Key field with the key that goes along with the e-mail address entered as the Key ID String on the Local Identity tab.

Now go back up to the Phase 1 tab, seen in Figure 13.27. These settings will match up with those set on the server tunnel's Phase 1 section. Set the Exchange Type to **aggressive**, the DH Exchange to **Group 2**, Cipher Algorithm to **3DES**, Hash Algorithm to **SHA1**, and Key Life Time limit to **86400**.

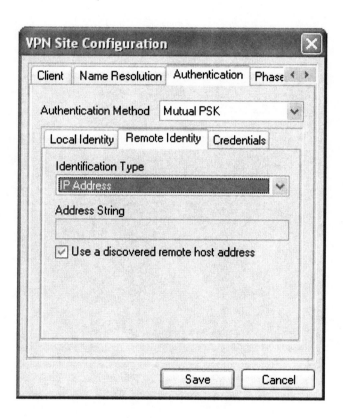

Figure 13.25: Client Setup: Authentication, Remote Identity

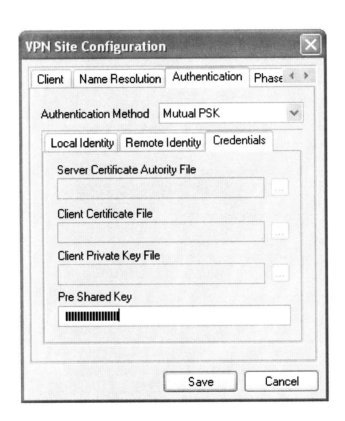

Figure 13.26: Client Setup: Authentication, Credentials

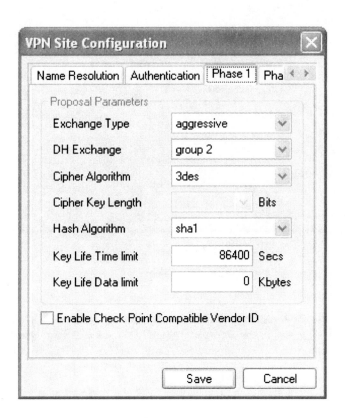

Figure 13.27: Client Setup: Phase 1

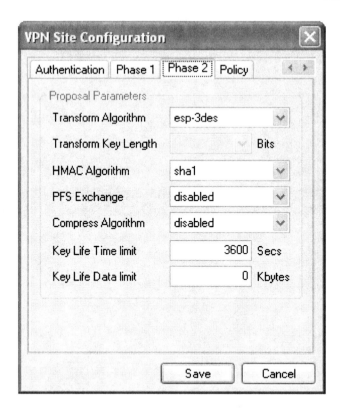

Figure 13.28: Client Setup: Phase 2

The settings on the Phase 2 tab will also be the same as those set on the mobile clients Phase 2 section, as can be seen in Figure 13.28. Set the Transform Algorithm to **esp-3des**, HMAC Algorithm is **SHA1**, PFS is **disabled**, Compress Algorithm is **disabled**, and Key Life Time limit is **3600**.

Finally there is the Policy tab, shown in Figure 13.29. This controls what traffic will be sent on the tunnel. Uncheck Obtain Topology Automatically, then click the Add button.

On the Topology Entry screen, seen in Figure 13.30, you need to specify what subnet will be on the other end of the tunnel. Set the Type to **Include**. For the Address, enter the network behind pfSense on the other side, and the Netmask that goes along with it. For our example that will be **192.168.1.0** and **255.255.255.0** respectively. Click OK.

When you click Save, you will be taken back to the main screen of the Shrew Soft client, and you have an opportunity to change the name of the connection, as in Figure 13.31.

It is a good idea to name the connection after the location to which it connects. In this case, I named it after the office where the tunnel leads as Figure 13.32 shows.

To connect to that VPN, click it once to select it and then click Connect. The VPN connect dialog will appear, and then click the Connect button on there as well. If the tunnel is successfully established, it will be indicated in the window. Figure 13.33 shows the output from a successful connection.

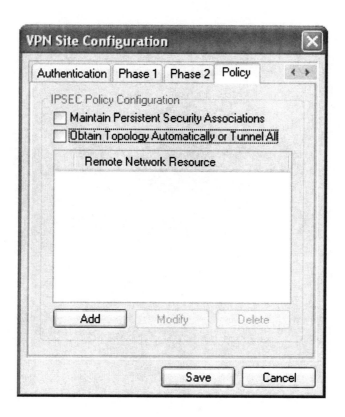

Figure 13.29: Client Setup: Policy

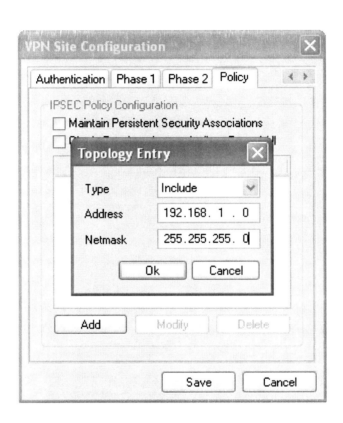

Figure 13.30: Client Setup: Policy, Add Topology

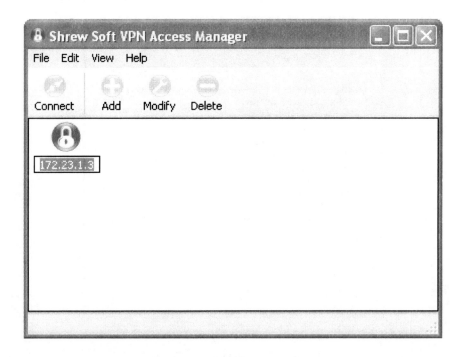

Figure 13.31: Client Setup: New Connection Name

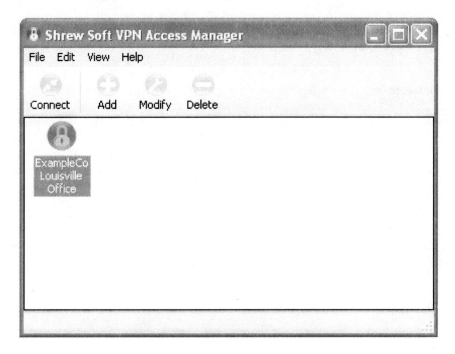

Figure 13.32: Ready To Use Connection

Figure 13.33: Connected Tunnel

You should now be able to contact systems at the other end of the tunnel. If it didn't come up right or pass traffic, double check all of the settings on both sides as they are listed here. Otherwise, continue on to the troubleshooting section.

13.5.2.2   TheGreenBow IPsec Client

TheGreenBow IPsec Client is a commercial VPN client for Windows which is compatible with pf-Sense. Instructions for configuring this client with pfSense can be found in the VPN gateway support section of their website. For more information about purchasing and configuring the client, visit their website. They offer a free 30 day trial of the client for those looking to evaluate it as a possible solution.

13.5.2.3   NCP Secure Entry Client

The Secure Entry Client by NCP is another commercial IPsec client for Windows, Windows Mobile, and Symbian. As it is standards-compliant, it can also connect to pfSense systems.

13.5.2.4   SSH Sentinel

SSH Sentinel is another standards-compliant IPsec client for Windows. Though SSH Sentinel does work with pfSense, its configuration is quite complex and the available free client is seven years old, having been released in 2002. Due to those factors, we do not recommend its use, and the Shrew Soft client should be used in its place.

13.5.2.5 IPSecuritas

IPSecuritas by Lobotomo Software is a freeware Mac OS X client for IPsec that some users have reported to work with pfSense.

13.5.2.6 Linux Clients

There are some freely available Linux clients, but they vary between distributions. Some are just front-ends to other utilities like **ipsec-tools**, but they should work as long as the client configurations are similar to the one demonstrated above.

13.5.2.7 Cisco VPN Client

The Cisco VPN Client does not currently work with pfSense because it requires xauth support. This should work with pfSense 2.0, however, since xauth will be available there.

13.6 Testing IPsec Connectivity

The easiest test for an IPsec tunnel is a ping from one client station behind the router to another on the opposite side. If that works, the tunnel is up and working properly.

As mentioned in Section 13.4.4, traffic initiated from pfSense will not normally traverse the tunnel without some extra routing, but there is a quick way to test the connection from the router console using the **ping** command while specifying a source address with the $-S$ parameter. Without using $-S$ or a static route, the packets generated by **ping** will not attempt to traverse the tunnel. This would be the syntax to use for a proper test:

```
# ping -S <Local LAN IP> <Remote LAN IP>
```

Where the `Local LAN IP` is an IP address on an internal interface within in the local subnet definition for the tunnel, and the `Remote LAN IP` is an IP on the remote router within the remote subnet listed for the tunnel. In most cases this is simply the LAN IP address of the respective pfSense routers. Given our site-to-site example above, this is what you would type to test from the console of the Site A router:

```
# ping -S 192.168.1.1 10.0.10.1
```

You should receive ping replies from Site B's LAN address if the tunnel is up and working properly. If you do not receive replies, move on to the troubleshooting section (Section 13.8).

13.7 IPsec and NAT-T

IPsec NAT-T encapsulates the ESP protocol traffic inside of UDP port 4500 traffic, because ESP frequently causes difficulties when used in combination with NAT. NAT-T support was added for a time in pfSense 1.2.3, except it brought out bugs in the underlying ipsec-tools software that caused regressions. One major regression was that renegotiation with some third party IPsec devices would fail. After considerable efforts to fix the problem, NAT-T support was pulled to eliminate the regressions and get 1.2.3 released. A 1.2.3-RC2 snapshot with NAT-T is available for those who wish to use it, with the caveat that it may cause renegotiation issues.

13.8 IPsec Troubleshooting

Due to IPsec's finicky nature, it isn't unusual for trouble to arise. Thankfully there are some basic (and some not so basic) troubleshooting steps that can be employed to track down potential problems.

13.8.1 Tunnel does not establish

The single most common cause of failed IPsec tunnel connections is a configuration mismatch. Often it is something small, such as a DH group set to 1 on side A and 2 on side B, or perhaps a subnet mask of /24 on one side and /32 on the other. Some routers (Linksys, for one) also like to hide certain options behind "Advanced" buttons or make assumptions. A lot of trial and error may be involved, and a lot of log reading, but ensuring that both sides match precisely will help the most.

Depending on the Internet connections on either end of the tunnel, it is also possible (especially with mobile clients) that a router involved on one side or the other does not properly handle IPsec traffic, primarily where NAT is involved. The problems are generally with the ESP protocol. NAT Traversal (NAT-T) encapsulates ESP in UDP port 4500 traffic to get around these issues, but is not currently available in pfSense.

In the case of a timeout on a mobile client, first check the service status at Status → Services. If the service is stopped, double check that Allow mobile clients is checked on VPN → IPsec, Mobile clients tab. If the service is running, check the firewall logs (Status → System Logs, Firewall tab) to see if the connection is being blocked, and if so, add a rule to allow the blocked traffic.

13.8.2 Tunnel establishes but no traffic passes

The top suspect if a tunnel comes up but won't pass traffic would be the IPsec firewall rules. If you are at Site A and cannot reach Site B, check the Site B router. Conversely, if you are at Site B and cannot contact Site A, check Site A. Before looking at the rules, be sure to check the firewall logs which are at Status → System Logs, on the Firewall tab. If you see blocked entries involving the subnets used in the IPsec tunnel, then move on to checking the rules. If there are no log entries indicating blocked packets, revisit the section on IPsec routing considerations in Section 13.4.2.

Blocked packets on the IPsec or enc0 interface indicate that the tunnel itself has established but traffic is being blocked by rules on the IPsec interface. Blocked packets on the LAN or other internal interface may indicate that an additional rule may be needed on that interface's ruleset to allow traffic from the internal subnet out to the remote end of the IPsec tunnel. Blocked packets on WAN or OPT WAN interfaces would prevent a tunnel from establishing. Typically this only happens when the automatic VPN rules are disabled. Adding a rule to allow the ESP protocol and UDP port 500 from that remote

IP address should allow the tunnel to establish. In the case of mobile tunnels, you will need to allow traffic from any source to connect to those ports.

Rules for the IPsec interface can be found under Firewall → Rules, on the IPsec tab. Common mistakes include setting a rule to only allow TCP traffic, which means things like ICMP ping and DNS would not work across the tunnel. See Chapter 6 for more information on how to properly create and troubleshoot firewall rules.

In some cases it may also be possible that a setting mismatch could also cause traffic to fail passing the tunnel. In one instance, I saw a subnet defined on one non-pfSense router as 192.168.1.1/24, and on the pfSense side it was 192.168.1.0/24. The tunnel established, but traffic would not pass until the subnet was corrected.

There could also be an issue with how the packets are being routed. Running a **traceroute** (**tracert** on Windows) to an IP on the opposite side of the tunnel may be enlightening. Repeat the test from both sides of the tunnel. Check the Section 13.4.2 section in this chapter for more information. When using **traceroute**, you will see that traffic which does enter and leave the IPsec tunnel will seem to be missing some interim hops. This is normal, and part of how IPsec works. Traffic which does not properly enter an IPsec tunnel will appear to leave the WAN interface and route outward across the Internet, which would point to either a routing issue such as pfSense not being the gateway (as in Section 13.4.2), an incorrectly specified remote subnet on the tunnel definition, or to a tunnel which has been disabled.

13.8.3   Some hosts work, but not all

If traffic between some hosts over the VPN functions properly, but some hosts do not, this is commonly one of four things.

1. Missing, incorrect or ignored default gateway — If the device does not have a default gateway, or has one pointing to something other than pfSense, it does not know how to properly get back to the remote network on the VPN (see Section 13.4.2). Some devices, even with a default gateway specified, do not use that gateway. This has been seen on various embedded devices, including IP cameras and some printers. There isn't anything you can do about that other than getting the software on the device fixed. You can verify this by running **tcpdump** on the inside interface of the firewall connected to the network containing the device. Troubleshooting with **tcpdump** is covered in Section 25.5, and an IPsec-specific example can be found in Section 25.5.3.2. If you see traffic going out the inside interface on the firewall, but no replies coming back, the device is not properly routing its reply traffic (or could potentially be blocking it via a firewall).

2. Incorrect subnet mask — If the subnet in use on one end is 10.0.0.0/24 and the other is 10.254.0.0/24, and a host has an incorrect subnet mask of 255.0.0.0 or /8, it will never be able to communicate across the VPN because it thinks the remote VPN subnet is part of the local network and hence routing will not function properly.

3. Host firewall — if there is a firewall on the target host, it may not be allowing the connections.

4. Firewall rules on pfSense — ensure the rules on both ends allow the desired network traffic.

13.8.4   Connection Hangs

Historically, IPsec has not gracefully handled fragmented packets. Many of these issues have been resolved over the years, but there may be some lingering problems. If hangs or packet loss are seen only when using specific protocols (SMB, RDP, etc.), the WAN MTU may need reduced. A reduced MTU will ensure that the packets traversing the tunnel are all of a size which can be transmitted whole. A good starting point would be 1300, and if that works slowly increase the MTU until you find the breaking point, then back off a little from there.

13.8.5   "Random" Tunnel Disconnects/DPD Failures on Embedded Routers

If you experience dropped IPsec tunnels on an ALIX or other embedded hardware, you may need to disable DPD on the tunnel. You may be able to correlate the failures to times of high bandwidth usage. This happens when the CPU on a low-power system is tied up with sending IPsec traffic or is otherwise occupied. Due to the CPU overload it may not take the time to respond to DPD requests or see a response to a request of its own. As a consequence, the tunnel will fail a DPD check and be disconnected.

13.8.6   IPsec Log Interpretation

The IPsec logs available at Status → System Logs, on the IPsec tab will contain a record of the tunnel connection process. In this section, we will demonstrate some typical log entries, both good and bad. The main things to look for are key phrases that indicate what part of a connection actually worked. If you see "ISAKMP-SA established", that means Phase 1 was completed successfully and a Security Association was negotiated. If "IPsec-SA established" is seen, then Phase 2 has also been completed and the tunnel should be up and working at that point.

In the following examples, the tunnel is being initiated from Site A.

13.8.6.1   Successful Connections

These are examples of successful tunnels, in both Main Mode and Aggressive.

13.8.6.1.1   Successful Main Mode Tunnel

Log output from Site A:

```
ERROR: such policy already exists. anyway replace it: 192.168.30.0/24[0] ↩
    192.168.30.1/32[0] proto=any dir=in
ERROR: such policy already exists. anyway replace it: 192.168.30.1/32[0] ↩
    192.168.30.0/24[0] proto=any dir=out
ERROR: such policy already exists. anyway replace it: 192.168.30.0/24[0] ↩
    192.168.32.0/24[0] proto=any dir=out
ERROR: such policy already exists. anyway replace it: 192.168.32.0/24[0] ↩
    192.168.30.0/24[0] proto=any dir=in
```

```
[ToSiteB]: INFO: IPsec-SA request for 172.16.3.41 queued due to no  ↩
    phase1 found.
[ToSiteB]: INFO: initiate new phase 1 negotiation:  ↩
    172.16.0.40[500]<=>172.16.3.41[500]
INFO: begin Identity Protection mode.
INFO: received Vendor ID: DPD
INFO: received broken Microsoft ID: FRAGMENTATION
[ToSiteB]: INFO: ISAKMP-SA established 172.16.0.40[500]-172.16.3.41[500]  ↩
    spi:cc32cfe26c6911bc:54c42149875f4c9b
[ToSiteB]: INFO: initiate new phase 2 negotiation:  ↩
    172.16.0.40[500]<=>172.16.3.41[500]
[ToSiteB]: INFO: IPsec-SA established: ESP  ↩
    172.16.3.41[0]->172.16.0.40[0] spi=94628762(0x5a3eb9a)
[ToSiteB]: INFO: IPsec-SA established: ESP  ↩
    172.16.0.40[500]->172.16.3.41[500] spi=240792694(0xe5a3476)
```

Log output from Site B:

```
ERROR: such policy already exists. anyway replace it: 192.168.32.0/24[0]  ↩
    192.168.32.1/32[0] proto=any dir=in
ERROR: such policy already exists. anyway replace it: 192.168.32.1/32[0]  ↩
    192.168.32.0/24[0] proto=any dir=out
ERROR: such policy already exists. anyway replace it: 192.168.32.0/24[0]  ↩
    192.168.30.0/24[0] proto=any dir=out
ERROR: such policy already exists. anyway replace it: 192.168.30.0/24[0]  ↩
    192.168.32.0/24[0] proto=any dir=in
[ToSiteA]: INFO: respond new phase 1 negotiation:  ↩
    172.16.3.41[500]<=>172.16.0.40[500]
INFO: begin Identity Protection mode.
INFO: received broken Microsoft ID: FRAGMENTATION
INFO: received Vendor ID: DPD
[ToSiteA]: INFO: ISAKMP-SA established 172.16.3.41[500]-172.16.0.40[500]  ↩
    spi:cc32cfe26c6911bc:54c42149875f4c9b
[ToSiteA]: INFO: respond new phase 2 negotiation:  ↩
    172.16.3.41[500]<=>172.16.0.40[500]
[ToSiteA]: INFO: IPsec-SA established: ESP  ↩
    172.16.0.40[0]->172.16.3.41[0] spi=240792694(0xe5a3476)
[ToSiteA]: INFO: IPsec-SA established: ESP  ↩
    172.16.3.41[500]->172.16.0.40[500] spi=94628762(0x5a3eb9a)
```

13.8.6.1.2   Successful Aggressive Mode Tunnel

Log output from Site A:

```
[ToSiteB]: INFO: IPsec-SA request for 172.16.3.41 queued due to no  ↩
    phase1 found.
[ToSiteB]: INFO: initiate new phase 1 negotiation:  ↩
    172.16.0.40[500]<=>172.16.3.41[500]
INFO: begin Aggressive mode.
INFO: received broken Microsoft ID: FRAGMENTATION
```

```
INFO: received Vendor ID: DPD
NOTIFY: couldn't find the proper pskey, try to get one by the peer's  ←
    address.
[ToSiteB]: INFO: ISAKMP-SA established 172.16.0.40[500]-172.16.3.41[500]  ←
    spi:fccacccc1b248084:90ce65662b86f1df
[ToSiteB]: INFO: initiate new phase 2 negotiation:  ←
    172.16.0.40[500]<=>172.16.3.41[500]
[ToSiteB]: INFO: IPsec-SA established: ESP  ←
    172.16.3.41[0]->172.16.0.40[0] spi=191124503(0xb645417)
[ToSiteB]: INFO: IPsec-SA established: ESP  ←
    172.16.0.40[500]->172.16.3.41[500] spi=113130323(0x6be3b53)
```

Log output from Site B:

```
[ToSiteA]: INFO: respond new phase 1 negotiation:  ←
    172.16.3.41[500]<=>172.16.0.40[500]
INFO: begin Aggressive mode.
INFO: received broken Microsoft ID: FRAGMENTATION
INFO: received Vendor ID: DPD
NOTIFY: couldn't find the proper pskey, try to get one by the peer's  ←
    address.
[ToSiteA]: INFO: ISAKMP-SA established 172.16.3.41[500]-172.16.0.40[500]  ←
    spi:fccacccc1b248084:90ce65662b86f1df
[ToSiteA]: INFO: respond new phase 2 negotiation:  ←
    172.16.3.41[500]<=>172.16.0.40[500]
[ToSiteA]: INFO: IPsec-SA established: ESP  ←
    172.16.0.40[0]->172.16.3.41[0] spi=113130323(0x6be3b53)
[ToSiteA]: INFO: IPsec-SA established: ESP  ←
    172.16.3.41[500]->172.16.0.40[500] spi=191124503(0xb645417)
```

13.8.6.2   Failed Connection Examples

These examples show failed connections for varying reasons. Particularly interesting parts of the log
entries will be emphasized.

13.8.6.2.1   Mismatched Phase 1 Encryption

Log output from Site A:

```
[ToSiteB]: INFO: IPsec-SA request for 172.16.3.41 queued due to no  ←
    phase1 found.
[ToSiteB]: INFO: initiate new phase 1 negotiation:  ←
    172.16.0.40[500]<=>172.16.3.41[500]
INFO: begin Identity Protection mode.
[ToSiteB]: ERROR: phase2 negotiation failed due to time up waiting for  ←
    phase1. ESP 172.16.3.41[0]->172.16.0.40[0]
INFO: delete phase 2 handler.
ERROR: phase1 negotiation failed due to time up. 96f516ded84edfca  ←
    :0000000000000000
```

Log output from Site B:

```
[ToSiteA]: INFO: respond new phase 1 negotiation:  ↩
    172.16.3.41[500]<=>172.16.0.40[500]
INFO: begin Identity Protection mode.
INFO: received broken Microsoft ID: FRAGMENTATION
INFO: received Vendor ID: DPD
ERROR: rejected enctype: DB(prop#1:trns#1):Peer(prop#1:trns#1) = 3DES- ↩
    CBC:AES-CBC
ERROR: no suitable proposal found.
ERROR: failed to get valid proposal.
ERROR: failed to pre-process packet.
ERROR: phase1 negotiation failed.
```

In this case, the log entry tells you exactly what the problem was: This side was set for 3DES encryption, and the remote side is set for AES. Set both to matching values and then try again.

13.8.6.2.2 Mismatched Phase 1 DH Group

In this instance, the log entries will be exactly as above, except that the emphasized line will instead be:

```
ERROR: rejected dh_group: DB(prop#1:trns#1):Peer(prop#1:trns#1) = 768- ↩
    bit MODP group:1024-bit MODP group
```

This error can be corrected by setting the DH group setting on both ends of the tunnel to a matching value.

13.8.6.2.3 Mismatched Pre-shared Key

A mismatched pre-shared key can be a little tougher to diagnose. An error stating the fact that this value is mismatched is not printed in the log, instead you will see a message such as this:

```
[ToSiteB]: NOTIFY: the packet is retransmitted by 172.16.3.41[500] (1).
[ToSiteB]: ERROR: phase2 negotiation failed due to time up waiting for ↩
    phase1. ESP 172.16.3.41[0]->172.16.0.40[0]
```

If you notice an error similar to the above, check that the pre-shared keys match up on both ends.

13.8.6.2.4 Mismatched Phase 2 Encryption

Log output from Site A:

```
[ToSiteB]: INFO: IPsec-SA request for 172.16.3.41 queued due to no ↩
    phase1 found.
[ToSiteB]: INFO: initiate new phase 1 negotiation:  ↩
    172.16.0.40[500]<=>172.16.3.41[500]
INFO: begin Identity Protection mode.
INFO: received Vendor ID: DPD
```

```
INFO: received broken Microsoft ID: FRAGMENTATION
[ToSiteB]: INFO: ISAKMP-SA established 172.16.0.40[500]-172.16.3.41[500] ↩
    spi:196ea30ce76dd794:ab8c960884b0aa46
[ToSiteB]: INFO: initiate new phase 2 negotiation: ↩
    172.16.0.40[500]<=>172.16.3.41[500]
ERROR: fatal NO-PROPOSAL-CHOSEN notify message, phase1 should be deleted ↩
    .
```

Log output from Site B:

```
[ToSiteA]: INFO: respond new phase 1 negotiation: ↩
    172.16.3.41[500]<=>172.16.0.40[500]
INFO: begin Identity Protection mode.
INFO: received broken Microsoft ID: FRAGMENTATION
INFO: received Vendor ID: DPD
[ToSiteA]: INFO: ISAKMP-SA established 172.16.3.41[500]-172.16.0.40[500] ↩
    spi:196ea30ce76dd794:ab8c960884b0aa46
[ToSiteA]: INFO: respond new phase 2 negotiation: ↩
    172.16.3.41[500]<=>172.16.0.40[500]
WARNING: trns_id mismatched: my:AES peer:3DES
ERROR: not matched
ERROR: no suitable policy found.
ERROR: failed to pre-process packet.
```

In these log entries, you can see that Phase 1 completed successfully ("ISAKMP-SA established") but failed during Phase 2. Furthermore, it states that it could not find a suitable proposal, and from the Site B logs we can see that this was due to the sites being set for different encryption types, AES on one side and 3DES on the other.

13.8.6.2.5 Other Mismatched Phase 2 Information

Some other Phase 2 errors such as mismatched PFS values or mismatched remote subnets will result in the same log output. In this case, there is little recourse but to check each option to ensure settings match up on both sides.

Log output from Site A:

```
[ToSiteB]: INFO: IPsec-SA request for 172.16.3.41 queued due to no ↩
    phase1 found.
[ToSiteB]: INFO: initiate new phase 1 negotiation: ↩
    172.16.0.40[500]<=>172.16.3.41[500]
INFO: begin Identity Protection mode.
INFO: received Vendor ID: DPD
INFO: received broken Microsoft ID: FRAGMENTATION
[ToSiteB]: INFO: ISAKMP-SA established 172.16.0.40[500]-172.16.3.41[500] ↩
    spi:2a20b780a9c021f7:976e7d4fdb3d4dfb
[ToSiteB]: INFO: initiate new phase 2 negotiation: ↩
    172.16.0.40[500]<=>172.16.3.41[500]
[ToSiteB]: ERROR: 172.16.3.41 give up to get IPsec-SA due to time up to ↩
    wait.
```

Log output from Site B:

```
[ToSiteA]: INFO: respond new phase 1 negotiation:   ↩
    172.16.3.41[500]<=>172.16.0.40[500]
INFO: begin Identity Protection mode.
INFO: received broken Microsoft ID: FRAGMENTATION
INFO: received Vendor ID: DPD
[ToSiteA]: INFO: ISAKMP-SA established 172.16.3.41[500]-172.16.0.40[500]   ↩
    spi:2a20b780a9c021f7:976e7d4fdb3d4dfb
[ToSiteA]: INFO: respond new phase 2 negotiation:   ↩
    172.16.3.41[500]<=>172.16.0.40[500]
ERROR: no policy found: 192.168.30.0/24[0] 192.168.32.0/24[0] proto=any   ↩
    dir=in
ERROR: failed to get proposal for responder.
ERROR: failed to pre-process packet.
```

The errors indicate that the proposals for phase 2 did not agree, and all values in the Phase 2 section should be checked as well as the remote subnet definitions.

Note

In some cases, if one side has PFS set to **off**, and the other side has a value set, the tunnel will still establish and work. The mismatch shown above may only be seen if the values mismatch, for example **1** vs. **5**.

13.8.6.3   Other Common Errors

Some error messages may be encountered in the IPsec logs. Some are harmless, and others are indicative of potential problems. Usually the log messages are fairly straightforward in meaning, and indicate various problems establishing a tunnel with reasons why. There are some, however, that are a little more obscure.

```
Feb 20 10:33:41  racoon: ERROR: failed to pre-process packet.
Feb 20 10:33:41  racoon: ERROR: failed to get sainfo.
```

This is most commonly seen when the local and/or remote subnet definitions are incorrectly specified, especially if the subnet mask is set incorrectly on one side.

```
racoon: ERROR: none message must be encrypted.
```

Indicates that there may be a problem with traffic arriving from the opposite end of the tunnel. Try restarting the **racoon** service on the far side router by browsing to Status → Services and clicking **Restart** next to **racoon**.

```
racoon: ERROR: can't start the quick mode, there is no ISAKMP-SA.
```

May indicate a problem with sending local traffic to the remote tunnel, because an ISAKMP Security Association has not been found. It may be necessary to restart the **racoon** service on one or both sides to clear this up.

```
racoon: INFO: request for establishing IPsec-SA was queued due to no  ↩
    phase1 found.
```

This is normal, and usually seen when a tunnel is first established. The system will first try to complete a phase 1 connection to the far side and then continue.

```
racoon: INFO: unsupported PF_KEY message REGISTER
```

This is harmless as well, and is typically found in the log shortly after the **racoon** daemon starts.

13.8.7 Advanced debugging

When negotiation is failing, especially when connecting to third party IPsec devices where it isn't as easy to completely match the settings between the two sides, sometimes the only way to get adequate information to resolve the problem is to run **racoon** in the foreground in debug mode. To do so, first log into your firewall using SSH and chose option **8** at the console menu for a command prompt. Run the following commands.

```
# killall racoon
```

Now wait about 5 seconds for the process to shut down, and launch it again using the following.

```
# racoon -F -d -v -f /var/etc/racoon.conf
```

The first line stops the existing **racoon** process. The second starts **racoon** in the foreground (-F), with debugging (-d), increased verbosity (-v), using configuration file /var/etc/racoon.conf (-f). Running it in the foreground causes it to display its logs in your SSH session, so you can watch what is happening in real time. To quit out of **racoon**, press **Ctrl-C** and the service will be stopped. After finishing with debugging, you will need to start racoon normally. The easiest way to do this is to browse to Status → Services in the web interface and click 🔄 next to **racoon**.

Note

This method of debugging is disruptive to all IPsec on the system, when you kill off **racoon** you will drop all IPsec connections. Because of the volume of logs you will have to sort through with multiple IPsec connections enabled, while debugging a problem with one of them it's easier if you can disable the others while troubleshooting. Generally this method of debugging is only done when bringing up a new IPsec connection.

13.9 Configuring Third Party IPsec Devices

You can connect any VPN device supporting standard IPsec with pfSense. It is being used in production in combination with numerous vendors' equipment, and should work fine with any IPsec capable devices in your network. Connecting devices from two different vendors can be troublesome regardless of the vendors involved because of configuration differences between vendors, in some cases bugs in the implementations, and the fact that some of them use proprietary extensions. This section offers some general guidance on configuring IPsec VPNs with third party devices, as well as specific examples on configuring Cisco PIX firewalls and IOS routers.

13.9.1   General guidance for third party IPsec devices

To configure an IPsec tunnel between pfSense and a device from another vendor, the primary concern is to ensure that your phase 1 and 2 parameters match on both sides. For the configuration options on pfSense, where it allows you to select multiple options you should usually only select one of those options and ensure the other side is set the same. The endpoints *should* negotiate a compatible option when multiple options are selected, however that is frequently a source of problems when connecting to third party devices. Configure both ends to what you believe are matching settings, and save and apply the changes on both sides.

Once you believe that the settings match on both ends of the tunnel, attempt to pass traffic over the VPN to trigger its initiation, then check your IPsec logs on both ends to review the negotiation. Depending on the situation, the logs from one end may be more useful than those from the opposite end, so it is good to check both and compare. You will find the pfSense side provides better information in some scenarios, while on other occasions the other device provides more useful logging. If the negotiation fails, determine whether it was phase 1 or 2 that failed and thoroughly review your settings accordingly, as described in Section 13.8.

13.9.2   Cisco PIX OS 6.x

The following configuration would be for a Cisco PIX running on 6.x as Site B from the example site-to-site configuration earlier in the chapter. See Section 13.4.1 for the Site A pfSense settings.

```
sysopt connection permit-ipsec
isakmp enable outside

!--- Phase 1
isakmp identity address
isakmp policy 1 encryption 3des
isakmp policy 1 hash sha
isakmp policy 1 group 2
isakmp policy 1 lifetime 86400
isakmp policy 1 authentication pre-share
isakmp key aBc123%XyZ9$7qwErty99 address 172.23.1.3 netmask  ↩
    255.255.255.255 no-xauth no-config-mode

!--- Phase 2
crypto ipsec transform-set 3desshai esp-3des esp-sha-hmac
access-list PFSVPN permit ip 10.0.10.0 255.255.255.0 192.168.1.0  ↩
    255.255.255.0
crypto map dyn-map 10 ipsec-isakmp
crypto map dyn-map 10 match address PFSVPN
crypto map dyn-map 10 set peer 172.23.1.3
crypto map dyn-map 10 set transform-set 3desshai
```

```
crypto map dyn-map 10 set security-association lifetime seconds 3600
crypto map dyn-map interface outside

!--- no-nat to ensure it routes via the tunnel
access-list nonat permit ip 10.0.10.0 255.255.255.0 192.168.1.0  ↵
    255.255.255.0
nat (inside) 0 access-list nonat
```

13.9.3 Cisco PIX OS 7.x, 8.x, and ASA

Configuration on newer revisions of the PIX OS and for ASA devices is similar to that of the older ones, but has some significant differences. The following example would be for using a PIX running OS version 7.x or 8.x, or an ASA device, as Site B in the site-to-site example earlier in this chapter. See Section 13.4.1 for the corresponding Site A settings.

```
crypto isakmp enable outside

!--- Phase 1
crypto isakmp policy 10
  authentication pre-share
  encryption 3des
  hash sha
  group 2
  lifetime 86400

tunnel-group 172.23.1.3 type ipsec-l2l
tunnel-group 172.23.1.3 ipsec-attributes pre-shared-key aBc123%  ↵
    XyZ9$7qwErty99

!--- Phase 2
crypto ipsec transform-set 3dessha1 esp-3des esp-sha-hmac
access-list PFSVPN extended permit ip 10.0.10.0 255.255.255.0  ↵
    192.168.1.0 255.255.255.0
crypto map outside_map 20 match address PFSVPN
crypto map outside_map 20 set peer 172.23.1.3
crypto map outside_map 20 set transform-set 3dessha1
crypto map outside_map interface outside

!--- no-nat to ensure it routes via the tunnel
access-list nonat extended permit ip 10.0.10.0 255.255.255.0 192.168.1.0  ↵
    255.255.255.0
nat (inside) 0 access-list nonat
```

13.9.4 Cisco IOS Routers

This shows a Cisco IOS-based router as Site B from the example site-to-site configuration earlier in the chapter. See section Section 13.4.1 for the Site A pfSense settings.

```
!--- Phase 1
crypto isakmp policy 10
  encr 3des
  authentication pre-share
  group 2
crypto isakmp key aBc123%XyZ9$7qwErty99 address 172.23.1.3 no-xauth

!--- Phase 2
access-list 100 permit ip 192.168.1.0 0.0.0.255 10.0.10.0 0.0.0.255
access-list 100 permit ip 10.0.10.0 0.0.0.255 192.168.1.0 0.0.0.255
crypto ipsec transform-set 3DES-SHA esp-3des esp-sha-hmac
crypto map PFSVPN 15 ipsec-isakmp
  set peer 172.23.1.3
  set transform-set 3DES-SHA
  match address 100

!--- Assign the crypto map to the WAN interface
interface FastEthernet0/0
  crypto map PFSVPN

!--- No-Nat so this traffic goes via the tunnel, not the WAN
ip nat inside source route-map NONAT interface FastEthernet0/0 overload
access-list 110 deny   ip 10.0.10.0 0.0.0.255 192.168.1.0 0.0.0.255
access-list 110 permit ip 10.0.10.0 0.0.0.255 any
route map NONAT permit 10
  match ip address 110
```

Chapter 14

PPTP VPN

pfSense can act as a PPTP VPN server as one of its three VPN options. This is an attractive option because the client is built into every Windows and OS X version released in the past decade. It can also provide passthrough services to an internal PPTP server.

For general discussion of the various types of VPNs available in pfSense and their pros and cons, see Chapter 12.

14.1 PPTP Security Warning

If you have not already, you should read Section 12.2.7 about VPN security. PPTP is widely used, but it is not the most secure VPN solution available.

14.2 PPTP and Firewall Rules

By default, when you have PPTP redirection or the PPTP server enabled, hidden firewall rules will be automatically added to WAN to permit TCP 1723 and GRE traffic from any source to the destination address. You can disable this behavior on pfSense 1.2.3 and later releases by checking the Disable all auto-added VPN rules box under System → Advanced. You may wish to do this if you know your PPTP clients will be connecting only from particular remote networks. This prevents potential abuse from arbitrary Internet hosts, though in deployments where users are mobile and will be connecting from numerous locations, it's impossible to know all the subnets users will be coming from so tightening the ruleset is impractical and will cause difficulties for your users.

14.3 PPTP and Multi-WAN

Unfortunately because of the way PPTP works, and the way PF works with the GRE protocol, it is only possible to run a PPTP server on your primary WAN interface

14.4   PPTP Limitations

The state tracking code in the underlying PF firewall software for the GRE protocol can only track a single session per public IP per external server. This means if you use PPTP VPN connections, only one internal machine can connect simultaneously to a PPTP server on the Internet. A thousand machines can connect simultaneously to a thousand different PPTP servers, but only one simultaneously to a single server. The only available work around is to use multiple public IPs on your firewall, one per client, or to use multiple public IPs on the external PPTP server. This is not a problem with other types of VPN connections.

This same limitation also means if you enable the PPTP Server or Redirection functionality, no clients NATed to your WAN IP address will be able to connect to any outside PPTP server. The work around to this is to NAT your clients' outbound Internet access to a different public IP address.

Both of these limitations are able to be worked around in most environments, however fixing this is a high priority for the pfSense 2.0 release. At the time of this writing, development work is happening to eliminate this limitation, though it is unknown if it will be successful.

14.5   PPTP Server Configuration

To configure the PPTP server, first browse to VPN → PPTP. Select Enable PPTP server.

14.5.1   IP Addressing

You will need to decide what IP addresses to use for the PPTP server and clients. The Remote address range is usually a portion of your LAN subnet, such as 192.168.1.128/28 (.128 through .143). Then select an IP address outside of that range for the Server address, such as 192.168.1.144 as shown in Figure 14.1.

Server address	192.168.1.144
	Enter the IP address the PPTP server should use on its side for all clients.
Remote address range	192.168.1.128 / 28
	Specify the starting address for the client IP address subnet.
	The PPTP server will assign 16 addresses, starting at the address entered above, to clients.

Figure 14.1: PPTP IP Addressing

Note
This subnet does not have to be contained within an existing subnet on your router. You may use a completely different set of IP addresses if desired.

14.5.2   Authentication

You can authenticate users from the local user database, or via RADIUS. RADIUS allows you to connect to another server on your network to provide authentication. This can be used to authenticate PPTP users from Microsoft Active Directory (see Section 24.1) as well as numerous other RADIUS capable servers.

If using RADIUS, check the Use a RADIUS server for authentication box and fill in the RADIUS server and shared secret. For authentication using the local user database, leave that box unchecked. You will have to add your users on the Users tab of the VPN → PPTP screen unless using RADIUS. See Section 14.5.6 below for more details on the built-in authentication system.

14.5.3   Require 128 bit encryption

You should require 128 bit encryption where possible. Most PPTP clients support 128 bit encryption, so this should be fine in most environments. PPTP is relatively weak at 128 bit, and significantly more so at 40 and 56 bit. Unless you absolutely must, you should never use anything less than 128 bit with PPTP.

14.5.4   Save changes to start PPTP server

After filling in the aforementioned items, click Save. This will save your configuration and launch the PPTP server. If you are authenticating your users with the local user database, click the Users tab and enter your users there.

14.5.5   Configure firewall rules for PPTP clients

Browse to Firewall → Rules and click the PPTP VPN tab. These rules control what traffic is permitted from PPTP clients. Until you add a firewall rule here, all traffic initiated from connected PPTP clients will be blocked. Traffic initiated from your LAN to the PPTP clients is controlled using your LAN firewall rules. Initially you may want to add an allow all rule here for testing purposes as shown in Figure 14.2, and once you verify functionality, restrict the ruleset as desired.

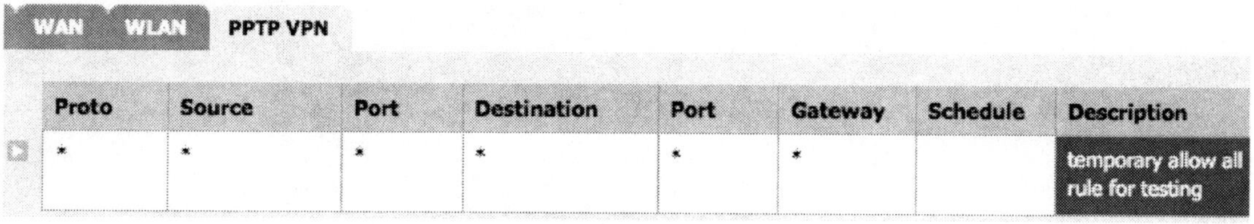

	Proto	Source	Port	Destination	Port	Gateway	Schedule	Description
	*	*	*	*	*	*		temporary allow all rule for testing

WAN   WLAN   PPTP VPN

Figure 14.2: PPTP VPN Firewall Rule

14.5.6   Adding Users

Adding users via RADIUS will vary from one implementation to another. This fact makes it beyond the scope of this section, but should be covered in the documentation for the particular RADIUS server being employed.

Adding users to pfSense's built-in PPTP users system is quite easy. First, click on VPN → PPTP, and then the Users tab. You will be presented with an empty users screen as shown in Figure 14.3. Click the ⊞ button to add a user.

Figure 14.3: PPTP Users Tab

After clicking ⊞, the user editing page will appear. Fill it in with the username and password for a user, as in Figure 14.4. You may also enter a static IP assignment if desired.

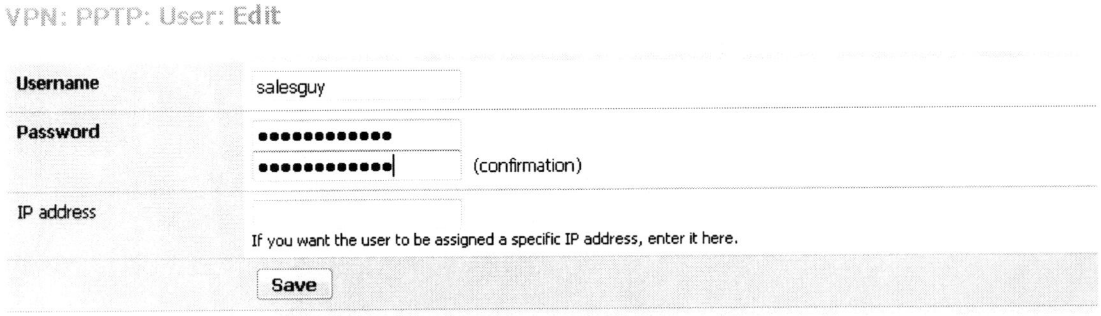

VPN: PPTP: User: Edit

Username	salesguy
Password	●●●●●●●●●●●●
	●●●●●●●●●●●● (confirmation)
IP address	
	If you want the user to be assigned a specific IP address, enter it here.
	Save

Figure 14.4: Adding a PPTP User

Click Save, and then the user list will return (Figure 14.5), but before the change will take effect, the Apply Changes button must first be clicked.

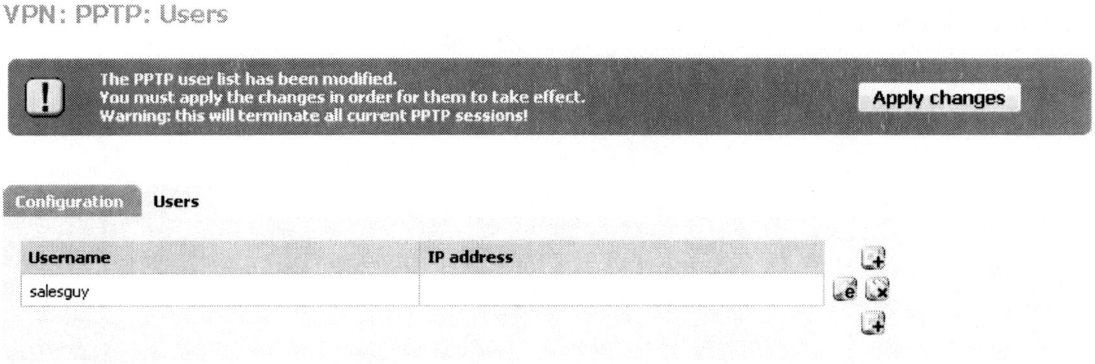

VPN: PPTP: Users

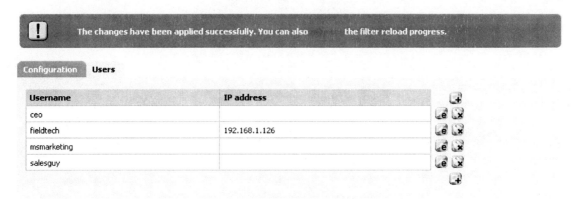

Figure 14.5: Applying PPTP Changes

Repeat that process for each user you would like to add, eventually you will have a rather full looking user list, as in Figure 14.6.

VPN: PPTP: Users

Figure 14.6: List of PPTP Users

If you need to edit an existing user, click . Users may be deleted by clicking .

14.6 PPTP Client Configuration

Now that your PPTP server is configured and ready, you will need to configure your PPTP clients. The following sections provide instructions on configuring Windows XP, Windows Vista and Mac OS X for connecting to a PPTP server.

14.6.1   Windows XP

Open Control Panel, and double click Network Connections (Figure 14.7).

Network
Connections

Figure 14.7: Network Connections

Under Network Tasks, click Create a new connection (Figure 14.8). At the welcome screen of the wizard, click Next.

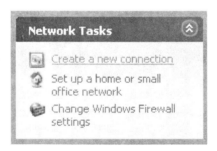

Figure 14.8: Network Tasks

Select Connect to the network at my workplace, as in Figure 14.9, and click Next.

Select Virtual Private Network connection, like Figure 14.10, then click Next.

Enter a name for the connection under Company Name, like that in Figure 14.11, and click Next.

Enter the WAN IP of the remote pfSense router under Host Name or IP Address, just like Figure 14.12, and click Next, then click Finish (Figure 14.13).

You now have a PPTP dial-up entry that works like any other dail-up connection. A prompt for the username and password, like that in Figure 14.14, will show up when the initial connection is attempted. It is best not to connect yet, however. Cancel this dialog if it appears and try again after following the rest of this section.

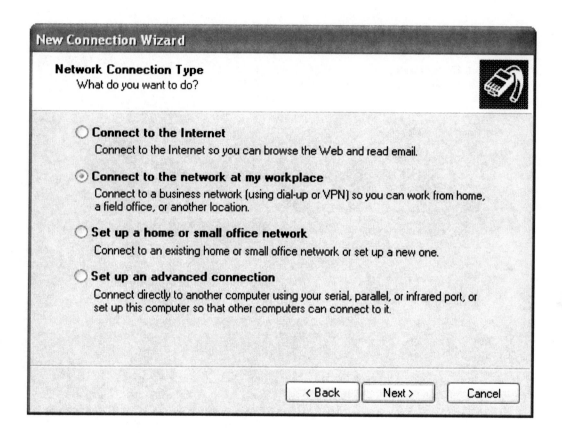

Figure 14.9: Workplace Connection

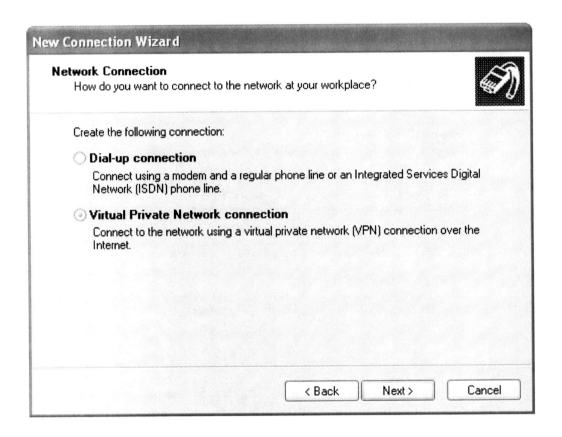

Figure 14.10: Connect to VPN

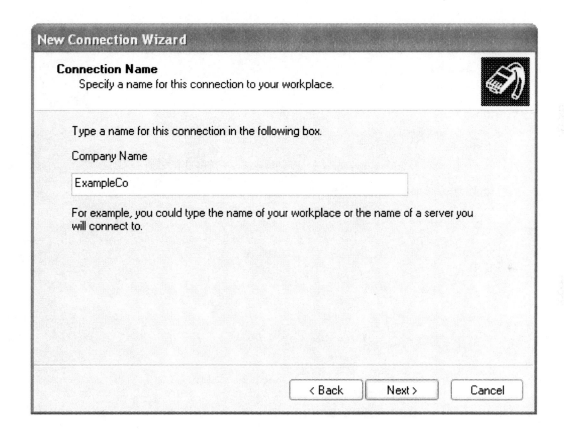

Figure 14.11: Connection Name

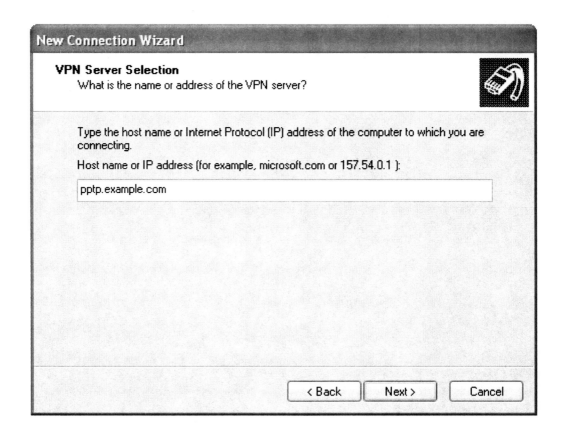

Figure 14.12: Connection Host

Figure 14.13: Finishing the Connection

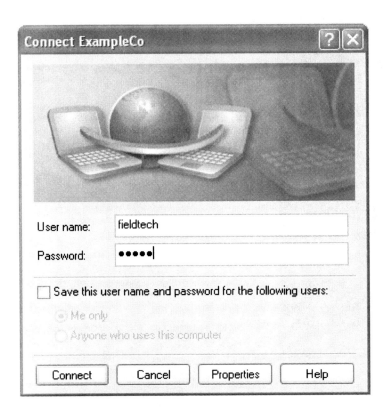

Figure 14.14: Connect Dialog

Figure 14.15: Connection Properties

There are some other settings that needs checked and perhaps adjusted. From within Network Connections, right click on the icon for the PPTP connection, then click Properties (Figure 14.15).

Click on the Security tab (Figure 14.16). Under Verify my identity as follows, make sure that Require secured password is chosen. Also ensure that Require data encryption (disconnect if none) is checked.

Now click on the Networking tab. As you can see in Figure 14.17, the Type of VPN drop down defaults to **Automatic**. What this really means is "try stuff until something works." PPTP is the last thing Windows will try, and there will be a delay of up to 30 seconds or more while it waits for the other options to time out, so you likely want to select **PPTP** here to avoid that delay and any complications that may arise from Windows' automatic methodology.

By default, this connection will send all traffic out through the PPTP connection as its gateway. This may or may not be desirable, depending on your intended configuration. This behavior is configurable, however. To change this, double click on Internet Protocol (TCP/IP), and click the Advanced button. Now uncheck Use default gateway on remote network as in Figure 14.18, then click OK on all the open windows. With this option unchecked, only traffic bound for the subnet of the PPTP connection will traverse the tunnel.

Now the PPTP connection will only send traffic destined for its subnet across the VPN. If you need to selectively route traffic, see Section 14.10.

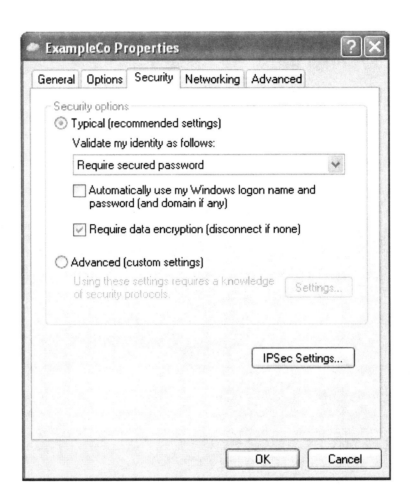

Figure 14.16: Security Tab

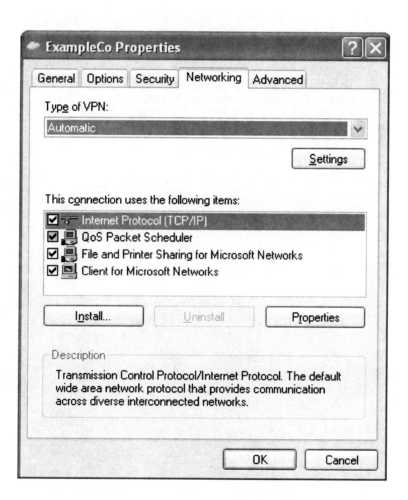

Figure 14.17: Networking Tab

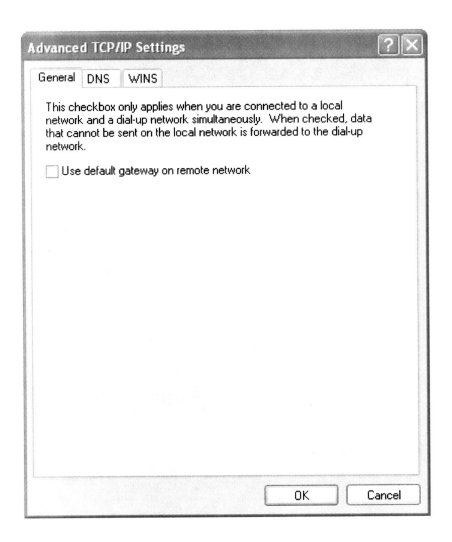

Figure 14.18: Remote Gateway Setting

14.6.2   Windows Vista

Figure 14.19: Vista Network Connections

Click on the Network Connection indicator icon in the system tray by the clock, then click Connect or Disconnect as seen in Figure 14.19.

Click Set up a connection or network (Figure 14.20), then click Connect to a workplace (Figure 14.21) and then Next.

Set up a connection or network
Open Network and Sharing Center

Figure 14.20: Setup A Connection

Figure 14.21: Connect to a Workplace

If prompted, choose No, create a new connection, and click Next.

Click Use my Internet connection (VPN) (Figure 14.22).

Figure 14.22: Connect using VPN

On the next screen, shown in Figure 14.23, enter the WAN IP of the remote pfSense router under Internet Address.

Enter a name for the connection under Destination name.

Check Don't Connect Now and click Next.

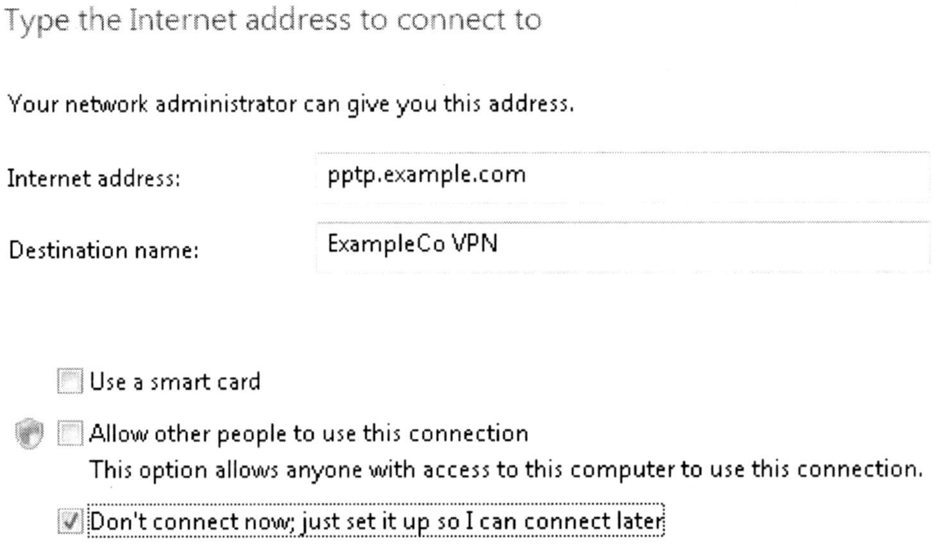

Type the Internet address to connect to

Your network administrator can give you this address.

Internet address: pptp.example.com

Destination name: ExampleCo VPN

☐ Use a smart card

🛡 ☐ Allow other people to use this connection
    This option allows anyone with access to this computer to use this connection.

☑ Don't connect now; just set it up so I can connect later

Figure 14.23: Connection Setup

Enter the username and password, as in Figure 14.24, then click Create. A screen like Figure 14.25 should appear indicating that the connection has been created.

Type your user name and password

User name:	fieldtech
Password:	•••••

☐ Show characters
☐ Remember this password

Domain (optional):

Figure 14.24: Authentication Settings

The connection is ready to use

➦ Connect now

Figure 14.25: Connection is Ready

You should now have a PPTP dial-up entry that works like any other dail-up connection. Quickly access this by clicking the Network Connection indicator icon in the system tray, click Connect or Disconnect, choose the VPN connection, and click Connect.

However, before connecting for the first time, there are some other settings to double check. First, click the Network Connection indicator icon in the system tray, and click Connect or Disconnect. Right click on the VPN connection that was just created, then click Properties as demonstrated in Figure 14.26.

Change to the Security tab (Figure 14.27). Under Verify my identity as follows, make sure that Require secured password is chosen. Also ensure that Require data encryption (disconnect if none) is checked.

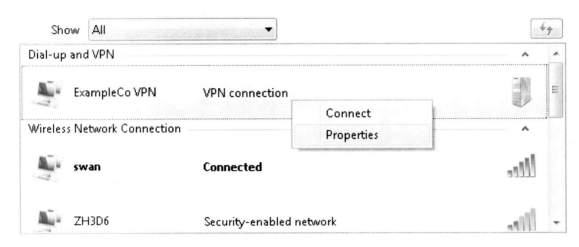

Figure 14.26: Get Connection Properties

Figure 14.27: VPN Security Settings

Now change to the Networking tab (Figure 14.28). It is probably best to uncheck Internet Protocol Version 6 (TCP/IPv6) at this point.

The Type of VPN drop down defaults to **Automatic**. What this really means is "try stuff until something works." PPTP is the last thing Windows will try, and there will be a delay of up to 30 seconds or more while it waits for the other options to time out, so you likely want to select **PPTP** here to avoid that delay and any complications that may arise from Windows' automatic methodology.

As with Windows XP, this connection will send all traffic out through the PPTP connection as its gateway. This may or may not be desirable, depending on your intended configuration. If you want all traffic to go across the tunnel, skip the rest of this section. Otherwise, click on Internet Protocol Version 4 (TCP/IPv4), then click Properties.

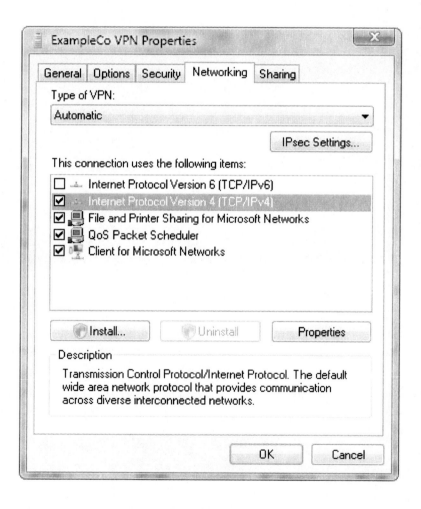

Figure 14.28: VPN Networking Settings

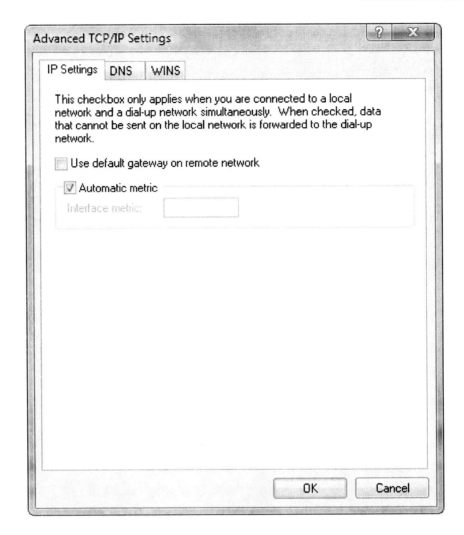

Figure 14.29: VPN Gateway

Click the Advanced button, and then uncheck Use default gateway on remote network as shown in Figure 14.29. Click OK or Close on all the windows that were just opened.

Now the PPTP connection will only send traffic destined for its subnet across the VPN. If you need to selectively route traffic, see Section 14.10.

14.6.3   Windows 7

The PPTP client setup procedure in the release version (RTM) of Windows 7 is virtually identical to Windows Vista.

14.6.4 Mac OS X

Open System Preferences, then click View → Network. Click the plus at the bottom of the list of your network adapters to add a new connection, which can be seen in Figure 14.30.

Figure 14.30: Add network connection

In the Interface drop down, select VPN, and for VPN Type select PPTP. Fill in the service name as desired and click Create. These choices are shown in Figure 14.31

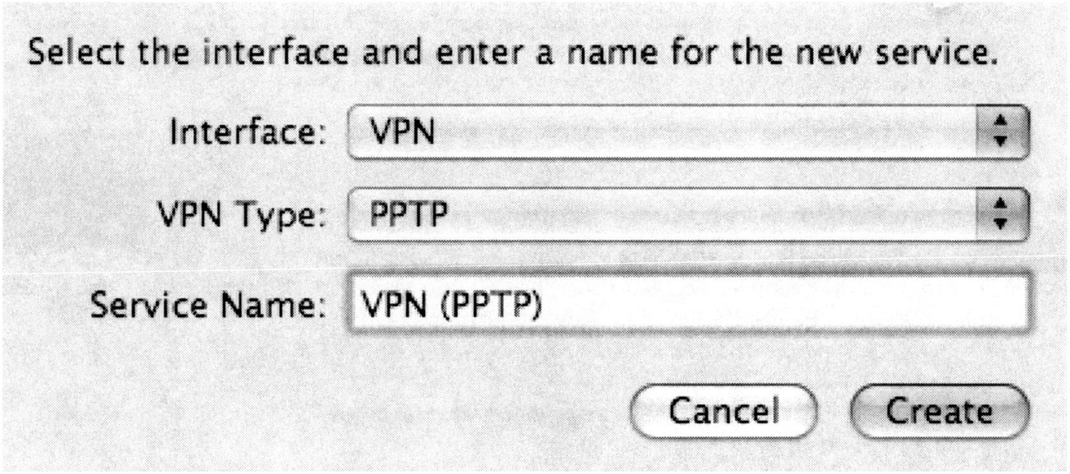

Select the interface and enter a name for the new service.

Interface: VPN

VPN Type: PPTP

Service Name: VPN (PPTP)

Cancel   Create

Figure 14.31: Add PPTP VPN connection

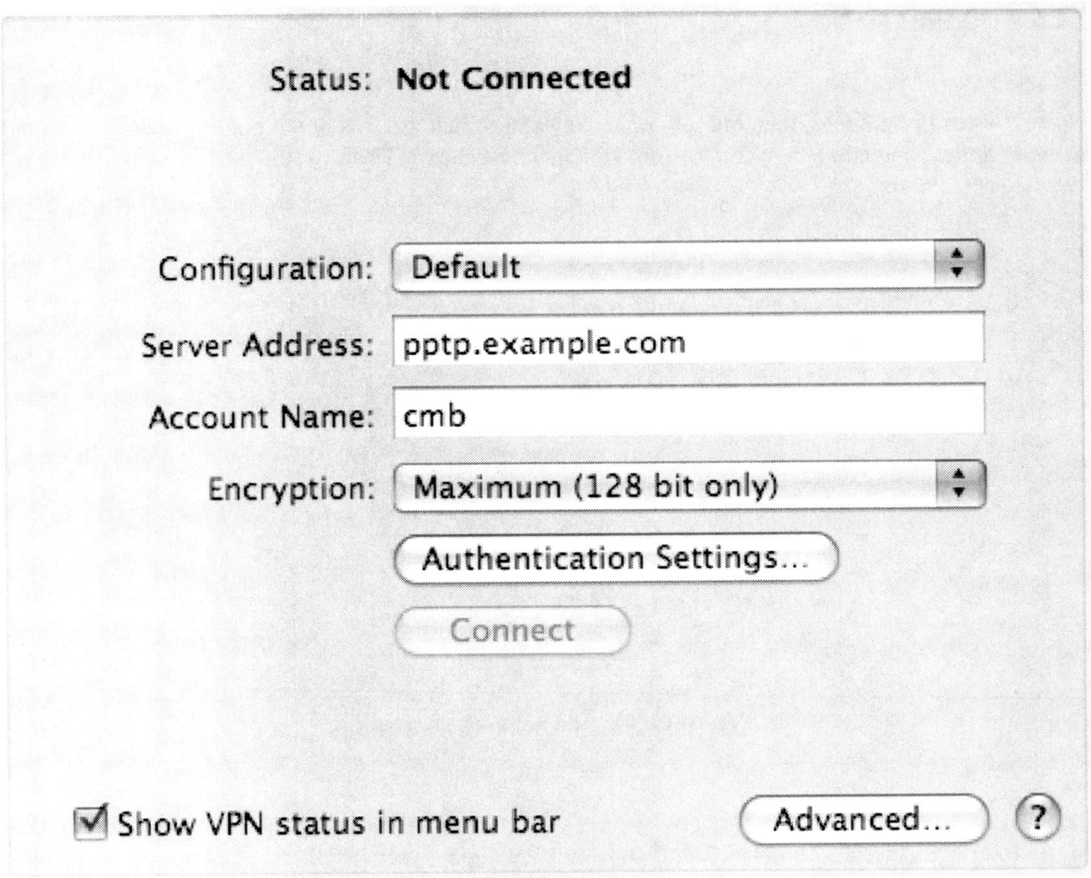

Status: Not Connected

Configuration: | Default ▲▼

Server Address: | pptp.example.com

Account Name: | cmb

Encryption: | Maximum (128 bit only) ▲▼

(Authentication Settings...)

(Connect)

☑ Show VPN status in menu bar   (Advanced...) (?)

Figure 14.32: Configure PPTP VPN connection

This will take you back to the Network screen where you finish configuration for the PPTP VPN connection. Fill in the server address, account name, and choose Maximum (128 bit only) for Encryption. An example is shown in Figure 14.32. Then click the Advanced button.

The Advanced screen has a number of options, some of them shown in Figure 14.33, though only one you may want to consider changing. The Send all traffic over VPN connection box is unchecked by default. If you want all the traffic from the client to traverse the VPN while connected, check this box. Click OK when finished.

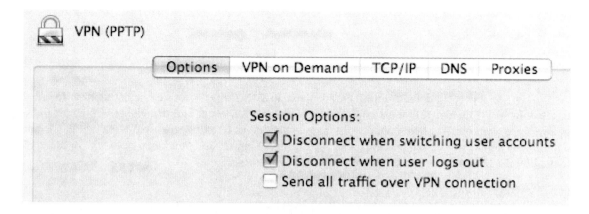

Figure 14.33: Advanced options

Since I checked Show VPN status in menu bar as shown in Figure 14.32, my connection now shows at the top of the screen. To connect, click on the name of your connection like that seen in Figure 14.34.

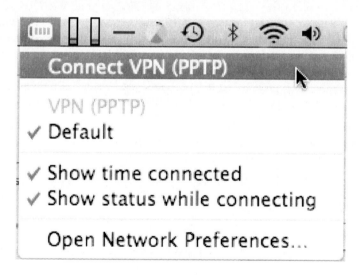

Figure 14.34: Connect to PPTP VPN

14.7 Increasing the Simultaneous User Limit

It is possible to increase the simultaneous user limit from the default hard coded 16, though only via hidden config.xml options. To increase your limit, browse to the Diagnostics → Backup/Restore screen, and click Download Configuration. Open the downloaded XML backup in a text editor and scroll down to <pptp>.

```
<pptp>
    <n_pptp_units>16</n_pptp_units>
    <pptp_subnet>28</pptp_subnet>
```

As you can see above, the default setting for 16 clients in a /28 subnet is located in that section. In order to allow for more clients, you must adjust both the connection count and the subnet. In the example below, there would be 32 client connections, and a block of 32 IP addresses used. Note that this is not a traditional subnet per se, rather a means of specifying a range inside of a larger network. Because of that, all of the IP addresses in the "subnet" definition are usable.

```
<pptp>
<n_pptp_units>32</n_pptp_units>
<pptp_subnet>27</pptp_subnet>
```

14.8   PPTP Redirection

PPTP redirection allows you to forward PPTP traffic destined to your WAN IP to an internal PPTP server. To enable it, select Redirect incoming PPTP connections to and enter your internal PPTP server's IP in the PPTP redirection box. This is functionally equivalent to adding Port Forward entries for TCP port 1723 and the GRE protocol to your internal PPTP server, which you can do instead if you prefer. Its existence is largely a hold over from m0n0wall, where the underlying IPFilter does not support forwarding the GRE protocol. It has been retained because of m0n0wall users' familiarity with the feature, and some users prefer the ease of a single entry rather than two port forward entries.

Firewall rules for the GRE protocol and TCP port 1723 are automatically added on the WAN. You do not need to enter any firewall rules when using PPTP redirection, unless you have Disable all auto-added VPN rules checked under System → Advanced.

14.9   PPTP Troubleshooting

This section covers troubleshooting steps for the most common problems users encounter with PPTP.

14.9.1   Cannot connect

First, ensure the client computer is connected to the Internet. If that succeeds, make note of the error you are receiving from the client. Windows (except Vista) will provide an error code that will help considerably in narrowing down the potential problems. Windows Vista removed this and hence makes it difficult to properly troubleshoot connection failures, but thankfully the same error codes that have been around for over a decade are back in Windows 7 (beta and RC). Troubleshooting with Vista is not recommended.

For those using non-Windows clients, the troublesome areas are generally the same, though you may have to try them all to determine the specific problem.

14.9.1.1 Error 619

Error 619 means something along the way is breaking your GRE traffic. This is almost always caused by the firewall the client is behind. If the client is also behind pfSense, first ensure that none of the scenarios outlined in Section 14.4 apply. If the firewall the client is behind is another product, you may need to enable PPTP passthrough or a similar setting for PPTP to function, if it can at all. In some cases, like 3G wireless providers assigning private IPs to customers, you will be stuck with choosing another VPN option.

14.9.1.2 Error 691

Error 691 is caused by an invalid username or password. This means the user is not entering the correct username or password in the PPTP client. Correct the username and/or password, matching up with the information configured in the local user database for PPTP, or on the RADIUS server.

14.9.1.3 Error 649

You may see error 649 when authenticating to RADIUS on a Microsoft Windows server using IAS. This means the account does not have permission to dial in, and the cause will likely be one of three things.

1. Dial in permission set to "Deny access" — go to the properties of the user's account in Active Directory Users and Computers and click the Dial-in tab. Depending on your preferred IAS configuration, you will want either **Allow access** or **Control access through remote access policy**.

2. User's password is expired — if the user's password is expired, they cannot log in over PPTP.

3. Incorrect IAS configuration — you may have configured remote access policies in IAS as such that users are not authorized to be connected.

14.9.2   Connected to PPTP but cannot pass traffic

Ensure you have added firewall rules to the PPTP VPN interface as described in Section 14.5.5.

Also ensure the remote subnet across the VPN is different from the local subnet. If you are trying to connect to a 192.168.1.0/24 network across VPN and the local subnet where the client is connected is also 192.168.1.0/24, traffic destined for that subnet will never traverse the VPN because it is on the local network. This is why it's important to choose a relatively obscure LAN subnet when using VPN, as discussed in Section 4.2.4.

14.10   PPTP Routing Tricks

If you only want selected subnets to be routed across the PPTP tunnel, it can still be done with some custom route commands on the client. The following technique works under Windows XP, Vista, and

Windows 7, but can probably be altered to work on most any platform. This assumes that you have already configured the client to not send all traffic across the connection (i.e. not using the remote gateway).

First, the PPTP client needs to be assigned a static address in the user profile. This can be done using the built-in authentication, or via RADIUS. This static address should be outside of the general assignment pool since this is not a reservation.

The trick is to route traffic destined for the remote subnets to the assigned PPTP address. This will cause traffic for those subnets to ride the tunnel to the other side. It isn't limited to subnets that are immediately reachable on the other side, either, as any subnet can be used. This is handy if you want to also route access to a third-party site through the VPN tunnel as well.

These commands can be typed at a command line, but are more at home in a batch file as in this example:

```
@echo off
route add 192.168.210.0 mask 255.255.255.0 192.168.1.126
route add    10.99.99.0 mask 255.255.255.0 192.168.1.126
route add    172.16.1.0 mask 255.255.252.0 192.168.1.126
pause
```

In that example, *192.168.1.126* is the static IP assigned to this particular PPTP client's username . These commands would route the three specified subnets across the PPTP connection, in addition to the subnet for the connection itself. The pause is optional, but may help to ensure that all the routes were added successfully. The batch file will need to be run each time the connection is established.

Note

On Windows Vista and Windows 7, these commands will need to be run as Administrator. If you created a shortcut to this batch file, its properties may be altered so it always runs in that manner. Alternately, you could right click on the batch file and choose Run As Administrator.

14.11   PPTP Logs

A record of login and logout events is kept on Status → System Logs, on the PPTP tab.

Last 150 PPTP VPN log entries			
Time	**Action**	**User**	**IP address**
Jul 17 12:46:26	◀	rick	
Jul 17 12:08:52	▶	rick	192.168.130.128

Figure 14.35: PPTP Logs

As seen in Figure 14.35, each login and logout should be recorded with a timestamp and username, and each login will also show the IP address assigned to the PPTP client.

Chapter 15

OpenVPN

OpenVPN is an open source SSL VPN solution that can be used both for client remote access and site to site connectivity. OpenVPN supports clients on a wide range of operating systems including all the BSDs, Linux, Mac OS X, Solaris and Windows 2000 and newer. Every OpenVPN connection, whether remote access or site to site, consists of a server and a client. In the case of site to site VPNs, one firewall acts as the server and the other as the client. It does not matter which firewall possesses these roles. Typically the primary location's firewall will provide server connectivity for all remote locations, whose firewalls are configured as clients. This is functionally equivalent to the opposite configuration — the primary location configured as a client connecting to servers running on the firewalls at the remote locations.

There are two types of authentication methods that can be used with OpenVPN: shared key and X.509. For shared key, you generate a key that will be used on both sides. X.509 is described further in the next section.

Note that while OpenVPN is a SSL VPN, it is not a "clientless" SSL VPN in the sense that commercial firewall vendors commonly refer to it. You will need to install the OpenVPN client on all your client devices. In reality no VPN solution is truly "clientless", and this terminology is nothing more than a marketing ploy. For more in depth discussion on SSL VPNs, this post from Matthew Grooms, an IPsec tools and pfSense developer, from the mailing list archives provides some excellent information: `http://marc.info/?l=pfsense-support&m=121556491024595&w=2`.

For general discussion of the various types of VPNs available in pfSense and their pros and cons, see Chapter 12.

15.1   Basic Introduction to X.509 Public Key Infrastructure

One of the authentication options for OpenVPN is using X.509 keys. An in depth discussion of X.509 and PKI is outside the scope of this book, and is the topic of a number of entire books for those interested in details. This section provides the very basic understanding you'll need for configuring OpenVPN. This is the preferred means of running remote access VPNs, because it allows you to revoke access to individual machines. With shared keys, you either have to create a unique server and port for each client, or distribute the same key to all clients. The former gets to be a management nightmare, and the latter is problematic in the case of a compromised key. If a client machine is compromised, stolen, or lost, or you otherwise wish to revoke the access of one person, you must re-issue the shared key to all clients. With a PKI deployment, if a client is compromised, or access needs to be revoked for any other reason, you can simply revoke that client's certificate. No other clients are affected.

With PKI, first a Certificate Authority (CA) is created. This CA then signs all of the individual certificates in your PKI. The CA's certificate is used on the OpenVPN servers and clients to verify the authenticity of certificates used. The CA's certificate can be used to verify the signing on certificates, but not to sign certificates. Signing certificates requires the CA's private key (`ca.key` when using easy-rsa, discussed later in this chapter). The privacy of the CA private key is what ensures the security of your PKI. Anyone with access to the CA private key can generate certificates to be used on your PKI, hence it must be kept secure. This key is never distributed to clients or servers.

Ensure you never copy more files to the clients than are needed, as this may result in the security of your PKI being compromised. Later sections in this chapter describe which files clients need to connect, and how to generate your certificates.

15.2   Generating OpenVPN Keys and Certificates

OpenVPN uses certificates or shared keys to encrypt and decrypt traffic. This section shows how to generate a shared key or certificates for use with OpenVPN. Later sections describe how to use these keys or certificates.

15.2.1   Generating Shared Keys

Shared key is the preferred method for site to site OpenVPN connections. To generate a shared key, browse to Diagnostics → Command and run the following command:

```
# openvpn --genkey --secret /tmp/shared.key
```

Then to display the key, run this:

```
# cat /tmp/shared.key
```

The key will look something like this:

```
#
# 2048 bit OpenVPN static key
#
-----BEGIN OpenVPN Static key V1-----
6ade12d55caacbbc5e086ccb552bfe14
4ca7f08230b7e24992685feba9842a03
44ee824c6ac4a30466aa85c0361c7d50
19878c55e6f3e7b552e03a807b21bad5
ce0ca22d911f08d16b21ea1114e69627
f9e8a6cd277ad13b794eef5e1862ea53
e7b0cba91e8f120fa983bdd8091281f6
```

```
610bf8c7eb4fed46875a67a30d25896f
0010d6d128ad607f3cbe81e2e257a48a
82abfca3f8f85c8530b975dca34bcfe4
69f0066a8abd114f0e2fbc077d0ea234
34093e7d72cc603d2f47207585f2bdec
ed663ad17db9841e881340c2b1f86d0a
45dc5b24823f47cc565196ceff4a46ca
34fc074959aa1ef988969cfdd6d37533
e5623222373d762a60e47165b04091c2
-----END OpenVPN Static key V1-----
```

Copy the key and paste it into your OpenVPN configuration.

After copying the key, you will want to delete it. To do so, run:

```
# rm /tmp/shared.key
```

15.2.2 Generating Certificates

For X.509 OpenVPN configurations, you first need to generate the certificates. If you have an existing PKI you will want to use it, and this section will not be relevant for you. Most pfSense users do not have an existing X.509 PKI, and the easiest means of setting one up is the easy-rsa scripts provided with OpenVPN.

15.2.2.1 Determining a home for easy-rsa

If you have an existing BSD or Linux system, you can download the latest version of OpenVPN on that system, extract it, and you will find the `easy-rsa` folder under the extracted OpenVPN folder. Similarly with Windows systems, the OpenVPN installation also installs easy-rsa, by default under `C:\Program Files\OpenVPN\easy-rsa`. You can also use easy-rsa directly on pfSense.

If you would rather run it in a virtual machine, the pfSense Tools virtual appliance includes the easy-rsa scripts.

The most serious PKI deployments of this nature commonly run on a dedicated system in a physically secure location that is not connected to any network at all, with keys copied as needed using removable storage. In most small to mid-sized environments this is impractical and rarely done. Keep in mind that a compromise of your PKI compromises the integrity of your entire OpenVPN infrastructure, so keep it on a system secured appropriately to the level of risk on your network.

15.2.2.2 Generating Certificates using pfSense

You can use easy-rsa on pfSense to generate your OpenVPN keys. The easy-rsa files included with OpenVPN assume the presence of the **bash** shell, which BSD operating systems don't include by default, so a custom easy-rsa package has been made available by pfSense developers if you wish to use it on your firewall. You will need SSH enabled on your firewall to use easy-rsa. To install, just run the following from a SSH session command prompt:

```
# fetch -o - http://files.pfsense.org/misc/easyrsa-setup.txt | /bin/sh
```

This will download the files, extract them, and remove the downloaded file. After doing this, you will be prompted to run the next step manually. Copy and paste the last line displayed to generate your certificates.

Note

If you have gone through this process previously, repeating this will wipe out all your existing certificates!

```
# cd /root/easyrsa4pfsense && ./PFSENSE_RUN_ME_FIRST
```

This will first prompt you for your location and organization information, to be used when generating the certificate authority and initial certificates, and as defaults when creating additional certificates in the future. It will then create your certificate authority, a server certificate, and one client certificate. These files can be found in the `/root/easyrsa4pfsense/keys/` directory.

15.2.2.2.1   Creating a client key

To create a new client key, run the following commands, where username is the name of the client (substitute the person's *username* here).

```
# cd /root/easyrsa4pfsense
# source vars
# ./build-key username
```

15.2.2.2.2   Creating a password protected client key

The process for creating a password protected client key is mostly the same as a non-password protected key. To do so, run the following commands:

```
# cd /root/easyrsa4pfsense
# source vars
# ./build-key-pass username
```

The password specified when creating the key will have to be entered by the user upon each connection to OpenVPN.

15.2.2.2.3   Copying keys from the firewall

After creating your keys, you need a means of transferring them for use in your server and client configurations. For keys used on pfSense, whether in a server or client configuration, the easiest way is to use the **cat** command in a SSH session and copy the resulting output. For example, to get the contents of the CA certificate, run:

```
# cat /root/easyrsa4pfsense/keys/ca.crt
```

Copy the output and paste it into the CA certificate box. Which certificate files to enter into each box of the OpenVPN configuration is covered later in the chapter.

For clients not on pfSense, you will want to download the appropriate certificate files from the system. This can be done using SCP, as described in Section 4.5.2 or in the web interface in the Diagnostics → Command screen. Fill in the appropriate filename in the File to download box, such as /root/ easyrsa4pfsense/keys/ca.crt for the CA certificate, and click Download. Repeat for each file needed. Another alternative is to backup the entire easy-rsa directory as described in the next section, and extract the backup to retrieve the required files.

15.2.2.2.4   Backing up easy-rsa

The easyrsa4pfsense folder is not backed up when you backup your configuration file. You will want to get a backup of this folder, as a loss of the data in the keys directory will make it impossible to generate new keys and revoke existing keys. The existing configuration will not stop working, but losing the ability to add or revoke keys will leave you stuck with recreating all your keys and re-issuing them to your clients. The easiest way to backup easy-rsa is using the Backup package to backup path /root/easyrsa4pfsense as shown in Figure 15.1. The Backup package is discussed further in Section 5.6.

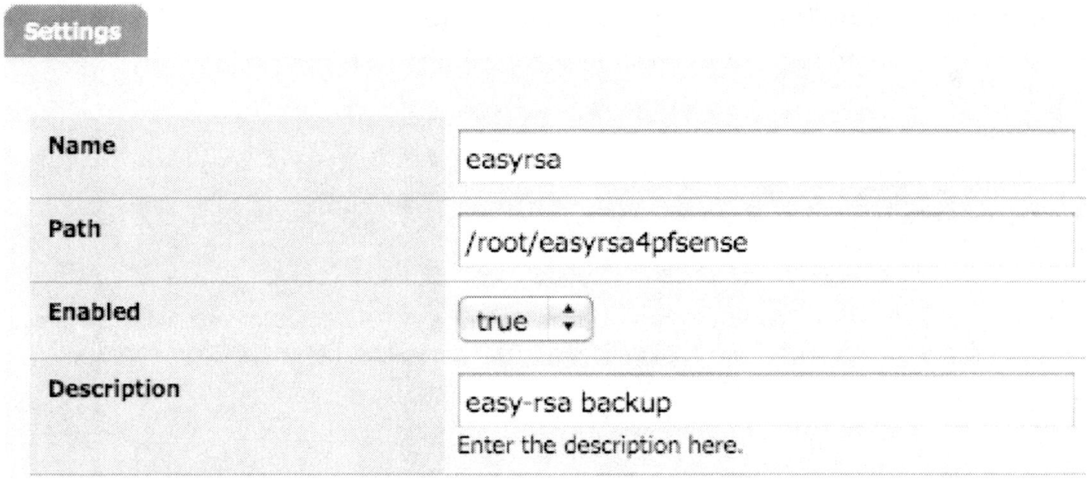

Name	easyrsa
Path	/root/easyrsa4pfsense
Enabled	true
Description	easy-rsa backup
	Enter the description here.

Figure 15.1: easy-rsa Backup

15.2.2.3   Using easy-rsa

If you prefer to use easy-rsa on a system other than pfSense, there are a few extra steps you must follow that the **easyrsa4pfsense** package handles automatically. These steps are applicable to BSD and Linux systems, though the process on Windows is largely the same. If using Windows, refer to the

README.txt in the `easy-rsa` folder for more information, and you can also follow these steps for the most part. To get started, download and extract OpenVPN from `http://openvpn.net`. Inside the extracted folder you will find the `easy-rsa` folder. For Windows, after running the OpenVPN installation, you will find the `easy-rsa` folder in `C:\Program Files\OpenVPN\`.

15.2.2.3.1 Setting up your information in vars

There is a file called `vars` included in the `easy-rsa` folder. Open this file in a text editor and go down to the bottom of the file. You will see something like the following.

```
export KEY_COUNTRY=US
export KEY_PROVINCE=Kentucky
export KEY_CITY=Louisville
export KEY_ORG="pfSense"
export KEY_EMAIL="pfsense@localhost"
```

You can edit these to match your location, organization and email, though you can also leave them as is if you want your certificates to be created using this information. Save `vars` after making any desired changes.

15.2.2.3.2 Create your CA

First, run **source vars** to load the easy-rsa environment variables. Then run **./clean-all** to ensure you are starting with a clean environment. Once you have created your CA, never run **clean-all** as it will delete your CA and all certificates.

```
# source vars
NOTE: when you run ./clean-all, it will be doing a rm -rf on /home/cmb/ ↩
    easyrsa4pfsense/keys
# ./clean-all
#
```

Now you are ready to run **./build-ca**, the command that creates your CA. Note the fields are already filled in using what you entered in `vars` previously. You can just hit **Enter** at each prompt.

```
# ./build-ca
Generating a 1024 bit RSA private key
...................................++++++
.....++++++
writing new private key to 'ca.key'
-----
You are about to be asked to enter information that will be incorporated
into your certificate request.
What you are about to enter is what is called a Distinguished Name or a ↩
    DN.
There are quite a few fields but you can leave some blank
For some fields there will be a default value,
If you enter '.', the field will be left blank.
-----
```

```
Country Name (2 letter code) [US]:
State or Province Name (full name) [Kentucky]:
Locality Name (eg, city) [Louisville]:
Organization Name (eg, company) [pfSense]:
Organizational Unit Name (eg, section) []:
Common Name (eg, your name or your server's hostname) []:
Email Address [pfsense@localhost]:
#
```

15.2.2.3.3 Generating your DH key

Next you will generate your DH key by running **./build-dh**. It warns it will take a long time, though that depends on the speed of your processor. This takes under 5 seconds on an Intel Core 2 Quad Q6600 processor, but it may take up to several minutes on 500 MHz and slower CPUs.

```
# ./build-dh
Generating DH parameters, 1024 bit long safe prime, generator 2
This is going to take a long time

.................+..............+.........................................
..................... .......................................+.+..................
....................................+....................+... ............................
...............................+..........................................  ......
....+.++*++*++*
```

15.2.2.3.4 Generating a server certificate and key

Now you need to create a certificate and key for your OpenVPN server using the **./build-key-server** command followed by the name you will use to reference the server (cosmetic only).

```
# ./build-key-server server
Generating a 1024 bit RSA private key
.................++++++
........++++++
writing new private key to 'server.key'
-----
You are about to be asked to enter information that will be incorporated
into your certificate request.
What you are about to enter is what is called a Distinguished Name or a  ↩
    DN.
There are quite a few fields but you can leave some blank
For some fields there will be a default value,
If you enter '.', the field will be left blank.
-----
Country Name (2 letter code) [US]:
State or Province Name (full name) [Kentucky]:
Locality Name (eg, city) [Louisville]:
Organization Name (eg, company) [pfSense]:
Organizational Unit Name (eg, section) []:
```

```
Common Name (eg, your name or your server's hostname) []: server
Email Address [pfsense@localhost]:

Please enter the following 'extra' attributes
to be sent with your certificate request
A challenge password []:
An optional company name []:
Using configuration from /home/cmb/easyrsa4pfsense/openssl.cnf
Check that the request matches the signature
Signature ok
The Subject's Distinguished Name is as follows
countryName             :PRINTABLE:'US'
stateOrProvinceName     :PRINTABLE:'Kentucky'
localityName            :PRINTABLE:'Louisville'
organizationName        :PRINTABLE:'pfSense'
commonName              :PRINTABLE:'server'
emailAddress            :IA5STRING:'pfsense@localhost'
Certificate is to be certified until Jan 18 07:18:22 2019 GMT (3650 days ↩
    )
Sign the certificate? [y/n]: y


1 out of 1 certificate requests certified, commit? [y/n] y
Write out database with 1 new entries
Data Base Updated
#
```

15.2.2.3.5   Generate client certificates

You will need to create a certificate for each client using the **build-key** command followed by the key name. The following example shows the creation of a client key for user *cmb*. You can name the client key however you desire. Using the username of the person who will use the key usually makes the most sense. For client connections that will reside on firewalls, you might want to use the hostname of the firewall that will use the key.

```
# ./build-key cmb
Generating a 1024 bit RSA private key
....................................................++++++
..........................++++++
writing new private key to 'cmb.key'
-----
You are about to be asked to enter information that will be incorporated
into your certificate request.
What you are about to enter is what is called a Distinguished Name or a ↩
    DN.
There are quite a few fields but you can leave some blank
For some fields there will be a default value,
If you enter '.', the field will be left blank.
-----
Country Name (2 letter code) [US]:
```

```
State or Province Name (full name) [Kentucky]:
Locality Name (eg, city) [Louisville]:
Organization Name (eg, company) [pfSense]:
Organizational Unit Name (eg, section) []:
Common Name (eg, your name or your server's hostname) []: cmb
Email Address [pfsense@localhost]:

Please enter the following 'extra' attributes
to be sent with your certificate request
A challenge password []:
An optional company name []:
Using configuration from /home/cmb/easyrsa4pfsense/openssl.cnf
Check that the request matches the signature
Signature ok
The Subject's Distinguished Name is as follows
countryName            :PRINTABLE:'US'
stateOrProvinceName    :PRINTABLE:'Kentucky'
localityName           :PRINTABLE:'Louisville'
organizationName       :PRINTABLE:'pfSense'
commonName             :PRINTABLE:'cmb'
emailAddress           :IA5STRING:'pfsense@localhost'
Certificate is to be certified until Jan 18 07:21:04 2019 GMT (3650 days ↩
    )
Sign the certificate? [y/n]: y


1 out of 1 certificate requests certified, commit? [y/n] y
Write out database with 1 new entries
Data Base Updated
#
```

You will need to repeat that process for each client being deployed. For users added in the future, you can run this again at any time.

15.3 OpenVPN Configuration Options

This section describes all of the available options with OpenVPN and when you may want or need to use them. Subsequent sections cover examples of configuring site to site and remote access VPNs with OpenVPN, using the most common options and a minimal configuration.

15.3.1 Server configuration options

This section describes each configuration option on the OpenVPN Server Edit screen.

15.3.1.1 Disable this tunnel

Check this box and click Save to retain the configuration, but not enable the server.

15.3.1.2   Protocol

Select TCP or UDP here. Unless there is a reason you must use TCP, such as the ability to bypass many firewalls by running an OpenVPN server on TCP port 443, you should use UDP. It is always preferable to use connectionless protocols when tunneling traffic. TCP is connection oriented, with guaranteed delivery. Any lost packets are retransmitted. This may sound like a good idea, but performance will degrade significantly on heavily loaded Internet connections, or those with consistent packet loss, because of the TCP retransmissions. You will frequently have TCP traffic within the tunnel. Where you have TCP wrapped around TCP, when a packet is lost, both the outer and inner lost TCP packets will be re-transmitted. Infrequent occurrences of this will be unnoticeable, but recurring loss will cause significantly lesser performance than if you were using UDP. You really do not want lost packets of encapsulated VPN traffic to be retransmitted. If the traffic inside the tunnel requires reliable delivery, it will be using a protocol such as TCP which ensures that and will handle its own retransmissions.

15.3.1.3   Dynamic IP

Checking this box adds the **float** configuration option to your OpenVPN configuration. This allows connected clients to retain their connection if their IP changes. For clients on Internet connections where the IP changes frequently, or mobile users who commonly move between different Internet connections, you will need to check this option. Where the client IP is static or rarely changes, not using this option offers a minuscule security improvement.

15.3.1.4   Local port

The local port is the port number OpenVPN will use to listen. Your firewall rules need to allow traffic to this port, and it must be specified in the client configuration. The port for each server must be unique.

15.3.1.5   Address pool

This is the pool of addresses to be assigned to clients upon connecting. The server's end of the Open-VPN configuration will use the first address in this pool for its end of the connection, and assign additional addresses to connected clients.

15.3.1.6   Use static IPs

If you check this option, the server will not assign IPs to clients. Usually this will not be used, though it is useful in combination with custom options for some hacks such as using bridging.

15.3.1.7   Local network

This field specifies what route, if any, is pushed to clients connecting to this server. If you need to push routes for more than one subnet, enter the first subnet here and see Section 15.10 for information on adding the remaining subnets.

15.3.1.8 Remote network

If a subnet is specified here, a route to this subnet via the other side of this OpenVPN connection will be added. This is used for site to site connectivity, and not for mobile clients. You can only enter one subnet here. If you need to add more than one Remote network subnet, enter the first here and see Section 15.10 for information on adding the remaining subnets.

15.3.1.9 Client-to-client VPN

If clients need to communicate between each other, check this option. Without this option, they can only send traffic to the server (and any connected network for which they have a route).

15.3.1.10 Cryptography

This is where you select the cryptographic cipher to be used for this connection. The default is BF-CBC, which is Blowfish 128 bit Cipher Block Chaining. This is OpenVPN's default, and is a fine choice for most scenarios. One common situation where you may want to change this is when you are using a hardware crypto accelerator, such as `glxsb` built into ALIX hardware, or a `hifn` card. In these cases, you will see increased performance by using a hardware accelerated cipher. For ALIX or other hardware with `glxsb`, choose **AES-CBC-128**. For `hifn` hardware, chose any of the 3DES or AES options. See Section 15.10.3 for more information on using crypto accelerators.

15.3.1.11 Authentication method

Here you select either PKI or shared key, depending on which you will use. Section 15.2 discusses these options in more detail.

15.3.1.12 Shared key

When using shared key authentication, you paste the shared key here.

15.3.1.13 PKI Options

The next five options are available for configuration when using PKI authentication. The first four are mandatory.

15.3.1.13.1 CA certificate

Paste the CA certificate here (`ca.crt` when using easyrsa).

15.3.1.13.2 Server Certificate

Paste the server certificate here (`server.crt` when using easyrsa).

15.3.1.13.3 Server key

Paste the server key here (`server.key` when using easyrsa).

15.3.1.13.4 DH parameters

Paste the DH parameters here (`dh1024.pem` when using easyrsa).

15.3.1.13.5 CRL

CRL is for the certificate revocation list. If you ever need to revoke access for one or more of your certificates, a CRL PEM file is created that gets pasted here. This file is called `crl.pem` when using easyrsa. This file is a complete list of all revoked certificates, so the contents of this field are replaced, not appended to, when you revoke certificates.

15.3.1.14 DHCP Options

There are eight different DHCP options that can be configured. These options behave the same as when configured in any DHCP server.

15.3.1.14.1 DNS Domain Name

This specifies the DNS domain name to be assigned to clients. To ensure name resolution works properly for hosts on your local network where DNS name resolution is used, you should specify your internal DNS domain name here. For Microsoft Active Directory environments, this should usually be your Active Directory domain name.

15.3.1.14.2 DNS server

Here you specify the DNS servers to be used by the client while connected to this server. For Microsoft Active Directory environments, this should specify your Active Directory DNS servers for proper name resolution and authentication when connected via OpenVPN.

15.3.1.14.3 WINS server

Specify the WINS servers to be used, if any.

15.3.1.14.4 NBDD server

This option is for the NetBIOS Datagram Distribution server, which is typically not used.

15.3.1.14.5 NTP server

This field specifies DHCP option 47, primary NTP server. It can be an IP address or FQDN.

15.3.1.14.6 NetBIOS node type

The NetBIOS node type controls how Windows systems will function when resolving NetBIOS names. It's usually fine to leave this to **none** to accept Windows' default.

15.3.1.14.7 NetBIOS scope

Enter the NetBIOS scope here if applicable. Usually this is left blank.

15.3.1.14.8 Disable NetBIOS

This option disables NetBIOS over TCP/IP on the client, and is usually not set.

15.3.1.15 LZO Compression

This check box enables LZO compression for your OpenVPN traffic. If this box is checked, the traffic crossing your OpenVPN connection will be compressed before being encrypted. This saves on bandwidth usage for many types of traffic, at the expense of increased CPU utilization on both the server and client. Generally this impact is minimal, and I suggest enabling this for nearly any usage of OpenVPN over the Internet. For high speed connections, such as the usage of OpenVPN across a LAN, high speed low latency WAN, or local wireless network, this may be undesirable, as the delay added by the compression may be more than the delay saved in transmitting the traffic. If nearly all of the traffic crossing your OpenVPN connection is already encrypted (such as SSH, SCP, HTTPS, amongst many other protocols), you should not enable LZO compression because encrypted data is not compressible and the LZO compression will cause slightly more data to be transferred than would be without compression. The same is true if your VPN traffic is almost entirely data that is already compressed.

15.3.1.16 Custom options

While the pfSense web interface supports all the most commonly used options, OpenVPN is very powerful and flexible and you may occasionally want or need to use options that are unavailable in the web interface. You can fill in these custom options here. These options are described further in Section 15.10.

15.3.1.17 Description

Enter a description for this server configuration, for your reference.

15.4 Remote Access Configuration

This section describes the process for configuring a X.509-based remote access VPN solution with OpenVPN.

15.4.1   Determine an IP addressing scheme

In addition to the internal subnets you will want clients to access, you need to choose an IP subnet to use for the OpenVPN connections. This is the subnet filled in under Interface IP in the server configuration. Connected clients will receive an IP address within this subnet, and the server end of the connection also receives an IP on this subnet, where the client directs traffic for subnets routed through the OpenVPN connection. As always when choosing internal subnets for a single location, this subnet should be CIDR summarizable with your internal subnets. The example network depicted here uses 172.31.54.0/24 for LAN, and 172.31.55.0/24 for OpenVPN. These two networks are summarized with 172.31.54.0/23, making routing easier to manage. CIDR summarization is discussed further in Section 1.7.5.

15.4.2   Example Network

Figure 15.2 shows the network configured in this example.

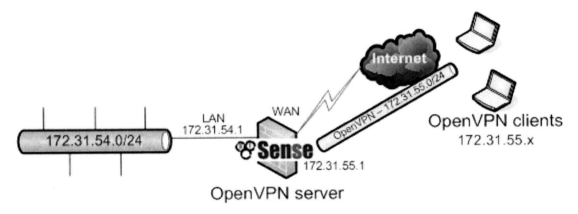

Figure 15.2: OpenVPN example remote access network

15.4.3   Server Configuration

Browse to VPN → OpenVPN and click ⬚ on the Server tab to add a new OpenVPN server. Most options will be left at their defaults. The following will need to be configured.

- Local Address — specify the subnet to be used for OpenVPN clients here. For this example, that is **172.31.55.0/24**.

- Authentication method — moving down the page a bit before moving back up, you need to change Authentication method from **Shared key** to **PKI**.

- Local network — move back up the page and specify Local network as the network reachable to the clients through the VPN. In this example that will be LAN, so **172.31.54.0/24** is specified here. Additional subnets can be specified with the **route** custom option described in Section 15.10.

- CA certificate — paste the `ca.crt` file from easy-rsa here.

- Server certificate — paste the `server.crt` file from easy-rsa here.

- Server key — paste the `server.key` file from easy-rsa here.

- DH parameters — paste the `dh1024.pem` file from easy-rsa here.

- LZO compression — unless this VPN is used with a high speed, low latency connection such as a local wired or wireless network, you will want to check this box to enable LZO compression.

- Description — fill in a description here for your reference.

These are the bare minimum options for most server configurations. The additional options may be desirable or necessary in some circumstances. Refer to Section 15.3 for more information on the other available options.

When finished configuring the options as desired, click Save to finish the server configuration. pfSense will start the OpenVPN server as soon as you click Save.

15.4.3.1 Permitting traffic to the OpenVPN server

Next, add a firewall rule to permit traffic to the OpenVPN server. Browse to Firewall → Rules, and to the WAN tab, then click [icon]. For the example configuration here, protocol **UDP** will be chosen, with **any** source, destination **WAN Address**, and destination port **1194**. This rule is depicted in Figure 15.3.

Figure 15.3: OpenVPN server WAN rule

If you know which source addresses your clients will be connecting from, you can specify a source network or alias rather than leaving the server open to the entire Internet. This is usually impossible where you have roaming clients. There is not much risk to leaving this open, however, as with certificate based authentication you have lesser risk of compromise than password-based solutions that are susceptible to brute forcing. This presumes a lack of security holes in OpenVPN itself, which to date has a solid security track record.

15.4.4 Client Installation

With the server configuration complete, OpenVPN now needs to be installed on the client system. The same OpenVPN installation can function as either a client or server, so there is only one installation routine. It functions as instructed in the configuration provided, which will be covered in the next section. This section provides an overview of installation on several common operating systems.

15.4.4.1   Windows Installation

The OpenVPN project provides an installer for Windows 2000 through Windows 7, downloadable from `http://openvpn.net/index.php/open-source/downloads.html`. At the time of this writing, the best version for most Windows users is 2.1_rc19. The 2.1 series, while not yet classified as stable, has proven to be stable in wide production use and includes a built in GUI. The current stable 2.0.9 version (what runs on pfSense) does not include a Windows GUI. The 2.1 client is fully compatible and stable with the 2.0.x version running on pfSense. The installation is straight forward, just accept all the defaults. The installation will create a new Local Area Connection on your system for the `tun` interface. This interface will be connected when the VPN is connected, and otherwise show as disconnected. No configuration of this interface is necessary, as its configuration will be pulled from the OpenVPN server.

Note

On Windows Vista and Windows 7 with UAC (User Account Control) enabled, you must right click the OpenVPN GUI icon and click Run as Administrator for it to work. It can connect without administrative rights, but it cannot add the route needed to direct traffic over the OpenVPN connection, leaving it unusable. You may also adjust the properties of the shortcut to always launch the program as Administrator. This option is found on the Compatibility tab of the shortcut properties.

15.4.4.2   Mac OS X Clients and Installation

There are three client options for Mac OS X. One is the simple OpenVPN command line client. Most users prefer a graphical client, and there are two options available for OS X. Tunnelblick is a free option available for download at `http://www.tunnelblick.net`. I have used it in the past with success. Another GUI option is the commercial Viscosity client available at `http://www.viscosityvpn.com`. At the time of this writing, it costs $9 USD for a single seat. If you use OpenVPN frequently, Viscosity is a much nicer client and well worth the cost.

Both Tunnelblick and Viscosity are easily installed, with no configuration options during installation.

15.4.4.3   FreeBSD Installation

If you have a stock FreeBSD installation, you can find OpenVPN in ports. To install, just run:

```
# cd /usr/ports/security/openvpn && make install clean
```

15.4.4.4   Linux Installation

Linux installation will vary depending on your preferred distribution and method of managing software installations. OpenVPN is included in the package repositories of most major Linux distributions. With all the various possibilities between countless distributions, and adequate information already available in other sources online, this book won't cover any specifics. Simply search the Internet for your distribution of choice and "**installing OpenVPN**" to find information.

15.4.5 Client Configuration

After installing OpenVPN, you need to copy the certificates to the client and create the client configuration file.

15.4.5.1 Copy certificates

Three files from easy-rsa are needed for each client: the CA certificate, the client certificate, and the client key. The CA certificate is `ca.key` in the easy-rsa keys directory. The client's certificate and key are named with the client name used when they were generated. The certificate for user *jdoe* is `jdoe.crt` and the key is `jdoe.key`. Copy `ca.crt`, `username.crt` and `username.key` to the OpenVPN `config` directory on the client.

15.4.5.2 Create Configuration

After copying the certificates to the client, the OpenVPN client configuration file must be created. This can be done with any plain text file editor, such as Notepad on Windows. The following shows the options most frequently used.

```
client
dev tun
proto udp
remote openvpn.example.com 1194
ping 10
resolv-retry infinite
nobind
persist-key
persist-tun
ca ca.crt
cert username.crt
key username.key
pull
verb 3
comp-lzo
```

The **remote** line specifies the host and port of the remote OpenVPN server. An IP address or FQDN can be specified here. The **proto** line specifies the protocol used by the OpenVPN connection. Change this line to **proto tcp** if you chose TCP rather than UDP for your OpenVPN server. The **ca**, **cert**, and **key** lines need to be modified accordingly for each client.

15.4.5.2.1 Distributing configuration and keys to clients

The easiest way to distribute the keys and OpenVPN configuration to clients is to package them in a zip file, or self-extracting zip automatically extracting to `C:\Program Files\OpenVPN\config`. This must be transmitted securely to the end user, and should never be passed over untrusted networks unencrypted.

15.4.5.3 Configuring Viscosity

When using the Viscosity client, you need not manually create the OpenVPN client configuration file as described in the previous section. Viscosity provides a GUI configuration tool that is used to generate the underlying OpenVPN client configuration shown in the previous section. First, copy the CA certificate, client certificate and client key to a folder of your choosing on the Mac. These files will be imported into Viscosity, and afterwards they can be deleted. Ensure this folder is kept secure, or has the files deleted once finished configuring Viscosity. Then launch Viscosity to begin the configuration.

Click the lock icon added to the menu bar at the top of the screen, and click Preferences to begin the configuration as shown in Figure 15.4.

Figure 15.4: Viscosity Preferences

Click the plus at the bottom right of the Preferences screen, and click New Connection as shown in Figure 15.5.

At the first configuration screen (Figure 15.6), enter a name for your connection, the IP address or hostname of the OpenVPN server, the port being used, and the protocol. Check Enable DNS support if you specified DNS servers in your server configuration. Click the Certificates tab when finished.

On the Certificates tab (Figure 15.7), the CA and user certificates and user key must be specified. The files can be downloaded to any location on the Mac's filesystem. After downloading them, click Select next to each of the three boxes to choose the appropriate file for each. The Tls-Auth box is left blank. Click the Options tab when finished.

On the Options tab (Figure 15.8), check Use LZO Compression if you enabled it on the server side. The remaining options can be left at their defaults. Click the Networking tab to continue.

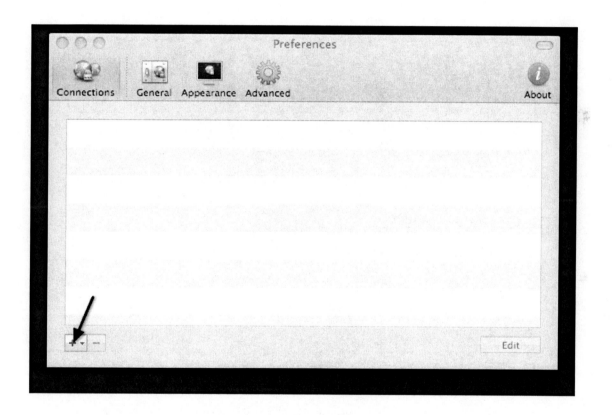

Figure 15.5: Viscosity Add Connection

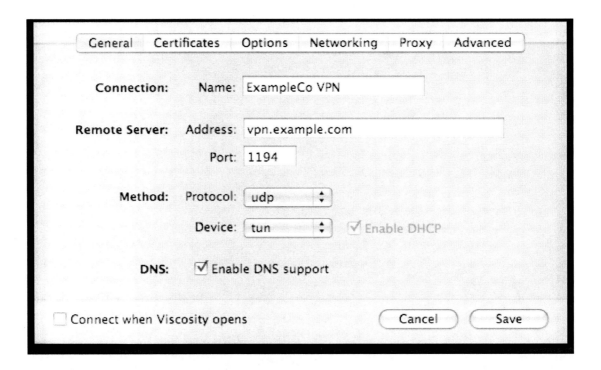

Figure 15.6: Viscosity Configuration: General

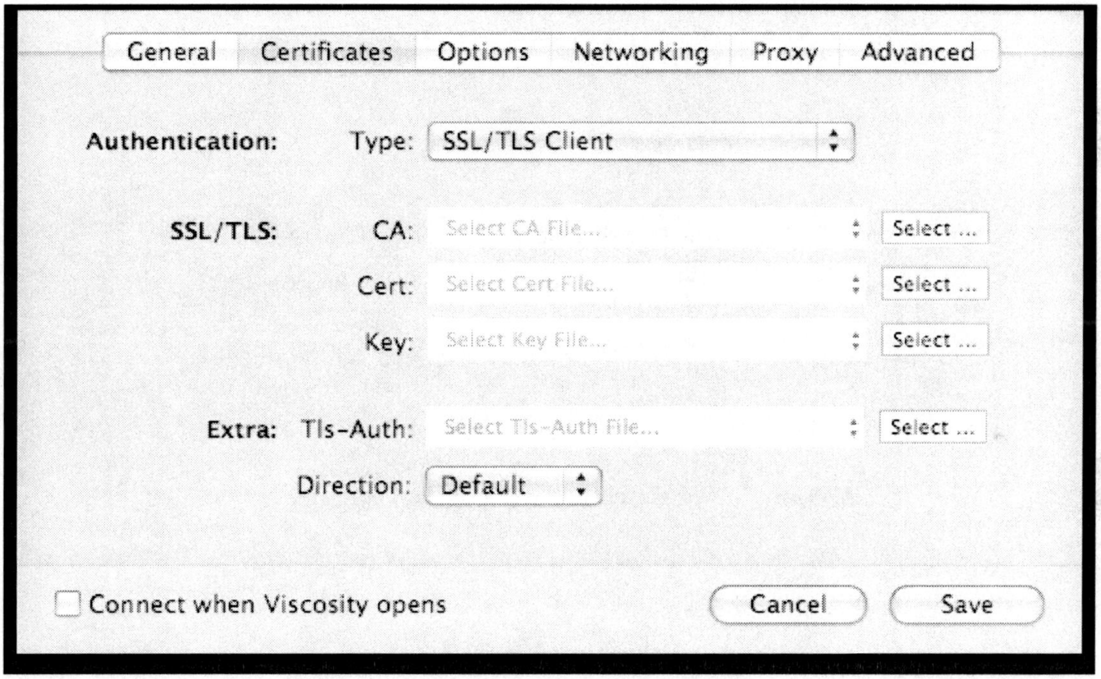

Figure 15.7: Viscosity Configuration: Certificates

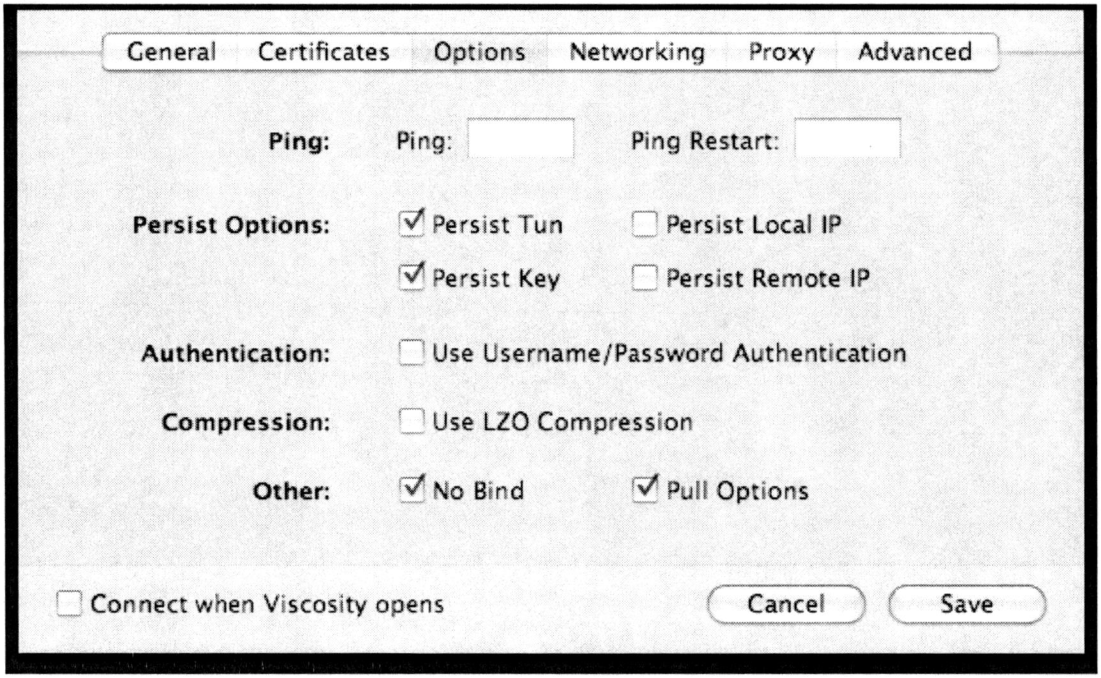

Figure 15.8: Viscosity Configuration: Options

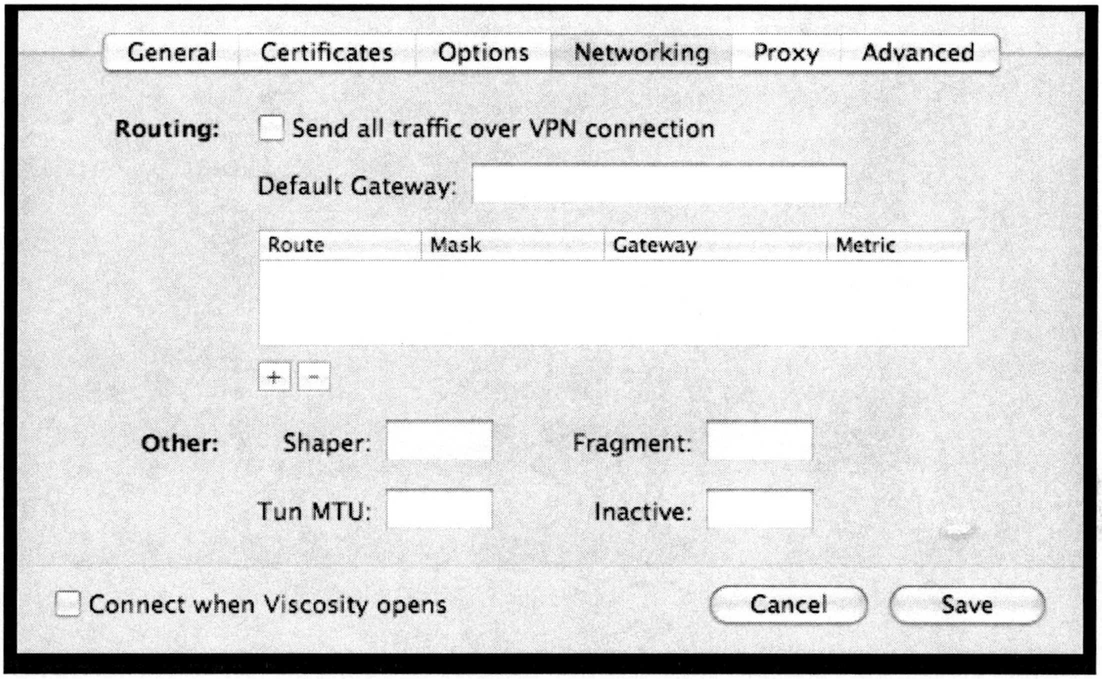

Figure 15.9: Viscosity Configuration: Networking

On the Networking tab (Figure 15.9), the primary option of interest is the Send all traffic over VPN connection check box. If you want to send all traffic through the VPN, check this box. The remaining configuration tabs can be disregarded in nearly all configurations. When finished, click Save to finish adding the new OpenVPN configuration.

Now you will have your just added OpenVPN configuration shown in the Preferences screen. Close the Preferences screen, then click the lock in the menu bar, and the name of your VPN connection to connect, as shown in Figure 15.10.

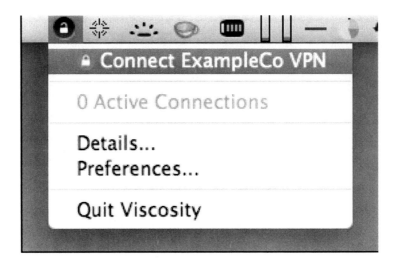

Figure 15.10: Viscosity connect

After a few seconds, the lock in the menu bar should turn green to show it connected successfully. By clicking on it, and clicking Details as shown in Figure 15.11, you can see information on the connection.

On the first screen (Figure 15.12), you see the connection status, connected time, the IP assigned to the client, and the IP of the server. A bandwidth graph is displayed at the bottom of the screen, showing the throughput in and out of the OpenVPN interface.

By clicking on the up/down arrows button in the middle of the details screen, you can see further network traffic statistics. This shows the traffic sent within the tunnel (TUN/TAP In and Out), as well as the total TCP or UDP traffic sent including the overhead of the tunnel and encryption. For connections using primarily small packets, the overhead is considerable with all VPN solutions. The stats shown in Figure 15.13 are from only a few pings traversing the connection. The traffic sent in bringing up the connection is also counted here, so the initial overhead is higher than what it will be after being connected for some time. Also, the typical VPN traffic will have larger packet sizes than 64 byte pings, making the total overhead and difference between these two numbers considerably less.

Clicking on the third icon in the middle of the Details screen shows the OpenVPN log file (Figure 15.14). If you have any trouble connecting, review the logs here to help determine the problem. See also Section 15.11.

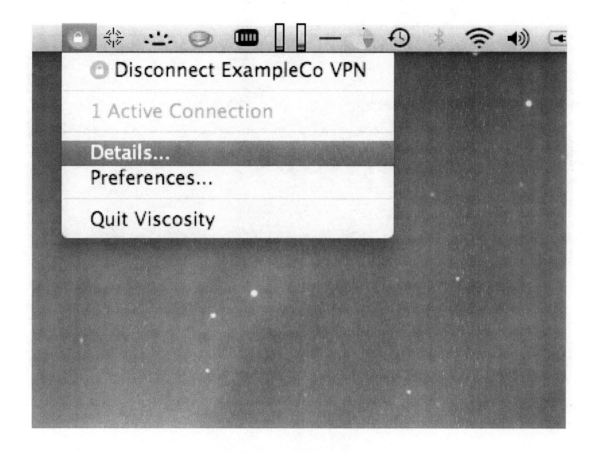

Figure 15.11: Viscosity menu

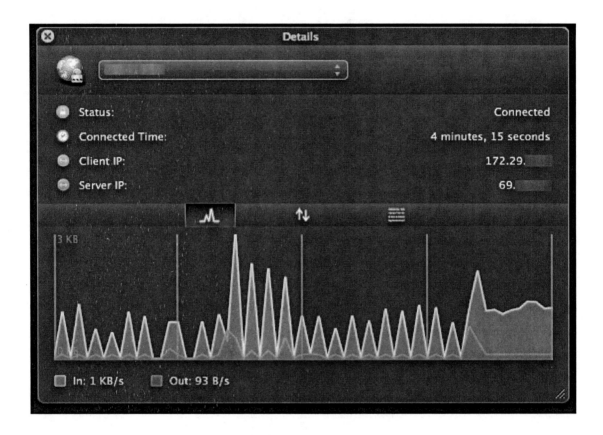

Figure 15.12: Viscosity details

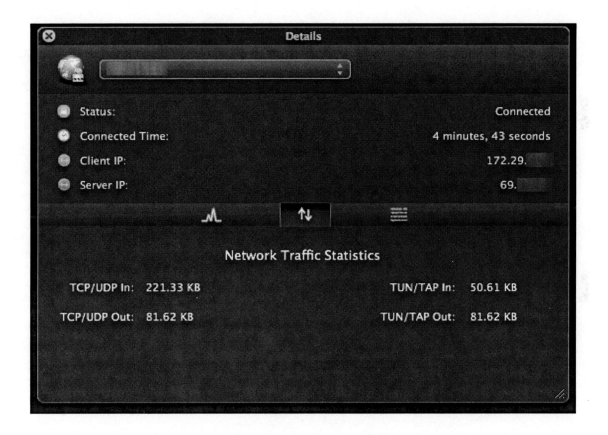

Figure 15.13: Viscosity details: Traffic Statistics

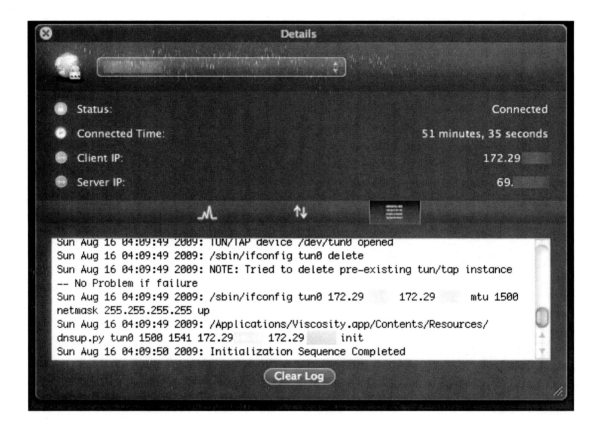

Figure 15.14: Viscosity details: Logs

15.5   Site to Site Example Configuration

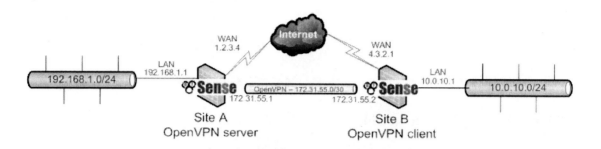

Figure 15.15: OpenVPN example site to site network

This section describes the process of configuring a site to site connection using shared keys. When configuring a site to site OpenVPN connection, one firewall will be the server and the other will be the client. Usually your main location will be the server side and the remote offices will act as clients, though the opposite is functionally equivalent. In addition to the subnets on both ends, as with the remote access OpenVPN configuration, there will be a dedicated subnet in use for the OpenVPN inter-connection between networks. The example configuration described here is depicted in Figure 15.15.

172.31.55.0/30 is used as the Address pool. The OpenVPN tunnel between the two firewalls gets an IP on each end out of that subnet, as illustrated in the diagram. The following sections describe how to configure the server and client sides of the connection.

15.5.1   Configuring Server Side

Browse to VPN → OpenVPN and click ⊞ on the Server tab. The following fields are configured, with everything else left at defaults.

- Address pool — Enter **172.31.55.0/30** here.

- Remote network — Enter **10.0.10.0/24** here.

- Shared key — Paste in the shared key for this connection here. Instructions on generating shared keys is provided in Section 15.2.1.

- Description — Enter something here to describe the connection.

That is everything that must be configured for the OpenVPN server to function in this scenario. Click Save.

Next you will need to add a firewall rule on WAN allowing access to the OpenVPN server. Specify the protocol **UDP**, source IP as the client's IP address if it has a static IP, or **any** if its IP is dynamic. Destination is the **WAN Address**, and destination port is **1194** in this instance. Figure 15.16 shows the firewall rule used for this example.

| | UDP | 4.3.2.1 | * | 1.2.3.4 | 1194 (OpenVPN) | * | | Allow site B OpenVPN |

Figure 15.16: OpenVPN example site to site WAN firewall rule

Apply changes after the firewall rule is added, and the server configuration is finished.

15.5.2   Configuring Client Side

On the client end, browse to VPN → OpenVPN and click ⊞ on the Client tab. The following fields are configured, with everything else left at defaults.

- Server address — Enter the public IP address or hostname of the OpenVPN server here.

- Remote network — Enter `192.168.1.0/24` here.

- Shared key — Paste in the shared key for the connection here, using the same key as on the server side.

- Description — Enter something here to describe the connection.

After filling in those fields, click Save. The configuration of the client is complete. No firewall rules are required on the client side because the client only initiates outbound connections. The server never initiates connections to the client.

Note

With remote access PKI configurations, frequently you do not define routes and other configuration options in the client configuration, but rather push those options from the server to the client. With shared key deployments, you must define routes and other parameters on both ends as needed (as described previously, and later in Section 15.10), you cannot push from client to server when using shared keys.

15.5.3   Testing the connection

The configuration is now complete and the connection should immediately be active upon saving on the client side. Try to ping across to the remote end to verify connectivity. If problems arise, refer to Section 15.11.

15.6   Filtering and NAT with OpenVPN Connections

By default, pfSense adds rules to the `tun` or `tap` interfaces being used by OpenVPN to allow all traffic in from connected OpenVPN clients. If you want to filter traffic from OpenVPN clients, you have to check Disable all auto-added VPN rules under System → Advanced (see Section 12.3 before doing this to review the ramifications). Then you assign the OpenVPN interface to an OPT interface and configure it accordingly. This section describes how to accomplish both filtering and NAT for OpenVPN clients.

15.6.1 Interface assignment and configuration

Browse to Interfaces → Assign and assign the appropriate `tun` or `tap` interface as an OPT interface. If you only have one OpenVPN connection and aren't using bridging as described in Section 15.9, your OpenVPN interface will be `tun0`. If you have multiple connections, and need to NAT or filter incoming traffic from OpenVPN clients, you will want to specify the device to be used for each connection in the custom options field. This is described in Section 15.10.2. You will have one OPT interface per OpenVPN server and client configured on the system. Figure 15.17 shows `tun0` assigned as OPT1.

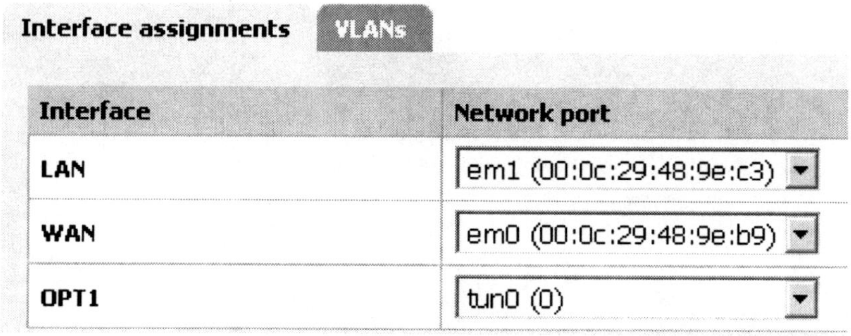

Interface assignments	VLANs
Interface	**Network port**
LAN	em1 (00:0c:29:48:9e:c3) ▾
WAN	em0 (00:0c:29:48:9e:b9) ▾
OPT1	tun0 (0) ▾

Figure 15.17: Assign tun0 interface

Now browse to the interface page for the previously assigned interface, Interfaces → OPT1 for the example shown in Figure 15.17. First check the Enable interface box at the top of the page, and enter an appropriate description in the Description field. In the IP address box enter **none**. This is a trick to not configure any IP information on the interface, which is necessary since OpenVPN itself must configure these settings on the `tun0` interface. Click Save to apply these changes. This does nothing to change the functionality of OpenVPN, it simply makes the interface available for firewall rule and NAT purposes.

15.6.2 Filtering with OpenVPN

Now that you have the OpenVPN interface assigned, browse to Firewall → Rules and click the tab for the OpenVPN interface you just assigned. Here you can add firewall rules just like any other interface that will apply to traffic initiated by OpenVPN clients. Remember that unless you check the Disable all auto-added VPN rules box under System → Advanced, allow all rules for the interface will be added that will override any rules you apply here. For more information on firewall rules, refer to Chapter 6.

15.6.3 NAT with OpenVPN

If you simply want to NAT your OpenVPN clients to your WAN IP so they can access the Internet using the OpenVPN connection, you need to enable Advanced Outbound NAT and specify an Outbound NAT rule for your Address Pool subnet(s). See Section 7.6 for more details on Outbound NAT.

With the OpenVPN interface assigned, NAT rules can also be applied the same as with any other interface. This is useful when you must connect two conflicting subnets. If you have two networks using a 192.168.1.0/24 LAN subnet that you need to connect using a site to site VPN, they cannot communicate across VPN without NAT (or bridging, as covered in Section 15.9, but that should really only be used for mobile clients and not site to site connections). Hosts on a 192.168.1.0/24 subnet will never reach the other end of the VPN to communicate with the remote 192.168.1.0/24 subnet, because that network is always treated as local. However with NAT, you can make the remote side function as if it were using a different IP subnet.

Note

This will work fine for many protocols, but for some that are commonly desirable across VPN connections, primarily SMB/CIFS file sharing between Windows hosts, will not function in combination with NAT. If you are using a protocol that is not capable of functioning with NAT, this is not a viable solution.

Figure 15.18 shows an example where both ends are using the same subnet. After assigning the `tun` interface to an OPT interface on both sides, as described in Section 15.6.1, 1:1 NAT can be applied.

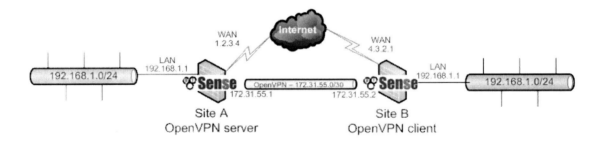

Figure 15.18: Site to site with conflicting subnets

The traffic from Site A will be translated to 172.16.1.0/24, and Site B will be translated to 172.17.1.0/24. A 1:1 NAT entry will be added on each end to translate the entire /24 range. To reach Site A from Site B, 172.16.1.x IP addresses will be used. The last octet in the 192.168.1.x IP will be translated to the last octet in the 172.16.1.x translated IP, so to reach 192.168.1.10 at Site A from Site B, you would use 172.16.1.10 instead. To reach 192.168.1.50 at Site B from Site A, you would use 172.17.1.50 instead. Figure 15.19 and Figure 15.20 show the 1:1 NAT configuration for each side, where the `tun` interface is assigned as OPT2.

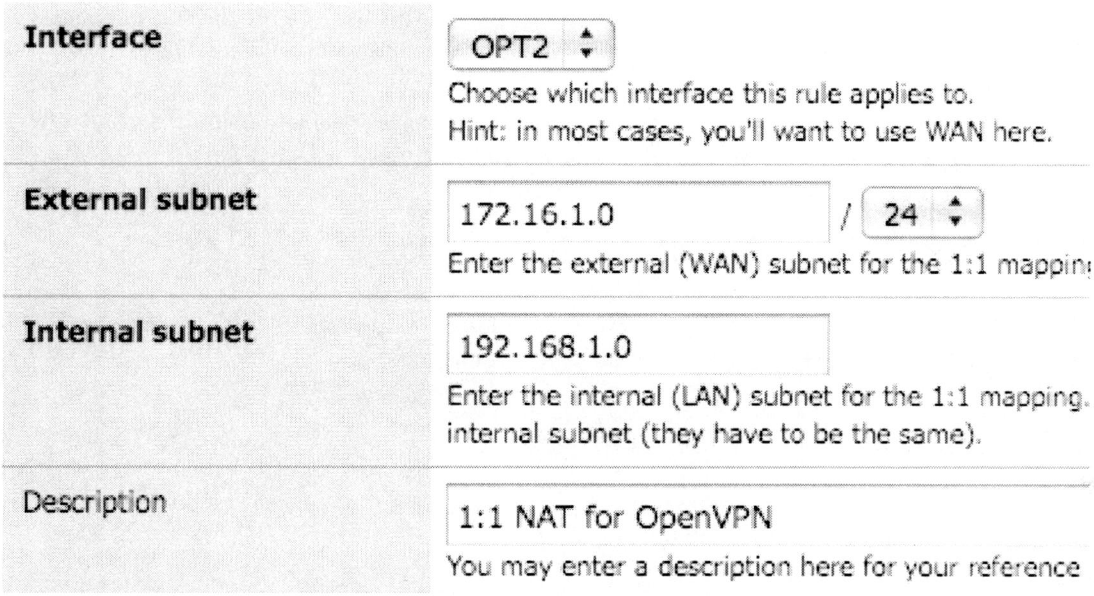

Interface

OPT2

Choose which interface this rule applies to.
Hint: in most cases, you'll want to use WAN here.

External subnet

172.16.1.0 / 24

Enter the external (WAN) subnet for the 1:1 mappin:

Internal subnet

192.168.1.0

Enter the internal (LAN) subnet for the 1:1 mapping.
internal subnet (they have to be the same).

Description

1:1 NAT for OpenVPN

You may enter a description here for your reference

Figure 15.19: Site A 1:1 NAT configuration

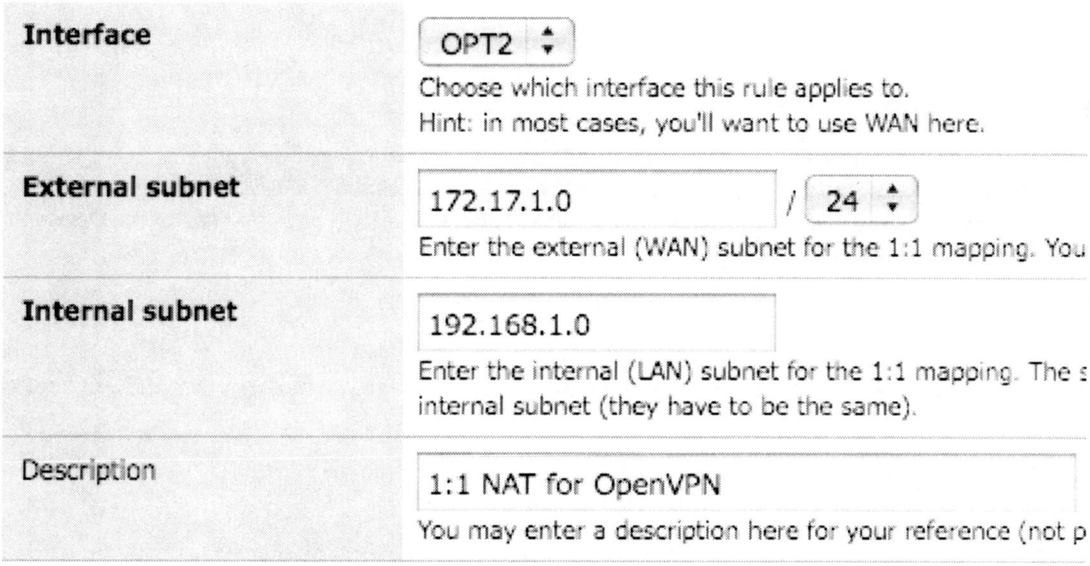

Interface

OPT2

Choose which interface this rule applies to.
Hint: in most cases, you'll want to use WAN here.

External subnet

172.17.1.0 / 24

Enter the external (WAN) subnet for the 1:1 mapping. You

Internal subnet

192.168.1.0

Enter the internal (LAN) subnet for the 1:1 mapping. The s
internal subnet (they have to be the same).

Description

1:1 NAT for OpenVPN

You may enter a description here for your reference (not p

Figure 15.20: Site B 1:1 NAT configuration

In the OpenVPN configuration on both sides, the Remote network must be specified as the translated IP subnet, not as 192.168.1.0/24. In this example, the Remote network at Site A is 172.17.1.0/24, and 172.16.1.0/24 at Site B.

After applying the NAT configuration changes and configuring the Remote network accordingly on both sides, the networks will be able to communicate using the translated subnets.

15.7 OpenVPN and Multi-WAN

OpenVPN is multi-WAN capable, with some caveats in some circumstances. This section covers multi-WAN considerations with OpenVPN server and client configurations.

15.7.1 OpenVPN servers and multi-WAN

OpenVPN servers can be used with any WAN connection, though the means of doing so will vary depending on the specifics of your configuration.

15.7.1.1 OpenVPN server using TCP

While TCP is generally not the preferred protocol for OpenVPN, as described earlier in this chapter, using TCP makes multi-WAN OpenVPN easier to configure. OpenVPN servers using TCP will work properly on all WANs where the firewall rules allow the traffic to the OpenVPN server. You need a rule on each WAN interface.

15.7.1.2 OpenVPN server using UDP

OpenVPN servers with UDP are also multi-WAN capable, but with some caveats that aren't applicable with TCP, because of the way pf's multi-WAN routing functions. Each WAN must have its own OpenVPN server. You can use the same certificates for all the servers. Only two parts of the OpenVPN configuration must change.

15.7.1.2.1 Address Pool

Each server must have a unique Address Pool that does not overlap with any other address pool or internal subnet.

15.7.1.2.2 Custom Option local

Each OpenVPN server must specify the IP of the WAN interface used by that server with the **local** custom option. The following example shows how to configure OpenVPN for WAN IP 1.2.3.4.

```
local 1.2.3.4
```

For connections with a dynamic IP, a hostname can alternatively be specified. The following shows an example for hostname openvpn.example.com.

```
local openvpn.example.com
```

15.7.1.2.3 Automatic Failover for Clients

Multiple remote servers can be configured on OpenVPN clients. If the first server cannot be reached, the second will be used. This can be used in combination with a multi-WAN OpenVPN server deployment to provide automatic failover for clients. If your OpenVPN servers are running on IPs 1.2.3.4 and 4.3.2.1, both using port 1194, the **remote** lines in your client configuration file will be as follows.

```
remote 1.2.3.4 1194
remote 4.3.2.1 1194
```

For clients configured on pfSense, the first **remote** is configured by the options given in the GUI. The second **remote** is specified in the custom options field.

15.7.2 OpenVPN Clients and Multi-WAN

OpenVPN clients configured on the firewall will follow the system routing table when making the connection to the OpenVPN server. This means by default, all clients will use the WAN interface. To use an OPT WAN interface, you must enter a static route to direct traffic to the remote endpoint of the OpenVPN connection.

Figure 15.21 illustrates the static route required when using the WAN2 interface to access an OpenVPN server running on IP 1.2.3.4, where the gateway of the WAN2 interface is 172.31.1.1.

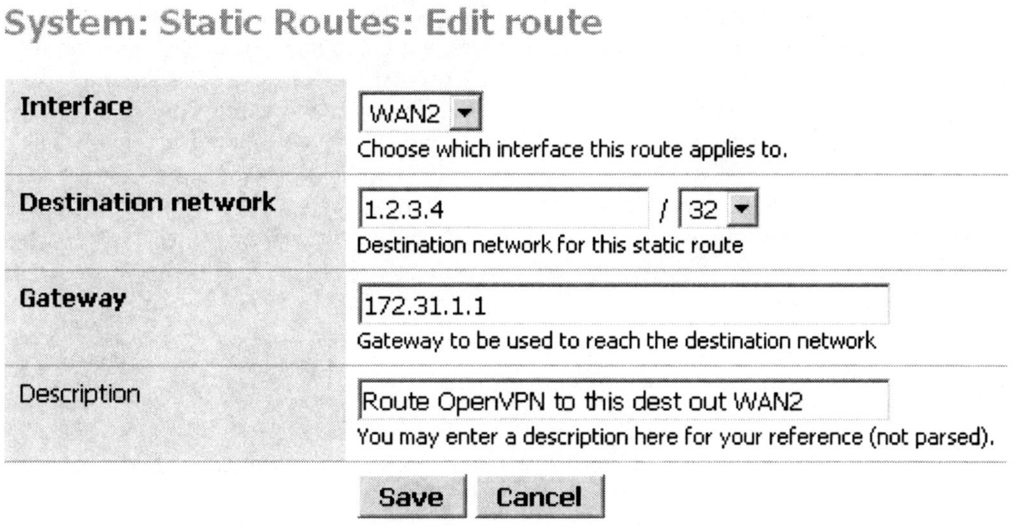

System: Static Routes: Edit route

Interface	WAN2 ▾ Choose which interface this route applies to.
Destination network	1.2.3.4 / 32 ▾ Destination network for this static route
Gateway	172.31.1.1 Gateway to be used to reach the destination network
Description	Route OpenVPN to this dest out WAN2 You may enter a description here for your reference (not parsed).

Save   Cancel

Figure 15.21: Example static route for OpenVPN Client on OPT WAN

15.8 OpenVPN and CARP

OpenVPN is interoperable with CARP. To provide a high availability OpenVPN solution with CARP, configure your clients to connect to a CARP VIP, and configure the OpenVPN server to use the CARP

IP with the **local** custom configuration option. In pfSense 1.2.x, the OpenVPN configuration cannot be synchronized with your secondary firewall, so you must manually enter it into both firewalls.
The connection state isn't retained between hosts, so clients must reconnect after failover occurs, but
OpenVPN will detect the connection failure and reconnect within a minute or so of failover. CARP is
discussed further in Chapter 20.

15.9   Bridged OpenVPN Connections

The OpenVPN configurations discussed to this point have all been routed, using t u n interfaces. This
is usually the preferable way of connecting VPN clients, but OpenVPN also offers the option of using t a p interfaces and bridging clients directly onto your LAN or other internal network. This can
make the remote clients appear to be on your local LAN. However the pfSense GUI was not designed
to accommodate such scenarios. There has been a hack used by some people, but it has significant
problems. A usable option will be available at some point — check http://doc.pfsense.org/
index.php/OpenVPN_Bridging for the latest information on OpenVPN bridging.

15.10   Custom configuration options

OpenVPN offers dozens of configuration options, many beyond the most commonly used fields that
are presented in the GUI. This is why the custom configuration options box exists. You can fill in an
unlimited number of additional configuration options, separated by semicolons. This section covers the
most frequently used custom options individually. There are many more, though rarely needed. The
OpenVPN man page details them all. Exercise caution when adding custom options, there is no input
validation applied to ensure the validity of options used. If an option is used incorrectly, the OpenVPN
client or server may not start. You can view the OpenVPN logs under Status → System logs on the
OpenVPN tab to ensure the options used are valid. Any invalid options will result in a log message Options error: Unrecognized option or missing parameter(s) followed by the
option that caused the error.

15.10.1   Routing options

To add additional routes for a particular OpenVPN client or server, you use the **route** custom configuration option. The following example adds a route for 10.50.0.0/24.

route 10.50.0.0 255.255.255.0

To add multiple routes, separate them with a semicolon:

route 10.50.0.0 255.255.255.0;route 10.254.0.0 255.255.255.0

The **route** configuration option is used to add routes locally. For an OpenVPN server configuration
using PKI, you can also push additional routes to clients. To push the routes for 10.50.0.0/24 and
10.254.0.0/24 to all clients, use the following custom configuration option.

push "route 10.50.0.0 255.255.255.0";push "route 10.254.0.0 255.255.255.0"

15.10.1.1 Redirecting the default gateway

OpenVPN also allows you to change the default gateway of the client to the OpenVPN connection, so all the traffic from the client is pushed across the VPN. This is great for untrusted local networks such as wireless hotspots, as it provides protection against numerous attacks that are a risk on untrusted networks. To do so, add the following custom option:

push "redirect-gateway def1"

You can also enter this as a custom option on the client side by using **redirect-gateway def1** without specifying **push**. (Note the option is the letters "**def**" followed by the digit *one*, not the letter "L".)

15.10.2 Specifying the interface

OpenVPN servers and clients use a tunnel type interface for each connection. This is all automatically handled by pfSense, but you can specify the device name to be used. Some users prefer to specify this, for example to assign the OpenVPN interface to an OPT interface on pfSense so filtering rules can be applied to incoming OpenVPN traffic. To do so, add a custom option such as **dev tun0**. Each OpenVPN client and server needs to use a unique device, so the next subsequent OpenVPN configuration would specify **dev tun1**, incrementing by one for each additional server or client.

15.10.3 Using hardware crypto accelerators

If you have a hardware crypto accelerator such as a hifn card or the onboard glxsb on the ALIX platform, add custom option **engine cryptodev** to take advantage of this hardware with Open-VPN. You must also be using a cryptography algorithm supported by your accelerator. For glxsb, that is only AES-128-CBC. Modern Hifn cards such as the Soekris vpn1411 support 3DES and 128, 192 and 256 bit AES.

15.10.4 Specifying IP address to use

The **local** custom option allows you to specify the IP address the OpenVPN service will use. This can be either an IP address, such as **local 1.2.3.4**, or a FQDN such as:

local myopenvpn.dyndns.org

This is mostly used in multi-WAN scenarios, as described in Section 15.7, or in combination with CARP VIPs.

15.11 Troubleshooting OpenVPN

Should you encounter any problems trying to use OpenVPN, this section provides information on troubleshooting the most common issues users encounter.

15.11.1   Some hosts work, but not all

If traffic between some hosts over the VPN functions properly, but some hosts do not, this is commonly one of four things.

1. Missing, incorrect or ignored default gateway — If the device does not have a default gateway, or has one pointing to something other than pfSense, it does not know how to properly get back to the remote network on the VPN. Some devices, even with a default gateway specified, do not use that gateway. This has been seen on various embedded devices, including IP cameras and some printers. There isn't anything you can do about that other than getting the software on the device fixed. You can verify this by running **tcpdump** on the inside interface of the firewall connected to the network containing the device. Troubleshooting with **tcpdump** is covered in Section 25.5. If you see traffic going out the inside interface on the firewall, but no replies coming back, the device is not properly routing its reply traffic (or could potentially be blocking it via a firewall).

2. Incorrect subnet mask — If the subnet in use on one end is 10.0.0.0/24 and the other is 10.254.0.0/24, and a host has an incorrect subnet mask of 255.0.0.0 or /8, it will never be able to communicate across the VPN because it thinks the remote VPN subnet is part of the local network and hence routing will not function properly.

3. Host firewall — if there is a firewall on the target host, it may not be allowing the connections.

4. Firewall rules on pfSense — ensure the rules on both ends allow the desired network traffic.

15.11.2   Check the OpenVPN logs

Browse to Status → System logs and click the OpenVPN tab to view the OpenVPN logs. Upon connecting, OpenVPN will log something similar to the following (the number following `openvpn` will differ, it is the process ID of the OpenVPN process making the connection).

```
openvpn[32194]: UDPv4 link remote: 1.2.3.4:1194
openvpn[32194]: Peer Connection Initiated with 192.168.110.2:1194
openvpn[32194]: Initialization Sequence Completed
```

If you do not see the `link remote` and `Peer Connection Initialized` messages upon trying to connect, the cause is likely either incorrect client configuration, so the client is not attempting to connect to the correct server, or incorrect firewall rules blocking the client's connection.

15.11.3   Ensure no overlapping IPsec connections

Because of the way IPsec ties into the FreeBSD kernel, any enabled IPsec connection matching the local and remote subnets that exists when IPsec is enabled (even if it is not up) will cause that traffic to never be routed across the OpenVPN connection. Any IPsec connections specifying the same local and remote networks must be disabled.

15.11.4 Check the system routing table

Browse to Diagnostics → Routes and review the routes added. For site to site VPNs, you should see routes for the remote network(s) to the appropriate `tun` or `tap` interface. If the routes are missing or incorrect, your Local Network, Remote Network, or custom options are not configured correctly. If you are using a shared key setup and not PKI, ensure that you are not using "push" commands are instead adding routes to both ends using "route" custom options, as in Section 15.10.1.

15.11.5 Test from different vantage points

If the connection shows as being up in the logs, but doesn't work from your LAN, try it from the firewall itself, first using the inside interface being used for the OpenVPN connection (typically LAN) as the ping source. If that doesn't work, SSH into the firewall and choose option 8 for a command prompt. Run **ping** **x.x.x.x** at the command line, replacing $x.x.x.x$ with an IP on the remote side of the VPN. This will cause the traffic to be initiated from the IP of the `tun` interface being used by OpenVPN. This can help narrow down routing problems on the remote network.

15.11.6 Trace the traffic with tcpdump

Using **tcpdump** to determine where the traffic is seen and where it isn't is one of the most helpful troubleshooting techniques. Start with the internal interface (commonly LAN) on the side where the traffic is being initiated, progress to the `tun` interface on that firewall, then the `tun` interface on the remote firewall, and finally the inside interface on the remote firewall. Determining where the traffic is seen and where it isn't can help greatly in narrowing down where the problem is located. Packet capturing is covered in detail in Chapter 25.

Chapter 16

Traffic Shaper

Traffic shaping, or network Quality of Service (QoS), is a means of prioritizing the network traffic traversing your firewall. Without traffic shaping, packets are processed on a first in/first out basis by your firewall. QoS offers a means of prioritizing different types of traffic, ensuring that high priority services receive the bandwidth they need before lesser priority services. The traffic shaper wizard in pfSense gives you the ability to quickly configure QoS for common scenarios, and custom rules may also be created for more complex tasks. For simplicity, the traffic shaping system in pfSense may also be referred to as the "shaper", and the act of traffic shaping may be called "shaping".

16.1   Traffic Shaping Basics

For those of you who are unfamiliar with traffic shaping, it is sort of like a bouncer at an exclusive club. The VIPs (Very Important Packets) always make it in first and without waiting. The regular packets have to wait their turn in line, and "undesirable" packets can be kept out until after the real party is over. All the while, the club is kept at capacity and never overloaded. If more VIPs come along later, some regular packets may need to be tossed out to keep the place from getting too crowded.

The way that shaping is accomplished in pf, and thus pfSense, may be a little counter-intuitive at first because the traffic has to be limited in a place where pfSense can actually control the flow. Incoming traffic from the Internet going to a host on the LAN (downloading) is actually shaped coming *out* of the LAN interface from the pfSense system. In the same manner, traffic going from the LAN to the Internet (uploading) is shaped when *leaving* the WAN.

There are traffic shaping queues, and traffic shaping rules. The queues are where bandwidth and priorities are actually allocated. Traffic shaping rules control how traffic is assigned into those queues. Rules for the shaper work similarly to firewall rules, and allow similar matching characteristics. If a packet matches a shaper rule, it will be assigned into the queues specified by that rule.

16.2   What the Traffic Shaper can do for you

The basic idea of traffic shaping, raising and lowering the priorities of packets, is a simple one. However, the number of ways in which this concept can be applied is vast. These are but a few common examples that have proven popular with our users.

16.2.1   Keep Browsing Smooth

Asymmetric links, where the download speed differs from the upload speed, are commonplace these days, especially with DSL. Some links are so out of balance that the maximum download speed is almost unattainable because it is difficult send out enough ACK (acknowledgement) packets to keep traffic flowing. ACK packets are transmitted back to the sender by the receiving host to indicate that data was successfully received, and to signal that it is OK to send more. If the sender does not receive ACKs in a timely manner, TCP's congestion control mechanisms will kick in and slow down the connection.

You may have noticed this situation before: When uploading a file over such a link, browsing and downloading slows to a crawl or stalls. This happens because the uploading portion of the circuit is full from the file upload, there is little room to send ACK packets which allow downloads keep flowing. By using the shaper to prioritize ACK packets, you can achieve faster, more stable download speeds on asymmetric links.

This is not as important on symmetric links where the upload and download speed are the same, but may still be desriable if the available outgoing bandwidth is heavily utilized.

16.2.2   Keep VoIP Calls Clear

If your Voice over IP calls use the same circuit as data, then uploads and downloads may degrade your call quality. pfSense can prioritize the call traffic above other protocols, and ensure that the calls make it through clearly without breaking up, even if you're streaming hi-def video from Hulu at the same time. Instead of the call breaking up, the speed of the other transfers will be reduced to leave room for the calls.

16.2.3   Reduce Gaming Lag

There are also options to give priority to the traffic associated with network gaming. Similar to prioritizing VoIP calls, the effect is that even if you are downloading while playing, the response time of the game should still be nearly as fast as if the rest of your connection were idle.

16.2.4   Keep P2P Applications In Check

By lowering the priority of traffic associated with known peer-to-peer ports, you can rest easier knowing that even if those programs are in use, they won't hinder other traffic on your network. Due to its lower priority, other protocols will be favored over P2P traffic, which will be limited when any other services need the bandwidth.

16.3   Hardware Limitations

Traffic shaping is performed with the help of ALTQ. Unfortunately, only a subset of all supported network cards are capable of using these features because the drivers must be altered to support shaping. The following network cards are capable of using traffic shaping, according to the man page for altq(4):

age(4), ale(4), an(4), ath(4), aue(4), awi(4), bce(4), bfe(4), bge(4), dc(4), de(4), ed(4), em(4), ep(4), fxp(4), gem(4), hme(4), ipw(4), iwi(4), jme(4), le(4), msk(4), mxge(4), my(4), nfe(4), npe(4), nve(4), ral(4), re(4), rl(4), rum(4), sf(4), sis(4), sk(4), ste(4), stge(4), udav(4), ural(4), vge(4), vr(4), wi(4), and xl(4).

16.4   Limitations of the Traffic Shaper implementation in 1.2.x

Wrapping a GUI around the underlying traffic shaping components in pfSense proved a very difficult task, and lacking functionality in the underlying system in some areas also limits its capabilities. The implementation that exists in 1.2.x works well, within its limits. The traffic shaper in pfSense 2.0 has been rewritten to address these limitations.

16.4.1   Only two interface support

The shaper only works correctly with deployments consisting of two interfaces, LAN and WAN. Multi-WAN, and networks with other OPT interfaces will not function as desired. The shaper in 2.0 does accommodate multiple interfaces properly.

16.4.2   Traffic to LAN interface affected

Traffic to the LAN IP is queued in the same fashion as traffic traversing the firewall. So if your web interface uses HTTPS, and your traffic shaper queue for HTTPS is filled, it will delay your traffic to the management interface the same as if your HTTPS request were going out to the Internet. If you use pings to the LAN IP from a monitoring system, you may see significant delay and jitter for this same reason.

By extension this also applies to other services offered by the pfSense router. Users of the squid proxy package have noticed that their local clients received data from the proxy only at the speed of their WAN, and so it never appeared to be caching data. In fact, it was caching data, but it was also shaping the traffic at the same time.

16.4.3   No application intelligence

The shaper is not capable of truly differentiating between protocols. Traffic using TCP port 80 is considered as HTTP, whether it's really HTTP or it's a P2P application using port 80. This can be a significant problem in some environments.

16.5 Configuring the Traffic Shaper With the Wizard

It is recommended that you configure the traffic shaper for the first time using the wizard, which will guide you through the process. Due to the complexity of the shaper queues and rules, it is not a good idea to attempt starting from scratch on your own. If you need custom rules, step through the wizard and approximate what you will need, then make the custom rules afterward. Each screen will setup unique queues, and rules that will control what traffic is assigned into those queues. Should you want to configure everything manually, simply specify your WAN speed at the first screen, then click Next through all the remaining screens without configuring anything.

16.5.1 Starting the Wizard

To get started with the Traffic Shaping Wizard, click on Firewall → Traffic Shaper. The wizard should start automatically as in Figure 16.1. If you have completed the shaping wizard before, or have custom rules, you will instead see the list of shaper rules. To erase the existing shaper rules and start from scratch, click on the EZ Shaper wizard tab which will relaunch the wizard pre-filled with your current settings. As you finish each screen of the wizard, click Next to continue to the following page.

Figure 16.1: Starting the Shaper Wizard

16.5.2 Networks and Speeds

This screen, as shown in Figure 16.2, is where you configure the network interfaces that will be the Inside and Outside from the point of view of the shaper, along with the Download and Upload speeds. Depending on your connection type, the true link speed may not be the actual usable speed. In the case of PPPoE, you have not only PPPoE overhead, but also overhead from the underlying ATM network link being used in most PPPoE deployments. By some calculations, between the overhead from ATM, PPPoE, IP, and TCP, you may lose as much as 13% of the advertised link speed.

When in doubt of what to set the speed to, be a little conservative. Reduce by 10-13% and work your way back up. If you have a 3Mbit/s line, set it for about 2700 and try it. You can always edit the resulting parent queue later and adjust the speed. If you set it low, the connection will be maxed out at exactly the speed you set. Keep nudging it up higher until you no longer get any performance gains.

pfSense Traffic Shaper Wizard

Setup network speeds

Inside:	LAN ▾ This is usually the LAN interface Inside interface for shaping your download speeds
Download:	3096 The download speed of your WAN link in Kbits/second. Note: PPPOE users should take into account PPPOE overhead and put a lower speed here.
Outside:	WAN ▾ This is usually the WAN interface Outside interface for shaping your upload speeds
Upload:	512 The upload speed of your WAN link in Kbits/second. Note: PPPOE users should take into account PPPOE overhead and put a lower speed here.

Figure 16.2: Shaper Configuration

16.5.3 Voice over IP

There are several options available for handling VoIP call traffic, shown in Figure 16.3. The first choice, Prioritize Voice over IP traffic, is self-explanatory. It will enable the prioritization of VoIP traffic and this behavior can be fine-tuned by the other settings below. There are a few well-known providers including Vonage, Voicepulse, PanasonicTDA, and Asterisk servers. If you have a different provider, you can choose **Generic**, or override this setting with the Address field by entering the IP of your VoIP phone or an Alias containing the IPs of all your phones.

You may also choose the amount of Bandwidth to guarantee for your VoIP phones. This will vary based on how many phones you have, and how much bandwidth each session will utilize.

pfSense Traffic Shaper Wizard

Enable:	☑ Prioritize Voice over IP traffic This will raise the priority of VOIP traffic above all other traffic.

VOIP specific settings

Provider:	Generic (lowdelay) ▾ Choose Generic if your provider isn't listed.
Address:	172.16.32.5 (Optional) If this is chosen, the provider field will be overridden. This allows you to just provide the IP address of the VOIP adaptor to prioritize. NOTE: You can also use a Firewall Alias in this location.
Bandwidth:	128Kbits/sec ▾ Total bandwidth guarantee for VOIP phone(s)

Figure 16.3: Voice over IP

16.5.4 Penalty Box

The penalty box, depicted in Figure 16.4, is a place to which you can relegate misbehaving users or devices that would otherwise consume more bandwidth than desired. These users are assigned a hard bandwidth cap which they cannot exceed. Check the Penalize IP or Alias to enable the feature, enter an IP or Alias in the Address box, and then enter upload and download limits in kilobits per second in their respective boxes.

pfSense Traffic Shaper Wizard	
Enable:	☑ Penalize IP or Alias This will lower the priority of traffic from this IP or alias.
PenaltyBox specific settings	
Address:	192.168.1.15 This allows you to just provide the IP address of the computer(s) to Penalize. NOTE: You can also use a Firewall Alias in this location.
BandwidthUp:	128 The upload limit in Kbits/second.
BandwidthDown:	512 The download limit Kbits/second.

Figure 16.4: Penalty Box

16.5.5 Peer-to-Peer Networking

The next screen, shown in Figure 16.5, will let you set controls over many peer-to-peer (P2P) networking protocols. By design, P2P protocols will utilize all available bandwidth unless limits are put in place. If you expect P2P traffic on your network, it is a good practice to ensure that other traffic will not be degraded due to its use. To penalize P2P traffic, first check Lower priority of Peer-to-Peer traffic.

Many P2P technologies deliberately try to avoid detection. Bittorrent is especially guilty of this behavior. It often utilizes non-standard or random ports, or ports associated with other protocols. You can check the p2pCatchAll option which will cause any unrecognized traffic to be assumed as P2P traffic and its priority lowered accordingly. You can set hard bandwidth limits for this traffic underneath the catchall rule. The upload and download bandwidth limits are set in Kilobits per second.

The remaining options are comprised of various known P2P protocols, more than 20 in all. Check each one that you would like to be recognized.

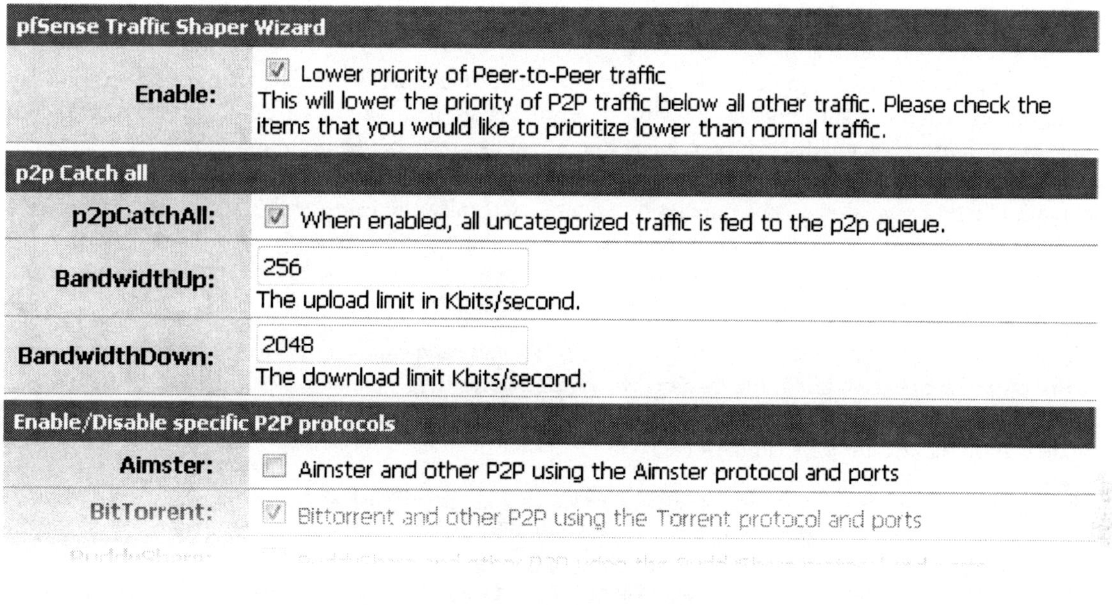

pfSense Traffic Shaper Wizard	
Enable:	☑ Lower priority of Peer-to-Peer traffic This will lower the priority of P2P traffic below all other traffic. Please check the items that you would like to prioritize lower than normal traffic.
p2p Catch all	
p2pCatchAll:	☑ When enabled, all uncategorized traffic is fed to the p2p queue.
BandwidthUp:	256 The upload limit in Kbits/second.
BandwidthDown:	2048 The download limit Kbits/second.
Enable/Disable specific P2P protocols	
Aimster:	☐ Aimster and other P2P using the Aimster protocol and ports
BitTorrent:	☑ Bittorrent and other P2P using the Torrent protocol and ports

Figure 16.5: Peer-to-Peer Networking

16.5.6 Network Games

Many games rely on low latency to deliver a good online gaming experience. If someone tries to download large files or game patches while playing, that traffic can easily swallow up the packets associated with the game itself and cause lag or disconnections. By checking the option to Prioritize network gaming traffic, as seen in Figure 16.6, you can raise the priority of game traffic so that it will be transferred first and given a guaranteed chunk of bandwidth. There are many games listed, check all those which should be prioritized. If your game is not listed here you may still want to check a similar game so that you will have a reference rule that may be altered later.

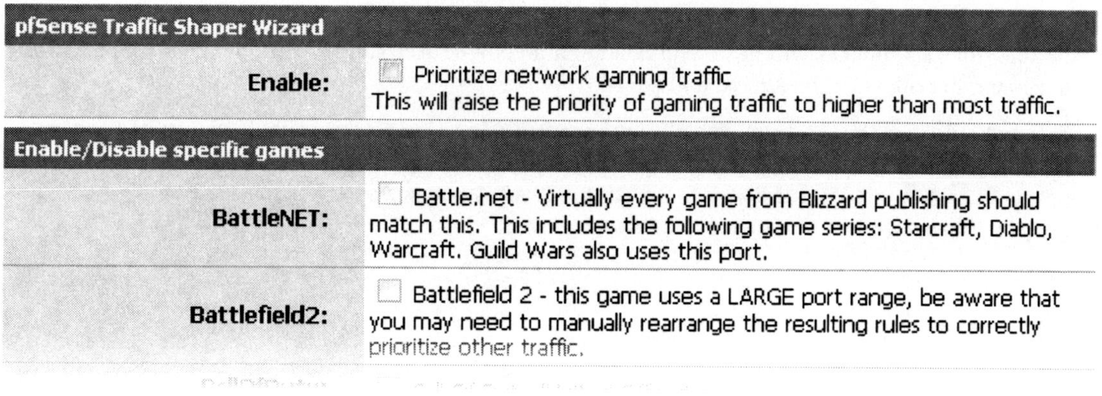

pfSense Traffic Shaper Wizard	
Enable:	☐ Prioritize network gaming traffic This will raise the priority of gaming traffic to higher than most traffic.
Enable/Disable specific games	
BattleNET:	☐ Battle.net - Virtually every game from Blizzard publishing should match this. This includes the following game series: Starcraft, Diablo, Warcraft. Guild Wars also uses this port.
Battlefield2:	☐ Battlefield 2 - this game uses a LARGE port range, be aware that you may need to manually rearrange the resulting rules to correctly prioritize other traffic.

Figure 16.6: Network Games

16.5.7   Raising or Lowering Other Applications

The last configuration screen of the shaper wizard, seen in Figure 16.7, lists many other commonly available application and protocols. How these protocols are handled will depend on the environment that this pfSense router will be protecting. Some of these may be desired, and others may not. For example, in a corporate environment, you may want to lower the priority of non-interactive traffic such as mail, where a slow down isn't noticed by anyone, and raise the priority of interactive services like RDP where poor performance is an impediment to people's ability to work. In a home, multimedia streaming may be more important, and other services can be lowered. Enable the option for Other networking protocols, and then pick and choose from the list.

There are more than 25 other protocols to choose from, and each can be given a **Higher priority**, **Lower priority**, or left at the **Default priority**. If you enabled p2pCatchAll, you will want to use this screen to ensure that these other protocols are recognized and treated normally, rather than penalized by the default p2pCatchAll rule.

pfSense Traffic Shaper Wizard	
Enable:	☑ Other networking protocols This will help raise or lower the priority of other protocols higher than most traffic.
Remote Service / Terminal emulation	
MSRDP:	Higher priority ▾ Microsoft Remote Desktop Protocol
VNC:	Higher priority ▾ Virtual Network Computing
AppleRemoteDesktop:	Default priority ▾ Apple Remote Desktop
PC Anywhere:	Default priority ▾ Symantec PC Anywhere

Figure 16.7: Raise or Lower Other Applications

16.5.8   Finishing the Wizard

All of the rules and queues will now be created, but not yet in use. By pressing the Finish button on the final screen, the rules will be loaded and active.

Shaping should now be activated for all new connections. Due to the stateful nature of the shaper, only new connections will have traffic shaping applied. In order for this to be fully active on all connections, you must clear the states. To do this, visit Diagnostics → States, click the Reset States tab, check Firewall state table, then click Reset.

16.6   Monitoring the Queues

In order to be sure that traffic shaping is working as intended, it may be monitored by browsing to Status → Queues. As can be seen in Figure 16.8, this screen will show each queue listed by name, its current usage, and some other related statistics.

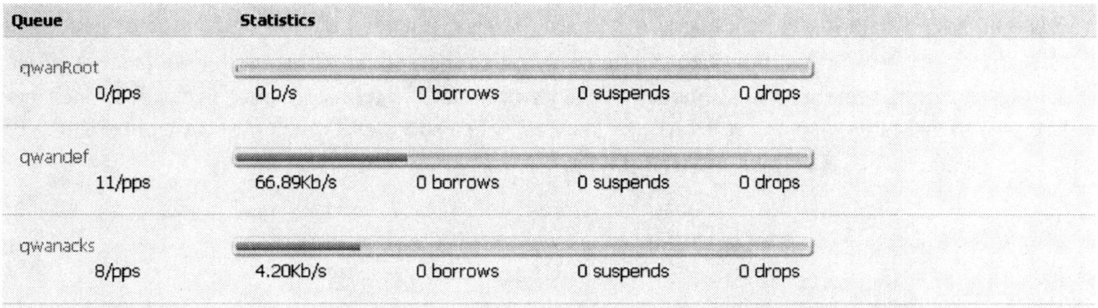

Figure 16.8: Basic WAN Queues

The graphical bar shows you how "full" a queue is. The rate of data in the queue is shown in both packets per second (pps) and bits per second (b/s). Borrows happen when a neighboring queue is not full and capacity is borrowed from there when needed. Drops happen when traffic in a queue is dropped in favor of higher priority traffic. It is normal to see drops, and this does not mean that a full connection is dropped, just a packet. Usually, one side of the connection will see that a packet was missed and then resend, often slowing down in the process to avoid future drops. The suspends counter indicates when a delay action happens. The suspends counter is not used by the shaping scheduler employed by pfSense in 1.2.x, and should likely be zero.

16.7 Advanced Customization

After using the shaper wizard, you may find that the rules it generates do not quite fit your needs. You may want to shape a service that is not handled by the wizard, a game that uses a different port, or there may be other services that need limited. Once the basic rules have been created by the wizard, it should be relatively easy to edit or copy those rules and create custom ones of your own.

16.7.1 Editing Shaper Queues

As mentioned in the summary, the queues are where bandwidth and priorities are actually allocated. Each queue is assigned a priority, from 0-7. When there is an overload of traffic, the higher numbered queues are preferred (e.g. 7) over the lower numbered queues (e.g. 1). Each queue is assigned either a hard bandwidth limit, or a percentage of the total link speed. The queues can also be assigned other attributes that control how they behave, such as being low-delay, or having certain congestion avoidance algorithms applied. Queues may be changed by going to Firewall → Traffic Shaper, and clicking the Queues tab. A list of rules will appear, like that in Figure 16.9

Editing queues is not for the weak of heart. It can be a complex task with powerful results, but without thorough understanding of the settings involved, it is best to stick with the queues generated by the wizard and alter their settings, rather than trying to make new ones from scratch.

When viewing the queues list, each queue will be shown along with the flags associated with the queue, its priority, allocated bandwidth, and name. To edit a queue, click 🖉, and to delete a queue click 🗙.

You should not attempt to delete a queue if it is still being referenced by a rule. To reorder queues in the list, check the box next to the queue to be moved, and then click the ⊠ button on the row which should be underneath the relocated queues. When you hover the mouse pointer over ⊠, a thick bar will appear to indicate where the rules will be inserted. The ordering of queues is strictly cosmetic. To add a new queue, click ⊞ at the bottom of the list.

Firewall: Shaper: Queues

Rules	Queues	EZ Shaper wizard

	Flags	Priority	Default	Bandwidth	Name		
☐		0	No	512 Kb	qwanRoot		⊠⊠⊠
☐		0	No	3096 Kb	qlanRoot		⊠⊠⊠
☐		1	Yes	1 %	qwandef		⊠⊠⊠
☐		1	Yes	1 %	qlandef		⊠⊠⊠
☐	ACK	7	No	25 %	qwanacts		⊠⊠⊠

Figure 16.9: Traffic Shaper Queues List

When editing a queue, each of the options should be carefully considered. If you are looking for more information about these settings than is mentioned here, visit the PF Packet Queueing and Prioritization FAQ.[1] The best available scheduler is Hierarchical Fair Service Curve (HFSC), and that is the only one available in pfSense 1.2.x.

The Bandwidth setting should be a fraction of the available bandwidth in the parent queue, but it must also be set with an awareness of the other neighboring queues. When using percentages, the total of all queues under a given parent cannot exceed 100%. When using absolute limits, the totals cannot exceed the bandwidth available in the parent queue.

Priority can be any number from 0-7. Queues with higher numbers are preferred when there is an overload, so situate your queues accordingly. For example, VoIP traffic should be of the highest priority, so it should be set to a 7. Peer-to-peer network traffic, which can be delayed in favor of other protocols, should be set at 1.

The Name for a queue must be between 1-15 characters and cannot contain spaces. The most common convention is to start the name of a queue with the letter "q" so that it may be more readily identified in the ruleset.

There are six different Scheduler options that may be set for a given queue:

- Default Queue

  Selects this queue as the default, the one which will handle all unmatched packets. Each interface should have one and only one default queue.

- ACK/low-delay Queue (ACK)

---

[1] `http://www.openbsd.org/faq/pf/queueing.html` and also available in *The OpenBSD PF Packet Filter* book.

At least one queue per interface should have this set. Typically this is reserved for — as the name implies — ACK packets which need to be handled specially at a high priority.

- Random Early Detection (RED)

A method to avoid congestion on a link; it will actively attempt to ensure that the queue does not get full. If the bandwidth is above the maximum given for the queue, drops will occur. Also, drops may occur if the average queue size approaches the maximum. Dropped packets are chosen at random, so the more bandwidth in use by a given connection, the more likely it is to see drops. The net effect is that the bandwidth is limited in a fair way, encouraging a balance. RED should only be used with TCP connections since TCP is capable of handling lost packets, and can resend when needed.

- Random Early Detection In and Out (RIO)

Enables RED with in/out, which will result in having queue averages being maintained and checked against for incoming and outgoing packets.

- Explicit Congestion Notification (ECN)

Along with RED, it allows the sending of control messages that will throttle connections if both ends support ECN. Instead of dropping the packets as RED will normally do, it will set a flag in the packet indicating network congestion. If the other side sees and obeys the flag, the speed of the ongoing transfer will be reduced.

- This is a parent queue

Allows this queue to be chosen as a parent of other queues.

The Service Curve (sc) is where you can fine tune the bandwidth requirements for this queue.

- m1

Burstable bandwidth limit

- d

Time limit for bandwidth burst, specified in milliseconds. (e.g. 1000 = 1 second)

- m2

Normal bandwidth limit

For instance, you need m1 bandwidth within d time, but a normal maximum of m2. Within the initial time set by d, m2 is not checked, only m1. After d has expired, if the traffic is still above m2, it will be shaped. Most commonly, m1 and d are left blank, so that only m2 is checked.

Each of these values may be set for the following uses:

- Upper Limit

Maximum bandwidth allowed for the queue. Will do hard bandwidth limiting. The m1 parameter here can also be used to limit bursting. In the timeframe d you will not get more than m1 bandwidth.

- Real Time

  Minimum bandwidth guarantee for the queue. This is only valid for child queues. The m1 parameter will always be satisfied in timeframe d, and m2 is the maximum that this discipline will allow to be used.

- Link Share

  The bandwidth share of a backlogged queue. Will share the bandwidth between classes if the Real Time guarantees have been satisfied. If you set the m2 value for Link Share, it will override the Bandwidth setting for the queue. These two settings are the same, but if both are set, Link Share's m2 is used.

By combining these factors, a queue will get the bandwidth specified by the Real Time factors, plus those from Link Share, up to a maximum of Upper Limit. It can take a lot of trial and error, and perhaps a lot of arithmetic, but it may be worth it to ensure that your traffic is governed as you see fit. For more information on m1, d, and m2 values for different scenarios, visit the pfSense Traffic Shaping forum.

Lastly, if this is a child queue, select the Parent queue from the list. Click Save to save the queue settings and return to the queue list, then click Apply Changes to reload the queues and activate the changes.

16.7.2   Editing Shaper Rules

Traffic shaping rules control how traffic is assigned into queues. If a packet matches a traffic shaper rule, it will be assigned into the queue specified by that rule. Packet matching is handled similarly to firewall rules, but with some additional fine-grained control. The edit the shaper rules, go to Firewall → Traffic Shaper, and click the Rules Tab. On that screen, shown in Figure 16.10, the existing rules will be listed with the interface direction, protocol, source, destination, target queues, and name.

On this screen also lies the master control for shaping. Uncheck Enable traffic shaper to disable the traffic shaper, then click Save. To remove the rules and queues created by the traffic shaper, and reset the shaper back to defaults, click Remove Wizard. The next time you visit Firewall → Traffic Shaper, the wizard will start again.

To edit a rule, click 🖉, and to delete a rule click ✖. Rules may be moved up or down a row at time by clicking ▲ to move up or ▼ to move down. To reorder multiple rules in the list, check the box next to the rules which should be moved, and then click the ◀ button on the row which should be underneath the relocated rules. The rules will then be moved above the chosen row. You can make a new rule based on another existing rule by clicking ⊞ next to the row with the rule you would like to copy. You will be presented with the rule editing screen pre-filled with the details from the existing rule. To add a new blank rule, click ⊞ at the bottom of the list.

Figure 16.10: Traffic Shaper Rules List

Each rule has several matching criteria which will aid in ensuring that the proper traffic is fed into the proper queues. Before setting the options to match, however, the Target queues must be defined. You must set both an Outbound Queue and an Inbound Queue. Packets matching this rule in the outbound direction will fall into the outbound queue, and packets matching this rule in the inbound direction will fall into the inbound queue. The packet's path is set by choosing an In Interface and Out Interface.

Now the actual matching criteria begin. Most of these options will look familiar from the firewall rules. For more detail on how to set the Protocol, Source, and Destination, refer back to Chapter 6. For now we'll focus on why you would set these instead of how. Which fields to set will depend upon the path implied by the In and Out Interfaces.

For instance, if the traffic will be originating from a host on the LAN, the In Interface should be LAN, and the Source would be set to the address or subnet of the LAN host. If the traffic will be going to a specific location, set the Destination accordingly, otherwise set to **Any**. For matching traffic for specific services, you should set the Destination port range appropriately. In this example, to match HTTP traffic, leave the Source port range set to **Any**, and set the Destination Port Range to HTTP. Rarely is it necessary to set a source port, as they are typically chosen at random.

Traffic will be matched going in and out by default, but you can use the Direction option to restrict this behavior. Remember, however, that this is set from the firewall's perspective.

IP Type of Service (TOS) "precedence bits" can be used to catch packets which have been tagged for special handling. There are three settings available here, and each of them may have one of three values. The three fields indicate a request for low delay, high throughput, or high reliability. For each of these, Yes means the flag *must* be set. No means the flag *must not* be set. Don't care means it will be ignored.

A subset of the TCP flags may also be matched. These indicate various states of a connection (or lack thereof). They can be matched on whether or not they are explicitly set, cleared, or either (don't care).

- SYN — Synchronize sequence numbers. Indicates a new connection attempt.

- ACK — Indicates ACKnowledgment of data. As discussed earlier, these are replies to let the sender know data was received OK.

- FIN — Indicates there is no more data from the sender, closing a connection.

- RST — Connection reset. This flag is set when replying to a request to open a connection on a port which has no listening daemon. Can also be set by firewall software to turn away undesirable connections.

- PSH — Indicates that data should be pushed or flushed, including data in this packet, by passing the data up to the application.

- URG — Indicates that the urgent field is significant, and this packet should be sent before data that is not urgent.

The final field, Description, is free-text and used to identify this rule. You may find it useful to indicate here what the queue's intention is (name of the application or protocol) as well as the direction the rule is set to match.

By combining as many of these parameters as needed, it should be possible to match almost any traffic you would need to queue. Click Save to finish up and return to the rule list, then click Apply Changes to reload the rules and activate them.

16.8   Troubleshooting Shaper Issues

Traffic Shaping/QoS is a tricky topic, and can prove difficult to get right the first time. There are some common pitfalls that people fall upon, which are covered in this section.

16.8.1   Why isn't Bittorrent traffic going into the P2P queue?

Bittorrent is known for not using much in the way of standard ports. Clients are allowed to declare which port others should use to reach them, which means chaos for network administrators trying to track the traffic based on port alone. In 1.2.x, pfSense doesn't have any way to examine the packets to tell what program the traffic appears to be, so it is forced to rely on ports. This is why it may be a good idea to use the P2P Catchall rule, and/or make rules for each type of traffic you want, and treat your default queue as low priority.

16.8.2   Why isn't traffic to ports opened by UPnP properly queued?

Traffic allowed in by the UPnP daemon will end up in the default queue. This happens because the rules generated dynamically by the UPnP daemon do not have any knowledge of queues unless UPnP is configured to send traffic into a specific queue. Depending on what you have using UPnP in your environment, this may be low priority traffic like Bittorrent, or high priority traffic like game consoles or voice chat programs like Skype. The queue can be set by going to Services → UPnP and entering a queue name into the Traffic Shaper Queue field.

16.8.3 How can I calculate how much bandwidth to allocate to the ACK queues?

This is a complex topic, and most people gloss over it and just guess a sufficiently high value. For more detailed explanations with mathematical formulas, check the Traffic Shaping section of the pfSense forums.[2] There is a sticky post in that board which describes the process in great detail, and there is also a downloadable spreadsheet which can be used to help ease the process.

16.8.4 Why is <x> not properly shaped?

As with other questions in this section, this tends to happen because of rules entered either internally or by other packages that do not have knowledge of queues. Since no queue is specified for a rule, it ends up in the default or root queue, and not shaped. You may need to disable the WebGUI/ssh anti-lockout rules and perhaps even replace the default LAN→ANY firewall rule with more specific options. In the case of packages, you may need to adjust how your default queue is handled.

---

[2] http://forum.pfsense.org/index.php/board,26.0.html

Chapter 17

Server Load Balancing

Two types of load balancing functionality are available in pfSense: Gateway and Server. Gateway load balancing enables distribution of Internet-bound traffic over multiple WAN connections. For more information on this type of load balancing, see Chapter 11. Server load balancing allows you to distribute traffic to multiple internal servers for load distribution and redundancy, and is the subject of this chapter.

Server load balancing allows you to distribute traffic between multiple internal servers. It is most commonly used with web servers and SMTP servers though can be used for any service that uses TCP.

While pfSense has replaced high end, high cost commercial load balancers including BigIP, Cisco LocalDirector, and more in serious production environments, pfSense 1.2.x is not nearly as powerful and flexible as these solutions. It is not suitable for deployments that require flexible monitoring and balancing configuration. For TCP monitoring, it simply checks that the specified TCP port is open. In the case of a web server, the server may not be returning any HTTP responses, or invalid ones, and there is no way to determine this. For large or complex deployments, you will commonly want a more powerful solution. However for basic needs, the functionality available in pfSense suits countless sites very well.

We are currently reviewing options for a more capable load balancer for the 2.0 release.

17.1 Explanation of Configuration Options

There are two portions of configuration for the server load balancer. Virtual Server Pools define the list of servers to be used, which port they listen on, and the monitoring method to be used. Virtual Servers define the IP and port to listen on, and the appropriate pool to direct the incoming traffic to that IP and port.

17.1.1 Virtual Server Pools

To configure Virtual Server Pools, browse to Services → Load Balancer. Click ⊞ to add a new pool. Each of the options on this page is discussed here.

- Name — Enter a name for the pool here. The name is how the pool is referenced later when configuring the virtual server that will use this pool.

- Description — Optionally enter a longer description for the pool here.

- Type — This should default to **Server**, which is what we need for this configuration.

- Behavior — Select **Load Balancing** to balance load between all the servers in the pool, or **Failover** to always use the first server in the pool unless it fails, then fall back to subsequent servers.

- Port — This is the port your servers are listening on internally. This can be different from the external port, which is defined later in the virtual server configuration.

- Monitor — This defines the type of monitor to use, which is how the balancer determines if the servers are up. Selecting **TCP** will make the balancer connect to the port previously defined in Port, and if it cannot connect to that port, the server is considered down. Choosing **ICMP** will instead monitor the defined servers by pinging them, and will mark them down if they do not respond to pings.

- Monitor IP — This field is not applicable with the server load balancer and is grayed out.

- Server IP Address — This is where you fill in the internal IP address of the servers in the pool. Enter them one at a time, clicking Add to pool afterwards.

- List — This field shows the list of servers you have added to this pool. You can remove a server from the pool by clicking on its IP address and clicking Remove from pool.

After populating all the fields as desired, click Save. Proceed to configuring the Virtual Server for this pool by clicking the Virtual Servers tab.

17.1.1.1   Virtual Servers

Virtual Servers is where you define the IP and port to listen on for forwarding traffic to the previously configured pool. Click ⊞ to add a new virtual server. Each of the options on this page is discussed below.

- Name — Enter a name for the virtual server here. This is simply for your reference.

- Description — Optionally enter a longer description for the virtual server here. This is also just for reference purposes.

- IP Address — This is where you enter the IP address that the virtual server will listen on. This is usually your WAN IP or a Virtual IP on WAN. It must be a static IP address. You can use a CARP VIP here for a high availability load balancer setup. For more information on high availability and CARP VIPs, refer to Chapter 20.

- Port — This is the port the virtual server will listen on. It can be different from the port your servers are listening on internally.

- Virtual Server Pool — This is where you select the previously configured pool. The connections to the IP Address and Port defined on this screen will be directed to the IPs and port configured in the pool.

- Pool Down Server — This is the server that clients are directed to if all the servers in your pool are down. You must enter something here. If you don't have an alternate server to send requests to, you can put one of the IPs of your pool servers in here, though the result will be inaccessibility if all the servers in the pool are down.

After filling in the fields appropriately, click Submit, then Apply Changes.

17.1.1.2   Firewall rules

The last step is to configure firewall rules to allow traffic to the pool. Just like in a NAT scenario, the firewall rules must permit traffic to the internal private IPs of the servers, as well as the port they are listening on internally. You should create an alias for the servers in the pool, and create a single firewall rule on the interface where the traffic destined to the pool will be initiated (usually WAN) allowing the appropriate source (usually any) to destination of the alias created for the pool. A specific example of this is provided in Section 17.2.4. For more information on firewall rules, refer to Chapter 6.

17.1.2   Sticky connections

There is one additional configuration option available for server load balancing, under the System → Advanced menu. Under Load Balancing, you will find Use sticky connections. Checking this box will ensure clients with an active connection to the pool are always directed to the same server for any subsequent connections. Once the client closes all active connections, and the closed state times out, the sticky connection is lost. This may be desirable for some web load balancing configurations where a particular client's requests should only go to a single server, for session or other reasons. Note this isn't perfect, as if the client's web browser closes all TCP connections to your server after loading a page and sits there for 10 minutes or more before loading the next page, the next page may be served from a different server. Generally this isn't an issue as most web browsers won't immediately close a connection, and the state exists long enough to not make it a problem, but if you are strictly reliant on a specific client never getting a different server in the pool regardless of how long the browser sits there inactive, you should look for a different load balancing solution.

17.2   Web Server Load Balancing Example Configuration

This section shows you how to configure the load balancer from start to finish for a two web server load balanced environment.

17.2.1   Example network environment

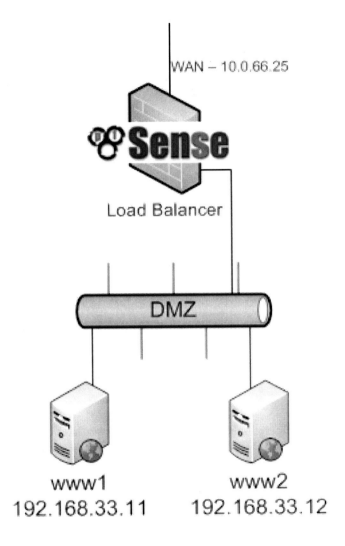

Figure 17.1: Server load balancing example network

Figure 17.1 shows the example environment configured in this section. It consists of a single firewall, using its WAN IP for the pool, with two web servers on a DMZ segment.

17.2.2   Configuring pool

To configure the pool, browse to Services → Load Balancer and click ⊞. Figure 17.2 shows the load balancing pool configuration for the two web servers, using a TCP monitor. After filling in all the fields appropriately, click Save.

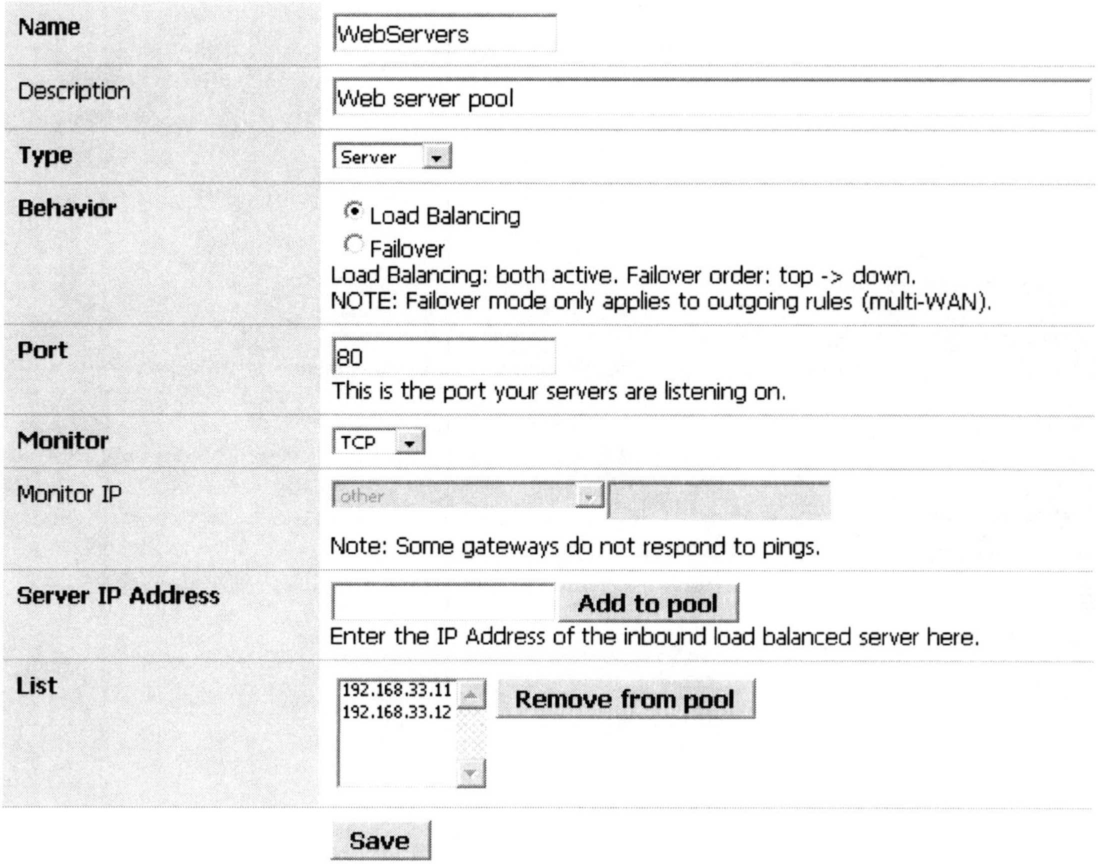

Name	WebServers
Description	Web server pool
Type	Server
Behavior	⦿ Load Balancing ◯ Failover Load Balancing: both active. Failover order: top -> down. NOTE: Failover mode only applies to outgoing rules (multi-WAN).
Port	80 This is the port your servers are listening on.
Monitor	TCP
Monitor IP	other Note: Some gateways do not respond to pings.
Server IP Address	Add to pool Enter the IP Address of the inbound load balanced server here.
List	192.168.33.11 192.168.33.12 Remove from pool

Save

Figure 17.2: Pool configuration

17.2.3   Configuring virtual server

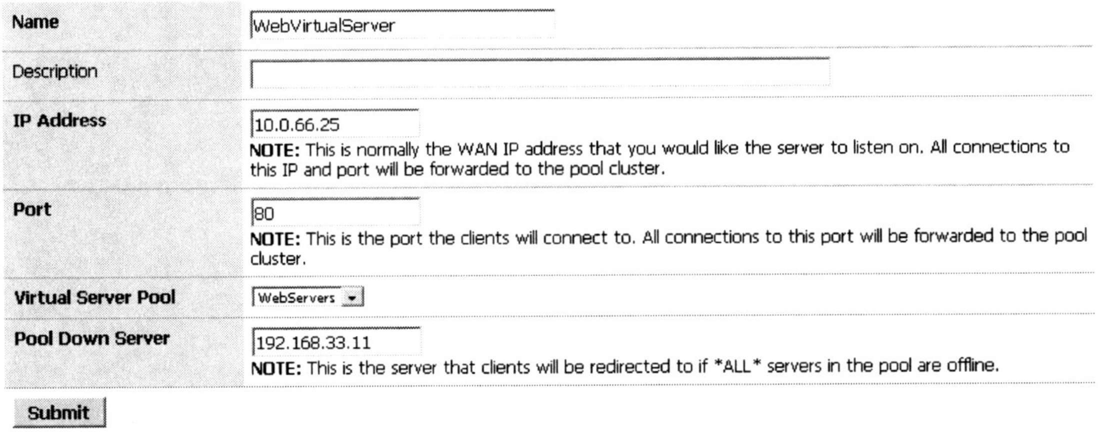

Name	WebVirtualServer
Description	
IP Address	10.0.66.25 **NOTE:** This is normally the WAN IP address that you would like the server to listen on. All connections to this IP and port will be forwarded to the pool cluster.
Port	80 **NOTE:** This is the port the clients will connect to. All connections to this port will be forwarded to the pool cluster.
Virtual Server Pool	WebServers ▼
Pool Down Server	192.168.33.11 **NOTE:** This is the server that clients will be redirected to if *ALL* servers in the pool are offline.

Submit

Figure 17.3: Virtual Server configuration

Back at the Load Balancer Pool screen, click the Virtual Servers tab and click ⊞ to add a new virtual server. Figure 17.3 shows the virtual server configuration to listen on the WAN IP (10.0.66.25) on port 80 and forward the traffic on that IP and port to the servers defined in the **WebServers** pool. For the Pool Down Server, this configuration uses one of the IPs of the servers in the **WebServers** pool because of lack of another option. In this case, if both of the pool servers are down, the virtual server is inaccessible. After filling in the fields here, click Submit, then Apply Changes.

17.2.4   Configuring firewall rules

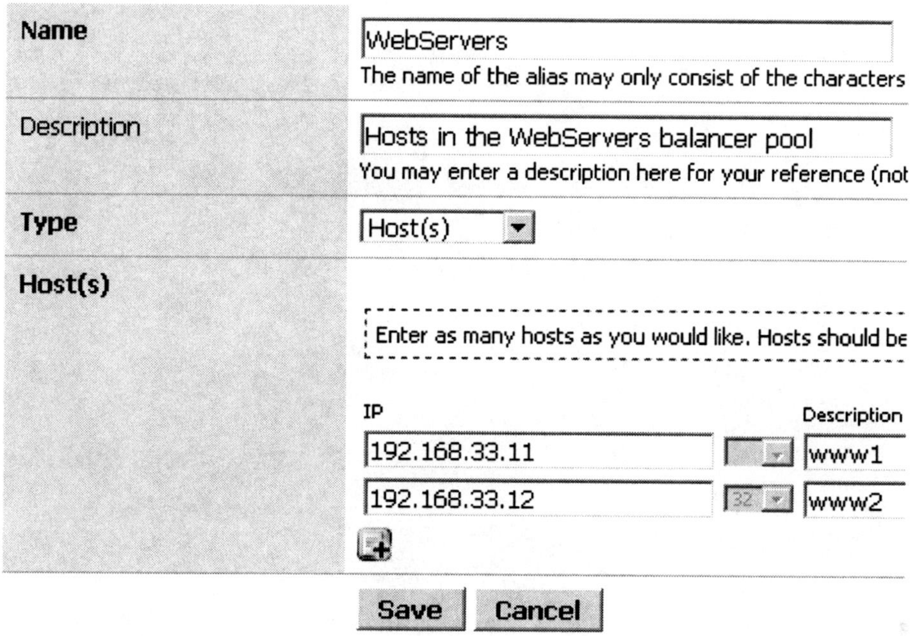

Name	WebServers
	The name of the alias may only consist of the characters
Description	Hosts in the WebServers balancer pool
	You may enter a description here for your reference (not
Type	Host(s) ▼
Host(s)	

Enter as many hosts as you would like. Hosts should be

IP		Description
192.168.33.11	▼	www1
192.168.33.12	32 ▼	www2

Save   Cancel

Figure 17.4: Alias for web servers

Now firewall rules must be configured to allow access to the servers in the pool. The rules must allow the traffic to the internal IP addresses and port being used, and no rules are necessary for the outside IP Address and Port used in the virtual server configuration. It is preferable to use an alias containing all the servers in the pool, so access can be allowed with a single firewall rule. Browse to Firewall → Aliases and click 🔲 to add an alias. Figure 17.4 shows the alias used for this example configuration, containing the two web servers.

Click Save after entering the alias, and Apply Changes. Then browse to Firewall → Rules and on the tab for the interface where the client traffic will be initiated (WAN in this case), click 🔲. Figure 17.5 shows a snippet of the firewall rule added for this configuration. The options not shown were left at their defaults, aside from Description.

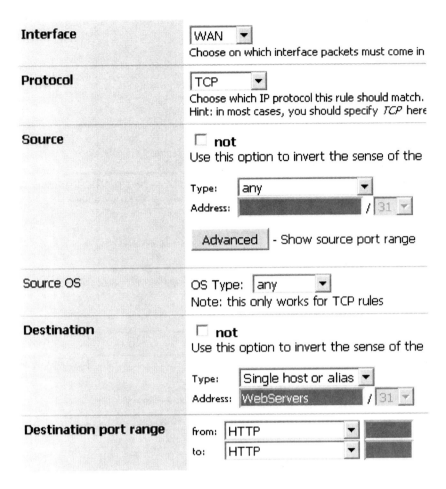

Figure 17.5: Adding firewall rule for web servers

Figure 17.6 shows the rule after it was added.

Figure 17.6: Firewall rule for web servers

17.2.5   Viewing load balancer status

Now that your load balancer is configured, to view its status, browse to Status → Load Balancer and click the Virtual Servers tab. Here you will see the status of each server in the pool (as shown in Figure 17.7). If the status has changed to online within the past five minutes, as it will after you first setup the load balancer, you will see "Online" is highlighted in a yellowish color. After five minutes have past, the status will change to green.

Name	Port	Servers	Status	Description
WebVirtualServer	80	192.168.33.11 192.168.33.12	Online Last change Jul 23 2009 08:21:47 Online Last change Jul 23 2009 08:21:47	Web server pool

Figure 17.7: Virtual Server status

If you stop the web server service on one of the servers or take the server off the network entirely if using ICMP monitors, you will see the status update to Offline and the server will be removed from the pool.

17.2.6 Verifying load balancing

To verify the load balancing, **curl** is the best option to ensure your web browser's cache and persistent connections do not affect the results of your testing. **curl** is available for every OS imaginable and can be downloaded from the curl website. To use it, simply run **curl http://*mysite*** replacing *mysite* with either the IP address or hostname of your site. You must do this from outside your network. The following illustrates an example of testing with **curl** from the WAN side.

```
# curl http://10.0.66.25
<html>

<head>
<title>.12</title>
</head>

<body>

<p> 192.168.33.12 - Server 2 </p>

</body>
</html>
```

When initially testing your load balancing, you will want to configure each server to return a page specifying its hostname, IP address, or both, so you will know which server you are hitting. If you do not have sticky connections enabled, you will get a different server each time you request a page with **curl** (with the exception of the scenario described in Section 17.3.2).

17.3 Troubleshooting Server Load Balancing

This section describes the most common issues users encounter with server load balancing, and how to troubleshoot them.

17.3.1   Connections not being balanced

Connections not being balanced is most always a failure of the testing methodology being used, and is usually specific to HTTP. Web browsers will commonly keep connections to a web server open, and hitting refresh just re-uses the existing connection. A single connection will never be changed to another balanced server. Another common issue is the cache of your web browser, where the browser never actually requests the page again. It's preferable to use a command line tool such as **curl** for testing of this nature, because it ensures you are never impacted by the problems inherent in testing with web browsers — it has no cache, and opens a new connection to the server each time it is run. More information on **curl** can be found in Section 17.2.6.

If you are using sticky connections, ensure you are testing from multiple source IPs. Tests from a single source IP will always go to a single server unless you wait long times in between connections.

17.3.2   Unequal balancing

Because of the way the underlying software functions, in low load environments, balancing will be unequal. The underlying **slbd** monitoring service resets its pf anchor on every monitor interval, which is every 5 seconds. This means every 5 seconds, the next connection will go to the first server in the pool. With very low load services where you frequently have one connection or fewer every 5 seconds, you will see very little load balancing. You still have full failover capabilities should one of the servers fail. This problem really solves itself though, as when your load increases to the point where balancing the load is important, it will be balanced equally. In production environments handling thousands of packets per second, the balancing is equal across the servers.

17.3.3   Down server not marked as offline

If a server goes down but is not marked as offline, it's because from the perspective of the monitoring that pfSense is doing, it isn't really down. If using a TCP monitor, that TCP port is accepting connections. The service on that port could be broken in numerous ways and still answer TCP connections. For ICMP monitors, this problem is exacerbated, as servers can be hung with no listening services at all and still answer to pings.

17.3.4   Live server not marked as online

If a server is online, but not marked as online, it's because it isn't online from the perspective of the firewall. The server must answer on the TCP port used or respond to pings sourced from the interface IP of the firewall interface closest to the server. For example if the server is on the LAN, the server must answer requests initiated from the firewall's LAN IP. To verify this for ICMP monitors, browse to Diagnostics → Ping and ping the server IP using the interface where the server is located. For TCP monitors, log into the firewall using SSH, or at the console, and choose console menu option **8**. At the command prompt, try to telnet to the port the server should be listening on. For example to test a web server in the example earlier in this chapter, you would run **telnet 192.168.33.11 80**.

A failed connection will sit there for a while trying to connect, while a successful connection will connect immediately. The following is an example of a failed connection.

```
# telnet 192.168.33.12 80
Trying 192.168.33.12...
telnet: connect to address 192.168.33.12: Operation timed out
telnet: Unable to connect to remote host
```

And here is an example of a successful connection.

```
# telnet 192.168.33.12 80
Trying 192.168.33.12...
Connected to 192.168.33.12.
Escape character is '^]'.
```

You will likely find that the connection fails, and will need to troubleshoot further on the server.

Chapter 18

Wireless

pfSense includes built in wireless capabilities that allow you to turn your pfSense install into a wireless access point, use a wireless 802.11 connection as a WAN connection, or both. This chapter also covers suggested means of securely accommodating external wireless access points, and how to securely deploy a wireless hotspot. In-depth coverage of 802.11 is outside the scope of this book. For those seeking such information, I recommend the book *802.11 Wireless Networks: The Definitive Guide*.

18.1   Recommended Wireless Hardware

There are a variety of wireless cards supported in FreeBSD 7.2, and pfSense includes support for every card supported by FreeBSD. Some are supported better than others. Most pfSense developers work with Atheros hardware, so it tends to be the most recommended hardware. Many have success with other cards as well, and Ralink is another popular choice. Other cards may be supported, but do not support all available features. In particular, some Intel cards can be used in infrastructure mode but cannot run in access point mode due to limitations of the hardware itself.

18.1.1   Wireless cards from big name vendors

Linksys, D-Link, Netgear and other major manufacturers commonly change the chipsets used in their wireless cards without changing the model number. There is no way to ensure a specific model card from these vendors will be compatible because you have no way of knowing which "minor" card revision you will end up with. While one revision of a particular model may be compatible and work well, another card of the same model may be incompatible. For this reason, we recommend avoiding cards from the major manufacturers. If you already have one, it's worth trying to see if it is compatible, but be warned if you purchase one because the "same" model worked for someone else, you may end up with a completely different piece of hardware that is incompatible.

18.1.2   Wireless drivers included in 1.2.3

This section lists the wireless drivers included in pfSense 1.2.3, and the chipsets that are supported by those drivers (pulling from the FreeBSD man pages for the drivers). Drivers in FreeBSD are referred to by their driver name, followed by (4), such as `ath(4)`. The (4) refers to kernel interfaces, in this case specifying a network driver. The drivers are listed in order of frequency of use with pfSense, based on mailing list and forum postings since the project's inception.

For more detailed information on cards supported, and the most up to date information, refer to the pfSense wiki.

18.1.2.1   ath(4)

Supports cards based on the Atheros AR5210, AR5211 and AR5212 chipsets.

18.1.2.2   ral(4)

Ralink Technology IEEE 802.11 wireless network driver — supports cards based on the Ralink Technology RT2500, RT2501 and RT2600 chipsets.

18.1.2.3   wi(4)

Lucent Hermes, Intersil PRISM and Spectrum24 IEEE 802.11 driver — supports cards based on Lucent Hermes, Intersil PRISM-II, Intersil PRISM-2.5, Intersil Prism-3, and Symbol Spectrum24 chipsets. These cards support only 802.11b.

18.1.2.4   awi(4)

AMD PCnetMobile IEEE 802.11 PCMCIA wireless network driver — supports cards based on the AMD 79c930 controller with Intersil (formerly Harris) PRISM radio chipset.

18.1.2.5   an(4)

Aironet Communications 4500/4800 wireless network adapter driver — supports Aironet Communications 4500 and 4800 wireless network adapters and variants.

18.2   Wireless WAN

You can assign your wireless card as your WAN interface, or an OPT WAN in a multi-WAN deployment. This section covers assigning and configuring a wireless interface as a WAN interface.

18.2.1   Interface assignment

If you have not already assigned your wireless interface, browse to Interfaces → Assign. Click Add to add an OPT interface for your wireless, or select it as WAN if desired. Figure 18.1 shows an Atheros card assigned as WAN.

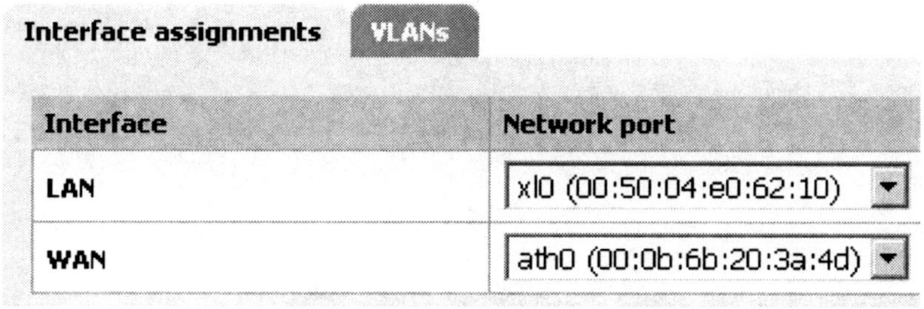

Interface	Network port
LAN	xl0 (00:50:04:e0:62:10)
WAN	ath0 (00:0b:6b:20:3a:4d)

Interface assignments   VLANs

Figure 18.1: Interface assignment — wireless WAN

18.2.2   Configuring your wireless network

Browse to the Interfaces menu for your wireless WAN interface. This example uses WAN, so I will browse to Interfaces → WAN. Select the type of configuration (DHCP, static IP, etc.), and scroll down under Wireless configuration. Choose Infrastructure (BSS) mode, fill in the SSID, and configure encryption such as WEP (Wired Equivalent Privacy) or WPA (Wi-Fi Protected Access) if used. Most wireless networks will not need any further configuration, but if yours does, make sure it's configured appropriate for the access point you will be using. Then click Save.

18.2.3   Checking wireless status

Browse to Status → Interfaces to see the status of the wireless interface just configured. You can tell whether the interface has successfully associated with the chosen access point by looking at the status of the interface. Status associated means it is connected successfully, as shown in Figure 18.2.

If it shows No carrier, it was unable to associate. Figure 18.3 shows an example of this, where I configured SSID **asdf**, a non-existent wireless network.

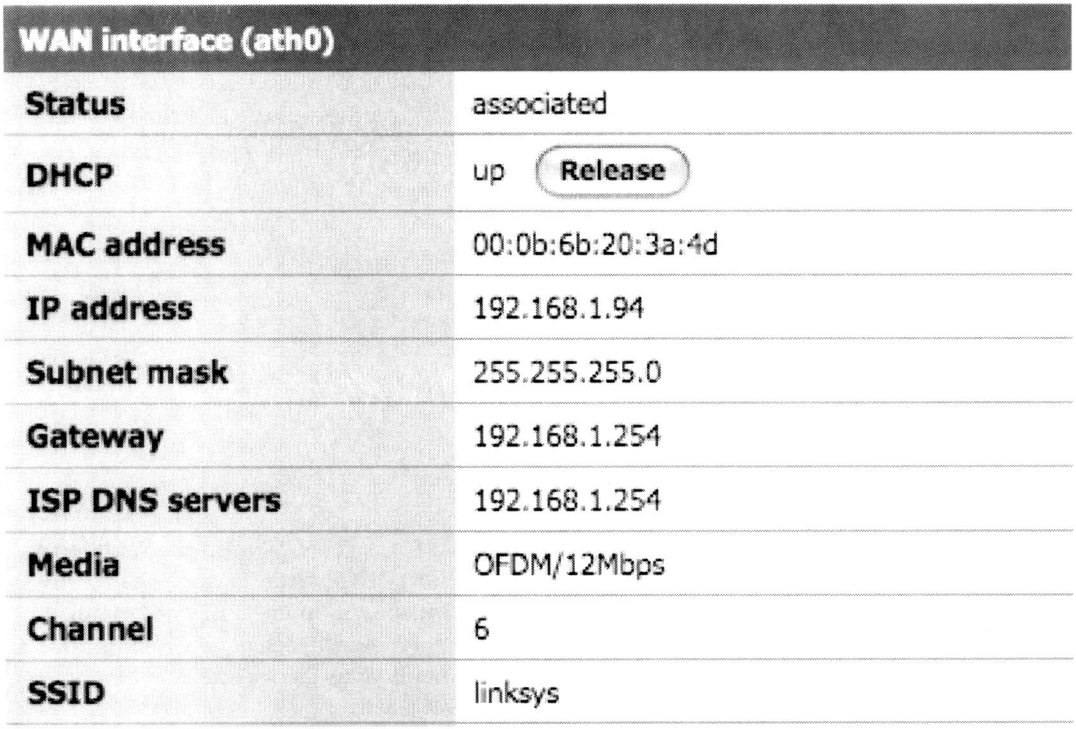

WAN interface (ath0)	
Status	associated
DHCP	up (Release)
MAC address	00:0b:6b:20:3a:4d
IP address	192.168.1.94
Subnet mask	255.255.255.0
Gateway	192.168.1.254
ISP DNS servers	192.168.1.254
Media	OFDM/12Mbps
Channel	6
SSID	linksys

Figure 18.2: Wireless WAN Associated

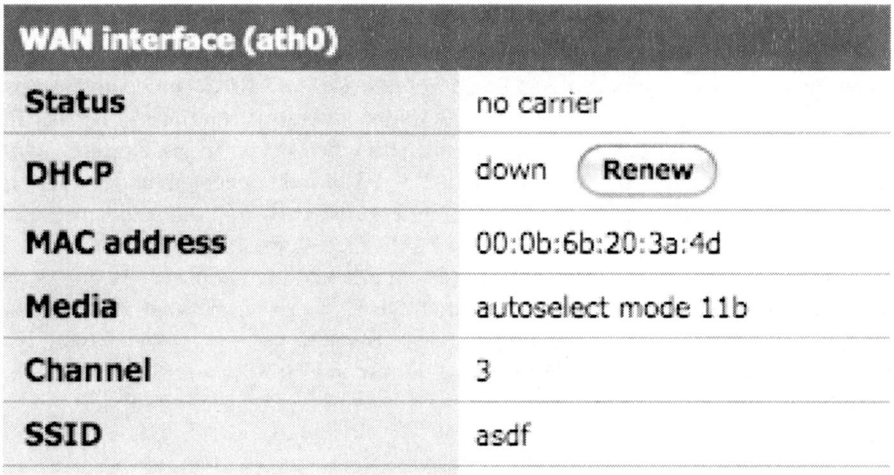

WAN interface (ath0)	
Status	no carrier
DHCP	down (**Renew**)
MAC address	00:0b:6b:20:3a:4d
Media	autoselect mode 11b
Channel	3
SSID	asdf

Figure 18.3: No carrier on wireless WAN

18.2.4 Showing available wireless networks and signal strength

By browsing to Status → Wireless, you can see the wireless networks visible to your firewall as shown in Figure 18.4. Your wireless interface must be configured before this menu item will appear.

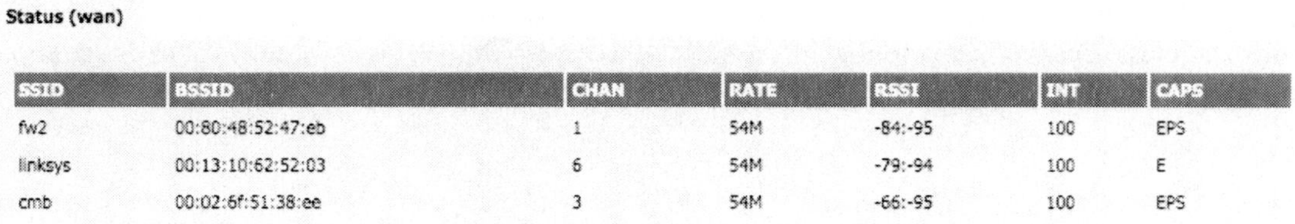

Status (wan)

SSID	BSSID	CHAN	RATE	RSSI	INT	CAPS
fw2	00:80:48:52:47:eb	1	54M	-84:-95	100	EPS
linksys	00:13:10:62:52:03	6	54M	-79:-94	100	E
cmb	00:02:6f:51:38:ee	3	54M	-66:-95	100	EPS

Figure 18.4: Wireless Status

18.3 Bridging and wireless

Only wireless interfaces in access point (hostap) mode will function in a bridged configuration. You can bridge a wireless interface in hostap to any other interface to combine the two interfaces on the same broadcast domain. You may wish to do this if you have devices or applications that must reside on the same broadcast domain to function properly. This is discussed in more depth in Section 18.4.3.1.

18.3.1   BSS and IBSS wireless and bridging

Because of the way wireless works in BSS (Basic Service Set) and IBSS (Independent Basic Service Set) mode, and the way bridging works, you cannot bridge a wireless interface in BSS or IBSS mode. Every device connected to a wireless card in BSS or IBSS mode must present the same MAC address. With bridging, the MAC address passed is the actual MAC of the connected device. This is normally desirable — it is just how bridging works. With wireless, the only way this can function is if all the devices behind that wireless card present the same MAC address on the wireless network. This is explained in depth by noted wireless expert Jim Thompson in a mailing list post.[1] As one example, when VMware Player, Workstation, or Server is configured to bridge to a wireless interface, it automatically translates the MAC address to that of the wireless card. Because there is no way to simply translate a MAC address in FreeBSD, and because of the way bridging in FreeBSD works, it is difficult to provide any workarounds similar to what VMware offers. At some point pfSense may support this, but it is not on the road map for 2.0.

18.4   Using an External Access Point

If you have an existing wireless access point, or a wireless router that you wish to only use as an access point now that pfSense is acting as your firewall, there are several ways to accommodate wireless in your network. This section covers the most commonly deployed scenarios.

18.4.1   Turning your wireless router into an access point

When replacing a simple wireless router such as a Linksys or D-Link or other home grade device with pfSense as a perimeter firewall, the wireless functionality can be retained by turning the wireless router into a wireless access point by following the steps described in this section. These are generic steps that need to be followed for any device. To find specifics for your wireless router, refer to its documentation.

18.4.1.1   Disable the DHCP server

First you will want to disable the DHCP server if it was previously in use. You will want pfSense to handle this function for your network, and having two DHCP servers on your network will cause problems.

18.4.1.2   Change the LAN IP

Next you will need to change the LAN IP to an unused IP on the subnet where your access point will reside (commonly LAN). It is probably using the same IP you will assign to the pfSense LAN interface, so it will require a different address. You will want to retain a functional IP on the access point for management purposes.

---

[1] `http://lists.freebsd.org/pipermail/freebsd-current/2005-October/056977.html`

18.4.1.3   Plug in the LAN interface

Most wireless routers bridge the wireless onto the internal LAN port or ports. This means the wireless will be on the same broadcast domain and IP subnet as the wired ports. For routers with an integrated switch, any of the switch ports will usually work. *You do not want to plug in the WAN or Internet port on your router!* This will put your wireless network on a different broadcast domain from the rest of your network, and will result in NATing traffic between your wireless and LAN and double NATing traffic between your wireless and the Internet. This is an ugly design, and will lead to problems in some circumstances, especially if you need to communicate between your wireless clients and your wired LAN.

Where you will plug in the LAN interface will depend on your chosen network design. The next sections cover your options and your considerations in which to choose.

18.4.2   Bridging wireless to your LAN

One common means of deploying wireless is to plug the access point directly into the same switch as your LAN hosts, where the AP bridges the wireless clients onto the wired network. This will work fine, but offers limited control over your wireless clients' ability to communicate with your internal systems.

18.4.3   Bridging wireless to an OPT interface

If you want more control over your wireless clients, adding an OPT interface to pfSense for your access point is the preferred solution. If you wish to keep your wireless and wired networks on the same IP subnet and broadcast domain, you can bridge the OPT interface to your LAN interface. This scenario is functionally equivalent to plugging the access point directly into your LAN switch, except since pfSense is in the middle, it can filter traffic from your wireless network to provide protection to your LAN hosts.

You can also put your wireless network on a dedicated IP subnet if desired, by not bridging the OPT interface on pfSense and assigning it with an IP subnet outside of your LAN subnet. This enables routing between your internal and wireless networks, as permitted by your firewall ruleset. This is commonly done on larger networks, where multiple access points are plugged into a switch that is then plugged into the OPT interface on pfSense. It is also preferable when you will force your wireless clients to connect to a VPN before allowing connections to internal network resources.

18.4.3.1   Choosing bridging or routing

The choice between bridging (using the same IP subnet as your LAN) or routing (using a dedicated IP subnet for wireless) for your wireless clients will depend on what services your wireless clients require. Certain applications and devices rely on broadcasts to function. Apple's AirTunes, as one example, will not function across two broadcast domains, so if you have AirTunes on your wireless network and want to use it from a system on your wired network, you must bridge your wired and wireless networks. Another example is media servers used by devices such as Xbox 360 and Playstation 3. These rely on multicast or broadcast traffic that can only function if your wired and wireless networks are bridged.

In many home network environments you will have applications or devices that require your wired and wireless networks to be bridged. In most corporate networks, there aren't any applications that require bridging. Which to choose depends on the requirements of network applications you use, as well as your personal preference.

There are some compromises to this, one example being the Avahi package. It can listen on two different broadcast domains and rebroadcast messages from one to the other in order to allow multicast DNS to work (aka Rendezvous or Bonjour) for network discovery and services. Having a WINS (Windows Internet Name Service) server is another example, as it will allow you to browse networks of Windows/SMB-enabled machines even when you are not in the same broadcast domain.

18.5 pfSense as an Access Point

With a wireless card that supports hostap mode (ath(4), ral(4) and wi(4)), pfSense can be configured as a wireless access point.

18.5.1 Should I use an external AP or pfSense as my access point?

Historically, the access point functionality in FreeBSD has suffered from serious compatibility problems with some wireless clients. With FreeBSD 7.x this has improved significantly, however there may still be some incompatible devices. These difficulties with client compatibility are not always limited to FreeBSD, but you may find that a cheap consumer grade wireless router turned access point provides better compatibility than FreeBSD's access point capabilities in some instances. I use pfSense access points at home with no trouble, with my MacBook Pro, Apple AirTunes, Mac mini G4, iPod Touch, Palm Treo, various Windows laptops, Xbox 360, and FreeBSD clients and it works very reliably across all these devices. There is the possibility of finding incompatible devices with any access point. FreeBSD is no exception and you may find this is more common with FreeBSD than other access points. In older versions of FreeBSD, particularly with m0n0wall on FreeBSD 4.x, I recommended not using FreeBSD access point functionality. Today it works well with almost every device and is probably suitable for your network.

This is subject to significant change with each FreeBSD release. An up to date listing of known incompatible devices and the most recent information on wireless compatibility can be found at http://www.pfsense.org/apcompat.

18.5.2 Configuring pfSense as an access point

The process of configuring pfSense to act as a wireless access point (AP) is relatively easy. Many of the options should be familiar if you have configured other wireless routers before, and some options may be new unless you have used some commercial-grade wireless equipment. There are dozens of ways to configure access points, and they all depend upon your environment. Here, we cover setting pfSense up as a basic AP that uses WPA2 encryption with AES. In this example, ExampleCo needs wireless access for some laptops in the conference room.

18.5.2.1 Preparing the Wireless Interface

Before doing anything else, ensure that the wireless card is in the router, and the antenna is firmly attached. As described earlier in this chapter, the wireless card must be assigned as an OPT interface and enabled before the remaining configuration can be completed.

18.5.2.2 Interface Description

When in use as an access point, naming it "WLAN" (Wireless LAN) or "Wireless" will make it easy to identify in the list of interfaces. If you have a unique SSID, you may find it more convenient to use that in the description instead. If pfSense will be driving multiple access points, there should be some way to distinguish them, such as "WLANadmin" and "WLANsales". We'll call this one `ConfRoom` for now.

18.5.2.3 Interface Type/IP Address

Since this will be an access point on a dedicated IP subnet, you will need to set the Type to `Static` and specify an IP Address and subnet mask. Since this is a separate subnet from the other interfaces, it can be `192.168.201.0/24`, a subnet that is otherwise unused in the ExampleCo network.

18.5.2.4 Wireless Standard

Depending upon hardware support, there are several choices available for the wireless Standard setting, including 802.11b, 802.11g, 802.11g turbo, 802.11a, and 802.11a turbo, and possibly others. For this example, we will choose `802.11g`.

18.5.2.5 Wireless Mode

Set the Mode field to `Access Point`, and pfSense will use hostapd to act as an AP.

18.5.2.6 Service Set Identifier (SSID)

This will be the "name" of the AP as seen by clients. You should set the SSID to something readily identifiable, yet unique to your setup. Keeping with the example, this can be named `ConfRoom`.

18.5.2.7 Limiting Access to 802.11g Only

The 802.11g only setting controls whether or not older 802.11b clients are able to associate with this access point. Allowing older clients may be necessary in some environments if devices are still around that require it. Some mobile devices such as the Nintendo DS and the Palm Tungsten C are only compatible with 802.11b and require a mixed network in order to work. The flip side of this is that you will see slower speeds as a result of allowing such devices on your network, as the access point will be forced to cater to the lowest common denominator when an 802.11b device is present. In our example conference room, people will only be using recently purchased company-owned laptops that are all capable of 802.11g, so we will check this option.

18.5.2.8   Intra-BSS Communication

If you check Allow intra-BSS communication, wireless clients will be able to see each other directly, instead of routing all traffic through the AP. If clients will only need access to the Internet, it is typically safer to uncheck this. In our scenario, people in the conference room may need to share files back and forth directly between laptops, so this will stay checked.

18.5.2.9   Hiding SSID (Disable SSID Broadcasting)

Normally, the AP will broadcast its SSID so that clients can locate and associate with it easily. This is considered by some to be a security risk, announcing to all who are listening that you have a wireless network available, but in most cases the convenience outweighs the security risk. The benefits of disabling SSID broadcasting are overblown by some, as it does not actually hide the network from anyone capable of using many freely available wireless security tools that easily find such wireless networks. For our conference room AP, we will leave this unchecked to make it easier for meeting attendees to find and use the service.

18.5.2.10   Wireless Channel Selection

When selecting a Channel, you will need to be aware of any nearby radio transmitters in similar frequency bands. In addition to wireless access points, there are also cordless phones, Bluetooth, baby monitors, video transmitters, microwaves, and many other devices that utilize the same 2.4 GHz spectrum that can cause interference. Often you can get away with using any channel you like, as long as your AP clients are near the antenna. The safest channels to use are 1, 6, and 11 since their frequency bands do not overlap each other. You may specify **Auto** to tell the card to pick an appropriate channel, however this functionality does not work with some wireless cards. If you choose **Auto** and things do not work, choose a specific channel instead. For this network, since there are no others around, we'll choose channel **1**.

18.5.2.11   Wireless Encryption

Three types of encryption are supported for 802.11 networks: WEP, WPA, and WPA2. WPA2 with AES is the most secure. Even if you are not worried about encrypting the over-the-air traffic (which you should be), it provides an additional means of access control. A WPA/WPA2 passphrase is also easier to work with then a WEP key on most devices; it acts more like a password than a really long string of hexadecimal characters. As with the choice between 802.11b and 802.11g, some older devices only support WEP or WPA, but most modern wireless cards and drivers will support WPA2.

For our conference room, they will use WPA2, and turn WEP off. To do this, uncheck Enable WEP, and check Enable WPA. To ensure that only WPA2 will be in use, set WPA Mode to **WPA2**. For our WPA Pre-Shared Key, we'll use **excoconf213**, and also set WPA Key Mode Management to **Pre-Shared Key**.

To use WPA2+AES, as desired for the conference room wireless, set WPA Pairwise to **AES**.

Note

To use WPA2 on a Windows XP wireless client, you must have a wireless driver that supports WPA2. If you are using Windows XP's Wireless Configuration interface, in order to associate with an access point running WPA2 you will need to upgrade the PC to Windows XP SP3 or install the patch from Microsoft Knowledge Base article 917021.

18.5.2.11.1 Wireless encryption weaknesses

WEP has had serious known security problems for years now, and should never be used unless it is the only option for wireless devices you must support. It's possible to crack WEP in a matter of minutes at most, and it should never be relied upon for security. WEP cannot be relied upon for anything more than keeping out Internet seekers with no technical skills.

TKIP (Temporal Key Integrity Protocol), part of AES, became a replacement for WEP after it was broken. It uses the same underlying mechanism as WEP, and hence is vulnerable to some similar attacks. Recently these attacks are becoming more practical. At the time of this writing it isn't nearly as easy to break as WEP, but you should still never use it unless you have devices that are incompatible with WPA or WPA2 using AES. WPA and WPA2 in combination with AES are not subject to these flaws in TKIP.

18.5.2.12 Finishing AP Settings

The previous settings should be enough to get a wireless access point running with 802.11g with WPA2 + AES encryption. There are other settings that can be used to fine-tune the AP's behavior, but they are not necessary for normal operation in most environments. When you have finished changing the settings, click Save, then Apply Changes.

18.5.2.13 Configuring DHCP

Now that we have created an entirely separate network, we will want to enable DHCP so that associating wireless clients can automatically obtain an IP address. Browse to Services → DHCP Server, click on the tab for your wireless interface (ConfRoom for our example setup). Check the box to enable, set whatever size range you will need, and any additional needed options, then click Save and Apply Changes. For more details on configuring the DHCP service, see Section 21.1.

18.5.2.14 Adding Firewall Rules

Since this wireless interface is an OPT interface, it will have no default firewall rules. At the very least you will need to have a rule to allow traffic from this subnet to whatever destination will be needed. Since our conference room users will need internet access and access to other network resources, a default allow rule will be fine in this case. To create the rule, go to Firewall → Rules, and click on the tab for the wireless interface (ConfRoom for this example). Add a rule to pass traffic of any protocol, with a source address of the ConfRoom subnet, and any destination. For more information about creating firewall rules, see Chapter 6.

18.5.2.15   Associating Clients

The newly configured pfSense AP should appear in the list of available access points from your wireless device, assuming you did not disable broadcasting of the SSID. You should be able to associate clients with it as you would any other access point. The exact procedure will vary between operating systems, devices, and drivers, but most manufacturers have streamlined the process to make it simple for everyone.

18.5.2.16   Viewing Wireless Client Status

When you have a wireless interface configured for access point mode, the associated clients will be listed on Status → Wireless.

18.6   Additional protection for your wireless network

In addition to strong encryption from WPA or WPA2 with AES, some users like to employ an additional layer of encryption and authentication before allowing access to network resources. The two most commonly deployed solutions are Captive Portal and VPN. These methods can be employed whether you use an external access point on an OPT interface or an internal wireless card as your access point.

18.6.1   Additional wireless protection with Captive Portal

By enabling Captive Portal on the interface where your wireless resides, you can require authentication before users can access network resources. In corporate networks, this is commonly deployed with RADIUS authentication to Microsoft Active Directory so users can use their Active Directory credentials to authenticate while on the wireless network. Captive Portal configuration is covered in Chapter 19.

18.6.2   Additional protection with VPN

Adding Captive Portal provides another layer of authentication, but does not offer any additional protection from eavesdropping of your wireless traffic. Requiring VPN before allowing access to the internal network and Internet adds another layer of authentication as well as an additional layer of encryption for your wireless traffic. The configuration for your chosen type of VPN will be no different from a remote access configuration, but you will need to configure the firewall rules on the pfSense interface to only allow VPN traffic from your wireless clients.

18.6.2.1   Configuring firewall rules for IPsec

Figure 18.5 shows the minimal rules required to allow only access to IPsec on the WLAN interface IP. Pings to the WLAN interface IP are also allowed to assist in troubleshooting.

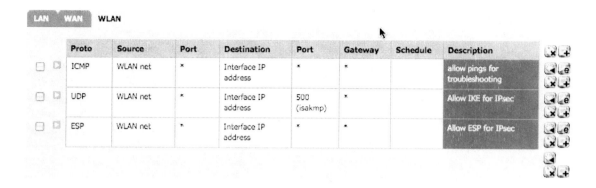

Figure 18.5: Rules to allow only IPsec from wireless

18.6.2.2 Configuring firewall rules for OpenVPN

Figure 18.6 shows the minimal rules required to allow access only to OpenVPN on the WLAN interface IP. Pings to the WLAN interface IP are also allowed to assist in troubleshooting. This assumes you are using the default UDP port 1194. If you choose another protocol or port, adjust the rule accordingly.

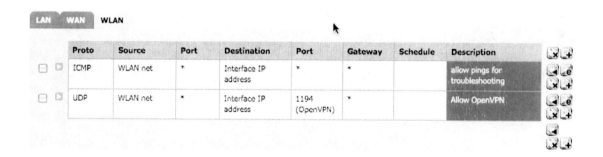

Figure 18.6: Rules to allow only OpenVPN from wireless

18.6.2.3 Configuring firewall rules for PPTP

Figure 18.7 shows the minimal rules required to allow access only to PPTP on the WLAN interface IP. Pings to the WLAN interface IP are also allowed to assist in troubleshooting.

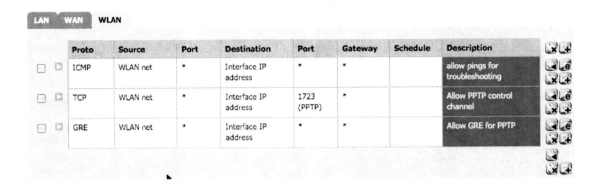

Figure 18.7: Rules to allow only PPTP from wireless

18.7   Configuring a Secure Wireless Hotspot

Your company or organization may wish to provide Internet access for customers or guests using your existing Internet connection. This can be a boon to your customers and business, but can also expose your private network to attack if not done properly. This section covers the common means of providing Internet access to guests and customers, while protecting your internal network.

18.7.1   Multiple firewall approach

For the best protection between your private network and public network, obtain at least two public IPs from your ISP, and use a second firewall for your public network. To accommodate this, you put a switch between your Internet connection and the WAN of both firewalls. This also has the benefit of putting your public network on a different public IP from your private network, so if you should receive a report of abuse, you will be able to easily differentiate whether it originated from your public or private network. The firewall protecting your private network will see your public network no differently than any Internet host.

18.7.2   Single firewall approach

In environments where the multiple firewall approach is cost prohibitive or otherwise undesirable, you can still protect your internal network by connecting your public network to an OPT interface on pfSense. You should assign a dedicated private IP subnet to this OPT interface, and configure your firewall rules to allow access to the Internet but not your internal network.

18.7.3   Access control and egress filtering considerations

Other than not allowing traffic from the publicly accessible network to the private network, there are additional things you should consider in the configuration of your hotspot.

18.7.3.1   Restrict network access

While many hotspots use open wireless networks with no other authentication, you should consider additional protections to prevent network abuse. On your wireless, consider using WPA or WPA2 and providing the passphrase to your guests or customers. Some will have the passphrase on a placard in the lobby or waiting area, posted in a guest room, or provide it upon request. Also consider implementing Captive Portal on pfSense (covered in Chapter 19). This helps prevent people in other offices and outside the building from using your wireless network.

18.7.3.2   Disable Intra-BSS communication

If your access point allows, you should not allow intra-BSS communication. This prevents wireless clients from communicating with other wireless clients, which protects your users from intentional attacks from other wireless users as well as unintentional ones such as worms.

18.7.3.3   Egress filtering

Consider what kind of egress policy to configure. The most basic, allowing access to the Internet without allowing access to the private network, is probably the most commonly deployed but you should consider additional restrictions. To avoid having your public IP address black listed because of infected visiting systems acting as spam bots, you should consider blocking SMTP. An alternative that still lets people use their SMTP email but limits the effect of spam bots is to create an allow rule for SMTP and specify Maximum state entries per host under Advanced Options on the Firewall: Rules: Edit page. Ensure the rule is above any other rules that would match SMTP traffic, and specify a low limit. Because connections may not always be properly closed by the mail client or server, you won't want to set this too low to prevent blocking legitimate users, but a limit of five connections should be reasonable. You may wish to specify Maximum state entries per host on all your firewall rules, but keep in mind that some protocols will require dozens or hundreds of connections to function. HTTP and HTTPS may require numerous connections to load a single web page depending on the content of the page and the behavior of the browser, so don't set your limits too low.

You will need to balance the desires of your users against the risks inherent in providing Internet access for systems you do not control, and define a policy that fits your environment.

18.8   Troubleshooting Wireless Connections

When it comes to wireless, there are a lot of things that can go wrong. From faulty hardware connections to radio interference to incompatible software/drivers, or simple settings mismatches, anything is possible, and it can be a challenge to make it all work on the first try. This section will cover some of the more common problems that have been encountered by pfSense users and developers.

18.8.1   Check the Antenna

Before spending any time diagnosing an issue, double and triple check the antenna connection. If it is a screw-on type, ensure it is fully tightened. For mini-PCI cards, ensure the pigtail connectors are properly connected and snapped in place. Pigtails on mini-PCI cards are fragile and easy to break. After disconnecting and reconnecting them a few times, you may need to replace them.

18.8.2   Try with multiple clients or wireless cards

To eliminate a possible incompatibility between pfSense's wireless functions and your wireless client, be sure to try it with multiple devices or cards first. If the same problem is repeatable with several different makes and models, it is more likely to be a problem with the configuration or related hardware than the client device.

18.8.3   Signal Strength is Low

If you have a weak signal, even when you are nearby the access point antenna, check the antenna again. For mini-PCI cards, if you only have one pigtail in use and there are two internal connectors, try hooking up to the other internal connector on the card. You can also try changing the Channel or adjusting the Transmit Power on the wireless interface configuration. For mini-PCI cards, check for broken ends on the fragile pigtail connectors where they plug into the mini-PCI card.

Chapter 19

Captive Portal

The Captive Portal feature of pfSense allows you to direct users to a web page before Internet access is permitted. From that page, you can either let users access the Internet after clicking through, or require authentication. The most common uses of Captive Portal are for wireless hot spots, or additional authentication before allowing access to internal networks from wireless clients. It can also be used with wired clients if desired.

19.1 Limitations

The captive portal implementation in pfSense does have some limitations. This section covers those, and the common ways of working around them where possible.

19.1.1 Can only run on one interface

You can only use the captive portal on one interface of your firewall. For networks where multiple IP subnets require Captive Portal functionality, you will need to use a router inside your captive portal install as illustrated in Figure 19.1.

19.1.2 Not capable of reverse portal

A reverse portal, requiring authentication for traffic coming into your network from the Internet, is not possible.

19.2 Portal Configuration Without Authentication

For a simple portal without authentication, all you need to do is check the Enable captive portal box, select an interface, and upload a HTML page with your portal contents as described in Section 19.5.12. You may wish to specify additional configuration options as detailed in Section 19.5.

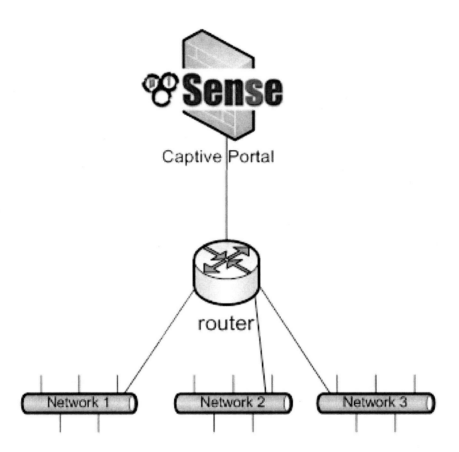

Figure 19.1: Captive Portal on multiple subnets

19.3 Portal Configuration Using Local Authentication

To setup a portal with local authentication, check the Enable captive portal box, select an interface, choose local authentication, and upload a HTML page with your portal contents as described in Section 19.5.12. You may wish to specify additional configuration options as detailed in Section 19.5. Then configure your local users on the Users tab of the Services → Captive Portal page.

19.4 Portal Configuration Using RADIUS Authentication

To setup a portal using RADIUS authentication, first configure your RADIUS server, then follow the same procedures as setting up a portal with local authentication, filling in the appropriate information for your RADIUS server. Read the next section for information on specific configuration options you may wish to use.

19.5 Configuration Options

This section describes each of the Captive Portal configuration options.

19.5.1 Interface

Here you select the interface captive portal will run on. This cannot be a bridged interface, and cannot be any WAN or OPT WAN interface.

19.5.2 Maximum concurrent connections

This field specifies the maximum number of concurrent connections per IP address. The default value is 4, which should suffice for most environments. This limit exists to prevent a single host from exhausting all resources on your firewall, whether inadvertent or intentional. One example where this would otherwise be a problem is a host infected with a worm. The thousands of connections issued will cause the captive portal page to be generated repeatedly if the host is not authenticated already, which would otherwise generate so much load it would leave your system unresponsive.

19.5.3 Idle timeout

If you want to disconnect idle users, fill in a value here. Users will be able to log back in immediately.

19.5.4 Hard timeout

To forcefully log off users after a specified period, enter a hard timeout value. You should enter either a hard timeout, idle timeout or both to ensure sessions are removed if users do not log off, as most likely will not. Users will be able to log back in immediately after the hard timeout, if their credentials are still valid (for local accounts, not expired, and for RADIUS authentication, user can still successfully authenticate to RADIUS).

19.5.5 Logout popup window

Check this box to enable a logout pop up window. Unfortunately, since most browsers have pop up blockers enabled, this window may not work for most of your users unless you control the computers and can exclude your portal in their pop up blocker.

19.5.6 Redirection URL

If you enter a URL here, after authenticating or clicking through the portal, users will be redirected to this URL rather than the one they originally tried to access. If this field is left blank, the user will be redirected to the URL the user initially tried to access.

19.5.7 Concurrent user logins

If this box is checked, only one login per user account is allowed. The most recent login is permitted and any previous logins under that username will be disconnected.

19.5.8 MAC filtering

This option allows you to disable the default MAC filtering. This is necessary in the case of multiple subnets behind a router using the portal, such as illustrated in Figure 19.1, as all users behind a router will show up to the portal as the router's MAC address.

19.5.9 Authentication

This section allows you to configure authentication if desired. If you leave No authentication selected, users will just have to click through your portal screen for access. If you require authentication, you can use either the local user manager or RADIUS authentication. Users for the local user manager are configured on the Users tab of the Services → Captive Portal page. RADIUS users are defined in your RADIUS server. For those with a Microsoft Active Directory network infrastructure, RADIUS can be used to authenticate captive portal users from your Active Directory using Microsoft IAS. This is described in Section 24.1. There are numerous other RADIUS servers that can also be used. RADIUS accounting can be enabled to send usage information for each user to the RADIUS server. Refer to documentation for your RADIUS server for more information.

19.5.10 HTTPS login

Check this box to use HTTPS for the portal page. If you check this you must enter a certificate and private key.

19.5.11 HTTPS server name

This field is where you specify the FQDN (hostname + domain) to be used for HTTPS. This needs to match the Common Name (CN) on your certificate to prevent your users from receiving certificate errors in their browsers.

19.5.12 Portal page contents

Here you upload a HTML page containing the portal page your users will see when trying to access the Internet before authenticating or clicking through the portal.

19.5.12.1 Portal page without authentication

This shows the HTML of a portal page that can be used without authentication.

```
<html>
<head>
<title>Welcome to our portal</title>
</head>
<body>
<p>Welcome to our portal</p>
<p>Click Continue to access the Internet</p>
<form method="post" action="$PORTAL_ACTION$">
  <input name="redirurl" type="hidden" value="$PORTAL_REDIRURL$">
  <input name="accept" type="submit" value="Continue">
</form>
</body>
</html>
```

19.5.12.2 Portal page with authentication

Here is an example portal page requiring authentication.

```
<html>
<head>
<title>Welcome to our portal</title>
</head>
<body>
<p>Welcome to our portal</p>
<p>Enter your username and password and click Login to access the  ↩
    Internet</p>
<form method="post" action="$PORTAL_ACTION$">
  <input name="auth_user" type="text">
  <input name="auth_pass" type="password">
  <input name="redirurl" type="hidden" value="$PORTAL_REDIRURL$">
  <input name="accept" type="submit" value="Login">
</form>
```

```
</body>
</html>
```

19.5.13 Authentication error page contents

Here you can upload a HTML page to be displayed on authentication errors. An authentication error occurs when a user enters a bad username or password, or in the case of RADIUS authentication, potentially an unreachable RADIUS server.

19.6 Troubleshooting Captive Portal

This section contains troubleshooting tips for the most common problem with captive portal.

19.6.1 Authentication failures

Authentication failures are normally the result of users entering an incorrect username or password. In the case of RADIUS authentication, these can occur because of connectivity problems to your RADIUS server, or problems on the RADIUS server itself. Check your RADIUS server's logs for indications of why access was denied, and ensure the firewall can communicate with the RADIUS server.

19.6.2 Portal Page never loads (times out) nor will any other page load

This has been reported to happen when using Captive Portal on a VLAN, but the parent interface of the VLAN is also assigned as another interface on pfSense. For example, if `vlan0` is VLAN tag 10 on `fxp1`, you cannot have `fxp1` assigned as any other interface, it must be left unused. This is the recommended configuration anyhow, and this problem is one more reason to follow that advice.

Chapter 20

Firewall Redundancy / High Availability

pfSense is one of very few open source solutions offering enterprise-class high availability capabilities with stateful failover, allowing the elimination of the firewall as a single point of failure. This is provided by the combination of CARP, pfsync, and pfSense's XML-RPC configuration synchronization, each of which will be explained in this chapter. Often this is simply referred to as CARP, though technically CARP is only part of the complete solution.

20.1   CARP Overview

Common Address Redundancy Protocol (CARP) was created by OpenBSD developers as a free, open redundancy solution for sharing IP addresses amongst a group of network devices. Similar solutions already existed, primarily the IETF standard for Virtual Router Redundancy Protocol (VRRP). However Cisco claims VRRP is covered by its patent on their Hot Standby Router Protocol (HSRP), and told the OpenBSD developers that it would enforce its patent. Hence, the OpenBSD developers created a new free, open protocol to accomplish essentially the same result without infringing on Cisco's patent. CARP became available in October 2003 in OpenBSD, and was later added to FreeBSD as well.

Each pfSense firewall in a CARP group has its own unique IP address assigned on each interface, and has the shared CARP VIPs assigned as well. These CARP IPs are only active if the firewall is currently the master. If a failure of any network interface is detected, the next designated firewall switches to master on all interfaces.

Note

Because each member of the CARP group must have an IP address in a subnet, plus the CARP IP address, at least three available IP addresses are required for each interface, and more IP addresses for additional group members. This also applies to your WAN interface, so be sure you have at least three available routable IP addresses from your ISP. The smallest routable block that includes 3 IP addresses is a /29, which has 8 addresses (6 usable).

20.2   pfsync Overview

pfsync enables the synchronization of the firewall state table from the master firewall to secondary firewalls. Changes on the primary's state table are sent out on the network to the secondary firewall(s). This uses multicast by default, though an IP address can be defined in the pfSense interface to force unicast updates for environments with only two firewalls where multicast traffic will not function properly (some switches block or break multicast). You can use any active interface for sending pfsync updates, however we recommend utilizing a dedicated interface for security and performance reasons. pfsync does not support any sort of authentication, so if you use anything other than a dedicated interface, it is possible for any user with local network access to insert states into your secondary firewall. In low throughput environments that aren't security paranoid, use of the LAN interface for this purpose is acceptable. Bandwidth required for this state synchronization will vary significantly from one environment to another, but could be as high as 10% of the throughput traversing the firewall depending on the rate of state insertions and deletions in your network.

The benefit of pfsync is you can fail over without losing your state table, which allows for seamless failover. In some environments, you won't notice the difference between failing over statefully and losing state during failover. In other networks, it can cause a significant but brief network outage.

20.2.1   pfsync and upgrades

Normally pfSense would allow firewall upgrades without any network disruption. Unfortunately, this isn't always the case with upgrades as the pfsync protocol has changed to accommodate additional functionality. This hopefully won't be the case again in the future, but if you are upgrading from pfSense 1.2 to 1.2.1 or higher, the underlying OS changed from FreeBSD 6.2 to 7.x and includes a newer pfsync. Always check the upgrade guide linked in all release announcements before upgrading to see if there are any special considerations for CARP users.

20.3   pfSense XML-RPC Sync Overview

pfSense's configuration synchronization allows you to make most configuration changes on only the primary firewall, which then replicates those changes over to the secondary automatically. The areas supported by this are firewall rules, firewall schedules, aliases, NAT, IPsec, Wake on LAN, static routes, load balancer, Virtual IPs, traffic shaper, and DNS forwarder. Other settings must be individually configured on the secondary firewall as needed, though the synchronization covers most if not all of what you will routinely change. Configuration synchronization should use the same interface as your pfsync traffic.

20.4   Example Redundant Configuration

This section describes the steps in planning for and configuring a simple three interface CARP configuration. The three interfaces are LAN, WAN, and pfsync. This is functionally equivalent to a two interface LAN and WAN deployment, with the pfsync interface being used solely to synchronize configuration and firewall states between the primary and secondary firewalls.

20.4.1 Determine IP Address Assignments

First you need to plan your IP address assignments. A good strategy is to use the lowest usable IP in the subnet as the CARP IP, the next subsequent IP as the primary firewall's interface IP, and the next IP as the secondary firewall's interface IP. You can assign these as desired, so choosing a scheme that makes the most sense to you is recommended.

20.4.1.1 WAN Addressing

The WAN addresses will be selected from those assigned by your ISP. For the example in Table 20.1, the WAN of the CARP pair is on a private network, and the addresses 10.0.66.10 through 10.0.66.12 will be used as the WAN IPs.

IP Address	Usage
10.0.66.10	CARP shared IP
10.0.66.11	Primary firewall WAN IP
10.0.66.12	Secondary firewall WAN IP

Table 20.1: WAN IP Address Assignments

20.4.1.2 LAN Addressing

The LAN subnet is 192.168.1.0/24. For this example, the LAN IPs will be assigned as shown in Table 20.2.

IP Address	Usage
192.168.1.1	CARP shared IP
192.168.1.2	Primary firewall LAN IP
192.168.1.3	Secondary firewall LAN IP

Table 20.2: LAN IP Address Assignments

20.4.1.3 pfsync Addressing

There will be no shared CARP IP on this interface because there is no need for one. These IPs are used only for communication between the firewalls. For this example, I will use 172.16.1.0/24 as the pfsync subnet. Only two IPs will be used, but I will use a /24 to be consistent with the other internal interface (LAN). For the last octet of the IP addresses, I chose the same last octet as that firewall's LAN IP for consistency.

In Figure 20.1 you can see the layout of this example CARP group. The primary and secondary each have identical connections to the WAN and LAN, and a crossover cable between them to connect the pfsync interfaces. In this basic example, the WAN switch and LAN switch are still potential single points of failure. Switching redundancy is covered later in this chapter in Section 20.8.

IP Address	Usage
172.16.1.2	Primary firewall LAN IP
172.16.1.3	Secondary firewall LAN IP

Table 20.3: pfsync IP Address Assignments

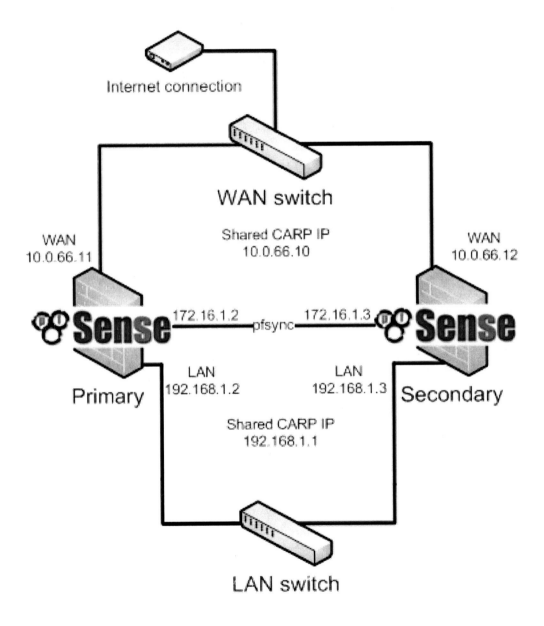

Figure 20.1: Example CARP network diagram

20.4.2   Configure the primary firewall

First we will get everything functioning as desired on the primary, then the secondary will be added. Leave the secondary firewall turned off until you get to that point.

20.4.2.1   Installation, interface assignment and basic configuration

Go through the installation and interface assignment no differently than you would for a single install. Assign the previously designated IP address to the LAN interface, and log into the web interface to continue. Go through the startup wizard, selecting your timezone, configuring the static IP previously designated for the primary firewall on the WAN, and setting your admin password. Continue to the next step after completing the startup wizard (refer back to Section 4.2 if needed).

20.4.2.2   Configuring the CARP Virtual IPs

Browse to Firewall → Virtual IPs and click 🔳 to add your first CARP VIP. The virtual IP editing screen will be displayed, as seen in Figure 20.2

Firewall: Virtual IP Address: Edit

Type	○ Proxy ARP ⦿ CARP ○ Other
Interface	WAN ▾
IP Address(es)	Type: Single address ▾ Address: 10.0.66.10 / 24 ▾ *This is the network's subnet mask. It does not specify a CIDR range.*
Virtual IP Password	●●●●●●●●●● Enter the VHID group password.
VHID Group	1 ▾ Enter the VHID group that the machines will share
Advertising Frequency	0 ▾ The frequency that this machine will advertise. 0 = master. Anything above 0 designates a backup.
Description	WAN CARP IP You may enter a description here for your reference (not parsed).

Figure 20.2: WAN CARP IP

For the Type, select **CARP**. The Interface should be set to **WAN**. For the IP Address, enter in the shared WAN IP address chosen earlier. In this example, it is **10.0.66.10**. The Virtual IP Password can be whatever you like, and as long as all your systems use pfSense with its configuration synchronization, you never need to know this password as it will automatically synchronize to your secondary firewall. You can generate a random password using a password generation tool, or bang randomly on the keyboard to create one. Each CARP IP on a pair of firewalls must use a unique VHID group (Virtual Host ID), and it also must be different from any VHIDs in active use on any directly connected network interface if CARP or VRRP is also present on other routers or firewalls on your network. If you have no other CARP or VRRP traffic present on your network, you may start at **1**. Otherwise, set it to the next available VHID on your network. The Advertising Frequency should be set according to this machine's role in the group. Since this one will be master, it should be set to **0**. On the backup system, this should be **1** or higher. For the Description, enter something relevant such as **WAN CARP IP**. Click Save when finished.

Firewall: Virtual IP Address: Edit

Type	○ Proxy ARP ⦿ CARP ○ Other
Interface	[LAN ▾]
IP Address(es)	Type: [Single address ▾]
	Address: [192.168.1.1] / [24 ▾] *This is the network's subnet mask. It does not specify a CIDR range.*
Virtual IP Password	[••••••••••••]
	Enter the VHID group password.
VHID Group	[2 ▾]
	Enter the VHID group that the machines will share
Advertising Frequency	[0 ▾]
	The frequency that this machine will advertise. 0 = master. Anything above 0 designates a backup.
Description	[LAN CARP IP]
	You may enter a description here for your reference (not parsed).

Figure 20.3: LAN CARP IP

Now click ⬚ to add another Virtual IP for the LAN (Figure 20.3). This time, set Type to **CARP**, Interface to **LAN**, and IP Address to the shared LAN IP, **192.168.1.1**. This Virtual IP Password is for a different IP group, so it does not have to match the one for WAN, and again you will never need to know this password. The VHID should be different from that of the WAN CARP IP, typically it is set one number higher, in this case **2**. Again, since this system is master the Advertising Frequency should be **0**. For the Description, enter **LAN CARP IP** or something similarly descriptive. Click Save when finished.

After saving the LAN CARP IP, you will see both VIPs in the list, as in Figure 20.4. Click Apply Changes and then both CARP IPs will be active.

20.4.2.3   Configure Outbound NAT for CARP

The next step will be to configure NAT so that clients on the LAN will use the shared WAN IP as the address. Browse to Firewall → NAT, and click the Outbound tab. Select the option to enable Manual Outbound NAT (Advanced Outbound NAT), then click Save.

A rule will appear that will NAT your LAN traffic to the WAN IP. You can adjust this rule to work with the CARP IP address instead. Click the ⬚ to the right of the rule. In the Translation section, select the WAN CARP IP address from the Address drop-down. Change the Description to mention that this rule

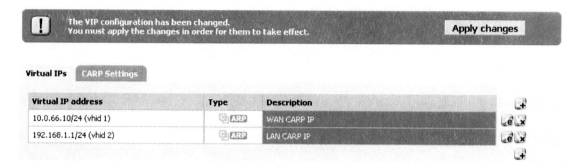

Figure 20.4: Virtual IP list

will NAT LAN to the WAN CARP. For reference, you may compare your outbound NAT rule settings to those in Figure 20.5

After you click Save on the NAT rule, and then click Apply Changes, new connections leaving the WAN will now be translated to the CARP IP. You can confirm this with a web site that displays the IP address from which is it being accessed, such as http://www.pfsense.org/ip.php.

You should also see the properly setup outbound NAT rule in the list, as in Figure 20.6.

20.4.2.4   Configure pfsync

The next task is to configure the pfsync interface that will be the line of communication between the primary and backup firewall. Navigate to Interfaces → OPT1 to set this up. If you do not have an OPT1 interface yet, you will need to assign it under Interfaces → (assign) (see Section 4.3.1).

Only a few options need to be set, as shown in Figure 20.7. The interface needs to be enabled, and it would help to use **pfsync** for its name. It should be set for a static IP, and given the address decided upon earlier for the primary side of pfsync, **172.16.1.2/24**.

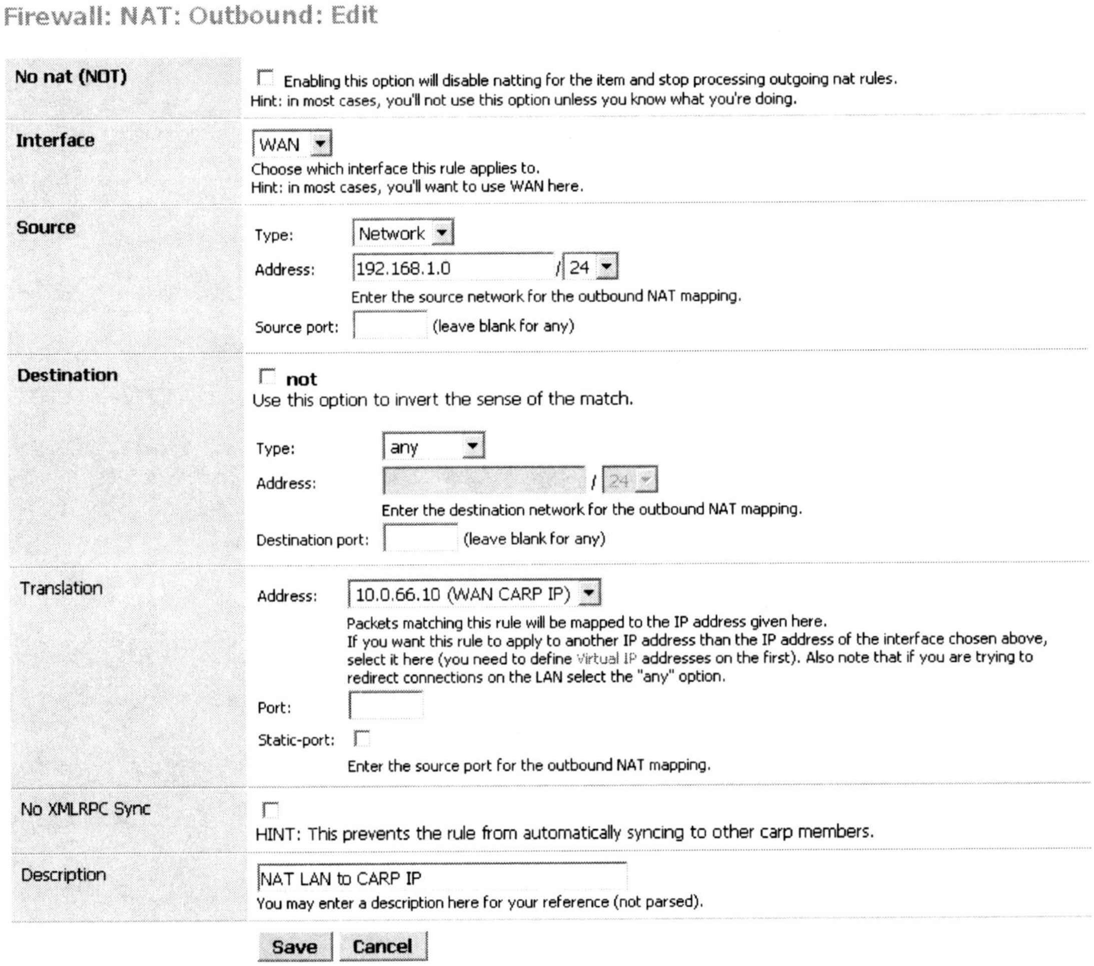

Firewall: NAT: Outbound: Edit

No nat (NOT)	☐ Enabling this option will disable natting for the item and stop processing outgoing nat rules. Hint: in most cases, you'll not use this option unless you know what you're doing.
Interface	WAN ▾ Choose which interface this rule applies to. Hint: in most cases, you'll want to use WAN here.
Source	Type: Network ▾ Address: 192.168.1.0 / 24 ▾ Enter the source network for the outbound NAT mapping. Source port: (leave blank for any)
Destination	☐ **not** Use this option to invert the sense of the match. Type: any ▾ Address: / 24 ▾ Enter the destination network for the outbound NAT mapping. Destination port: (leave blank for any)
Translation	Address: 10.0.66.10 (WAN CARP IP) ▾ Packets matching this rule will be mapped to the IP address given here. If you want this rule to apply to another IP address than the IP address of the interface chosen above, select it here (you need to define Virtual IP addresses on the first). Also note that if you are trying to redirect connections on the LAN select the "any" option. Port: Static-port: ☐ Enter the source port for the outbound NAT mapping.
No XMLRPC Sync	☐ HINT: This prevents the rule from automatically syncing to other carp members.
Description	NAT LAN to CARP IP You may enter a description here for your reference (not parsed).

Save   Cancel

Figure 20.5: Outbound NAT Entry

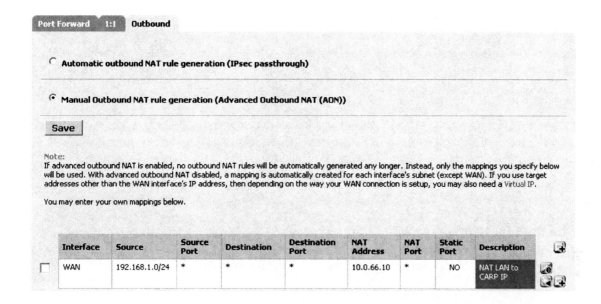

Figure 20.6: Advanced Outbound NAT Configuration

Interfaces: Optional 1 (OPT1)

Optional Interface Configuration

☑ **Enable Optional 1 interface**

Description	pfsync
	Enter a description (name) for the interface here.

IP configuration

Bridge with	none ▼
IP address	172.16.1.2 / 24 ▼
Gateway	
	If you have multiple WAN connections, enter the next hop gateway (router) IP address here. Otherwise, leave this option blank.

Figure 20.7: pfsync Interface Configuration

When you have finished entering the information for the pfsync interface, click Save.

The pfsync interface will also need a firewall rule to allow traffic from the backup. Go to Firewall → Rules, and click the pfsync tab. Add a new firewall rule that will allow traffic of any protocol from any source to any destination. Since this will only be a direct private connection with a crossover cable, it is safe to allow all traffic from the pfsync peer.

20.4.2.5   Modifying the DHCP Server

If pfSense is acting as a DHCP server, you need to instruct it to assign a CARP IP as the gateway IP. Otherwise pfSense will use its default behavior of assigning the IP configured on that interface as the gateway. That IP is specific to the primary firewall, so you need to change to a CARP IP for failover to work for your DHCP client systems.

Browse to Services → DHCP Server. Change the Gateway field to **192.168.1.1**, the shared CARP LAN IP. Set the Failover peer IP to the actual LAN IP of the backup system, **192.168.1.3**. This will allow the DHCP service on both systems to maintain a common set of leases.

Save, then Apply Changes.

20.4.3   Configuring the secondary firewall

Next the interfaces, IP addresses, and firewall rules on the secondary need to be configured.

20.4.3.1   Interface assignment and IP addressing

Before plugging in the WAN, LAN, or pfsync interfaces, power on the system and go through the installation and interface assignment as you did for the primary firewall. Set the LAN IP from the console to the previously designated backup LAN IP of **192.168.1.3**, set the DHCP settings the same as the primary, and then it should be safe to plug in the network connections.

You should then login to the web interface and go through the setup wizard, just as was done on the primary. Configure the WAN IP, and set the admin password to the same value as that on the primary.

You will also need to setup the sync interface as in Section 20.4.2.4, but with the IP address chosen for the backup system

20.4.3.2   Firewall rules

You will need a temporary firewall rule to allow the initial configuration sync to happen. Go to Firewall → Rules, and click the pfsync tab. Add a new firewall rule that will allow traffic of any protocol from any source to any destination. Put "temp" in the description so you can be sure that it has been replaced later. The rule should look like Figure 20.8

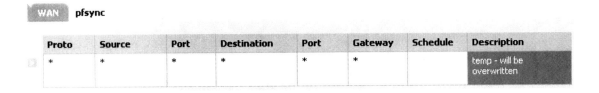

Proto	Source	Port	Destination	Port	Gateway	Schedule	Description
*	*	*	*	*	*		temp - will be overwritten

Figure 20.8: Firewall rule on pfsync interface

20.4.4   Setting up configuration synchronization

The final step is to configure the configuration synchronization between the primary and backup. On the master firewall only, go to Firewall → Virtual IPs, and click on the CARP Settings tab.

Check Synchronize Enabled, and pick `pfsync` as the Synchronize Interface. For the pfsync sync peer IP, enter the IP address for the backup system's pfsync interface, `172.16.1.3`. Check all of the remaining boxes on the screen, and enter the backup system's pfsync IP again in Synchronize to IP. Finally, enter the WebGUI admin password in the Remote System Password box. Click Save when finished.

When the synchronization settings are saved on the primary, it will automatically copy the settings from the primary to the backup for each selected option on the CARP Settings page. This includes the proper outbound NAT settings for CARP, the firewall rules for the pfsync interface, and even the CARP VIPs. Within 30 seconds, the initial configuration sync should have finished.

The DHCP server settings are not synchronized, so changes on the backup system will be necessary to set the CARP IP as the gateway, and to use the primary's LAN IP address as the DHCP failover peer, as in Section 20.4.2.5.

If the settings synchronized from the primary to the backup, then you know that the sync interface is connected and working properly. If not, you can go to Diagnostics → Ping, pick the pfsync interface, and attempt to ping the pfsync IP address of the opposing system. If that does not work, check that you are using a crossover cable and/or have a link light on the pfsync interface of both systems.

The CARP pair will now be active, but you will still need to check the status and test that failover is working properly. Skip down to Section 20.6 for the rest.

Note

You should *not* configure synchronization from the backup firewall to the master firewall. There are protections that should prevent this synchronization loop from causing harm, but it will clutter your logs with error messages and should never be configured this way.

20.5   Multi-WAN with CARP

You can also deploy CARP for firewall redundancy in a multi-WAN configuration, as long as all your WAN interfaces have at least 3 static IPs each. This section details the VIP and NAT configuration needed for a dual WAN CARP deployment. This section only covers topics specific to CARP and multi-WAN.

20.5.1   Determine IP Address Assignments

For this example, four IPs will be used on each WAN. Each firewall needs an IP, plus one CARP IP for Outbound NAT, plus one for a 1:1 NAT that will be used for an internal mail server in the DMZ segment.

20.5.1.1   WAN and WAN2 IP Addressing

Table 20.4 and Table 20.5 show the IP addressing for both WANs. In most environments these will be public IPs.

IP Address	Usage
10.0.66.10	Shared CARP IP for Outbound NAT
10.0.66.11	Primary firewall WAN IP
10.0.66.12	Secondary firewall WAN IP
10.0.66.13	Shared CARP IP for 1:1 NAT

Table 20.4: WAN IP Addressing

IP Address	Usage
10.0.64.90	Shared CARP IP for Outbound NAT
10.0.64.91	Primary firewall WAN2 IP
10.0.64.92	Secondary firewall WAN2 IP
10.0.64.93	Shared CARP IP for 1:1 NAT

Table 20.5: WAN2 IP Addressing

20.5.1.2   LAN Addressing

The LAN subnet is 192.168.1.0/24. For this example, the LAN IPs will be assigned as follows.

IP Address	Usage
192.168.1.1	CARP shared IP
192.168.1.2	Primary firewall LAN IP
192.168.1.3	Secondary firewall LAN IP

Table 20.6: LAN IP Address Assignments

20.5.1.3   DMZ Addressing

The DMZ subnet is 192.168.2.0/24. For this example, the LAN IPs will be assigned as follows in Table 20.7.

20.5.1.4   pfsync Addressing

There will be no shared CARP IP on this interface because there is no need for one. These IPs are used only for communication between the firewalls. For this example, 172.16.1.0/24 will be used as

IP Address	Usage
192.168.2.1	CARP shared IP
192.168.2.2	Primary firewall DMZ IP
192.168.2.3	Secondary firewall DMZ IP

Table 20.7: DMZ IP Address Assignments

the pfsync subnet. Only two IPs will be used, but a /24 is used to be consistent with the other internal interfaces. For the last octet of the IP addresses, the same last octet as that firewall's LAN IP is chosen for consistency.

IP Address	Usage
172.16.1.2	Primary firewall LAN IP
172.16.1.3	Secondary firewall LAN IP

Table 20.8: pfsync IP Address Assignments

20.5.2 NAT Configuration

The NAT configuration when using CARP is the same as without it, though you need to use only CARP VIPs, or public IPs in a subnet routed to one of your CARP IPs to ensure these addresses are always accessible. See Chapter 7 for more information on NAT configuration.

20.5.3 Firewall Configuration

With Multi-WAN you need a policy for the local network to route to the default gateway otherwise when you attempt to send traffic to the CARP address it will instead go out a secondary WAN connection.

You need to add a rule at the *top* of the firewall rules for all internal interfaces which will direct traffic for all local networks to the default gateway. The important part is the gateway needs to be default for this rule and not one of the failover or load balance connections. The destination for this rule should be the local LAN network, or an alias containing any locally reachable networks.

20.5.4 Multi-WAN CARP with DMZ Diagram

Due to the additional WAN and DMZ elements, a diagram of this layout is much more complex as can be seen in Figure 20.9.

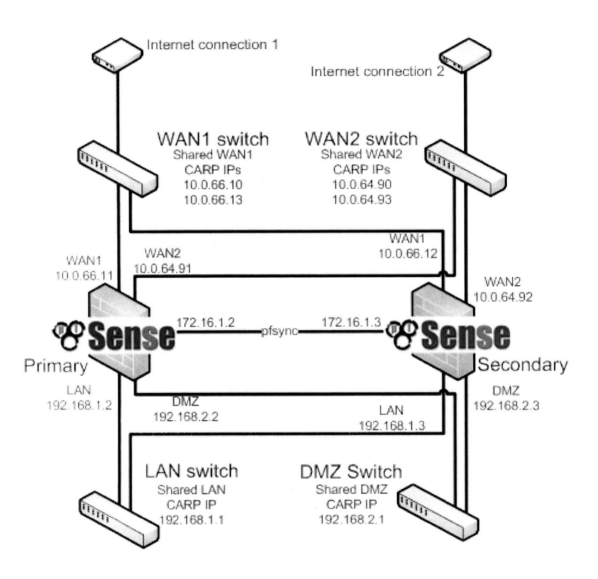

Figure 20.9: Diagram of Multi-WAN CARP with DMZ

20.6 Verifying Failover Functionality

Since using CARP is about high availability, it should be thoroughly tested before being placed into production. The most important part of that testing is making sure that the CARP peers will failover gracefully during system outages.

If any actions in this section do not work as expected, see Section 20.10.

20.6.1 Check CARP status

On both systems, navigate to Status → CARP (failover). The primary should show MASTER for the status of all CARP VIPs. The backup system should show BACKUP as the status. If the backup system instead shows DISABLED, click the Enable CARP button, and then refresh the Status → CARP (failover) page. It should now show up correctly.

20.6.2 Check Configuration Replication

Navigate to key locations on the backup router, such as Firewall → Rules and Firewall → NAT and ensure that rules created only on the primary system are being replicated to the backups.

If you followed the example earlier in this chapter, you should see that your "temp" firewall rule on the pfsync interface has been replaced by the rule from the primary.

20.6.3 Check DHCP Failover Status

If you have configured DHCP failover, its status can be checked by going to Status → DHCP Leases. A new section will appear at the top of the page containing the status of the DHCP Failover pool, as in Figure 20.10.

Failover Group	My State	Since	Peer State	Since
"dhcp0"	normal	2009/07/21 16:33:03	normal	2009/07/21 12:24:34

Figure 20.10: DHCP Failover Pool Status

20.6.4 Test CARP Failover

Now for the real failover test. Before starting, make sure that you can surf from a client behind the CARP pair with both pfSense firewalls online and running. Once that is confirmed to work, it would be an excellent time to make a backup.

For the actual test, unplug the primary from the network or shut it down. You should be able to keep surfing the Internet through the backup router. Check Status → CARP (failover) again on the backup and it should now report that it is MASTER for the LAN and the WAN CARP VIPs.

Now bring the primary system back online and it should regain its role as MASTER, and the backup system should demote itself to BACKUP once again, and Internet connectivity should still work properly.

You should test the CARP pair in as many failure scenarios as possible. Some other individual tests may include:

- Unplug the WAN or LAN cable

- Pull the power plug of the primary

- Disable CARP on the primary

- Test with each system individually (power off backup, then power back on and shut down the primary)

- Download a file or try streaming audio/video during the failover

- Try a continuous ping to an Internet host during the failover

20.7   Providing Redundancy Without NAT

As mentioned earlier, only CARP VIPs provide redundancy and they can only be used in conjunction with NAT. You can also provide redundancy for routed public IP subnets with CARP. This section describes this type of configuration, which is common in large networks, ISP and wireless ISP networks, and co-location environments.

20.7.1   Public IP Assignments

You will need at least a /29 public IP block for the WAN side of pfSense, which provides six usable IP addresses. Only three are required for a two firewall deployment, but this is the smallest IP subnet that will accommodate three IP addresses. Each firewall requires one IP, and you need at least one CARP VIP on the WAN side.

The second public IP subnet will be routed to one of your CARP VIPs by your ISP, co-location provider, or your upstream router if you control that portion of the network. Because this subnet is being routed to a CARP VIP, the routing will not be dependent upon a single firewall. For the depicted example configuration in this chapter, a /23 public IP subnet will be used and it will be subnetted into two /24 networks.

20.7.2   Network Overview

The example network depicted here is a co-location environment consisting of two pfSense installs with four interfaces each — WAN, LAN, DBDMZ, and pfsync. This network contains a number of web and database servers. It is not based on any real network, but there are countless production deployments similar to this.

20.7.2.1   WAN Network

The WAN side is where your network connects to the upstream network, either your ISP, co-location provider, or your upstream router.

20.7.2.2   LAN Network

LAN in pfSense is a fixed interface name, and it is a required interface in 1.2. LAN is not an appropriately descriptive name for this segment in this deployment. The LAN segment in this network contains web servers, and would be more appropriately described as a DMZ or web server segment, but will be LAN here because of this restriction. You may wish to add a fifth interface to the firewalls in this circumstance, and leave the interface assigned as LAN unplugged so your interfaces have more descriptive names. pfSense 2.0 allows renaming of the LAN interface, so this won't be a consideration in the future. Frequently VLANs are used in these types of deployments, in which case you can assign an unused VLAN to LAN, and use an appropriately named OPT interface for this internal network, rather than LAN.

20.7.2.3   DBDMZ Network

This segment is an OPT interface and contains the database servers. It is common to segregate the web and database servers into two networks in hosting environments. The database servers should never require direct access from the Internet, and hence are less subject to compromise than your web servers.

20.7.2.4   pfsync Network

The pfsync network in this diagram is used to replicate pfSense configuration changes via XML RPC and for pfsync to replicate state table changes between the two firewalls. As described earlier in this chapter, a dedicated interface for this purpose is recommended.

20.7.2.5   Network Layout

Figure 20.11 illustrates this network layout, including all routable IP addresses, a LAN, and the Database DMZ.

Note

Segments containing database servers typically do not need to be publicly accessible, and hence would more commonly use private IP subnets, but the example illustrated here can be used regardless of the function of the two internal subnets.

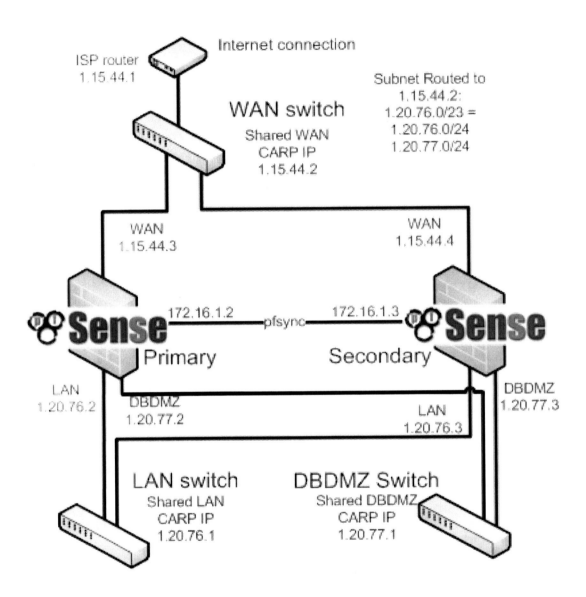

Figure 20.11: Diagram of CARP with Routed IPs

20.8 Layer 2 Redundancy

The diagrams earlier in this chapter did not describe layer 2 (switch) redundancy, to avoid throwing too many concepts at readers simultaneously. Now that you have an understanding of hardware redundancy with pfSense, this section covers the layer 2 design elements you should consider when planning a redundant network. This chapter assumes a two system deployment, though this scales to as many installations as you require.

If both your redundant pfSense systems are plugged into the same switch on any interface, that switch becomes a single point of failure. To avoid this single point of failure, the best choice is to deploy two switches for each interface (other than the dedicated pfsync interface).

The Routed IPs diagram is network-centric, not showing the switch infrastructure. The Figure 20.12 illustrates how that environment looks with a redundant switch infrastructure.

20.8.1 Switch Configuration

When using multiple switches, you should interconnect them. As long as you have a single connection between the two switches, and do not bridge on either of the firewalls, this is safe with any type of switch. Where using bridging, or where multiple interconnections exist between the switches, care must be taken to avoid layer 2 loops. You will need a managed switch that is capable of using Spanning Tree Protocol (STP) to detect and block ports that would otherwise create switch loops. When using STP, if an active link dies, e.g. switch failure, then a backup link can automatically be brought up in its place.

In pfSense 2.0, support will also be added for the `lagg(4)` link aggregation and link failover interface which will also allow you to have multiple network interfaces plugged into one or more switches for more fault tolerance.

20.8.2 Host Redundancy

It is more difficult to obtain host redundancy for your critical systems inside the firewall. Each system could have two network cards and a connection to each group of switches using Link Aggregation Control Protocol (LACP) or similar vendor-specific functionality. Servers could also have multiple network connections, and depending on the OS you may be able to run CARP on a set of servers so that they would be redundant as well. Providing host redundancy is more specific to the capabilities of your switches and your server operating system, which is outside the scope of this book.

20.8.3 Other Single Points of Failure

When trying to design a fully redundant network, there are many single points of failure that sometimes get missed. Depending on the level of uptime you are hoping to achieve, there are more and more things to consider than a simple switch failure. Here are a few more examples for redundancy on a wider scale:

- Each redundant segment should have isolated power.

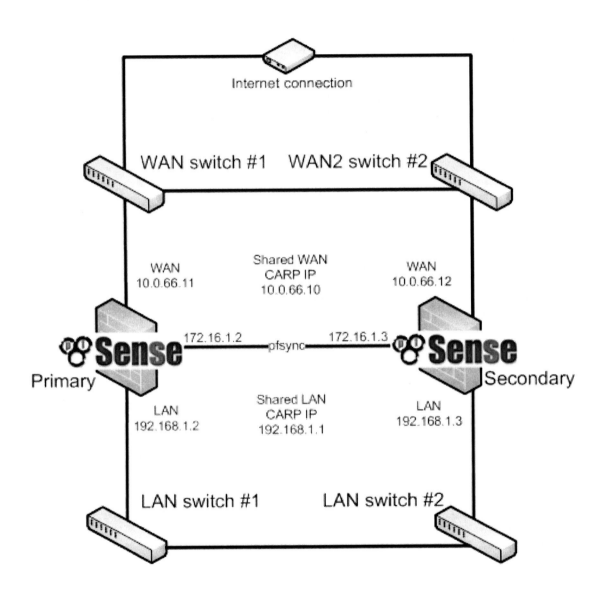

Figure 20.12: Diagram of CARP with Redundant Switches

- Redundant systems should be on separate breakers.
- Use multiple UPS banks/generators.
- Use multiple power providers, entering opposite sides of the building where possible.

- Even a Multi-WAN configuration is no guarantee of Internet uptime.

  - Use multiple Internet connection technologies (DSL, Cable, T1, Fiber, Wireless).
  - If any two carriers use the same pole/tunnel/path, they could both be knocked out at the same time.

- Have backup cooling, redundant chillers or a portable/emergency air conditioner.

- Consider placing the second set of redundant equipment in another room, another floor, or another building.

- Have a duplicate setup in another part of town or another city. Why buy one when you can buy two for twice the price?

- I hear hosting is cheap on Mars, but the latency is killer.

20.9   CARP with Bridging

CARP is not currently compatible with bridging in a native capacity. It requires a lot of manual intervention. The details of the process can be found in Section 9.5.2.

20.10   CARP Troubleshooting

CARP is a very complex technology, and with so many different ways to configure a failover cluster, it can be tricky to get things working properly. In this section, some common (and not so common) problems will be discussed and hopefully solved for the majority of cases. If you still have issues after reading this section, there is a dedicated CARP/VIPs board on the pfSense Forum.

Before going much farther, take the time to check all members of the CARP cluster to ensure that they have consistent configurations. Often, it helps to walk through the example setup, double checking all of the proper settings. Repeat the process on the backup members, and watch for any places where the configuration should be different on the backups. Be sure to check the CARP status (Section 20.6.1) and ensure CARP is enabled on all cluster members.

Errors relating to CARP will be logged in Status → System Logs, on the System tab. Check those logs on each system involved to see if there are any messages relating to XMLRPC sync, CARP state transitions, or other related errors.

20.10.1   Common Misconfigurations

There are three very common misconfigurations that happen which prevent CARP from working properly.

20.10.1.1   Use a different VHID on each CARP VIP

A different VHID must be used on each CARP VIP you create. Unfortunately it isn't always that simple. CARP is a multicast technology, and as such anything using CARP on the same network segment must use a unique VHID. VRRP also uses a similar protocol as CARP, so you also must ensure there are no conflicts with VRRP VHIDs, such as if your provider or another router on your network is using VRRP.

The best way around this is to use a unique set of VHIDs. If you are on a known safe private network, start numbering at 1. If you are on a network where VRRP or CARP are conflicting, you may have to consult with the administrator of that network to find a free block of VHIDs.

20.10.1.2   Incorrect Times

Check that all systems involved are properly synchronizing their clocks and have valid time zones, especially if running in a Virtual Machine. If the clocks are too far apart, some synchronization tasks like DHCP failover will not work properly.

20.10.1.3   Incorrect Subnet Mask

You must use the real subnet mask for a CARP VIP, **not** /32. This must match the subnet mask for the IP address on the interface to which the CARP IP is assigned.

20.10.1.4   IP Address for CARP Interface

The interface upon which the CARP IP resides must already have another IP defined directly on the interface (VLAN, LAN, WAN, OPT) before it can be utilized.

20.10.2   Incorrect Hash Error

There are a few reasons why this error might pop up in the system logs, some more worrisome than others.

If CARP is not working properly when you see this error, it could be due to a configuration mismatch. Ensure that for a given VIP, that the VHID, password, and IP address/subnet mask all match.

If your settings appear to be proper and CARP still does not work while generating this error message, then there may be multiple CARP instances on the same broadcast domain. You may need to disable CARP and monitor the network with **tcpdump** (Chapter 25) to check for other CARP or CARP-like traffic, and adjust your VHIDs appropriately.

If CARP is working properly, and you see this message when the system boots up, it may be disregarded. It is normal for this message to be seen when booting, as long as CARP continues to function properly (primary shows MASTER, backup shows BACKUP for status).

20.10.3 Both Systems Appear as MASTER

This will happen if the backup cannot see the CARP advertisements from the master. Check for firewall rules, connectivity trouble, switch configurations. Also check the system logs for any relevant errors that might lead to a solution. If you are seeing this in a Virtual Machine (VM) Product such as ESX, see Section 20.10.5.

20.10.4 Master system is stuck as BACKUP

In some cases, this is may happen normally for about 5 minutes after a system comes back to life. However, certain hardware failures or other error conditions can cause a server to silently take on a high advskew of 240 in order to signal that it still has a problem and should not become master. You can check this from the shell or Diagnostics → Command.

```
# ifconfig carp0
carp0: flags=49<UP,LOOPBACK,RUNNING> mtu 1500
   inet 10.0.66.10 netmask 0xffffff80
   carp: BACKUP vhid 1 advbase 1 advskew 240
```

In that case, you should isolate that firewall and perform further hardware testing.

20.10.5 Issues inside of Virtual Machines (ESX)

When using CARP inside of a Virtual Machine, especially VMware ESX, some special configurations are needed:

1. Enable promiscuous mode on the vSwitch.

2. Enable "MAC Address changes".

3. Enable "Forged transmits".

Additionally there is a bug in VMware's virtual switch functionality where multicast traffic gets looped back to the sending system where multiple physical NICs are connected to a vSwitch. CARP does not ignore such traffic, since on a normally functioning network that will never happen, and sees it as another host claiming to be the master. Hence both firewalls will always be stuck in backup mode. There are some patches being tested to provide a work around for CARP in this situation, and VMware has been notified of the vSwitch bug, so it may not be a problem in the future.

20.10.6 Configuration Synchronization Problems

Double check the following items when problems with configuration synchronization are encountered:

- The username must be the same on all nodes.

- The password in the configuration synchronization on the master must match the password on the backup.

- The WebGUI must be on the same port on all nodes.

- The WebGUI must be using the same protocol (HTTP or HTTPS) on all nodes.

- You must permit traffic to the WebGUI port on the interface that you are syncing to.

- The pfsync interface must be enabled and configured on all nodes.

- Remove **all** special characters from every description that you are syncing: NAT rules, Firewall rules, Virtual IPs, etc. This should no longer pose a problem, but should you have difficulties it is a good thing to try.

- Verify that **only** the master sync node has the sync options enabled.

- Ensure no IP address is specified in the Synchronize To IP on the backup node.

20.10.7 CARP and Multi-WAN Troubleshooting

If you have trouble reaching CARP VIPs from when dealing with Multi-WAN, double check that you have a rule such as one mentioned in Section 20.5.3

20.10.8 Removing a CARP VIP

If a CARP IP needs to be removed for whatever reason, the host system must be rebooted. Removing a CARP IP from a live system can result in a kernel panic or other system instability. More recent versions of pfSense will warn about this fact, and prompt for a reboot when a CARP VIP removal is attempted.

Chapter 21

Services

The base install of pfSense comes along with a set of services which add some fundamental functionality and flexibility to the firewall system. As the name implies, the options found within control services that the router will provide to clients, or in the case of routing services, other routers as well. These services include providing DHCP addressing, DNS resolution and Dynamic DNS, SNMP, UPnP and much more. This chapter covers the services available in the base system. There are many more services that can be added with packages, which will be covered later in the book.

21.1   DHCP Server

The DHCP server assigns IP addresses and related configuration options to client PCs on your network. It is enabled by default on the LAN interface, and with the default LAN IP of 192.168.1.1, the default scope range would be 192.168.1.10 through 192.168.1.199. In its default configuration, pfSense assigns its LAN IP as the gateway and DNS server if the DNS Forwarder is enabled. There are many options available to adjust in the WebGUI.

21.1.1   Configuration

To alter the behavior of the DHCP server, go to Services → DHCP Server. From there you can alter the behavior of the DHCP server, along with static IP mappings and some related options like static ARP.

21.1.1.1   Choosing an Interface

On the DHCP configuration page there is a tab for each non-WAN interface. Each interface has its own separate DHCP server configuration, and they may be enabled or disabled independently of one another. Before making any changes, ensure that you are looking at the tab for the right interface.

21.1.1.2   Service Options

The first setting on each tab tells pfSense whether or not to handle DHCP requests on that interface. To enable DHCP on the interface, check the Enable DHCP server on [name] interface box. To disable the service, uncheck that same box.

Normally, the DHCP server will answer requests from any client which requests a lease. In most environments this is normal and acceptable behavior, but in more restricted or secure environments this behavior is undesirable. With the Deny unknown clients option set, only clients with static mappings defined will receive leases, which is a more secure practice but is much less convenient.

Note

This will protect against low-knowledge users and people who casually plug in devices. Be aware, however, that a user with knowledge of your network could hardcode an IP address, subnet mask, gateway, and DNS which will still give them access. They could also alter/spoof their MAC address to match a valid client and still obtain a lease. Where possible, couple this setting with static ARP entries, access control in a switch that will limit MAC addresses to certain switch ports for increased security, and turn off or disable switch ports which you know should not be in use.

The IP address for the interface being configured is also shown, along with its subnet mask. Underneath that line the available range of IP addresses for that subnet mask is printed, which may help determine what starting and ending addresses to use for the DHCP pool range.

21.1.1.3   Address Range (DHCP Pool)

The two boxes for Range tell pfSense what will be the first and last address for use as a DHCP pool. The range must be entered with the lower number first, followed by the higher number. For example, the default LAN DHCP range is based off of the subnet for the default LAN IP address. It would be **192.168.1.10** to **192.168.1.199**. This range can be as large or as small as your network needs, but it must be wholly contained within the subnet for the interface being configured.

21.1.1.4   WINS Servers

Two WINS Servers (Windows Internet Name Service) may be defined that will be passed on to clients. If you have one or more WINS servers available, enter their IP addresses here. The actual servers do not have to be on this subnet, but be sure that the proper routing and firewall rules are in place to let them be reached by client PCs. If this is left blank, no WINS servers will be sent to the client.

21.1.1.5   DNS Servers

The DNS Servers may or may not need filled in, depending on your setup. If you are using the DNS Forwarder built into pfSense to handle DNS, leave these fields blank and pfSense will automatically assign itself as the DNS server for client PCs. If the DNS forwarder is disabled and these fields are left blank, pfSense will pass on whichever DNS servers are assigned to it under System → General Setup.

If you wish to use custom DNS Servers instead of the automatic choices, fill in the IP addresses for up to two DNS servers here. (See Section 24.2 for an example.) In networks with Windows servers, especially those employing Active Directory, it is recommended to use those servers for client DNS. When using the DNS forwarder in combination with CARP, specify the CARP IP on this interface here.

21.1.1.6 Gateway

The Gateway option may also be left blank if pfSense is the gateway for your network. Should that not be the case, fill in the IP address for the gateway to be used by clients on this interface. When using CARP, fill in the CARP IP on this interface here.

21.1.1.7 DHCP Lease Times

The Default lease time and Maximum lease time control how long a DHCP lease will last. The default lease time is used when a client does not request a specific expiration time. If the client does specify how long it wants a lease to last, the maximum lease time setting will let you limit that to a reasonable amount of time. These values are specified in seconds, and the default values are 7200 seconds (2 hours) for the default time, and 86400 seconds (1 day) for the maximum time.

21.1.1.8 Failover

If this system is part of a failover setup such as a CARP cluster, enter the Failover peer IP address next. This should be the real IP address of the other system in this subnet, not a shared CARP address.

21.1.1.9 Static ARP

The Enable Static ARP entries checkbox works similarly to denying unknown MAC addresses from obtaining leases, but takes it a step further in that it would also restrict any unknown machine from communicating with the pfSense router. This would stop would-be abusers from hardcoding an unused address on this subnet, circumventing DHCP restrictions.

Note
When using static ARP, be careful to ensure that all systems that need to communicate with the router are listed in the static mappings list before activating this option, especially the system being used to connect to the pfSense WebGUI.

21.1.1.10 Dynamic DNS

For Dynamic DNS settings, click the Advanced button to the right of that field. To enable this function, check the box and then fill in a domain name for the DHCP hostnames. If you are using pfSense's DNS forwarder, you may instead leave this option blank and configure the setting inside of the DNS forwarder setup.

21.1.1.11   NTP Servers

To specify NTP Servers (Network Time Protocol Servers), click the Advanced button to the right of that field, and enter IP addresses for up to two NTP servers.

21.1.1.12   Network Booting

To view the Enable Network booting settings, click the Advanced button to the right of that field. You may then check the box to turn on the feature, and then enter an IP address from which boot images are available, and a filename for the boot image. Both of these fields must be configured for network booting to work properly.

21.1.1.13   Save Settings

After making these changes, be sure to click Save before attempting to create static mappings. The settings will be lost if you navigate away from this page without saving first.

21.1.1.14   Static Mappings

Static DHCP mappings allow you to express a preference for which IP address will be assigned to a given PC, based on its MAC address. In network where unknown clients are denied, this also serves as a list of "known" clients which are allowed to receive leases or have static ARP entries. Static mappings can be added in one of two ways. First, from this screen, click 🔲 and you will be presented with a form for adding a static mapping. The other method is to add them from the DHCP leases view, which is covered later in this chapter.

Of the four fields on this screen, only the MAC address is necessary. By entering only the MAC address, it will added to the list of known clients for use when the Deny unknown clients option is set. There is a link beside the MAC address field that will copy the MAC address of the PC being used to access the WebGUI. This is provided as a convenience, versus obtaining the MAC address in other, more complicated, ways.

Note

The MAC address can be obtained from a command prompt on most platforms. On UNIX-based or UNIX-work-alike operating systems including Mac OS X, typing "`ifconfig -a`" will show the MAC address for each interface. On Windows-based platforms, "`ipconfig /all`" will show the MAC address. The MAC address may also sometimes be found upon a sticker on the network card, or near the network card for integrated adapters. For hosts on the same subnet, the MAC can be determined by pinging the IP address of the host and then running "`arp -a`".

The IP address field is needed if this will be a static IP mapping instead of only informing the DHCP server that the client is valid. This IP address is really a *preference*, and not a reservation. Assigning an IP address here will not prevent someone else from using the same IP address. If this IP address is in use when this client requests a lease, it will instead receive one from the general pool. For this reason, the pfSense WebGUI does not allow you to assign static IP mappings inside of your DHCP pool.

A Hostname may also be set, and it does not have to match the actual hostname set on the client. The hostname set here will be used when registering DHCP addresses in the DNS forwarder.

The Description is cosmetic, and available for your use to help track any additional information about this entry. It could be the name of the person who uses the PC, its function, the reason it needed a static address, or the administrator who added the entry. It may also be left blank.

Click Save to finish editing the static mapping and return to the DHCP Server configuration page.

21.1.2 Status

You will find the status of the DHCP server service itself under Status → Services. If it is enabled, its status should be shown as Running, as in Figure 21.1. The buttons on the right side allow you to restart or stop the DHCP server service. Restarting should never be necessary as pfSense will automatically restart the service when configuration changes are made that require a restart. Stopping the service is also likely never necessary, as the service will stop when you disable all instances of the DHCP server.

Service	Description	Status	
dnsmasq	DNS Forwarder	▢ Running	⟳ ▸
dhcpd	DHCP Service	▢ Running	⟳ ▸

Figure 21.1: DHCP Daemon Service Status

21.1.3 Leases

You can view the currently assigned leases at Diagnostics → DHCP leases. This screen shows the assigned IP address, the MAC address it is assigned to, the hostname (if any) that the client sent as part of the DHCP request, the beginning and end times of the lease, whether the machine is currently online, and whether the lease is active, expired, or a static registration.

21.1.3.1 View inactive leases

By default, only active and static leases are shown, but you may see everything, including the expired leases, by clicking the Show all configured leases button. To reduce the view back to normal, click the Show active and static leases only button.

21.1.3.2 Wake on LAN Integration

If you click on the MAC address, or the Wake on LAN button to the right of the lease, pfSense will send a Wake on LAN packet to that host. For more details about Wake on LAN, see Section 21.8.

21.1.3.3   Add static mapping

To make a dynamic lease into a static mapping, click the ⊞ to the right of the lease. This will pre-fill the MAC address of that host into the "Edit static mapping" screen. You'll need to add the desired IP address, hostname and description and click **Save**. Any existing leases for this MAC address will be cleared out of the leases file when saving the new entry.

21.1.3.4   Delete a lease

While viewing the leases, you may delete an inactive or expired lease manually by clicking the ⊠ button at the end of a line. This option is not available for active or static leases, only for offline or expired leases.

21.1.4   DHCP Service Logs

The DHCP daemon will log its activity to Status → System Logs, on the DHCP tab. Each DHCP request and response will be displayed, along with other status and error messages.

21.2   DHCP Relay

DHCP requests are broadcast traffic. Broadcast traffic is limited to the broadcast domain where it is initiated. If you need to provide DHCP service on a network segment without a DHCP server, you use DHCP relay to forward those requests to a defined server on another segment. It is not possible to run both a DHCP server and a DHCP Relay at the same time. To enable the DHCP relay you must first disable the DHCP server on each interface.

Once the DHCP server is disabled, visit Services → DHCP Relay. As with the DHCP server, there is a tab for each interface. Click on the interface upon which you want run the DHCP relay, then check the box next to Enable DHCP relay on [name] interface, which will also let you set the other available options.

If you check Append circuit ID and agent ID to requests, the DHCP relay will append the circuit ID (pfSense interface number) and the agent ID to the DHCP request. This may be required by the DHCP server on the other side, or may help distinguish where the requests originated.

The option to Proxy requests to DHCP server on WAN subnet does just what it says. If activated, it will pass DHCP requests from clients on this interface to the DHCP server which assigned the IP address to the WAN interface. Alternately, you may fill in the IP address of the DHCP server to which the requests should be proxied.

21.3   DNS Forwarder

The DNS Forwarder in pfSense is a caching DNS resolver. It is enabled by default, and uses the DNS servers configured in System → General Setup, or those obtained from your ISP for dynamically configured WAN interfaces (DHCP, PPPoE, and PPTP). For static IP WAN connections, you must enter DNS servers in System → General Setup or during the setup wizard for the DNS forwarder to function. You can also use statically configured DNS servers with dynamically configured WAN interfaces by unchecking the "Allow DNS server list to be overridden by DHCP/PPP on WAN" box on the System → General Setup page.

In prior versions, pfSense initially tried the first configured DNS server when attempting to resolve a DNS name, and moved on to subsequently configured DNS servers if the first failed to resolve. This could cause long delays if one or more of the available DNS servers was unreachable. In pfSense 1.2.3 and later this behavior has been changed to query all DNS servers at once, and the only the first response received is used and cached. This results in much faster DNS service, and can help smooth over problems that stem from DNS servers which are intermittently slow or have high latency.

21.3.1 DNS Forwarder Configuration

The DNS forwarder configuration is found under Services → DNS Forwarder.

21.3.1.1 Enable DNS Forwarder

Checking this box turns on the DNS forwarder, or uncheck if you wish to disable this functionality.

21.3.1.2 Register DHCP leases in DNS forwarder

If you want your internal machine names for DHCP clients to resolve in DNS, check this box. This only works for machines that specify a host name in their DHCP requests.

21.3.1.3 Register DHCP static mappings in DNS forwarder

This works the same as the Register DHCP leases in DNS forwarder option, except that it registers the DHCP static mapping addresses.

21.3.1.4 Host Overrides

The first section at the bottom of the DNS forwarder screen is where you can specify overrides for DNS host name resolution. Here you can configure a specific host name to resolve differently than it otherwise would via the DNS servers used by the DNS forwarder. This is useful for split DNS configurations (see Section 7.5.2), and as a semi-effective means of blocking access to certain specific websites.

Figure 21.2 illustrates a DNS override for an internal web server (example.com and www.example.com) as well as an example of blocking access to myspace.com and www.myspace.com.

Host	Domain	IP	Description
	example.com	192.168.1.100	www override
	myspace.com	127.0.0.1	hack block
www	myspace.com	127.0.0.1	hack block
www	example.com	192.168.1.100	www override

Figure 21.2: DNS Override Example

Note

It is not recommended to use strictly the DNS override functionality as a means of blocking access to certain sites. There are countless ways to get around this. It will stop non-technical users, but is very easy to get around for those with more technical aptitude.

21.3.1.5   Domain Overrides

Domain overrides are found at the bottom of the DNS Forwarder screen. This allows you to specify a different DNS server to use for resolving a specific domain.

One example of where this is commonly deployed is in small business networks with a single internal server with Active Directory, usually Microsoft Small Business Server. The DNS requests for the Active Directory domain name must be resolved by the internal Windows Server for Active Directory to function properly. Adding an override for the Active Directory domain pointing to the internal Windows server's IP address ensures these records are resolved properly whether clients are using pfSense as a DNS server or the Windows Server itself.

In an Active Directory environment, your systems should always use your Windows DNS server as their primary DNS server so dynamic name registration functions properly. In environments with only one Windows DNS server, you should enable the DNS forwarder with an override for your Active Directory domain and use pfSense as the secondary DNS server for your internal machines. This ensures DNS resolution (except for Active Directory) does not have a single point of failure, and loss of the single server won't mean a complete Internet outage. The loss of a single server in such an environment will usually have significant consequences, but users will be more apt to leave you alone to fix the problem if they can still check out their lolcats, MySpace, Facebook, et al in the mean time.

Another common use of DNS overrides is to resolve internal DNS domains at remote sites using a DNS server at the main site accessible over VPN. In such environments you usually want to resolve all DNS queries at the central site for centralized control over DNS, however some organizations prefer letting Internet DNS resolve with pfSense at each site, and only forwarding queries for internal domains to the central DNS server. Note you will need a static route for this to function over IPsec. See Section 13.4.4 for more information.

21.4   Dynamic DNS

The Dynamic DNS client in pfSense allows you to register the IP address of your WAN interface with a variety of dynamic DNS service providers. This is useful when you want to remotely access dynamic

IP connections, most commonly used to connect to a VPN, web server, or mail server.

Note

This only works on your primary WAN interface. Any OPT interfaces cannot utilize the built in Dynamic DNS client. You can also only register one Dynamic DNS name. pfSense 2.0 supports as many different dynamic DNS services as you desire, allows registration of OPT WAN IPs, and enables the registration of your real public IP in environments where pfSense receives a private IP for WAN and is NATed upstream.

21.4.1 Using Dynamic DNS

pfSense allows registration with nine different dynamic DNS providers as of version 1.2.3. You can see the available providers by clicking the Service type drop down box. You can find out more about those providers by searching for their name to find their web site. Most offer a basic level service at no cost, and some offer additional premium services at a cost.

Once you decide on a provider, visit their website, register for an account and setup a hostname. The procedures for this vary for each provider, but they have instructions on their websites. After configuring your hostname with the provider, you then configure pfSense with those settings.

21.4.1.1 Service Type

Select your dynamic DNS provider here.

21.4.1.2 Hostname

Enter the hostname you created with your dynamic DNS provider.

21.4.1.3 MX

An MX (Mail Exchanger) record is how Internet mail servers know where to deliver mail for your domain. Some dynamic DNS providers will let you configure this via your dynamic DNS client. If yours does, enter the host name of the mail server that will receive Internet email for your dynamic DNS domain.

21.4.1.4 Wildcards

Enabling wildcard DNS on your dynamic DNS name means all host name queries will resolve to the IP address of your dynamic DNS host name. For example, if your host name is example.dyndns.org, enabling wildcard will make *.example.dyndns.org (a.example.dyndns.org, b.example.dyndns.org, etc.) resolve the same as example.dyndns.org.

21.4.1.5   Username and Password

This is where you enter the username and password for your dynamic DNS provider.

21.4.2   RFC 2136 Dynamic DNS updates

The RFC 2136 dynamic DNS updates functionality allows you to register a hostname on any DNS server supporting RFC 2136 updates. This can be used to update hostnames on BIND and Windows Server DNS servers, amongst others.

This can run simultaneously with one of the previously discussed dynamic DNS service providers, however is also limited to a single configuration and will only register the WAN IP, not those of any OPT WAN interfaces.

21.5   SNMP

The Simple Network Management Protocol (SNMP) daemon will allow you to remotely monitor some pfSense system parameters. Depending on the options chosen, you can monitor network traffic, network flows, pf queues, and general system information such as CPU, memory, and disk usage. The SNMP implementation used by pfSense is **bsnmpd**, which by default only has the most basic management information bases (MIBs) available, and is extended by loadable modules.[1] In addition to the SNMP daemon, it can also send traps to an SNMP server for certain events. These vary based on the modules loaded. For example, network link state changes will generate a trap if you have the MIB II module loaded. The SNMP service can be configured by browsing to Services → SNMP.

The easiest way to see what data is available would be to run **snmpwalk** against the pfSense system from another host with **net-snmp** or an equivalent installed. The full contents of the MIBs available are beyond the scope of this book, but there are plenty of print and online resources for SNMP, and some of the MIB trees are covered in RFCs. For example, the Host Resources MIB is defined by RFC 2790.

21.5.1   SNMP Daemon

These options dictate if, and how, the SNMP daemon will run. To turn the SNMP daemon on, check Enable. Once Enable has been checked, the other options may then be changed.

21.5.1.1   Polling Port

SNMP connections are all UDP, and SNMP clients default to using UDP port 161. This setting will cause the daemon to listen on a different port, and your SNMP client or polling agent should be changed to match.

---

[1] http://people.freebsd.org/~harti/bsnmp/

21.5.1.2   System location

This text field specifies what string will be returned when the system's location is queried via SNMP. You may follow whatever convention is needed for your organization. For some devices a city or state may be close enough, while others may need more specific detail such as which rack and position in which the system resides.

21.5.1.3   System contact

The system contact is also a text field that can be set however your needs require. It could be a name, an e-mail address, a phone number, or whatever is needed.

21.5.1.4   Read Community String

With SNMP, the community string acts as a kind of username and password in one. SNMP clients will need to use this community string when polling. The default value of "public" is common, so you should consider changing it to something else in addition to restricting access to the SNMP service with firewall rules.

21.5.2   SNMP Traps

To instruct the SNMP daemon to send SNMP traps, check Enable. Once Enable has been checked, the other options may then be changed.

21.5.2.1   Trap server

The trap server is the hostname or IP address to which SNMP traps should be forwarded.

21.5.2.2   Trap server port

By default, SNMP traps are set on UDP port 162. If your SNMP trap receiver is set for a different port, adjust this setting to match.

21.5.2.3   SNMP trap string

This string will be sent along with any SNMP trap that is generated.

21.5.3   Modules

The loadable modules available here allow the SNMP daemon to understand and respond to queries for more system information. Each module loaded will consume additional resources. As such, ensure that only the modules that will actually be used are loaded.

21.5.3.1 MibII

This module provides information specified in the standard MIB II tree, which covers networking information and interfaces. Having this module loaded will, among other things, let you query network interface information including status, hardware and IP addresses, the amount of data transmitted and received, and much more.

21.5.3.2 Netgraph

The netgraph module provides some netgraph-related information such as netgraph node names and statuses, hook peers, and errors.

21.5.3.3 PF

The pf module gives access to a wealth of information about pf. The MIB tree covers aspects of the ruleset, states, interfaces, tables, and ALTQ queues.

21.5.3.4 Host Resources

This module covers information about the host itself, including uptime, load average and processes, storage types and usage, attached system devices, and even installed software.

21.5.4 Bind to LAN interface only

This option will make the SNMP daemon listen on the LAN interface only. This eases communications over IPsec VPN tunnels, as it eliminates the need for the previously mentioned static route, but it also helps provide some extra security by reducing the service's exposure on other interfaces.

21.6 UPnP

Universal Plug and Play (UPnP) is a network service which allows software and devices to configure each other when attaching to a network. This includes creating their own NAT port forwards and associated firewall rules. The UPnP service on pfSense, found at Services → UPnP, will enable client PCs and other devices such as game consoles to automatically allow required traffic to reach them. There are many popular programs and systems which support UPnP, such as Skype, uTorrent, mIRC, IM clients, PlayStation 3, and XBox 360.

UPnP employs the Simple Service Discovery Protocol (SSDP) for network discovery, which uses UDP port 1900. The UPnP daemon used by pfSense, **miniupnpd**, also uses TCP port 2189. You may need to allow access to these services with firewall rules, especially if you have removed the default LAN-to-any rule, or in bridged configurations.

21.6.1 Security Concerns

The UPnP service is a classic example of the "Security vs. Convenience" trade-off. UPnP, by its very nature, is insecure. Any program on the network could allow in and forward any traffic — a potential security nightmare. On the other side, it can be a chore to enter and maintain NAT port forwards and their associated rules, especially when it comes to game consoles. There is a lot of guesswork and research involved to find the proper ports and settings, but UPnP *just works* and requires little administrative effort. Manual port forwards to accommodate these scenarios tend to be overly permissive, potentially exposing services that should not be open from the Internet. The port forwards are also always on, where UPnP may be temporary.

There are access controls present in the UPnP service configuration, which will help lock down who and what is allowed to make alterations. Over and above the built-in access controls, you can further control access with firewall rules. When properly controlled, UPnP can also be a little more secure by allowing programs to pick and listen on random ports, instead of always having the same port open and forwarded.

21.6.2 Configuration

The UPnP service is configured by browsing to Services → UPnP. Enable the service by checking the Enable UPnP box. When you are finished making any needed changes, which are described in the remainder of this section, click Save. The UPnP service will then be started automatically.

21.6.2.1 Interfaces

This setting lets you to pick the interfaces upon which UPnP is allowed to listen. More than one interface may be chosen by holding down **Ctrl** while clicking the additional interfaces. Deselecting an interface works the same way, hold **Ctrl** while clicking to remove the selection. If an interface is bridged to another, UPnP should only be selected on the "parent" interface, not the one which is bridged. For example, if you have OPT1 bridged to LAN, only enable UPnP on LAN.

21.6.2.2 Maximum Speeds

Starting with pfSense version 1.2.3, you may now set maximum download and upload speeds for ports opened by UPnP. These speeds are set in Kilobits per second, so to limit a download to 1.5Mbit/s, you would enter **1536** into the Maximum Download Speed field.

21.6.2.3 Override WAN address

By default, the UPnP service will configure port forwards and firewall rules to the WAN address. This setting will let you enter an alternate IP address, such as a secondary WAN address or a shared CARP address.

21.6.2.4   Traffic Shaping Queue

By default, rules created by UPnP will not assign traffic into a shaper queue. By entering the name of a queue into this field, traffic that passes due to a UPnP-created rule will fall into this queue. Choose the queue wisely, as any UPnP enabled device or program will use this queue. It could be Bittorrent, or it could be a game console, so choose a queue that has a priority that fits best with the traffic you expect to be most common.

21.6.2.5   Log Packets

When this box is checked, the port forwards generated by UPnP will be set to log, so that each connection made will have an entry in the firewall logs, found at Status → System Logs, on the Firewall tab.

21.6.2.6   Use System Uptime

By default, the UPnP daemon reports the service uptime when queried rather than the system uptime. Checking this option will cause it to report the actual system uptime instead.

21.6.2.7   Default Deny

If the By default deny access to UPnP option is enabled, then UPnP will only allow access to clients matching the access rules. This is a more secure method of controlling the service, but as discussed above, is also less convenient.

21.6.2.8   UPnP User Permissions

There are four fields for specifying user-defined access rules. If the default-deny option is chosen, you must set rules to allow access. Rules are formulated using the following format:

<allow|deny> <external port|port range> <internal IP|IP/CIDR> <internal port|port range>

21.6.2.8.1   UPnP User Permission Example 1

Deny access to port 80 forwarding from everything on the LAN, 192.168.1.1, with a /24 subnet.

deny 80 192.168.1.1/24 80

21.6.2.8.2   UPnP User Permission Example 2

Allow 192.168.1.10 to forward any unprivileged port.

allow 1024-65535 192.168.1.10 1024-65535

21.6.3 Status

The status of the UPnP service itself may be viewed at Status → Services. This will show if the service is running or stopped, and allow you to stop, start or restart the service. This should all be handled automatically, but may be controlled manually if needed. A list of currently forwarded ports and clients like that in Figure 21.3 may be viewed under Status → UPnP.

Status: UPnP Status

Clear

Port	Protocol	Internal IP	Description
58091	udp	192.168.10.245	Teredo
38343	udp	192.168.10.22	Skype UDP at 192.168.10.22:38343 (888)
38343	tcp	192.168.10.22	Skype TCP at 192.168.10.22:38343 (888)
50064	udp	192.168.10.245	Teredo
6909	tcp	192.168.10.22	uTorrent (TCP)
6909	udp	192.168.10.22	uTorrent (UDP)

Figure 21.3: UPnP status screen showing client PCs with forwarded ports

When the service is running it should also show up when you browse the network using a UPnP-aware Operating System like Windows 7 or Windows Vista, as shown by Figure 21.4. You can right click on the router's icon and then click View device webpage to open up the WebGUI in your default browser. If you right click on the router and click Properties, it will also show the pfSense version and IP address of the router.

◢ Network Infrastructure (3)

FreeBSD router   pfSense router

Linksys WRT54G

Figure 21.4: pfSense system as seen by Windows 7 when browsing the Network

21.6.4 Troubleshooting

Most issues with UPnP tend to involve bridging. In this case it is important that you have specific firewall rules to allow UPnP on UDP port 1900. Since it is multicast traffic, the destination should be the broadcast address for the subnet, or in some cases making it **any** will be necessary. Consult your firewall logs at Status → System Logs, on the firewall tab, to see if traffic is being blocked. Pay particular attention to the destination address, as it may be different than expected.

Further trouble with game consoles may also be alleviated by switching to manual outbound NAT and enabling Static Port. See Section 7.6.2 for more details.

21.7   OpenNTPD

The OpenNTPD service is a Network Time Protocol (NTP) daemon which will listen for requests from clients and allow them to synchronize their clock with that of the pfSense system. By running a local NTP server and using it for your clients, it reduces the load on the lower-stratum servers and can ensure that your systems can always reach a time server. Before delegating this task to your pfSense system, it is a good practice to ensure that it has an accurate clock and keeps time reasonably.

There is not much to configuring the OpenNTPD server, available at Services → OpenNTPD. Check the Enable box, pick which Interfaces it should listen upon, and click Save. More than one interface may be chosen by holding down **Ctrl** while clicking the additional interfaces. Deselecting an interface works the same way, hold **Ctrl** while clicking to remove the selection. The service will be started immediately, however there will be a several minute delay before it will service NTP requests, as the service ensures its time is accurate before answering requests.

OpenNTPD logs are kept under Status → System Logs, on the OpenNTPD tab. OpenNTPD has very little logging, unless there is a problem the service will never generate any log entries.

21.8   Wake on LAN

The Wake on LAN (WOL) page at Services → Wake on LAN can be used to wake up computers from a powered-off state by sending special "Magic Packets". The NIC in the computer that is to be woken up must support WOL and has to be configured properly. Typically there is a BIOS setting to enable WOL, and non-integrated adapters likely need a WOL cable connected between the NIC and a WOL header on the motherboard.

WOL has many potential uses. Typically, workstations and servers are kept running because of services they provide, files or printers they share, or for convenience. Using WOL would allow these to remain powered off, and conserve power. Should a service be required, the system can be woken up when needed. Another example would be if someone needs remote access to a system, but the user shut it down. Using WOL the machine can be awoken, and may then be accessed once it has booted.

WOL offers no inherent security. Any system on the same layer 2 network may transmit a WOL packet, and the packet will be accepted and obeyed. It is best to only configure WOL in the BIOS for machines that need it, and disable it in all others. There are a couple of vendor-specific WOL extensions that provide some extra security, but nothing universally supported.

21.8.1 Wake Up a Single Machine

To wake up a single machine, choose the Interface through which it can be reached, and enter the system's MAC address in the format of $xx:xx:xx:xx:xx:xx$. When you click Send, pfSense will transmit a WOL Magic Packet out the chosen interface, and if everything went as planned, the system should wake up. Keep in mind that systems will take some time to boot. It may be several minutes before the target system is available.

21.8.2 Storing MAC Addresses

To store a MAC address for later convenience, click the by the list of stored MAC addresses, and you will see a blank edit screen. Pick the Interface through which it can be reached, and enter the system's MAC address in the format of $xx:xx:xx:xx:xx:xx$. A description may also be entered for later reference, for example "Pat's PC" or "Sue's Server". Click Save when finished and you will be returned to the main WOL page and your new entry should be visible in the list at the bottom of the page.

Maintaining the entries is similar to other tasks in pfSense: Click to edit an existing entry, and click to remove an entry.

21.8.3 Wake a Single Stored Machine

To send a WOL Magic Packet to a system that has been previously stored, click its MAC address in the list of stored systems. The MAC address should be highlighted as a link. You will be taken back to the WOL page, with the system's interface and MAC address pre-filled in the form. Click Send and the Magic Packet will be sent.

21.8.4 Wake All Stored Machines

On the WOL page, there is a button which can be used to send a WOL Magic Packet to all stored systems. Click the button and the requests will be sent, with no other intervention required.

21.8.5 Wake from DHCP Leases View

To send a WOL Magic Packet from the DHCP Leases view at Diagnostics → DHCP leases, click its MAC address in the list of leases, which should be highlighted as a link. The WOL link will only be active for systems whose status is shown as "offline". You will be taken back to the WOL page, with the system's interface and MAC address pre-filled in the form. Click Send and the Magic Packet will be sent.

21.8.6   Save from DHCP Leases View

You can copy a MAC address to a new WOL mapping entry while viewing the DHCP leases at Diagnostics → DHCP leases. Click the button at the end of line, and you will be taken to the WOL entry edit screen with that system's information pre-filled in the form. Add a description, and then click Save.

21.9   PPPoE Server

pfSense can act as a PPPoE server and accept/authenticate connections from PPPoE clients on a local interface, acting as an access concentrator. This can be used to force users to authenticate before gaining network access, or otherwise control their login behavior. This is found under Services → PPPoE Server. You will find that this configuration is very similar to the PPTP VPN server (Chapter 14).

To turn on this feature, you must first select Enable PPPoE server. Then choose which Interface on which to offer this service. Set the Subnet Mask which should be assigned to PPPoE clients and the Number of PPPoE Users to allow. Now enter the Server Address which is the IP address which the pfSense system will send to the PPPoE clients to use as their gateway. Enter an IP address in the Remote Address Range box and that will be used together with the Subnet Mask set earlier to define the network used by the PPPoE clients.

The remaining options are for authentication via RADIUS. If you wish to pass the authentication requests on to a RADIUS server, fill in the information on the lower half of the screen. If you would instead prefer to use local authentication, then Save the settings and click the Users tab to add local users. Click to add a user and then fill in the username, password, and an optional IP address.

See Section 24.1 for information on setting up RADIUS on a Windows server, but you may use whichever RADIUS server you prefer.

Chapter 22

System Monitoring

As important as the services provided by pfSense is the data and information that pfSense lets you see. Sometimes it seems that commercial routers go out of their way to hide as much information as possible from users, but pfSense can provide almost as much information as anyone could ever want (and then some).

22.1   System Logs

pfSense logs quite a bit of data by default, but does so in a manner that will not overflow the storage on the router. The logs are found under Status → System Logs in the WebGUI, and under /var/log/ on the filesystem. Some components such as DHCP and IPsec, among others, generate enough logs that they have their own logging tabs to reduce the clutter in the main system log and ease troubleshooting for these individual services. To view these other logs, click the tab for the subsystem you want to view.

pfSense logs are contained in a binary circular log or *clog* format. These files are a fixed size, and never grow. As a consequence of this, the log will only hold a certain amount of entries, and the old entries are continually pushed out of the log as new ones are added. If this is an issue for you or your organization, you may adjust the log settings to copy these entries to another server with syslog where they may be permanently retained or rotated with less frequency. See Section 22.1.3 later in this section for information about syslog.

22.1.1   Viewing System Logs

The system logs can be found under Status → System Logs, on the System tab. This will include log entries generated by the host itself in addition to those created by some services and packages which do not have their logs redirected to other tabs/log files.

As you can see by the example entries in Figure 22.1, there are log entries from the SSH daemon, the avahi package, and the dynamic DNS client. Many other subsystems will log here, but most will not overload the logs at any one time. Typically if a service has many log entries it will be moved to its own tab/log file. Also note in this example that the logs are configured to appear in reverse order, and the newest entries appear at the top of the list. See the next section to find out how to configure the logs for reverse order.

Aug 5 18:15:57	avahi-daemon[38307]: Found user 'avahi' (UID 1003) and group 'avahi' (GID 1003).
Aug 5 18:15:41	avahi-daemon[44110]: Leaving mDNS multicast group on interface em0.IPv4 with address 192.168.10.1.
Aug 5 18:15:41	avahi-daemon[44110]: Leaving mDNS multicast group on interface tun0.IPv4 with address 192.168.100.2.
Aug 5 18:15:41	avahi-daemon[44110]: Got SIGTERM, quitting.
Aug 5 18:15:32	sshd[38258]: Accepted password for admin from 192.168.10.10 port 64864 ssh2
Aug 5 01:01:02	php: : phpDynDNS: No Change In My IP Address and/or 25 Days Has Not Past. Not Updating Dynamic DNS Entry.
Aug 5 01:01:02	php: : DynDns: Cached IP: 72.69.194.6
Aug 5 01:01:02	php: : DynDns: Current WAN IP: 72.69.194.6
Aug 5 01:01:02	php: : DynDns: _detectChange() starting.
Aug 5 01:01:02	php: : DynDns: updatedns() starting
Aug 5 01:01:02	php: : DynDns: Running updatedns()

Figure 22.1: Example System Log Entries

22.1.2   Changing Log Settings

Log settings may be adjusted by going to Status → System Logs and using the Settings tab. Here you will find several options to choose from that control how logs are displayed.

The first option, Show log entries in reverse order, controls the order in which logs are displayed on the various logging tabs. With this option checked, the newest entries will be at the top of the log output. When this option is unchecked, the oldest entries will be at the top. Certain people find both of these methods useful and easier to follow, so you can pick whichever setting you prefer.

The next setting, Number of log entries to show, only controls how many log lines are displayed on each tab. The actual logs may contain more data, so this can be adjusted up or down a bit if needed.

Normally, every packet blocked by the firewall's default deny rule is logged. If you do not want to see these log entries, uncheck the Log packets blocked by the default rule option.

The Show raw filter logs option controls the output of the Firewall logs tab. When checked, the output will not be interpreted by the log parser, and will instead be displayed in its raw format. Sometimes this can aid in troubleshooting, or if you need support the raw log will give a technician more information than is normally seen in the default firewall log output. The raw logs are harder to read and interpret than the parsed logs, so this is typically left unchecked most of the time.

Click Save when you are done making changes. The remaining options on this screen are discussed in the following section.

22.1.3   Remote Logging with Syslog

The other options under Status → System Logs on the Settings tab are for using syslog to copy log entries to a remote server. Because the logs kept by pfSense on the router itself are of a finite size, copying these entries to a syslog server can help with troubleshooting and long-term monitoring. The logs on the router are cleared upon reboot, so having a remote copy can also help diagnose events that occur just before a router restarts.

Some corporate or legislative policies dictate how long logs must be kept for firewalls and similar devices. If your organization requires long-term log retention, you will need to configure a syslog server to receive and retain these logs.

To start logging remotely, check Enable syslog'ing to remote syslog server, and fill in an IP address for your syslog server next to Remote Syslog Server. If you would also like to disable local logging, you can check Disable writing log files to the local ram disk but this is not generally recommended.

The syslog server is typically a server that is directly reachable from your pfSense system on a local interface. Logging can also be sent to a server across a VPN, but may need some extra configuration (see Section 13.4.4) You should not send syslog data directly across your WAN connection, as it is plain text and could contain sensitive information.

Check the boxes for the log entries you would like copied to the syslog server. You can choose to remotely log system events, firewall events, DHCP service events, Portal auth, VPN events and Everything.

Be sure to click Save when you are finished making changes.

If you do not have a syslog server, it is fairly easy to set one up. See Section 24.3 for information on setting up Kiwi Syslog on Windows. Almost any UNIX or UNIX-like system can be used as a syslog server. FreeBSD is described in the following section, but others may be similar.

22.1.3.1 Configuring a Syslog Server on FreeBSD

Setting up a syslog server on FreeBSD requires only a couple steps. In these examples, replace $192.-$
$168.1.1$ with the IP address of your firewall, replace $exco\text{-}rtr$ with the hostname of your firewall, and replace $exco\text{-}rtr.example.com$ with the full hostname and domain of your firewall. I use $19\text{-}2.168.1.1$ in these examples because it is recommended to do this with the *internal* address of your router, not a WAN type interface.

First, you will likely need an entry in /etc/hosts that contains the address and name of your firewall, like so:

```
192.168.1.1            exco-rtr       exco-rtr.example.com
```

Then you need to adjust **syslogd**'s startup flags to accept syslog messages from the firewall. Edit /etc/rc.conf and add this line if it doesn't exist, or add this option to the existing line for the setting:

```
syslogd_flags=" -a 192.168.1.1 "
```

Lastly, you'll need to add some lines to /etc/syslog.conf that will catch log entries from this host. Underneath any other existing entries, add the following lines:

```
!*
+*
+exco-rtr
*.*                                          /var/log/exco-rtr.log
```

Those lines will reset the program and host filters, and then set a host filter for your firewall (use its short name as entered in `/etc/hosts`). If you are familiar with syslog, you can look at `/etc/syslog.conf` on the pfSense router and also filter the logs for various services into separate log files on the syslog server.

After these changes you will need to restart **syslogd**. On FreeBSD this is just one simple command:

```
# /etc/rc.d/syslogd restart
```

You should now be able to look at the log file on the syslog server and see it populating with log entries as activity happens on the firewall.

22.2   System Status

The main page of a pfSense system is also the System Status page (Status → System, shown in Figure 22.2). It contains some basic system information such as the name of the router, the version of pfSense that is being run, the platform (Section 1.6), uptime, state table size (Section 4.5.9.6), MBUF usage, CPU usage, memory usage, swap space usage, and disk usage. The counters on the page update every few seconds automatically, so refreshing the page is not necessary.

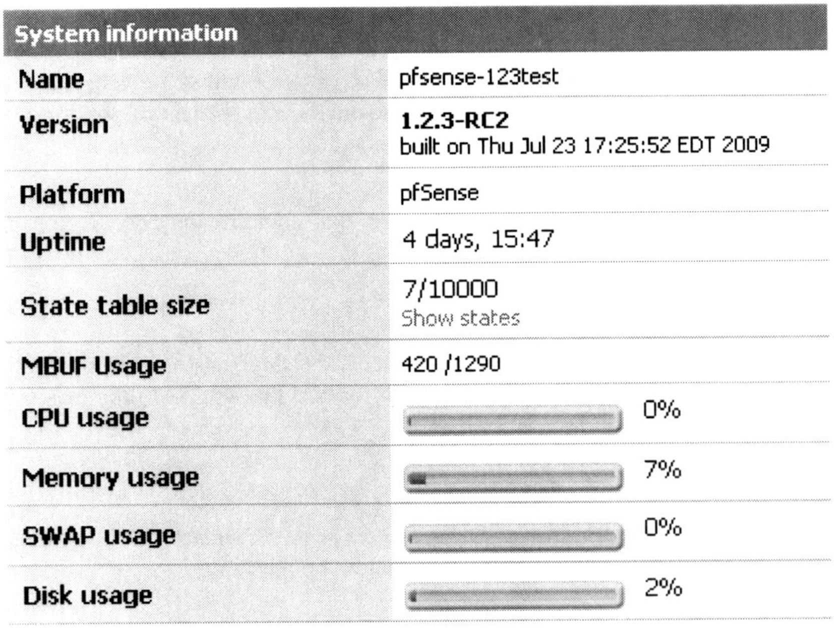

System information	
Name	pfsense-123test
Version	**1.2.3-RC2** built on Thu Jul 23 17:25:52 EDT 2009
Platform	pfSense
Uptime	4 days, 15:47
State table size	7/10000 Show states
MBUF Usage	420 /1290
CPU usage	0%
Memory usage	7%
SWAP usage	0%
Disk usage	2%

Figure 22.2: System Status

WAN interface (re0)	
Status	up
PPPoE	up [Disconnect]
MAC address	00:e0:4c:15:02:58
IP address	72.69.19.6
Subnet mask	255.255.255.255
Gateway	10.34.29.1
ISP DNS servers	68.238.0.12 68.238.112.12
Media	100baseTX <full-duplex>
In/out packets	27294223/22072735 (1.16 GB/225.52 MB)
In/out errors	0/0
Collisions	0

LAN interface (em0)	
Status	up
MAC address	00:08:74:1b:aa:de
IP address	192.168.10.1
Subnet mask	255.255.255.0
Media	100baseTX <full-duplex>
In/out packets	22552432/27777672 (195.82 MB/1.13 GB)
In/out errors	0/0
Collisions	0

Figure 22.3: Interface Status

22.3   Interface Status

The status of the network interfaces may be viewed at Status → Interfaces. In the first part of Figure 22.3, a PPPoE WAN connection has been made and the IP, DNS, etc has been obtained. You can also see the network interface's MAC address, media type, in/out packets, errors, and collisions. Dynamic connection types like PPPoE and PPTP have a Disconnect button when connected and a Connect button when offline. Interfaces obtaining an IP from DHCP have a Release button when there is an active lease, and a Renew button when there is not.

In the lower part of the image, you can see the LAN connection. Since this is a normal interface with a static IP, only the usual set of items are shown.

If an interface's status says "no carrier" then it typically means that the cable is not plugged in or the device on the other end is malfunctioning in some way. If any errors are shown, they are typically physical in nature: cabling or port errors. The most common suspect is cables, and they are easy and cheap to replace.

22.4   Service Status

Many system and package services show the status of their daemons at Status → Services. Each service is shown with a name, a description, and the status, as seen in Figure 22.4. The status is usually listed as Running or Stopped. From this view, a running service may be restarted by clicking 🔄 or stopped by clicking 🔳. A stopped service may be started by clicking ▶. Normally, it is not necessary to control services in this manner, but occasionally there may be maintenance or troubleshooting reasons for doing so.

Service	Description	Status	
avahi	Not available.	☐ Running	🔄 🔳
dnsmasq	DNS Forwarder	☐ Running	🔄 🔳
ntpd	NTP clock sync	☐ Running	🔄 🔳
dhcpd	DHCP Service	☐ Running	🔄 🔳
bsnmpd	SNMP Service	☐ Running	🔄 🔳
miniupnpd	UPnP Service	☐ Running	🔄 🔳
racoon	IPsec VPN	☐ Running	🔄 🔳

Figure 22.4: Services Status

22.5   RRD Graphs

RRD Graphs are another useful set of data provided by pfSense. While the router is running it keeps track of various bits of data about how the system performs, and then stores this data in Round-Robin Database (RRD) files. Graphs of this data are available from Status → RRD Graphs. On that screen there are six tabs, each of which are covered in this section: System, Traffic, Packets, Quality, Queues, and Settings.

Each graph is available in several times spans, and each of these is averaged over a different period of time based on how much time is being covered in a given graph. Also on each graph will be a legend and a summarization of the data being shown (minimums, averages, maximums, current values, etc.). Graphs are available in a 4 hour range with a 1 minute average, a 16 hour range with a 1 minute average, a 2 day range with a 5 minute average, a 1 month range with a 1 hour average, a 6 month range with a 12 hour average, and a 1 year range with a 12 hour average.

Many graphs can be viewed in Inverse style or Absolute style. With Inverse style, the graph is split down the middle horizontally and incoming traffic is shown going up from the center, and outgoing traffic is shown going down from the center. With Absolute style, the values are superimposed.

In Figure 22.5, you can see that it is a 16 hour inverse graph of traffic on the WAN, which has had a maximum use of 1.74Mbit/s average during a 1 minute period.

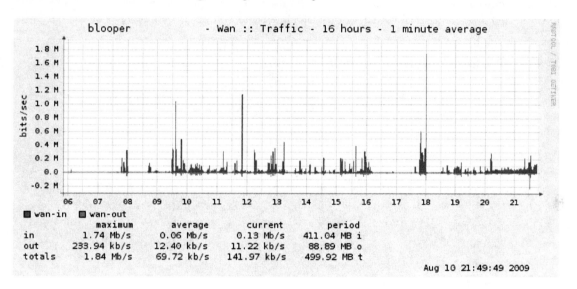

Figure 22.5: WAN Traffic Graph

22.5.1 System Graphs

The graphs under the System tab show a general overview of the system utilization, including CPU usage, total throughput, and firewall states.

22.5.1.1 Processor Graph

The processor graph shows CPU usage for user and system processes, interrupts, and the number of running processes.

22.5.1.2   Throughput Graph

The throughput graph shows the incoming and outgoing traffic totalled up for all interfaces.

22.5.1.3   States Graph

The states graph is a bit more complex. It shows the number of system states but also breaks down the value in several ways. It shows the filter states from firewall rules, NAT states from NAT rules, the count of unique active source and destination IP addresses, and the number of state changes per second.

22.5.2   Traffic Graphs

Traffic graphs will show the amount of bandwidth used on each available interface in bits per second notation, and there is also an Allgraphs choice which will show all of the traffic graphs on a single page.

22.5.3   Packet Graphs

The packet graphs work much like the traffic graphs, except instead of reporting based on bandwidth used, it reports the number of packets per second (pps) passed.

22.5.4   Quality Graphs

The quality graph tracks the quality of WAN or WAN-like interface (those with a gateway specified, or using DHCP). Shown on these graphs are the response time from the gateway in milliseconds, as well as a percentage of lost packets. Any loss on the graph indicates connectivity issues or times of excessive bandwidth use.

22.5.5   Queue Graphs

The queue graphs are a composite of each traffic shaper queue. Each individual queue is shown, represented by a unique color. You can view either the graph of all queues, or the graph representing the drops from all queues.

22.5.6   Settings

The RRD graphs can be customized to better suit your preferences. You can even turn them off if you prefer to use some external graphing solution instead. Click Save when finished making changes.

22.5.6.1   Enable Graphing

Check the box to turn on graphing, or remove the check to disable graphing.

22.5.6.2 Default Category

The Default Category option picks which tab will show up first when you click on Status → RRD Graphs.

22.5.6.3 Default Style

The Default Style option picks which style of graphs to use by default, Inverse or Absolute.

22.6 Firewall States

As discussed in Section 6.1.2, pfSense is a stateful firewall and uses one state to track each connection to and from the system. These states may be viewed in several ways, either in the WebGUI or from the console.

22.6.1 Viewing in the WebGUI

Viewing the states from the WebGUI can be done by visiting Diagnostics → States (Figure 22.6). Here you will see the protocol for each connection, its Source, Router, and Destination, and its connection state. When dealing with NAT entries, the three entries in the middle column represent the system which made the connection, the IP address and port pfSense is using for the NAT connection, and the remote system to which the connection has been made.

Individual states may be removed by clicking the ⊠ at the end of their row.

tcp	192.168.10.10:53650 -> 72.69.194.6:41047 -> 168.143.168.68:443	FIN_WAIT_2:FIN_WAIT_2	⊠
udp	224.0.0.251:5353 <- 192.168.10.17:5353	NO_TRAFFIC:SINGLE	⊠
tcp	207.45.186.18:80 <- 192.168.10.11:1289	ESTABLISHED:ESTABLISHED	⊠
tcp	192.168.10.11:1289 -> 72.69.194.6:52740 -> 207.45.186.18:80	ESTABLISHED:ESTABLISHED	⊠

Figure 22.6: Example States

22.6.2 Viewing with pftop

pftop is available from the system console menu, and offers a live view of the state table along with the total amount of bandwidth consumed by each state. There are several ways to alter the view while watching pftop. Press **h** to see a help screen that explains the available choices. The most common uses are using **0** through **8** to select different views, **space** for an immediate update, and **q** to quit.

22.7   Traffic Graphs

Real time traffic graphs drawn with SVG (Scalable Vector Graphics) are available that constantly update. You can find them under Status → Traffic Graphs, and an example of the graph can be found in Figure 22.7. These will allow you to see traffic as it happens, and give a much clearer view of what is happening "now" than relying on averaged data from the RRD graphs.

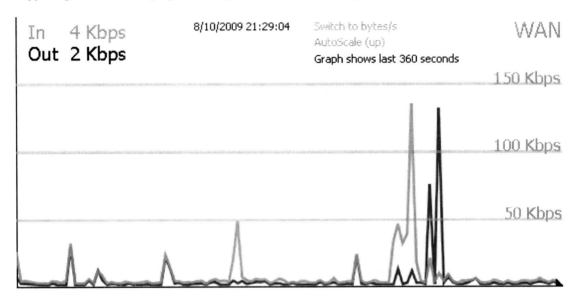

Figure 22.7: Example WAN Graph

Only one interface is visible at a time, and you can choose which one to view from the Interface dropdown list. Once an interface is chosen, the page will automatically refresh and start displaying the new graph. The Dashboard feature in pfSense 2.0 (also available as a beta package in 1.2) enables the simultaneous display of multiple traffic graphs on a single page.

Chapter 23

Packages

The pfSense package system provides the ability to extend pfSense without adding bloat and potential security vulnerabilities to the base distribution. Packages are only supported on full installs, not the live CD and older embedded platforms. The newer embedded versions which are based on NanoBSD now have the capability of running some packages. Certain packages may also be built into the base system, such as the SIP Proxy package. To see the packages available, browse to System → Packages.

23.1 Introduction to Packages

Many of the packages have been written by the pfSense community and not by the pfSense development team. The available packages vary quite widely, and some are more mature and well-maintained than others. There are packages which install and provide a GUI interface for third-party software, such as Squid, and others which extend the functionality of pfSense itself, like the Dashboard package which backports some functionality from pfSense 2.0.

Note

These pfSense packages are different than the FreeBSD Ports packages which are covered in Section 24.4 in the Third Party Software chapter.

By far the most popular package available for pfSense is for the Squid Proxy Server. It is installed more than twice as often as the next most popular package: Squidguard, which is a content filter that works with Squid to control access to web resources by users. Not surprisingly, the third most popular package is Lightsquid, which is a Squid log analysis package that lets you view the web sites which have been visited by users behind the proxy.

Some other examples of available packages (which are not Squid related) are:

- Bandwidth monitors that show traffic by IP address like Rate, BandwidthD, NTOP, and Darkstat.

- Extra services like a DNS server, TFTP server, FreeRADIUS, and FreeSWITCH (a VoIP PBX).

435

- Proxies for other services like SIP, IGMP, and IMSpector.

- System utilities like NUT for monitoring a UPS, LCDProc for using an LCD, and phpSysInfo.

- Popular third-party utilities like nmap, iperf, and arping.

- BGP Routing, Cron editing, Nagios and Zabbix agents, and many, many others.

As of this writing there are more than 50 different packages available; too many to cover them all in this book! If you would like to see the full list, it will be available from within your pfSense system by browsing to System → Packages.

You may notice that the packages screen may take a little longer to load than other pages in the web interface. This is because it fetches the XML package information from our servers before the page is rendered to provide the most up to date package information. If your firewall does not have a functional Internet connection including DNS resolution, this will fail and notify you, as in Figure 23.1. If you have previously successfully retrieved the package information, it will be displayed from cache, but you may not have the most recent information. This is usually caused by a missing or incorrect DNS server configuration. For static IP connections, verify working DNS servers are entered on the System → General Setup page. For those with dynamically assigned connections, ensure the servers assigned by your ISP are functioning. You may wish to override these dynamically assigned servers with OpenDNS or another DNS server.

Figure 23.1: Package information retrieval failed

A growing number of packages have a Package Info link in the package list, pointing to a site with more information on that specific package. You should read the information in the Package Info link before installing a package. After installation, you can find the most recent Package Info link for each installed package on the Installed Packages tab.

23.2 Installing Packages

Packages are installed from System → Packages. The listings there, exemplified by Figure 23.2, will show a package's name, category, version and status, a package information link, and a short description. Pay very close attention to Status before installing packages, some packages are experimental and should never be installed on critical production systems. You should also keep the installed packages to the bare minimum required for your deployment.

Package Name	Category	Status	Package Info	Description	
AutoConfigBackup	Services	BETA 1.15 platform: 1.2	Package Info	Automatically backs up your pfSense configuration. All contents are encrypted on the server. Requires pfSense Premium Support Portal Subscription from https://portal.pfsense.org	

Figure 23.2: Package Listing

Packages are installed by clicking the ⊞ button to the right of their entry. Upon clicking ⊞, you will be taken to the package installation screen where the install progress will be displayed (Figure 23.3).

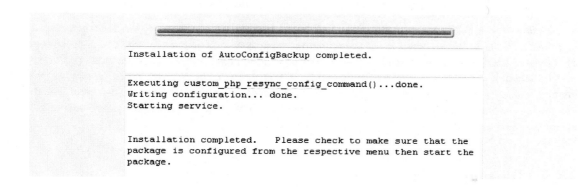

```
Installation of AutoConfigBackup completed.

Executing custom_php_resync_config_command()...done.
Writing configuration... done.
Starting service.


Installation completed.   Please check to make sure that the
package is configured from the respective menu then start the
package.
```

Figure 23.3: Post-Install Package Screen

23.3 Reinstalling and Updating Packages

Packages are reinstalled and updated the same way. Start by going to System → Packages, and clicking the Installed packages tab. The listings there should look like Figure 23.4. Find the package you want to reinstall or update in the list. If there is a newer version available than you have installed, the Package Version column will be highlighted in red stating the old and new versions. Click 🔳 to update or reinstall the package.

Another reinstallation choice would be to reinstall just the XML GUI components of a package, which can be done by clicking 🔳 next to the package entry. Unless instructed to do so by a developer, you shouldn't use this option as it can miss updates to the binaries that the latest GUI components may require.

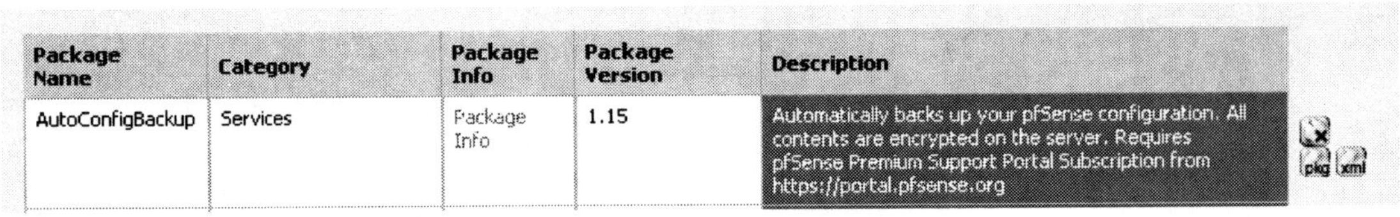

Package Name	Category	Package Info	Package Version	Description
AutoConfigBackup	Services	Package Info	1.15	Automatically backs up your pfSense configuration. All contents are encrypted on the server. Requires pfSense Premium Support Portal Subscription from https://portal.pfsense.org

Figure 23.4: Installed Package List

23.4 Uninstalling Packages

To uninstall a package, browse to System → Packages, and click the Installed packages tab. Find the package in the list, and click the ⊗ button. The package will then be removed from the system.

Some experimental packages overwrite files distributed with the base system. These packages cannot be uninstalled, as doing so would break the remaining base system. The package entry may still show the uninstall icon, but they will still be present after their attempted removal. Packages with this quirk will be labeled as such in their description field. If you upgrade the system, it will overwrite the changes made by these packages, so this is a possible means of uninstallation. Be very careful with any packages that cannot be uninstalled, they are generally meant for experimentation on non-critical systems.

23.5 Developing Packages

Packages are relatively simple to develop, and you may find that either you or your organization may benefit from developing a package that does not exist. For those interesting in creating their own packages, resources are available on the pfSense Documentation Wiki. If you create a package and think it may be of use to others, contact us and your work can be evaluated for inclusion into the package system for everyone to see.

Chapter 24

Third Party Software and pfSense

While this book is focused on pfSense, there are a number of third party software packages that can be configured to interoperate with pfSense or augment its functionality. In this context, *third party software* refers to software available from other vendors or sources which can be used together with pfSense, but is not considered part of the "pfSense system". These are different from pfSense packages, which are extra software that runs on the pfSense system and integrates into the system's GUI.

24.1   RADIUS Authentication with Windows Server

Windows 2000 Server and Windows Server 2003 can be configured as a RADIUS server using Microsoft's Internet Authentication Service (IAS). This allows you to authenticate the pfSense PPTP server, Captive Portal, or PPPoE server from your Windows Server local user accounts or Active Directory.

24.1.1   Choosing a server for IAS

IAS requires a minimal amount of resources and is suitable for addition to an existing Windows Server in most environments. Microsoft recommends installing it on an Active Directory domain controller to improve performance in environments where IAS is authenticating against Active Directory. It is also possible to install it on a member server, which may be desirable in some environments to reduce the attack footprint of your domain controllers — each network-accessible service provides another potential avenue for compromising your server. IAS does have a solid security record, especially compared to other things that must be running on your domain controllers for Active Directory to function, so this isn't much of a concern in most network environments. Most environments install IAS on one of their domain controllers.

24.1.2   Installing IAS

On the Windows Server, go to Control Panel, Add/Remove Programs, and choose Add/remove Windows Components. Scroll down and click on Networking Services, then click Details. Check Internet

Authentication Service in the Networking Services list and click OK. Then click Next and IAS will be installed. You may need to provide the Server CD for this installation to complete. When the installation is completed, click Finish.

24.1.3   Configuring IAS

To configure IAS, bring up the IAS MMC snap-in under Administrative Tools, Internet Authentication Service. First a RADIUS client will be added for pfSense, then remote access policies will be configured.

24.1.3.1   Adding a RADIUS Client

Right click on RADIUS Clients and click New RADIUS Client, as shown in Figure 24.1.

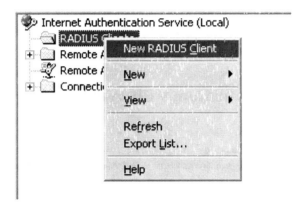

Figure 24.1: Add new RADIUS client

Enter a "friendly name" for your firewall, like shown in Figure 24.2, which can be your hostname or FQDN. The Client address field must be the IP address that pfSense will initiate its RADIUS requests from, or a FQDN that will resolve to that IP address. This will be the IP address of the interface closest to the RADIUS server. If the RADIUS server is reachable via your LAN interface, this will be the LAN IP. In deployments where pfSense is not your perimeter firewall, and your WAN interface resides on the internal network where your RADIUS server resides, the WAN IP address is what you must enter here. Fill in the Friendly name and pfSense address, then click Next.

Leave Client-Vendor set to **RADIUS Standard**, and fill in a shared secret, as shown in Figure 24.3. This shared secret is what you will enter on pfSense later. Click Finish.

Now you have completed your IAS configuration. You can see the RADIUS Client you just added as in Figure 24.4.

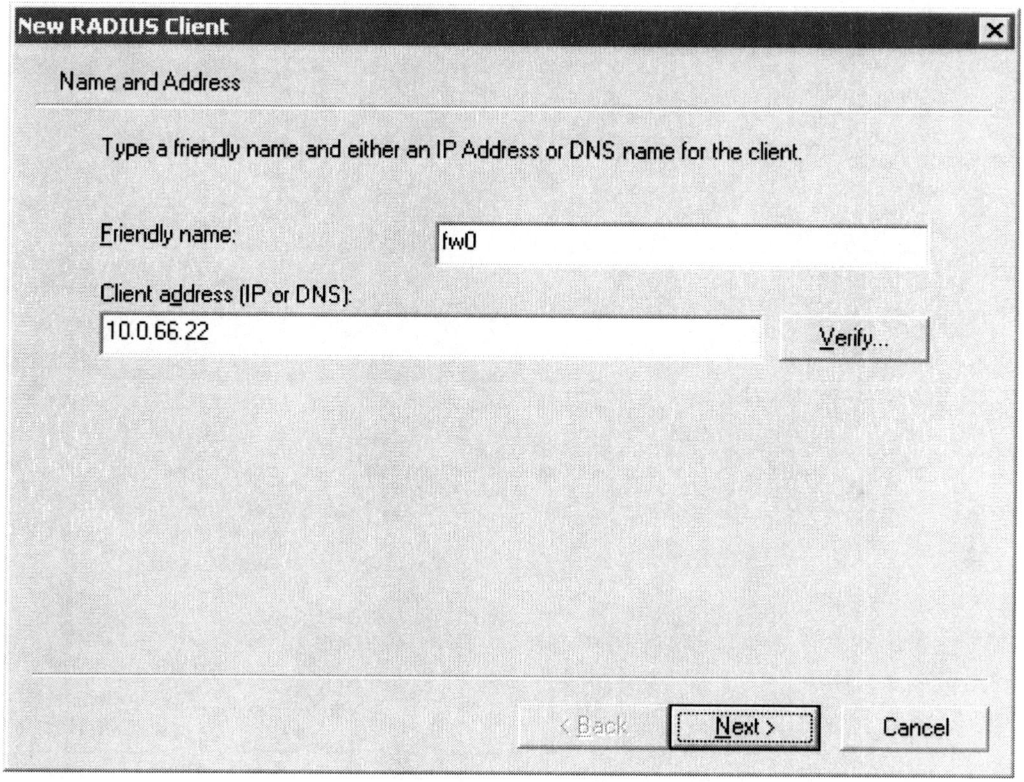

Figure 24.2: Add new RADIUS client — name and client address

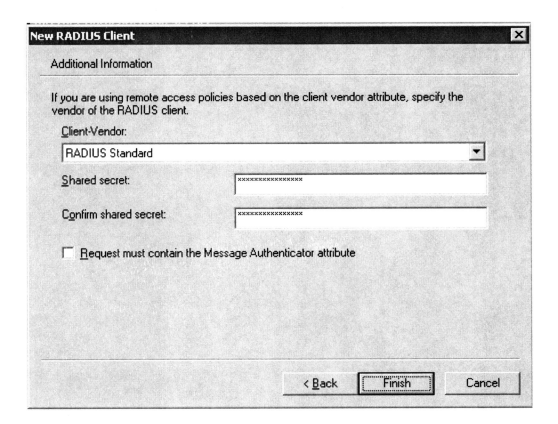

Figure 24.3: Add new RADIUS client — Shared secret

Friendly Name	Address	Protocol	Client-Vendor
fw0	10.0.66.22	RADIUS	RADIUS Standard

Figure 24.4: Listing of the RADIUS Client

Now you are ready to configure pfSense with the RADIUS information configured here, using the IP address of the IAS server, and the shared secret configured previously. Refer to the portion of this book describing the service you wish to use with RADIUS for more guidance. RADIUS can be used for Captive Portal (Section 19.4), the PPTP server (Section 14.5.2), and the PPPoE server (Section 21.9), and also in some packages.

24.1.3.2 Configuring Users and Remote Access Policy

Whether a user can authenticate via RADIUS is controlled using Remote Access Permission on each user's account under the Dial-in tab in the account properties in Active Directory Users and Computers. There you can specify to allow or deny access, or control access through Remote Access Policy. You have the option of specifying access here for each user by specifying allow or deny. For small environments with basic requirements, this may be preferable. Remote access policies scale better for environments with more users, as you can simply place a user in a specific Active Directory group to allow VPN access, and also offer more advanced capabilities such as time of day restrictions.

More information on remote access policies can be found in Microsoft's documentation at `http://technet.microsoft.com/en-us/library/cc785236%28WS.10%29.aspx`.

After configuring users and remote access policies as desired, you are ready to test the service you are using with RADIUS on pfSense.

24.1.3.3 Troubleshooting IAS

Should authentication fail, this section describes the most common problems users encounter with IAS.

24.1.3.3.1 Verify port

First ensure the default port 1812 is being used. If your IAS server was previously installed, it may have been configured with non-standard ports. In the IAS MMC console, right click on Internet Authentication Service (Local) at the top left of the MMC console and click Properties. Then click the Ports tab. You can specify multiple ports by separating them with a comma (as shown in Figure 24.5). Port 1812 must be one of the ports configured for Authentication. If you are using RADIUS accounting functionality as well, port 1813 must be one of the ports specified in Accounting.

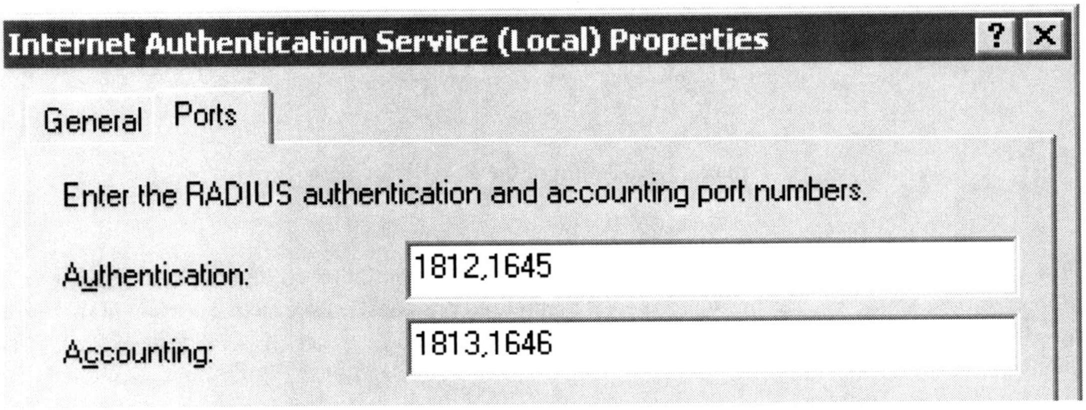

Figure 24.5: IAS Ports

24.1.3.3.2   Check Event Viewer

When a RADIUS authentication attempt is answered by the server, IAS logs to the System log in Event Viewer with the result of the authentication request and, if access is denied, the reason it was denied. In the Description field of the event properties, the Reason line tells why authentication failed. The common two failures are: bad username and password, when a user enters incorrect credentials; and "remote access permission for the user account was denied" when the user account is set to Deny access or the remote access policies configured in IAS do not allow access for that user. If IAS is logging that authentication was successful, but the client is receiving a bad username or password message, the RADIUS secret configured in IAS and pfSense does not match.

24.2   Free Content Filtering with OpenDNS

pfSense doesn't include any content filtering software at the time of this writing, but there is a great free option in integrating OpenDNS. First you need to configure your network to use OpenDNS's DNS servers for all recursive queries.[1]

24.2.1   Configuring pfSense to use OpenDNS

Visit the System → General Setup page, enter OpenDNS's two DNS servers there, and uncheck the "Allow DNS server list to be overridden by DHCP/PPP on WAN" box (Figure 24.6).

---

[1] Note: I am in no way affiliated with OpenDNS, just a very satisfied user of their services in multiple locations, and I have had numerous people thank me for referring me to them. They truly have an impressive offering.

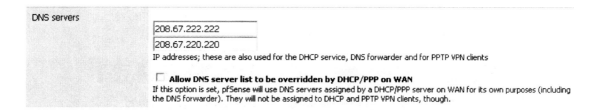

Figure 24.6: Configuring OpenDNS on pfSense

If your internal machines use pfSense's DNS forwarder as their only DNS server, this is all you need to change to use OpenDNS for your name resolution.

24.2.2 Configure internal DNS servers to use OpenDNS

If your internal machines use an internal DNS server, it needs to be configured to send its recursive queries to OpenDNS's servers. I will explain how to accomplish this with Windows Server's DNS server.

24.2.2.1 Configuring Forwarders in Windows Server DNS

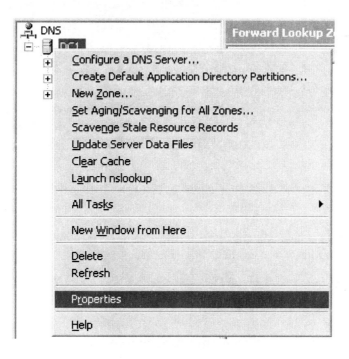

Figure 24.7: Windows Server DNS Properties

Open the DNS MMC snap-in under Administrative Tools, DNS. Right click on the server's name and click Properties, as shown in Figure 24.7.

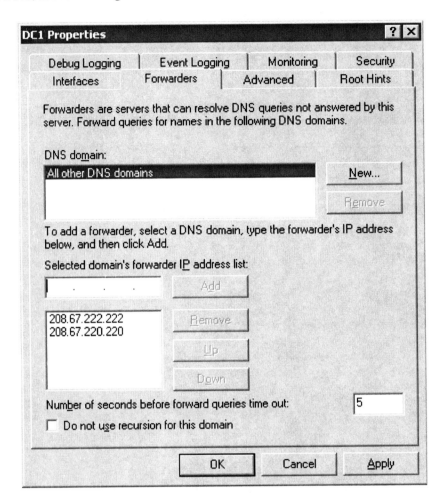

Figure 24.8: Windows Server DNS Forwarders

Select the Forwarders tab, and add OpenDNS's two DNS servers in the forwarder list for "All other DNS domains" as in Figure 24.8, then click OK.

Then repeat this for each of your internal DNS servers.

24.2.3   Configuring OpenDNS Content Filtering

Now you need to configure your content filtering as desired on the OpenDNS site.

24.2.3.1   Sign up for an OpenDNS account

Browse to `http://www.opendns.com` and click the Sign In link. Then click the "Create a free account" link and go through the account creation process.

24.2.3.2   Define your network(s) in OpenDNS

Figure 24.9: Add a network

OpenDNS first needs to be able to determine which DNS queries are from your network to be able to filter according to the policies defined in your account. After logging into your OpenDNS account, click the Networks tab (Figure 24.9). It will automatically show the public IP your HTTPS session is coming from, with a button to add this network to your account. Click the Add this network button.

This will bring up a window prompting whether your IP is static or dynamic (Figure 24.10). If you have a dynamic IP connection, you will have to run the OpenDNS Updater for Windows on a machine inside your network to ensure your address is kept up to date with OpenDNS. Your IP address is the only means of identification OpenDNS has of your network. If your IP is not correct in your OpenDNS settings, your content filtering will not function as configured in your account.

For static IP connections, uncheck the "Yes, it is dynamic" box and give the connection a name (Figure 24.11). For static IP connections, you don't need to run the updater client.

After adding your network to your account, you will see it in your network list like that in Figure 24.12.

Your network is now ready to use OpenDNS, though you still need to configure your desired content filtering settings.

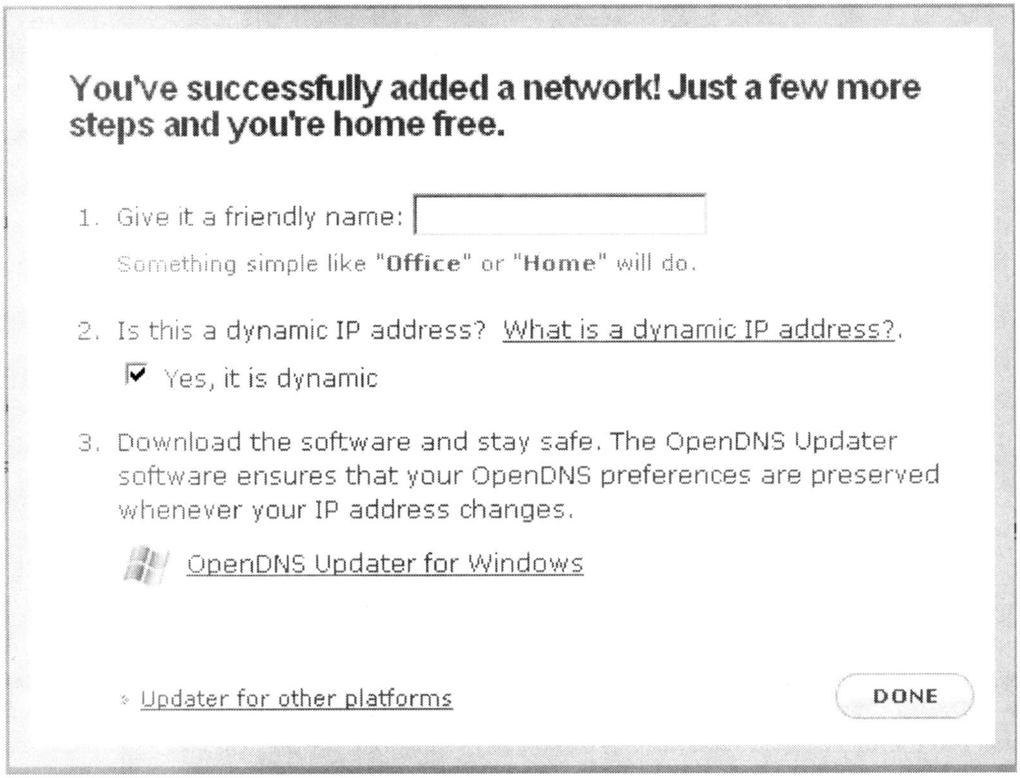

You've successfully added a network! Just a few more steps and you're home free.

1. Give it a friendly name: [   ]

   Something simple like "**Office**" or "**Home**" will do.

2. Is this a dynamic IP address? <u>What is a dynamic IP address?</u>.

   ☑ Yes, it is dynamic

3. Download the software and stay safe. The OpenDNS Updater software ensures that your OpenDNS preferences are preserved whenever your IP address changes.

   <u>OpenDNS Updater for Windows</u>

   › <u>Updater for other platforms</u>   (DONE)

Figure 24.10: Adding a dynamic IP connection

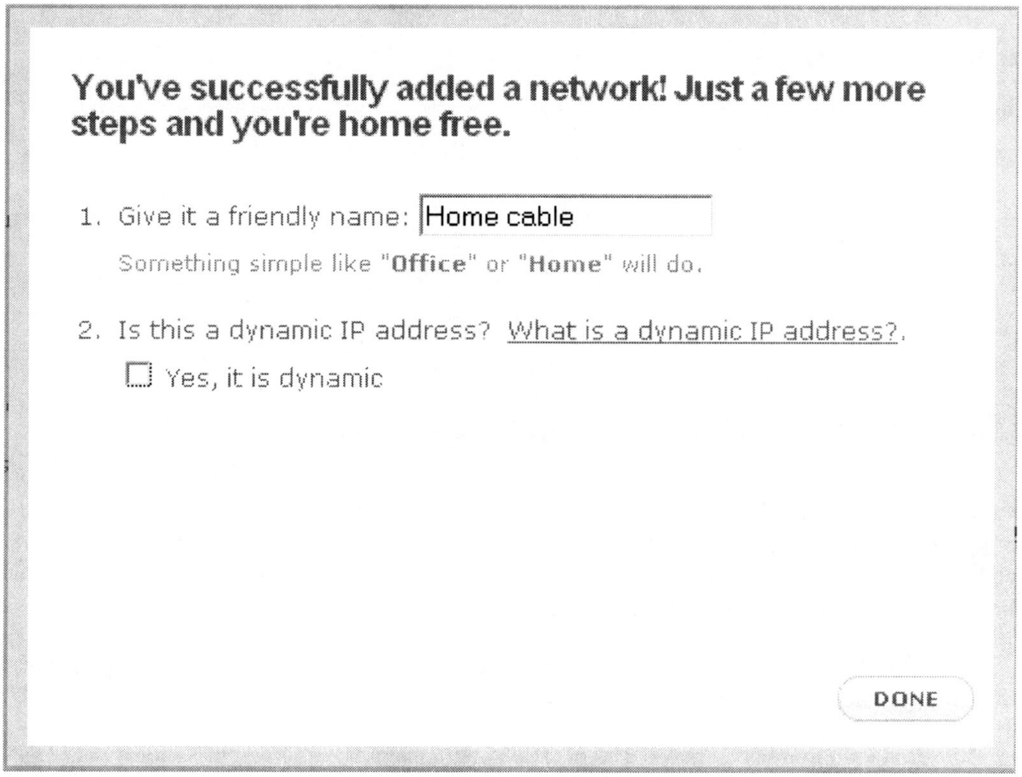

You've successfully added a network! Just a few more steps and you're home free.

1. Give it a friendly name: Home cable

   Something simple like "**Office**" or "**Home**" will do.

2. Is this a dynamic IP address? What is a dynamic IP address?.

   ☐ Yes, it is dynamic

DONE

Figure 24.11: Adding a static IP connection

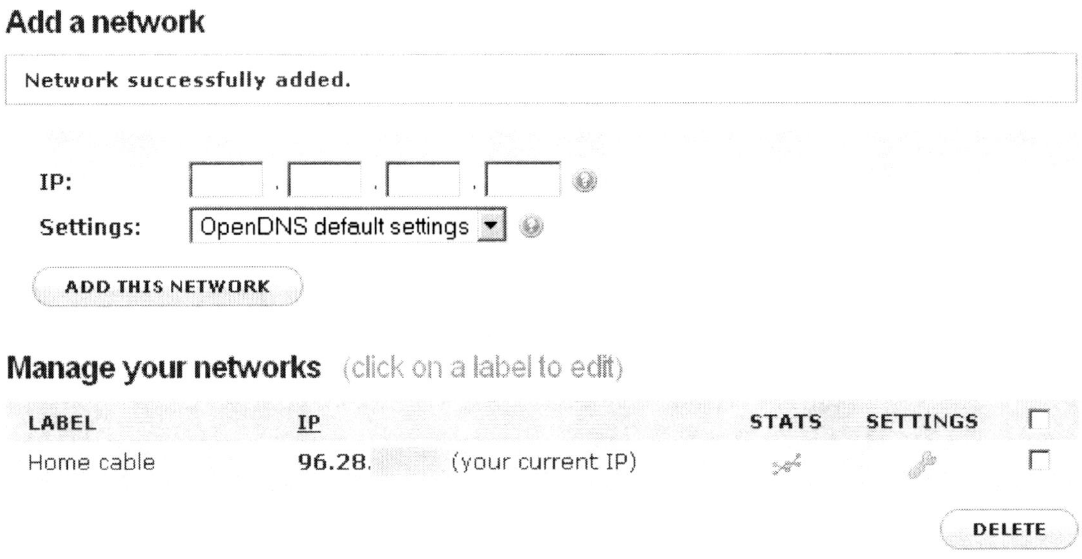

Add a network

Network successfully added.

IP: [ ] . [ ] . [ ] . [ ] ⓘ

Settings: OpenDNS default settings ▾ ⓘ

(ADD THIS NETWORK)

Manage your networks (click on a label to edit)

LABEL	IP		STATS	SETTINGS	☐
Home cable	**96.28.**	(your current IP)	✕	⚙	☐

(DELETE)

Figure 24.12: Network successfully added

24.2.3.3   Configuring content filtering settings for your account

To configure your content filtering settings, click the Settings tab at the top of the OpenDNS website. A list of levels like that in Figure 24.13 should appear. You will see your current filtering level is Minimal, which blocks only known phishing sites. You can select from four different pre-defined filtering levels, or choose Custom and select which categories you wish to block.

You can also block or allow specific domains, overriding your overall content filtering configuration, at the bottom of this screen (Figure 24.14).

OpenDNS provides a number of other configuration settings allowing you great control over DNS for your network. Their site contains a number of knowledge base and support articles detailing some of the possibilities, and all of the functionality is well described throughout the management interface. You don't have to stop at just content filtering — review everything else OpenDNS has to offer, as you may be able to put it to good use.

24.2.4   Configuring your firewall rules to prohibit other DNS servers

Now that your internal systems are all using OpenDNS as their DNS service, you will want to configure your firewall rules so no other DNS servers can be accessed. Otherwise internal users could simply change their machines (if they have the user rights to do so) to use a different DNS server that does not enforce your content filtering and other restrictions.

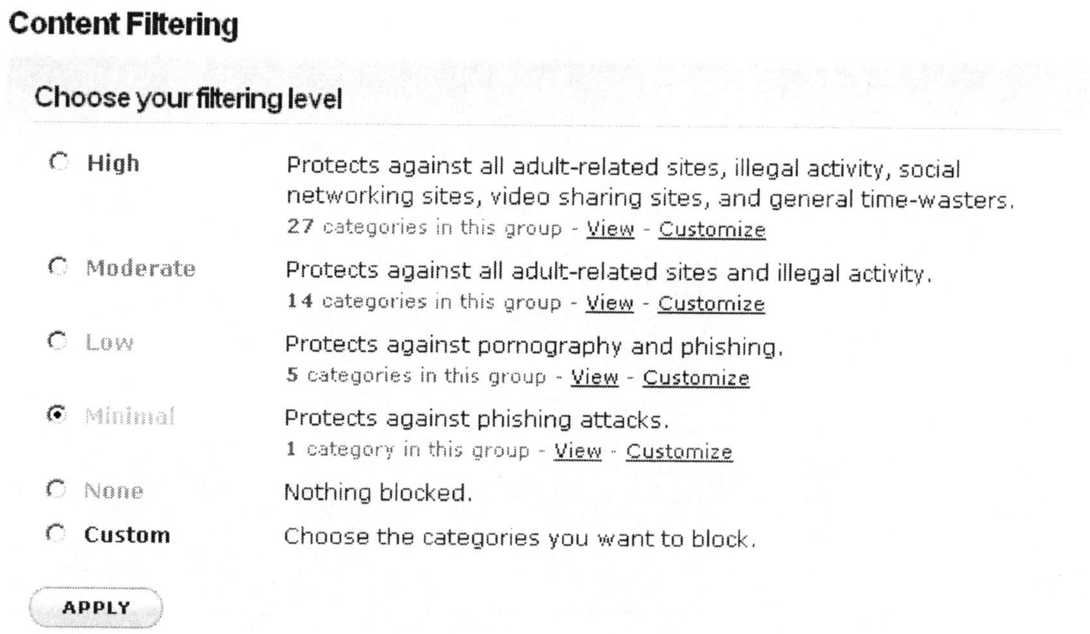

Content Filtering

Choose your filtering level

○ **High**   Protects against all adult-related sites, illegal activity, social networking sites, video sharing sites, and general time-wasters.
27 categories in this group - Ⅴiew - Customize

○ Moderate   Protects against all adult-related sites and illegal activity.
14 categories in this group - Ⅴiew - Customize

○ Low   Protects against pornography and phishing.
5 categories in this group - Ⅴiew - Customize

◉ Minimal   Protects against phishing attacks.
1 category in this group - Ⅴiew - Customize

○ None   Nothing blocked.

○ **Custom**   Choose the categories you want to block.

(APPLY)

Figure 24.13: Content filtering level

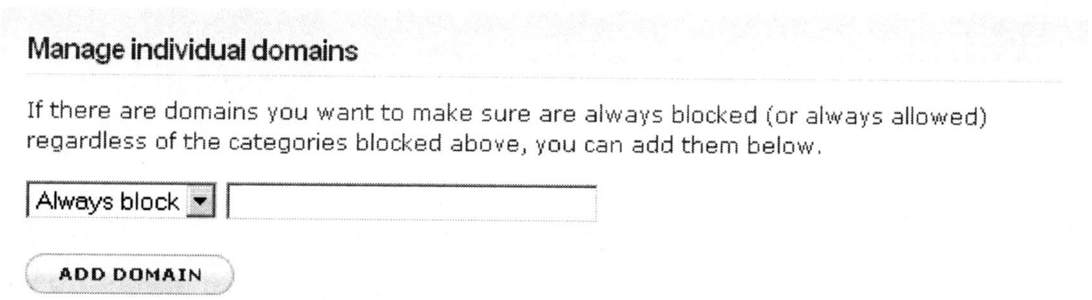

Manage individual domains

If there are domains you want to make sure are always blocked (or always allowed) regardless of the categories blocked above, you can add them below.

| Always block ▼ | |

(ADD DOMAIN)

Figure 24.14: Manage individual domains

24.2.4.1   Create a DNS Servers alias

First you will want to create an alias containing the DNS servers that internal machines are allowed to query, like the one in Figure 24.15. The LAN IP is listed because this example network uses the DNS forwarder as its internal DNS server, and this allows DNS queries from the LAN to the LAN IP. It also allows recursive queries from internal DNS servers, and the direct assignment of OpenDNS's DNS servers on internal machines. Note that unless you disable the anti-lockout rule, it isn't necessary to add the LAN IP here, but I recommend adding it regardless for clarity. Refer to Section 6.5.1.1 for more information.

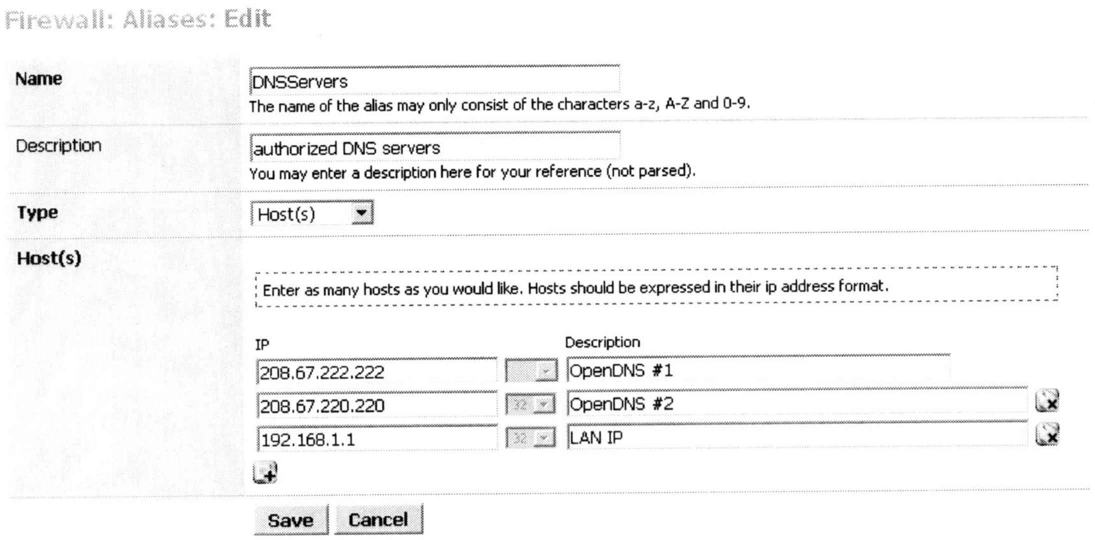

Firewall: Aliases: Edit

Name	DNSServers
	The name of the alias may only consist of the characters a-z, A-Z and 0-9.
Description	authorized DNS servers
	You may enter a description here for your reference (not parsed).
Type	Host(s)
Host(s)	Enter as many hosts as you would like. Hosts should be expressed in their ip address format.

IP		Description
208.67.222.222		OpenDNS #1
208.67.220.220	32	OpenDNS #2
192.168.1.1	32	LAN IP

Save   Cancel

Figure 24.15: DNS servers alias

24.2.4.2   Configure firewall rules

Now you need to configure your LAN rules to allow DNS destined for the previously created alias, and block DNS to other destinations if any of your other rules would permit DNS, such as the default LAN rule. As discussed in the firewall chapter, I prefer using reject rules for traffic blocked on internal interfaces. The ruleset in Figure 24.16 is kept short and simple for the sake of illustration — I recommend significantly stronger egress filtering than this shows, as described in the firewall chapter.

Figure 24.16: LAN rules to restrict DNS

24.2.5 Finishing Up and Other Concerns

And that's it. You now have a free content filtering solution integrated with pfSense in a means that makes it very difficult for the average user to get around. Note it isn't impossible to get around, especially with as permissive of a ruleset as the example above shows. There are several possibilities for tunneling DNS through that ruleset, with VPN connections, SSH port forwarding, and more. But if you allow any traffic through your firewall, that's always going to be a possibility. Properly locked down end user machines in combination with the above provides a strong content filtering solution that's difficult to get around.

24.3 Syslog Server on Windows with Kiwi Syslog

pfSense can send logs to an external server via the syslog protocol (Section 22.1.3). For Windows users, Kiwi Syslog Server[2] is a nice free option for collecting logs from your pfSense installs. It can be installed as a service for long term log collection, or run as an application for shorter term needs. It is compatible with both server and desktop versions of Windows 2000 and newer. The installation is straight forward, and doesn't require much configuration. Help can be found in its documentation after installation.

24.4 Using Software from FreeBSD's Ports System (Packages)

Because pfSense is based on FreeBSD, for a veteran FreeBSD system administrator many familiar FreeBSD packages can also be used. Installing software this way is not for the inexperienced, as it could have unintended side-effects, and is not recommended nor supported. Many parts of FreeBSD are not included, so library and other issues can be encountered. pfSense does not include a compiler in the base system for many reasons, and as such software cannot be built locally. However, you can install packages from FreeBSD's pre-built package repository.

---

[2] http://www.kiwisyslog.com/

24.4.1   Concerns/Warnings

Before you decide to install additional software to pfSense that is not a sanctioned package, there are some topics that need to be taken into account.

24.4.1.1   Security Concerns

Any extra software added to a firewall is a security problem, and should be evaluated fully before installation. If the need outweighs the risk, it may be worth taking. Official pfSense packages are not immune to this problem either. Any additional service is another potential attack vector.

24.4.1.2   Performance Concerns

Most pfSense systems are run on hardware that can handle the traffic load with which they are tasked. If you find that you have horsepower to spare, it may not hurt the system to add additional software. That said, be mindful of the resources that will be consumed by the added software.

24.4.1.3   Conflicting Software

If you install a package which duplicates functionality found in the base system, or replaces a base system package with a newer version, it could cause unpredictable system instability. Ensure that the software you are after does not already exist in the pfSense system before trying to install anything.

24.4.1.4   Lack of Integration

Any extra software installed will not have GUI integration. For some, this is not a problem, but there have been people who expected to install a package and have a GUI magically appear for its configuration. These packages will need to be configured by hand. If this is a service, that means also making sure that any startup scripts are altered to accommodate the methods used by pfSense.

There have also been cases where software has installed additional web pages that are not protected by pfSense's authentication process. Test any installed software to ensure that access is protected or filtered in some manner.

24.4.1.5   Lack of Backups

When installing packages in this manner, you must ensure that you backup any configuration or other needed files for this software. These files will not be backed up during a normal pfSense backup and could be lost or changed during a firmware update. You can use the add-on package described in Section 5.6 to backup arbitrary files such as these.

24.4.2 Installing Packages

To install a package, you must first make sure that the proper package site will be used. pfSense is compiled against a specific FreeBSD-RELEASE branch, and the packages there can become stale within a short amount of time. To work around this, specify the path to the set of packages for FreeBSD-STABLE before attempting to install a package:

```
# setenv PACKAGESITE=ftp://ftp.freebsd.org/pub/FreeBSD/ports/i386/ ↩
    packages-7-stable/
# pkg_add -r tcpflow
```

Or you can supply a full URL to a package:

```
# pkg_add -r ftp://ftp.freebsd.org/pub/FreeBSD/ports/i386/packages-7- ↩
    stable/Latest/iftop.tbz
```

The package should download and install, along with any needed dependencies.

It is also possible to build a custom package on another computer running FreeBSD and then copy/install the generated package file onto a pfSense system. Due to the complexity of this topic, it won't be covered here.

24.4.3 Maintaining Packages

You can view a list of all installed packages like so:

```
# pkg_info
```

To delete an installed package, you must specify its name fully or use a wildcard:

```
# pkg_delete lsof-4.82,4
# pkg_delete tcpflow-\*
```

Chapter 25

Packet Capturing

Capturing packets is the most effective means of troubleshooting problems with network connectivity. Packet capturing (or "sniffing") tools like **tcpdump** show what is "on the wire" — coming in and going out of an interface. Seeing how traffic is received by the firewall and how it leaves the firewall is a great help in narrowing down problems with firewall rules, NAT entries, and other networking issues. In this chapter, we cover obtaining packet captures from the WebGUI, with **tcpdump** at the command line in a shell, and using Wireshark.

25.1   Capture frame of reference

Keep in mind that packet captures show what is on the wire. It is the first to see traffic when receiving packets and last to see traffic when sending packets as they flow through the firewall. It sees traffic before firewall, NAT, and all other processing on the firewall happens for traffic coming into that interface, and after all that processing occurs for traffic leaving that interface. For incoming traffic, captures will show traffic that makes it to that interface on your firewall regardless of whether that traffic will be blocked by your firewall configuration. Figure 25.1 illustrates where **tcpdump** and also the WebGUI packet capture interface ties into the processing order.

25.2   Selecting the Proper Interface

Before you can start any packet capture, you need to know from where the capture should be taken. A packet capture will look different depending upon the interface chosen, and in certain scenarios it's better to capture on one specific interface, and in others, running multiple simultaneous captures on different interfaces is preferable. In using **tcpdump** at the command line, you will need to know the "real" interface names that go with the friendly names shown in the WebGUI. You may recall these from when the interfaces were originally assigned, but if not, you may visit Interfaces → (assign) and make a note of which physical interfaces, such as fxp0, correspond with the pfSense interfaces, such as WAN. Table 25.1 lists some interface names that you may encounter, depending on your configuration.

457

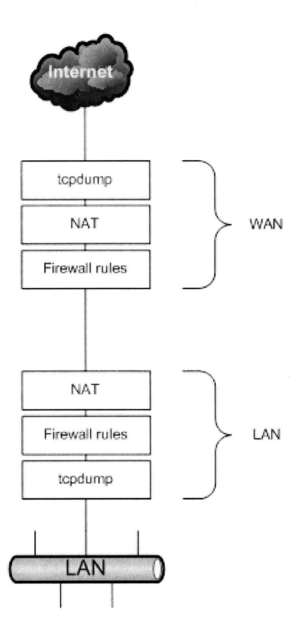

Figure 25.1: Capture reference

Real/Physical Name	Friendly Name
ng0 ... ng$<x>$	WAN (PPPoE or PPTP WAN), or PPTP clients
enc0	IPsec, encrypted traffic
tun0 ... tun$<x>$	OpenVPN, encrypted traffic
lo0	Loopback Interface
pfsync0	pfsync interface — used internally
pflog0	pf logging — used internally

Table 25.1: Real Interface vs. Friendly Names

When selecting an interface, you will typically want to start with where the traffic flows into pfSense. For example, if you are having trouble connecting to a port forward from outside your network, start with the WAN interface since that is where the traffic originates. Alternately, if you have a client PC which cannot reach the Internet, start with the LAN interface. When in doubt, try multiple interfaces and filter for the IP addresses or ports in question.

25.3 Limiting capture volume

When capturing packets, it is important to limit the volume of packets captured, but still ensure all relevant traffic for the problem being troubleshooted is captured. On most networks, when capturing without filtering the traffic captured, even with captures from short time frames, you end up with huge amounts of data to dig through to find the problem. You can filter post-capture by using display filters in Wireshark, but filtering appropriately at the time of capture is preferable to keep the capture file size down. Filters are discussed later in this chapter.

25.4 Packet Captures from the WebGUI

The WebGUI offers an easy-to-use front end to **tcpdump** that will let you get packet captures which can then be viewed or downloaded for deeper analysis in Wireshark. Because of its simplicity, it can only offer a few limited options for filtering desired traffic, which may complicate the task depending on the traffic level on your network and filtering needs. That said, for many people it is enough and gets the job done. If you feel limited by the options available, feel free to skip down to the next section on using **tcpdump** directly.

25.4.1 Getting a Packet Capture

First, browse to Diagnostics → Packet Capture to start the process. From there, choose the Interface on which you would like to capture traffic. If you would like to filter traffic going to or from a specific host, enter its IP address in the Host Address field. The Port may also be limited if you are capturing TCP or UDP traffic.

You can adjust Packet Length captured if desired. Usually you will want the full packet, but for captures run over longer periods of time where the headers matter more than the payload of the packets, limiting this to 64 bytes or so will result in a much smaller capture file that may still have adequate data for troubleshooting purposes. The Count box determines how many packets to capture before stopping. If you did not limit the capture in any way, bear in mind that this may be pretty "noisy" and you may need to increase this much larger than the default of **100**.

The Level of Detail option only affects the output as shown when the capture is finished. It does not change the level of detail in the capture file if you choose to download it when completed.

It is not generally recommended to check Reverse DNS Lookups when performing a capture as it will delay the output as reverse DNS is performed. Also it is commonly easier to troubleshoot when viewing IP addresses instead of hostnames, and reverse DNS can sometimes be inaccurate. This can be useful on occasion though.

Press Start to begin capturing data. The screen will display "Packet Capture is running" across the bottom, indicating the capture is in process. Press Stop to end the capture and view the output. If you specified a maximum packet count it will stop automatically when that count is reached, or you can click **Stop** to end it at any time.

25.4.2 Viewing the Captured Data

The capture output can be viewed in the WebGUI, or downloaded for later viewing in a program such as Wireshark. For more detail on using Wireshark to view a capture file, see Section 25.6.1 later in this chapter. Click Download Capture to download this file for later viewing.

The output shown in the Packets Captured frame are shown in standard **tcpdump** style.

25.5   Using tcpdump from the command line

tcpdump is the command line packet capture utility provided with most UNIX and UNIX-like operating system distributions, including FreeBSD. It is also included with pfSense, and usable from a shell on the console or by SSH. It is an exceptionally powerful tool, but that also makes it daunting to the uninitiated user. The **tcpdump** binary in FreeBSD 7.2 supports 36 different command line flags, limitless possibilities with filter expressions, and its man page, providing only a brief overview of all its options, is nearly 30 printed 8.5x11" pages long. After learning to use it, you must also know how to interpret the data it provides, which can require an in-depth understanding of networking protocols.

A comprehensive review of packet capturing and interpretation of the results is outside the scope of this book. Indeed, entire books have been written on this subject alone. For those with a thirst for more than basic knowledge in this area, some recommendations for additional reading are provided at the end of this chapter. This section is intended to provide an introduction to this topic, and leave you with enough knowledge for basic troubleshooting.

25.5.1   tcpdump command line flags

The following table shows the most commonly used command line flags with **tcpdump**. Each option will be discussed in further detail in this section.

Flag	Description
`-i <interface>`	Listen on `<interface>`, .e.g. `-i fxp0`
`-n`	Do not resolve IPs using reverse DNS.
`-w <filename>`	Save capture in pcap format to <filename>, e.g. `-w /tmp/wan.pcap`
`-s`	Snap length — amount of data to be captured from each frame
`-c <packets>`	Exit after receiving a specific number of packets.
`-p`	Don't put the interface in promiscuous mode.
`-v`	Verbose
`-e`	Print link-layer header on each line. Shows the source and destination MAC address, and VL⁄

Table 25.2: Commonly used tcpdump flags

25.5.1.1   -i flag

The `-i` flag specifies the interface on which **tcpdump** will listen. You use FreeBSD's interface name here, such as `fxp0`, `em0`, `rl0`, etc.

25.5.1.2   -n flag

Do not resolve IPs using reverse DNS. When this option is not specified, **tcpdump** will perform a reverse DNS (PTR) lookup for each IP address. This generates a significant amount of DNS traffic in captures displaying large volumes of traffic. You may wish to disable this to avoid adding load to your DNS servers. I prefer to always use `-n` because it eliminates the delay between a packet's capture and its display that is caused by performing the reverse lookup. Also IP addresses tend to be easier to read and understand than their PTR records. That is a matter of personal preference though, and in environments I am familiar with where I know the PTR records will provide the actual host names of the devices, I may run captures without `-n` to show the hostnames.

Another reason to use `-n`, though you should never capture in any environment where this is remotely a concern, is if you want to be "sneaky." One means of detecting packet capturing is looking for spikes and patterns in DNS PTR lookups.

25.5.1.3   -w flag

tcpdump allows you to save capture files in pcap format, for later analysis, or analysis on another system. This is commonly done from command line only devices like pfSense so the file can be copied to a host running Wireshark or another graphical network protocol analyzer and reviewed there. When saving to a file using `-w`, the frames will not be displayed in your terminal as they otherwise are. (See Section 25.6 about using Wireshark with pfSense.)

25.5.1.4   -s flag

By default, when capturing to a file, **tcpdump** will only save the first 64 bytes of each frame. This is enough to get the IP and protocol header for most protocols, but limits the usability of capture files. By

Flag	Description
-s 500	Capture the first 500 bytes of each frame
-s 0	Capture each frame in its entirety

Table 25.3: Example uses of tcpdump -s

using the −s flag, you can tell tcpdump how much of the frame to capture, in bytes. This is called the snap length.

You will usually want to use −s 0 when capturing to a file for analysis on another system. The only exception to this is scenarios where you need to capture a significant amount of traffic over a longer period of time. If you know the information you are seeking is in the header, you can save only the default 64 bytes of each frame and get the information you need, while significantly reducing the size of the resulting capture file.

25.5.1.5   -c flag

You can instruct tcpdump to capture a certain number of frames and then exit by using the −c flag. Example usage: tcpdump will exit after capturing 100 frames by specifying −c 100.

25.5.1.6   -p flag

Normally when capturing traffic with **tcpdump**, it puts your network interface into promiscuous mode. When not running in promiscuous mode, your NIC only receives frames destined for its own MAC address, as well as broadcast and multicast addresses. When switched into promiscuous mode, the interface shows every frame on the wire. In a switched network, this generally has little impact on your capture. In networks where the device you are capturing from is connected to a hub, using −p can significantly limit noise in your capture when the only traffic of interest is that to and from the system from which you are capturing.

25.5.1.7   -v flag

The −v flag controls the detail, or verbosity, of the output. Using more "v" options yields more detail, so you can use −v, −vv, or −vvv to view even more detail in the output printed to the console. This option does not affect the detail stored in a capture file when using the −w switch, but will instead cause the process to report the number of packets captured every 10 seconds.

25.5.1.8   -e flag

Normally tcpdump does not show any link layer information. Specify −e to display the source and destination MAC addresses, and VLAN tag information for any traffic tagged with 802.1q VLANs.

25.5.1.8.1 Example capture without -e

This capture shows the default output, containing no link layer information.

```
# tcpdump -ni em0 -c 5
tcpdump: verbose output suppressed, use -v or -vv for full protocol ↩
    decode
listening on em0, link-type EN10MB (Ethernet), capture size 96 bytes
23:18:15.830706 IP 10.0.64.210.22 > 10.0.64.15.1395: P ↩
    2023587125:2023587241(116) ack 2091089207 win 65535
23:18:15.830851 IP 10.0.64.210.22 > 10.0.64.15.1395: P 116:232(116) ack ↩
    1 win 65535
23:18:15.831256 IP 10.0.64.15.1395 > 10.0.64.210.22: . ack 116 win 65299
23:18:15.839834 IP 10.0.64.3 > 224.0.0.18: VRRPv2, Advertisement, vrid ↩
    4, prio 0, authtype none, intvl 1s, length 36
23:18:16.006407 IP 10.0.64.15.1395 > 10.0.64.210.22: . ack 232 win 65183
5 packets captured
```

25.5.1.8.2 Example capture using -e

Here you see the link layer information included. Note the source and destination MAC addresses in addition to the source and destination IP addresses.

```
# tcpdump -ni em0 -e -c 5
tcpdump: verbose output suppressed, use -v or -vv for full protocol ↩
    decode
listening on em0, link-type EN10MB (Ethernet), capture size 96 bytes
23:30:05.914958 00:0c:29:0b:c3:ed > 00:13:d4:f7:73:d2, ethertype IPv4 (0 ↩
    x0800), length 170: 10.0.64.210.22 > 10.0.64.15.1395: P ↩
    2023592509:2023592625(116) ack 2091091355 win 65535
23:30:05.915110 00:0c:29:0b:c3:ed > 00:13:d4:f7:73:d2, ethertype IPv4 (0 ↩
    x0800), length 170: 10.0.64.210.22 > 10.0.64.15.1395: P 116:232(116) ↩
    ack 1 win 65535
23:30:05.915396 00:13:d4:f7:73:d2 > 00:0c:29:0b:c3:ed, ethertype IPv4 (0 ↩
    x0800), length 60: 10.0.64.15.1395 > 10.0.64.210.22: . ack 116 win ↩
    65299
23:30:05.973359 00:00:5e:00:01:04 > 01:00:5e:00:00:12, ethertype IPv4 (0 ↩
    x0800), length 70: 10.0.64.3 > 224.0.0.18: VRRPv2, Advertisement, ↩
    vrid 4, prio 0, authtype none, intvl 1s, length 36
23:30:06.065200 00:13:d4:f7:73:d2 > 00:0c:29:0b:c3:ed, ethertype IPv4 (0 ↩
    x0800), length 60: 10.0.64.15.1395 > 10.0.64.210.22: . ack 232 win ↩
    65183
5 packets captured
```

25.5.2 tcpdump Filters

On most firewalls, **tcpdump** with no filters will produce so much output that it will prove very difficult to find traffic of interest. There are numerous filtering expressions available that allow you to limit the traffic displayed or captured to only what you are interested in.

25.5.2.1 Host filters

To filter for a specific host, append `host` and the IP address to the **tcpdump** command. To filter for host 192.168.1.100 you can use the following command.

```
# tcpdump -ni em0 host 192.168.1.100
```

That will capture all traffic to and from that host. If you only wish to capture traffic being initiated by that host, you can use the `src` directive.

```
# tcpdump -ni em0 src host 192.168.1.100
```

Similarly, you can also filter for traffic destined to that IP address by specifying `dst`.

```
# tcpdump -ni em0 dst host 192.168.1.100
```

25.5.2.2 Network filters

Network filters let you narrow down your capture to a specific subnet using the `net` expression. Following `net`, you can specify a dotted quad (`192.168.1.1`), dotted triple (`192.168.1`), dotted pair (`192.168`) or simply a number (`192`). A dotted quad is equivalent to specifying `host`, a dotted triple uses a subnet mask of 255.255.255.0, a dotted pair uses 255.255.0.0, and a number alone uses 255.0.0.0.

The following command displays traffic to or from any host with a 192.168.1.x IP address.

```
# tcpdump -ni em0 net 192.168.1
```

The next command is an example that will capture traffic to or from any host with a 10.x.x.x IP address.

```
# tcpdump -ni em0 net 10
```

Those examples will capture all traffic to or from the specified network. You can also specify `src` or `dst` the same as with `host` filters to capture only traffic initiated by or destined to the specified network.

```
# tcpdump -ni em0 src net 10
```

It is also possible to specify a CIDR mask as an argument to `net`.

```
# tcpdump -ni em0 src net 172.16.0.0/12
```

25.5.2.3 Protocol and port filters

Narrowing down by host or network frequently isn't adequate to eliminate unnecessary traffic from your capture. Or you may not care about the source or destination of traffic, and simply wish to capture a certain type of traffic. In other cases you may want to filter out all traffic of a specific type to reduce noise.

25.5.2.3.1 TCP and UDP port filters

To filter on TCP and UDP ports you use the `port` directive. This captures both TCP and UDP traffic using the specified port either as a source or destination port. It can be combined with `tcp` or `udp` to specify the protocol, and `src` or `dst` to specify a source or destination port.

25.5.2.3.1.1 Capture all HTTP traffic

```
# tcpdump -ni em0 tcp port 80
```

25.5.2.3.1.2 Capture all DNS traffic

Capture all DNS traffic (usually UDP, but some queries use TCP).

```
# tcpdump -ni em0 port 53
```

25.5.2.3.2 Protocol filters

You can filter by specific protocols using the `proto` directive. Protocol can be specified using the IP protocol number or one of the names `icmp`, `igmp`, `igrp`, `pim`, `ah`, `esp`, `vrrp`, `udp`, or `tcp`. Specifying `vrrp` will also capture CARP traffic as the two use the same IP protocol number. One common usage of the `proto` directive is to filter for CARP traffic. Because the normal protocol names are reserved words, they must be escaped with one or two backslashes, depending on the shell. The shell available in pfSense requires two backslashes to escape these protocol names. If you receive a syntax error, check that the protocol name is properly escaped. The following capture will show all CARP and VRRP traffic on the `em0` interface, which can be useful to ensure CARP traffic is being sent and received on the specified interface.

```
# tcpdump -ni em0 proto \\vrrp
```

25.5.2.4 Negating a filter match

In addition to matching specific parameters, you can negate a filter match by specifying `not` in front of the filter expression. If you are troubleshooting something other than CARP and its multicast heartbeats are cluttering your capture output, you can exclude it as follows.

```
# tcpdump -ni em0 not proto \\vrrp
```

25.5.2.5 Combining filters

You can combine any of the aforementioned filters using `and` or `or`. The following sections provide some examples.

25.5.2.5.1   Display all HTTP traffic to and from a host

To display all HTTP traffic from the host 192.168.1.11, use the following command.

```
# tcpdump -ni em0 host 192.168.1.11 and tcp port 80
```

25.5.2.5.2   Display all HTTP traffic to and from multiple hosts

To display all HTTP traffic from the hosts 192.168.1.11 and 192.168.1.15, use the following command.

```
# tcpdump -ni em0 host 192.168.1.11 or host 192.168.1.15 and tcp port 80
```

25.5.2.6   Filter expression usage

Filter expressions must come after every command line flag used. Adding any flags after a filter expression will result in a syntax error.

25.5.2.6.1   Incorrect ordering

```
# tcpdump -ni en1 proto \\vrrp -c 2
tcpdump: syntax error
```

25.5.2.6.2   Correct ordering

```
# tcpdump -ni en1 -c 2 proto \\vrrp
tcpdump: verbose output suppressed, use -v or -vv for full protocol  ↵
    decode
listening on en1, link-type EN10MB (Ethernet), capture size 96 bytes
18:58:51.312287 IP 10.0.64.3 > 224.0.0.18: VRRPv2, Advertisement, vrid  ↵
    4, prio 0, authtype none, intvl 1s, length 36
18:58:52.322430 IP 10.0.64.3 > 224.0.0.18: VRRPv2, Advertisement, vrid  ↵
    4, prio 0, authtype none, intvl 1s, length 36
2 packets captured
80 packets received by filter
0 packets dropped by kernel
```

25.5.2.7   More on Filters

This section covered the most commonly used **tcpdump** filter expressions, and probably covers all the syntax you will need. However this barely scratches the surface of the possibilities. There are many documents on the web that cover **tcpdump** in general and filtering specifically. See Section 25.8 at the end of this chapter for links to additional references on the subject.

25.5.3   Practical Troubleshooting Examples

This section details an approach preferred by us for troubleshooting a few specific problems. There are multiple ways to approach any problem, but packet capturing can rarely be beat for its effectiveness. Examining the traffic on the wire provides a level of visibility into what is really happening on the network

25.5.3.1   Port forward not working

You just added a port forward, and are trying to use it from a host on the Internet, but no dice. The troubleshooting steps outlined in Section 7.9.1 offers one way to approach this, but sometimes packet capturing is the only or easiest way to find the source of the problem.

25.5.3.1.1   Start from WAN

First you need to make sure the traffic is getting to your WAN interface. Start a **tcpdump** session on your WAN interface, and watch for the traffic to come in.

```
# tcpdump -ni vlan0 tcp port 5900
tcpdump: verbose output suppressed, use -v or -vv for full protocol  ↩
    decode
listening on vlan0, link-type EN10MB (Ethernet), capture size 96 bytes
11:14:02.444006 IP 172.17.11.9.37219 > 10.0.73.5.5900: S  ↩
    3863112259:3863112259(0) win 65535 <mss 1260,nop,nop,sackOK>
```

In this case, we see a packet come in from the WAN, so it is making it that far. Note that the first part of the TCP handshake, a packet with only SYN set (the S shown), is reaching us. If the port forward is working you will see a SYN ACK packet in reply to the SYN. With no return traffic visible, it could be a firewall rule or the target system may be unreachable (turned off, not listening on the specified port, host firewall blocking the traffic, etc.).

25.5.3.1.2   Check Internal Interface

The next step would be to run a **tcpdump** session on the internal interface associated with the port forward.

```
# tcpdump -ni fxp0 tcp port 5900
tcpdump: verbose output suppressed, use -v or -vv for full protocol  ↩
    decode
listening on fxp0, link-type EN10MB (Ethernet), capture size 96 bytes
11:14:38.339926 IP 172.17.11.9.2302 > 192.168.30.5.5900: S  ↩
    1481321921:1481321921(0) win 65535 <mss 1260,nop,nop,sackOK>
```

Looking at the internal traffic, we see that the connection did leave the inside interface, and the local IP address was translated correctly. If this local address matches what you expected, then both the port forward and the firewall rule are working properly, and connectivity to the local PC should be confirmed by other means. If you saw no output at all, then there is a problem with the firewall rule or the port forward may have been incorrectly defined. For this example, I had unplugged the PC.

25.5.3.2   IPsec tunnel will not connect

Because **tcpdump** has some awareness of the protocols being used, it can be very helpful in figuring out problems with IPsec tunnels. The next few examples will show how certain error conditions may present themselves when monitoring with **tcpdump**. The IPsec logs may be more helpful in some cases, but this can confirm what is actually being seen by the router. For encrypted traffic such as IPsec, packet capturing of the traffic is of less value as you cannot examine the payload of the captured packets without additional parameters, but it is helpful to determine if traffic from the remote end is reaching your firewall and which phases complete.

This first tunnel has an unreachable peer:

```
# tcpdump -ni vr0 host 192.168.10.6
tcpdump: verbose output suppressed, use -v or -vv for full protocol  ↩
    decode
listening on vr0, link-type EN10MB (Ethernet), capture size 96 bytes

19:11:11.542976 IP 192.168.10.5.500 > 192.168.10.6.500: isakmp: phase 1  ↩
    I agg
19:11:21.544644 IP 192.168.10.5.500 > 192.168.10.6.500: isakmp: phase 1  ↩
    I agg
```

This tunnel attempt has a mismatched PSK, notice how it attempts to move to phase 2, but then stops:

```
# tcpdump -ni vr0 host 192.168.10.6
tcpdump: verbose output suppressed, use -v or -vv for full protocol  ↩
    decode
listening on vr0, link-type EN10MB (Ethernet), capture size 96 bytes
19:15:05.566352 IP 192.168.10.5.500 > 192.168.10.6.500: isakmp: phase 1  ↩
    I agg
19:15:05.623288 IP 192.168.10.6.500 > 192.168.10.5.500: isakmp: phase 1  ↩
    R agg
19:15:05.653504 IP 192.168.10.5.500 > 192.168.10.6.500: isakmp: phase 2/ ↩
    others I inf[E]
```

Now Phase 1 is OK but there is a mismatch in the Phase 2 information. It will repeatedly attempt phase 2 traffic but you won't see any traffic on the tunnel.

```
# tcpdump -ni vr0 host 192.168.10.6
tcpdump: verbose output suppressed, use -v or -vv for full protocol  ↩
    decode
listening on vr0, link-type EN10MB (Ethernet), capture size 96 bytes
19:17:18.447952 IP 192.168.10.5.500 > 192.168.10.6.500: isakmp: phase 1  ↩
    I agg
19:17:18.490278 IP 192.168.10.6.500 > 192.168.10.5.500: isakmp: phase 1  ↩
    R agg
19:17:18.520149 IP 192.168.10.5.500 > 192.168.10.6.500: isakmp: phase 1  ↩
    I agg
19:17:18.520761 IP 192.168.10.6.500 > 192.168.10.5.500: isakmp: phase 2/ ↩
    others R inf[E]
19:17:18.525474 IP 192.168.10.5.500 > 192.168.10.6.500: isakmp: phase 2/ ↩
    others I inf[E]
```

```
19:17:19.527962 IP 192.168.10.5.500 > 192.168.10.6.500: isakmp: phase 2/ ↩
   others I oakley-quick[E]
```

Finally, a fully working tunnel with two-way traffic after Phase 1 and Phase 2 have completed!

```
#  tcpdump -ni vr1 host 192.168.10.6
tcpdump: verbose output suppressed, use -v or -vv for full protocol  ↩
   decode
listening on vr1, link-type EN10MB (Ethernet), capture size 96 bytes
21:50:11.238263 IP 192.168.10.5.500 > 192.168.10.6.500: isakmp: phase 1  ↩
   I agg
21:50:11.713364 IP 192.168.10.6.500 > 192.168.10.5.500: isakmp: phase 1  ↩
   R agg
21:50:11.799162 IP 192.168.10.5.500 > 192.168.10.6.500: isakmp: phase 1  ↩
   I agg
21:50:11.801706 IP 192.168.10.5.500 > 192.168.10.6.500: isakmp: phase 2/ ↩
   others I inf[E]
21:50:11.812809 IP 192.168.10.6.500 > 192.168.10.5.500: isakmp: phase 2/ ↩
   others R inf[E]
21:50:12.820191 IP 192.168.10.5.500 > 192.168.10.6.500: isakmp: phase 2/ ↩
   others I oakley-quick[E]
21:50:12.836478 IP 192.168.10.6.500 > 192.168.10.5.500: isakmp: phase 2/ ↩
   others R oakley-quick[E]
21:50:12.838499 IP 192.168.10.5.500 > 192.168.10.6.500: isakmp: phase 2/ ↩
   others I oakley-quick[E]
21:50:13.168425 IP 192.168.10.5 > 192.168.10.6: ESP(spi=0x09bf945f,seq=0 ↩
   x1), length 132
21:50:13.171227 IP 192.168.10.6 > 192.168.10.5: ESP(spi=0x0a6f9257,seq=0 ↩
   x1), length 132
21:50:14.178820 IP 192.168.10.5 > 192.168.10.6: ESP(spi=0x09bf945f,seq=0 ↩
   x2), length 132
21:50:14.181210 IP 192.168.10.6 > 192.168.10.5: ESP(spi=0x0a6f9257,seq=0 ↩
   x2), length 132
21:50:15.189349 IP 192.168.10.5 > 192.168.10.6: ESP(spi=0x09bf945f,seq=0 ↩
   x3), length 132
21:50:15.191756 IP 192.168.10.6 > 192.168.10.5: ESP(spi=0x0a6f9257,seq=0 ↩
   x3), length 132
```

25.5.3.3 Traffic traversing an IPsec tunnel

With some extra settings to initialize the process, you can also view traffic traversing your IPsec tunnels. This can help determine if traffic is attempting to reach the far end by using the tunnel. In versions prior to the 1.2.3 release, before **tcpdump** will work on the IPsec interface you had to set two **sysctl** variables that control what is visible to **tcpdump**. If you are using 1.2.3 release or newer, **tcpdump** will work without any extra handling.

In the following example, a host on one side of the tunnel is successfully sending an ICMP echo request (ping) to the far side, and receiving replies.

```
#  sysctl -w net.enc.out.ipsec_bpf_mask=0x00000001
```

```
net.enc.out.ipsec_bpf_mask: 0000000000 -> 0x00000001
# sysctl -w net.enc.in.ipsec_bpf_mask=0x00000001
net.enc.in.ipsec_bpf_mask: 0000000000 -> 0x00000001
# tcpdump -ni enc0
tcpdump: WARNING: enc0: no IPv4 address assigned
tcpdump: verbose output suppressed, use -v or -vv for full protocol ↩
    decode
listening on enc0, link-type ENC (OpenBSD encapsulated IP), capture size ↩
    96 bytes
22:09:18.331506 (authentic,confidential): SPI 0x09bf945f:
            IP 10.0.20.1 > 10.0.30.1:
            ICMP echo request, id 14140, seq 0, length 64
22:09:18.334777 (authentic,confidential): SPI 0x0a6f9257:
            IP 192.168.10.6 > 192.168.10.5: IP 10.0.30.1 > ↩
                10.0.20.1:
            ICMP echo reply, id 14140, seq 0, length 64 (ipip-proto ↩
                -4)
22:09:19.336613 (authentic,confidential): SPI 0x09bf945f:
            IP 10.0.20.1 > 10.0.30.1:
            ICMP echo request, id 14140, seq 1, length 64
22:09:19.339590 (authentic,confidential): SPI 0x0a6f9257:
            IP 192.168.10.6 > 192.168.10.5: IP 10.0.30.1 > ↩
                10.0.20.1:
            ICMP echo reply, id 14140, seq 1, length 64 (ipip-proto ↩
                -4)
```

If traffic was not properly entering the tunnel, you would not see any output. If there is a firewall or internal routing issue on the far side, you may see traffic leaving but nothing returning.

25.5.3.4   Troubleshooting Outbound NAT

For complex environments where Advanced Outbound NAT is needed, **tcpdump** can be of great assistance in troubleshooting your Outbound NAT configuration. One good capture to use is to look for traffic with private IP addresses on your WAN interface, as everything you see on your WAN should be NATed to a public IP. The following capture will display any traffic with RFC 1918 IP addresses as the source or destination. This will show any traffic that is not matching one of your outbound NAT rules, providing information to help review your Outbound NAT configuration to find the problem.

```
# tcpdump -ni em0 net 10 or net 192.168 or net 172.16.0.0/12
```

25.6   Using Wireshark with pfSense

Wireshark, formerly known as Ethereal, is a GUI protocol analysis and packet capture tool that can be used to view and capture traffic much like **tcpdump**. It is Open Source software, freely available at http://www.wireshark.org/. It can also be used to analyze capture files generated by the pfSense WebGUI, **tcpdump**, Wireshark, or any other software that writes files in the standard pcap file format.

25.6.1   Viewing Packet Capture File

To view a capture file in Wireshark, start the program and then go to File → Open. Locate the capture file, and then click the Open button. You can also double click on any file with a `.pcap` extension in Windows and OS X with default settings after the Wireshark installation. You will see a screen similar to Figure 25.2 in which the data from the capture file is displayed.

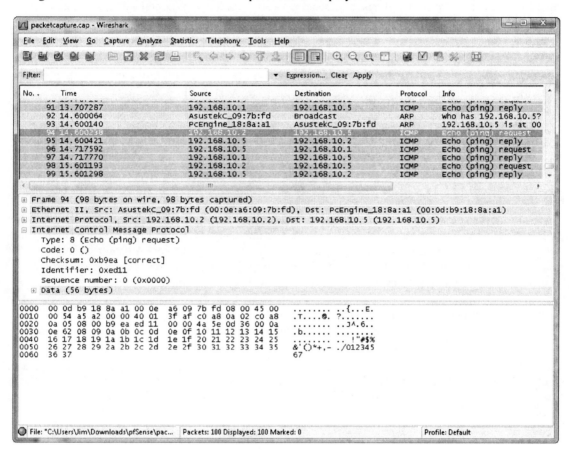

Figure 25.2: Wireshark Capture View

As seen in Figure 25.2, a list summarizing the packets in the capture file will be shown in the top list, with one packet per line. If there are too many, you can filter the results using the Filter box on the toolbar. When you click on a packet, the lower frames will show the details of what was contained within. The first lower pane shows a break-down of the packet's structure, and each of these items can be expanded for more detail. If the packet is of a supported protocol, in some cases it can interpret the data and show even more details. The bottom pane shows a hexadecimal and ASCII representation of the data contained in the packet.

Viewing the capture this way, it is easy to see the flow of traffic with as much or as little detail as needed.

25.6.2   Wireshark Analysis Tools

While some problems will require considerable knowledge of how the underlying protocols function, the analysis tools built into Wireshark helps lessen that need for many protocols. Under the Analyze and Statistics menus, you will find a few options that automate some of the analysis and provide summarized views of what is contained in the capture. The Expert Info options under the Analyze menu show a list of Errors, Warnings, Notes and network conversations contained in the capture.

Note

You will commonly see errors in Wireshark for incorrect checksums. This is because most NICs add the checksum in hardware directly before putting it on the wire. This is the only exception to the earlier note saying what you see in a packet capture is what is on the wire. Traffic sent out from the system where the capture is taken will have incorrect checksums where they are done in hardware, though traffic coming in from a remote system should always have correct checksums. You can turn off checksum offloading to ensure you are seeing traffic as the host is putting it on the wire, though usually this is something you simply ignore. Should you need to verify checksums, you will usually want to capture traffic from another system using a network tap or switch span port.

The Telephony menu is one example of automated analysis Wireshark can perform to make it easy to see problems with VoIP. In this particular case, VoIP traffic was traversing a MPLS WAN circuit with the provider's routers attached to an OPT interface of pfSense on both sides. A capture from the OPT interface on the initiating end showed no loss, indicating the traffic was being sent to the provider's router, but the OPT interface on the opposite end showed considerable packet loss in one direction when multiple simultaneous calls were active. These packet captures helped convince the provider of a problem on their network, and they found and fixed a QoS configuration problem on their side. When viewing a packet capture containing RTP traffic, click **Telephony**, **RTP**, **Show all streams** to see this screen.

Src IP addr ▾	Src port	Dest IP addr	Dest port	SSRC	Payload	Packets	Lost	Max Delta (ms)	Max Jitter (ms)	Mean Jitter (ms)	Pb?
10	13114	192	2244	0x63B69143	ITU-T G.711 PCMU	2103	0 (0.0%)	20.07	0.12	0.01	X
192.1	2244	1	13114	0x6F1D173B	ITU-T G.711 PCMU	1646	477 (22.5%)	179.89	51.24	1.84	X
10	11224	192	2268	0x2247C8D8	ITU-T G.711 PCMU	1321	0 (0.0%)	99.99	5.03	0.07	X
192.1	2268	1	11224	0x6C5B26A1	ITU-T G.711 PCMU	879	460 (34.4%)	340.79	49.96	2.67	X
10	17924	192	2242	0x393CBA89	ITU-T G.711 PCMU	480	0 (0.0%)	20.04	0.15	0.01	X
192.1	2242	1	17924	0x6177246E	ITU-T G.711 PCMU	133	366 (73.3%)	339.79	71.38	9.17	X

Figure 25.3: Wireshark RTP Analysis

25.6.3   Remote Realtime Capture

From a UNIX host that has Wireshark available, you can run a realtime remote capture by redirecting the output from an SSH session. This has been tested and known to work on FreeBSD and Ubuntu.

In order to use this technique, SSH must be enabled on the pfSense system and you will need to use an SSH key (see Section 4.5.2). The key must first be loaded into **ssh-agent** or generated without a passphrase because the redirection will not allow you to enter a password. Using **ssh-agent** is highly recommended, as any key without a passphrase is very insecure.

Before you attempt this technique, be sure that you can connect to your pfSense router using an SSH key without needing to type the passphrase. The first time you connect, you will be prompted to save the host key, so that must also be done before you try to start wireshark. You may start **ssh-agent** from a terminal window or shell like so:

```
# eval `ssh-agent`
Agent pid 29047
# ssh-add
Enter passphrase for /home/jim/.ssh/id_rsa:
Identity added: /home/jim/.ssh/id_rsa (/home/jim/.ssh/id_rsa)
```

Then start an SSH session as usual:

```
# ssh root@192.168.1.1
The authenticity of host '192.168.1.1 (192.168.1.1)' can't be  ←
   established.
DSA key fingerprint is 9e:c0:b0:5a:b9:9b:f4:ec:7f:1d:8a:2d:4a:49:01:1b.
Are you sure you want to continue connecting (yes/no)? yes
Warning: Permanently added '192.168.1.1' (DSA) to the list of known  ←
   hosts.

*** Welcome to pfSense 1.2.3-pfSense on exco-rtr ***
[...]
```

After you have confirmed that the SSH connection works, start the remote capture as follows:

```
# wireshark -k -i <(ssh root@192.168.1.1 tcpdump -i vr0 -U -w - not tcp  ←
   port 22)
```

Where the IP address part is the address of your pfSense system. The "**not tcp port 22**" part will exclude the traffic from your SSH session, which will otherwise clog the capture output. The above is written in "bash-style" syntax, but may work with other shells. You can adjust the **tcpdump** arguments for the interface, and add additional expressions, but the -U and -w - are necessary so that it writes the output to stdout, and writes each packet as it arrives.

See also the Capture Setup/Pipes page on the Wireshark wiki for other related techniques.

25.7 Plain Text Protocol Debugging with tcpflow

tcpflow is another package similar to **tcpdump** which will let you view the text contents of packets in realtime instead of the packet headers and other transport information. **tcpflow** uses similar syntax to **tcpdump**, with one notable exception: By default it writes the packet text to files instead of the console. To watch output on the console, use the -c option.

While not available on a stock pfSense installation, **tcpflow** may be added from the command line by installing the FreeBSD package. It is a small package with no dependencies, so installing it should not harm the system. To install **tcpflow** on pfSense, run the following command from a pfSense shell:

```
# pkg_add -r tcpflow
# rehash
```

If you were having trouble with an FTP connection from a LAN, you could monitor the control channel on the WAN side like so:

```
# tcpflow -i vlan0 -c host 172.17.11.9 and port 21
tcpflow[13899]: listening on vlan0
172.017.011.009.00021-010.000.073.005.23747: 220 Welcome to ExampleCo  ↩
    web FTP service
010.000.073.005.23747-172.017.011.009.00021: USER fieldtech
172.017.011.009.00021-010.000.073.005.23747: 331 Please specify the  ↩
    password.
010.000.073.005.23747-172.017.011.009.00021: PASS abc123
172.017.011.009.00021-010.000.073.005.23747: 230 Login successful.
010.000.073.005.23747-172.017.011.009.00021: PORT 10,0,73,5,194,240
172.017.011.009.00021-010.000.073.005.23747: 200 PORT command successful  ↩
    . Consider using PASV.
010.000.073.005.23747-172.017.011.009.00021: NLST
172.017.011.009.00021-010.000.073.005.23747: 150 Here comes the  ↩
    directory listing.
172.017.011.009.00021-010.000.073.005.23747: 226 Directory send OK.
```

As you can see from this output, it is easy to monitor the flow of plain text control protocols like FTP. You can see commands and output going in both directions, and most importantly you can see that the FTP proxy did its job and translated the PORT command to use the WAN IP address of pfSense instead, allowing active mode to work properly. If you instead saw the LAN IP address listed in the PORT command, you would know to check the FTP proxy settings or switch to PASV mode on the client.

Having **tcpflow** around has been very handy in my experience, and it makes a good complement to **tcpdump** when you want to focus on the contents of the packets rather than their structure.

25.8   Additional References

This capture only scratches the surface of the possibilities with packet captures. Here are some additional resources for those interested in more in-depth knowledge. Packet capturing is a very powerful means of troubleshooting network connectivity issues, and you will find your troubleshooting skills greatly improved if you learn the possibilities in more depth.

Computer Networking: Internet Protocols in Action by Jeanna Matthews

Tcpdump Filters by Jamie French

Tcpdump Advanced Filters by Sebastien Wains

Tcpdump Filters by Marios Iliofotou

FreeBSD Man Page for **tcpdump**

Appendix A

Menu Guide

This guide to the standard menu choices available in pfSense should help to quickly identify the purpose of a given menu option, and refer to places in the book where those options are discussed in further detail.

Packages can add items to any menu, so you may have to check all of them to locate the menu options for any installed packages. Typically, packages install under the Services menu but there are plenty of them that occupy other menus as well.

A.1   System

The System menu contains choices for the system itself, general and advanced options, firmware updates, add-on packages, and static routes.

Advanced
> Advanced system settings for the firewall, hardware, SSH, SSL certificates, and many others. See Section 4.5.

Firmware
> Upgrade or change the system firmware version. (e.g. update from pfSense 1.2.2 to 1.2.3). See Section 3.7.3.1.

General Setup
> General system settings such as hostname, domain, DNS servers, etc. See Section 4.4.

Packages
> Additional software add-ons for pfSense to expand its functionality. See Chapter 23.

Setup wizard
> The Setup Wizard guides you through the process of performing the basic initial setup. See Section 4.2.

Static routes
> Static Routes let pfSense know how to reach non-local subnets via locally reachable routers. See Section 8.1.

A.2   Interfaces

The Interfaces menu has items for assigning interfaces, and an item for each assigned interface. WAN and LAN will always appear, while others appear as OPTx or the name they have been given.

(assign)

> Assign interfaces to logical roles (e.g. LAN, WAN, OPT), and create/maintain VLANs. See Section 4.3.1 and Chapter 10.

WAN

> Configure the WAN interface. See Section 4.3.2.

LAN

> Configure the LAN interface. See Section 4.3.3.

OPTx

> Configure any additional optional interfaces. See Section 4.3.3.

A.3   Firewall

The Firewall menu items are for configuring various parts of the firewall rules, NAT rules, and their supporting structure.

Aliases

> Lets you manage collections of IP addresses, networks, or ports to simplify rule creation and management. See Section 6.3.

NAT

> Maintain NAT rules that control port forwards, 1:1 NAT, and outbound NAT behavior. See Chapter 7.

Rules

> Configure firewall rules. There should be one tab on this screen for each configured interface. See Section 6.2.

Schedules

> Setup time-based rule schedules. See Section 6.9.

Traffic Shaper

> Configure traffic shaping/Quality of Service (QoS) settings. See Chapter 16.

Virtual IPs

> Configure Virtual IP addresses to let pfSense handle traffic for more than one IP address per interface, typically for NAT rules or CARP failover. See Section 6.8.

A.4 Services

The Services menu contains items which allow you to control various services provided by daemons running on pfSense. See Chapter 21.

Captive portal

Controls the Captive Portal service which allows you to direct users to a web page first for authentication before permitting Internet access. See Chapter 19.

DNS forwarder

Configures pfSense's built-in caching DNS resolver. See Section 21.3.

DHCP relay

Configures the DHCP relay service which will proxy DHCP requests from one network segment to another. See Section 21.2.

DHCP server

Configures the DHCP service which provides automatic IP address configuration for clients on Internal interfaces. See Section 21.1.

Dynamic DNS

Configures Dynamic DNS services (dyndns) which will update a remote system when this pf-Sense router's WAN IP address has changed. See Section 21.4.

Load Balancer

Configures the Load Balancer, which in Gateway mode will balance outgoing connections across multiple WAN links, or in Server mode will balancing incoming connections across multiple servers. See Chapter 17.

OLSR

Configures Optimized Link State Routing, a dynamic mesh linking daemon, which supports wireless mesh networks.

PPPoE Server

Configure the PPPoE server which allow pfSense to accept and authenticate connections from PPPoE clients. See Section 21.9.

RIP

Configures the RIP routing daemon. See Section 8.3.1.

SNMP

Configures the Simple Network Management Protocol (SNMP) daemon to allow network-based collection of statistics from this router. See Section 21.5.

UPnP

Configure the Universal Plug and Play (UPnP) service which can automatically configure NAT and firewall rules for devices which support the UPnP standard. See Section 21.6.

OpenNTPD

Configure the Network Time Protocol server daemon. See Section 21.7.

Wake on LAN
    Configure Wake on LAN services which allow you to remotely wake up client PCs reachable
    from the pfSense system. See Section 21.8.

A.5   VPN

The VPN menu contains items pertaining to Virtual Private Networks (VPNs), including IPsec, Open-
VPN and PPTP. See Chapter 12.

IPsec
    Configure IPsec VPN tunnels, mobile IPsec options and users, and certificates. See Chapter 13.

OpenVPN
    Configure OpenVPN servers and clients, as well as client-specific configuration. See Chapter 15.

PPTP
    Configure PPTP services and users, or relay. See Chapter 14.

A.6   Status

The Status menu allows you to check the status of various system components and services, as well as
view logs.

Captive Portal
    When Captive Portal is enabled, you can view user status here. See Chapter 19.

CARP (failover)
    View the status of CARP IP addresses on this system. Will show MASTER/BACKUP status.
    See Section 20.6.1.

DHCP leases
    View a list of all DHCP leases assigned by this router. You can also delete offline leases, send
    Wake on LAN requests to offline systems, or create static leases from current entries. See Sec-
    tion 21.1.3.

Filter Reload Status
    Shows the status of any filter reload requests that are (or were) pending. The filter is reloaded
    whenever changes are applied. If no changes have been made, this screen should simply report
    that an update has been completed.

Interfaces
    Lets you view the hardware status for network interfaces, equivalent to using **ifconfig** on the
    console. See Section 22.3.

IPsec
    Views the status of any configured IPsec tunnels. See Chapter 13.

Load Balancer

Views the status of the Load Balancer pools. For gateway load balancing, see Section 11.9.1. For server load balancing see Section 17.2.5.

Package logs

View logs from certain supported packages.

Queues

View the status of the traffic shaping queues. See Section 16.6.

RRD Graphs

View graphed data for system statistics such as bandwidth used, CPU usage, firewall states, and so on. See Section 22.5.

Services

Monitor the status of system and package services/daemons. See Section 22.4.

System

A shortcut back to the main page of the pfSense router that displays general system information. See Section 22.2.

System logs

View logs from the system and system services such as the firewall, DHCP, VPNs, etc. See Section 22.1.

Traffic graph

View a dynamic SVG-based realtime traffic graph for an interface. See Section 22.7.

UPnP

View a list of any currently active UPnP port forwards. See Section 21.6.

Wireless

View a list of any currently available wireless networks in range. See Section 18.2.4.

A.7 Diagnostics

Items under the Diagnostics menu perform various diagnostic and administrative tasks.

ARP Tables

View a list of systems as seen locally by the router. The list includes an IP address, MAC address, Hostname, and the Interface where the system was seen.

Backup/Restore

Backup and restore configuration files. See Section 5.2, Section 5.5.1, and Section 5.5.2.

Command Prompt

Execute shell commands or PHP code, and upload/download files to the pfSense system. **Use with caution**.

Edit File

Edit a file on the pfSense system.

Factory defaults

Resets the configuration back to default. Be aware, however, that this does not alter the filesystem or uninstall package files; it only changes configuration settings.

Halt system

Shut down the router and turn off the power where possible.

NanoBSD

Only visible on the NanoBSD (embedded) platform. Allows cloning of the working slice over to the alternate slice, and choose which one should be used to boot the router.

Ping

Send three ICMP echo requests to a given IP address, sent via a chosen interface. Does not support multi-wan.

Reboot system

Reboot the pfSense router. Depending on the hardware, this could take several minutes.

Routes

Shows the contents of the system's routing table. See Section 8.4.1.

States

View the currently active firewall states. See Section 22.6.1.

Traceroute

Trace the route taken by packets between the pfSense router and a remote system. See Section 8.4.2.

Packet Capture

Perform a packet capture to inspect traffic, and then view or download the results. See Section 25.4.

Index

CPSIA information can be obtained at www.ICGtesting.com
Printed in the USA
LVOW130027011011

248588LV00003B/28/P